THE FIRST SOUTH AMERICANS

THE UNIVERSITY OF UTAH PRESS

Salt Lake City

The First
South Americans

The Peopling of a Continent from the Earliest Evidence to High Culture

Danièle Lavallée

Translated by Paul G. Bahn

Originally published as *Promesse d'Amérique: La préhistoire de l'Amérique du Sud*
© 1995, Hachette

English translation © 2000 by The University of Utah Press
All rights reserved

06 05 04 03 02 01 00
5 4 3 2 1

Library of Congress Cataloging-in-Publication Data

Lavallée, Danièle.
    [Promesse d'Amérique. English]
    The first South Americans : the peopling of a continent from the
earliest evidence to high culture / Danièle Lavallée, ; translated by
Paul G. Bahn.
        p. cm.
    Includes bibliographical references and index.
    ISBN 0–87480–665–8 (pbk. : alk. paper)
    1. Indians of South America—Antiquities.   2. Indians of South
America—History.   3. South America—Antiquities.   I. Title.
    F2229 .L4313 2000
    980´.012—dc21   00–010190

Contents

Preface to the English-language Edition

I WROTE THIS BOOK AT THE REQUEST OF A FRENCH PUBLISHER WHO wished to produce a general work devoted to the prehistory of South America. It was first published in France in 1995.

I state this at the outset because some may see me as an intruder in their domain: America from the far north to the southern tip. Yet the tradition of French research in Latin America began in the nineteenth century on the initiative of the Société Américaine de France, which held the First International Congress of Americanists in Nancy in 1875. Americanist research continues actively in France, even if there are comparatively few of us carrying it out.

A highly detailed book would have spoken only to a very small number of readers, and at great length. To keep things within reason, I chose a simpler presentation, though perhaps excessively so in the eyes of specialists. My account is based on a few examples, selected because they are among the most demonstrative and best supported by the facts, rather than on an exhaustive listing of all known data, some of which still need verification.

I have also given systematic preference to studies or excavation monographs that combine abundance and reliability of data with a rigorous chronology supported by C14 analyses. I have purposely omitted sites where excavations are still under way or have only been partially published or whose chronology has not yet been verified by "absolute" dating through C14 measurement, even though many of them seem very promising. In the same way, no one with an interest in the South American past should be astonished at the omission of some site or another that is considered a "key reference" but whose study dates back several decades. If the data it yielded have remained unique and have maintained their validity, then the site has its place in this book. But if analogous sites have yielded information since then that is more complete or more precise, then they have replaced it here.

Since its publication in France in 1995, the text has been altered slightly with a view to a North American audience in order to take account of various remarks and, as far as possible, to update it. Though it should be obvious, I must specify that this is anything but a textbook. I claim the right to be less than exhaustive in the presentation of data, to express personal opinions, and to take sides, instead of restricting myself to a strict description of reported facts or to an interminable bibliographical compilation. Moreover, I want to make it clear that the bibliographical updating of this book ends in 1998 and likewise has no pretensions to being exhaustive. I have refrained from inundating readers with an accumulation of references intended only to show that I have read everything. One can never read everything, and it will always be easy to unearth a book or article somewhere that I have failed to cite.

Because this is not a textbook, I have also kept discussion of theoretical developments to their essentials. Such things can easily be found elsewhere. Underlying the whole of my work, however, is a strong epistemological position honoring the primacy of field data. Some may see this approach as too "empirical." This is fully intentional. As André Leroi-Gourhan taught us, excavation constitutes "archaeology's fundamental research activity." It is our duty to establish the facts with a view to putting them together in a meaningful way. In fact, this is doubtless one of the fundamental differences that separate French archaeologists from our Anglo-Saxon colleagues, in whose eyes the development of a theoretical framework and of a prior conceptual plan sometimes seems more important than the examination and confrontation of observed facts.

It is my assertion that the peopling of America stretches back beyond the sacred date of 12,000 B.P. (before present). This having been stated at the outset, it is also worth wondering about the motivations (probably unconscious) that make this date an impassable threshold for some. The five years separating the first edition of this book from its English-language edition have been particularly rich in events that have stirred up our little scientific world and helped to strengthen the case for the antiquity of human arrival. One can mention, merely in regard to the initial peopling, the validation given to the Monte Verde site (at last!), the unexpected discoveries made in Brazilian Amazonia, and research in molecular genetics which, even though it has as yet produced something of a cacophony of results, brings tremendous hope for clarification.

TIME

This book considers prehistory in the European sense, that is to say, the whole period stretching from the first traces of human presence to the emergence of the first "civilizations." The same distinction is not used in America, where the term "prehistory" includes all cultural manifestations preceding the invasion by Europeans in the sixteenth century, including the most evolved

Pre-Columbian civilizations. It is important to be specific about this fundamental semantic difference from the outset, because it explains my choice to
present and discuss the cultural development of the whole of South America
from its initial peopling to the emergence of the first Andean "high culture,"
that of Chavín. I present this civilization only briefly because it lies outside
the chronological framework that I have laid out.

But why stop at Chavín? In some books about the oldest cultural developments, the authors make a distinction around the appearance of pottery
and therefore speak of a "preceramic" period. This distinction is only valid
for the Andean area. On the scale of the entire continent, the appearance of
pottery in no case constitutes a chronological marker, insofar as it arose at
very different times in different regions, between the fourth and first millennia B.C. Further, the use of fired-clay vessels, even though it constituted an
important technological innovation, scarcely revolutionized the way of life
of the peoples who adopted or invented it. Some groups came to know it
only in the twelfth or thirteenth centuries A.D., while others never used it.
Other specialists, with a broader canvas, see the start of American "civilization" as the emergence, toward the end of the second millennium B.C., of
Chavín's "high culture." This is the solution I have chosen here.

The blossoming of Chavín—a society that most South Americanists recognize as the beginning of "civilization"—reflects a decisive expansion of
cultural development and the emergence of complex society, even if it only
involved a limited part of the South American continent. When around 1200
B.C. Andean societies entered the era of the "high civilizations," elsewhere
there were societies of sedentary farmers, fisher-gatherers who did not know
agriculture, and hunter-gatherers who remained seminomadic: a cultural
mosaic with no equivalent anywhere else in the world.

A few clarifications are necessary regarding the presentations of dates.
The chronology is that of radiocarbon. This dating method, involving the
measurement of the C_{14} content of organic residues—plant remains, bone,
shell—was developed by William Libby in 1950 (for which he received the
Nobel Prize in chemistry) and has permitted the establishment of a relatively precise chronological framework. "Relatively" because a C_{14} date is
never exact but is followed by a statistical margin of error or sigma, the size
of which is generally proportional to the antiquity of the date. Hence, this
margin will be several centuries for dates of around 10,000 years ago, but
only a few dozen years for more recent dates. A C_{14} date is expressed in years
B.P.—that is, by convention, before 1950, the date when the method was
finalized.

One other detail: I do not use "calibrated" dates (that is, dates readjusted
through comparison with the calibration curve, itself obtained by comparison with dendrochronology dates). It is not that I doubt the validity of this
method but simply that a comparison between a calibrated date and a
noncalibrated date can lead to serious errors, especially if the quoted author

has omitted to specify this "detail," a scenario that occurs with some frequency in the regions that concern us here.

SPACE

The territory to be covered here is indeed immense: 7,600 kilometers from north to south, from the Caribbean shores of Venezuela and Colombia to the broken extremity of Tierra del Fuego, and 6,000 kilometers from east to west, from Brazil to Ecuador—almost 18 million square kilometers enclosing an extraordinary diversity of terrain, climate, and landscape. The continent is dominated and divided into two very unequal parts by a formidable barrier, the Andean Cordillera, the world's greatest mountain system after the Himalayas. The Andes are more than 8,000 kilometers long but scarcely more than 150 kilometers wide in Ecuador and 600 at their widest point at the latitude of Arica in Chile. They bristle with icy peaks and volcanoes that soar to between 6,000 and 7,000 meters (6,272 meters for Chimborazo in Ecuador, 6,746 meters for Huascarán in Peru, 6,959 meters for Aconcagua in Chile). Among the mountain chains, which are roughly oriented north-south and more or less parallel, there stretch vast, high plateaus—known as *páramos* in Colombia and Ecuador, punas in Peru and Argentina, and extended to altiplano in Bolivia—whose altitude varies between 3,500 and 4,800 meters, higher in the central part (Peru and Bolivia) where they also reach their maximum extent. This is an austere domain, with a harsh climate and poor soils, and yet it has never represented an obstacle for humans who traveled through it and settled there about 12,000 or 13,000 years ago. On either side of the Cordillera are two opposite worlds. West, lies a narrow coastal band with a succession of superhumid forests from north to south; then savannas that are gradually transformed by increasing aridity into desert; then, once again, more clement and green lands; and, finally, the hostile, rain-drenched, and windswept world of the area around the Magellan Straits. East, there is the dense expanse of the great equatorial forest. At its edges, it gradually gives way to the grassy Colombian and Venezuelan *llanos* in the north and, to the south, the scrub of the Bolivian and Paraguayan *pajonales* and the dry savanna and light forest of the Brazilian *caatinga* and *cerrado*. Farther to the south, the monotonous and marshy grassland of the Argentine pampa is conquered by the cold and gives way to the vast, arid steppe of Patagonia.

Little by little, people occupied this mosaic of territories over the course of thousands of years, sometimes yielding to the constraints of the environment but sometimes managing to control and transform it. This was accomplished with rates and methods whose diversity equaled that of the natural settings.

PEOPLE

To the complexity of a natural world with a thousand facets came the strategies implemented by humans to survive in it and even attempt its control. This addition was of unequal tempo. A precocious cultural growth in one place would contrast with a slower development in another or, elsewhere, a real or apparent stagnation.

From our distant perspective, the unequal value of the available data for the prehistoric South Americans is an important element. The inequality is due not only to the inherent difficulties in this type of research. (Obviously a camp of prehistoric fisher-gatherers in the Chilean desert, where material traces have been preserved under a few centimeters of sand, is easier to detect and excavate than the subtle impression left by a bivouac of hunter-gatherers in the Amazonian forest.) There are also differences in approach and perception of data on the part of the archaeologists themselves. Such differences are often a result of training and the material means available.

In this book I occasionally use data collected in the 1930s or 1940s, as they remain unique references for the region in question. For the most part they were obtained from simple, small-scale test pits. Moreover, numerous excavations, including relatively recent ones, have been carried out by arbitrary stratigraphy based on depth measurement. It was only later that excavations taking into account "natural" units or levels over large areas were carried out—all of which calls attention to this specific point: the comparison of information obtained by varied methods is always difficult and sometimes impossible. Inequalities in numerical importance or value of the data collected, linked to the constraints of the natural environment, are gradually diminishing, thanks in part to advances in research techniques. But it remains true that enormous portions of South American territory are still practically unexplored from the archaeological point of view.

In prehistory, and doubtless far more than in any other historical discipline, all synthesis is highly provisional. Every day new discoveries come along to destroy what was true or exemplary the day before. Conversely, new facts turn up to support long-established hypotheses or reinforce interpretations that had hitherto seemed rash and controversial. Again, this volume in no way claims to set out a complete inventory of the subject. As I have taken the liberty of being biased, this work is not exempt from the expression of personal positions. At the same time, I do not claim that they reflect the general opinion of a scientific community whose positions are, moreover, often in conflict.

Finally, I have deliberately left aside certain aspects of the South American past, rock art for example. This is not because I am oblivious to its beauty, its richness, or its significant information value but because this art deserves to be displayed, highlighted, and interpreted exhaustively and at great length.

Several of my colleagues have already done this far better than I could have done in the limited space available to me here.

Another domain that I chose not to include, except in scattered instances, is that of the Antilles, a physically fragmented world extending in an arc from Central America (to which it is most usually attached) to South America, to which the Lesser Antilles indisputably belong from the geographical point of view. The same division can be observed from the cultural point of view, because the string of Caribbean islands never constituted a unified territory during the Pre-Columbian past, even if large island groups were at times unified by similar cultures. Some cultural traits were borrowed from the regions to the north and east, from Nicaragua to Florida, and others from the south, from the Atlantic facade extending from Venezuela to the Guyanas. Disentangling the contribution and importance of each of these influences would have carried me way too far, since this is a domain in which the geographic division is accompanied by a great inequality of archaeological data. On the other hand, I have paid particular attention, when it seemed possible, to retracing and following the cultural trajectories that usually transcended present-day political frontiers; to discovering the lines of force that determined their principal aspects, be they the ways in which space was occupied or the variability in technology; and lastly (and not the least of my concerns) to evaluating the still immense gaps in our knowledge.

Paris, October 1999

1

THE DISCOVERY OF A WORLD?

EUROPE INVENTS AMERICA

A Castilla y a León
Nuevo mundo dío Colón

[To Castile and León
Columbus gave a new world]

SO READS THE MOTTO ADOPTED BY CHRISTOPHER COLUMBUS FOR HIS COAT
of arms. How much truth does this proud phrase actually contain? Was Columbus really the first to touch the shores of the New World? He was doubtless the first to reveal its existence to an amazed Europe but certainly not the
first to land there. On the occasion of the quincentenary of the "Discovery
of America" (a better term would be the "meeting of two worlds"), thousands of pages were devoted to this figure, to his voyages, and to his real or
alleged discoveries. It is not so much the man and his enterprise that are of
interest to us here but rather his expedition's most important result for the
archaeologist: the meeting with *Homo americanus* and his culture, and
the meaning that both of these assumed in the eyes of sixteenth-century
Europeans.

Numerous sailors could have reached—and several of them doubtless
did reach—America before Christopher Columbus. As A. Ronsin (1979) reminds us, in ancient times Phoenicians and Carthaginians were venturing
into the Atlantic beyond the Pillar of Hercules (the straits of Gibraltar) to
the Cassiterides (the Isles of Scilly) to seek the tin needed for making bronze.
Around 330 B.C., the Phoenician navigator Pytheas even reached Norway
and perhaps Iceland, the mysterious Thule of medieval legends. All the his-
torians of ancient times—Herodotus, Strabo, Diodorus of Sicily, Pliny the
Elder—evoke lands to the west, beyond the Mediterranean, which are the
Canaries (the Blessed Islands of the Phoenicians) and the Azores. Plato de-

scribes an immense sunken continent, Atlantis. Later, during the Early Middle Ages, Celtic monks traveled the North Atlantic, from Scotland to Iceland, and Saint Brendan may have reached the coast of Newfoundland. Finally, in the tenth century, the Vikings, seeking new lands, settled in the "Green Land" (Greenland) and then even farther west in Labrador. At any rate, medieval geography, fed by these imaginary or utterly real tales of travel, gave credence to the idea that beyond the great ocean, to the west, there existed other lands. This is how, out of an accumulation of errors, credulity, and ignorance, there was to arise among the navigators of the late fifteenth century "the urgent desire to find the western oceanic route" (ibid.: 17). They would be aided in this by advances in navigation: the adoption of the mixed-rigging caravel, a combination of square and lateen sails that enabled one to navigate whatever the wind direction; knowledge of astronomical navigation, including generalized use of the compass and the astrolabe which, although often difficult to use on the high seas, were of significant help to pilots; and, finally, the existence of an abundant marine cartography, especially the work of the Genoese and then the Portuguese. Moreover, Christopher Columbus was a very skilful mapmaker.

When at the end of the fifteenth century the Ottoman empire's takeover of Constantinople and then of the Balkans compelled European maritime trade to modify its hitherto circum-Mediterranean networks, the great concern became that of finding the most direct route to India and China, from which came spices, dyes, and other precious materials, and hence it was to the west that people looked. However, the continent that the navigators were to discover was, as Ronsin, writes, "an unknown which they thought they knew" (ibid.: 43). Certainly a world existed beyond the great ocean, but it was not the one of which they dreamed.

On 12 October 1492 Columbus landed at Guanahani (Watling, in the Bahamas) and took possession of the island in the name of the queen of Castile, as he was to do for all the lands he was subsequently to discover: in that same year, the islands of the Bahamas, Cuba—which he thought to be China—and Haiti (fig. 1); from 1493 to 1500, in the course of his second and third voyages, Dominica, Guadeloupe, Puerto Rico, and Jamaica; and finally Trinidad and the coast of the mainland at the mouth of the Orinoco. For the first time, on 4 August 1498, he set foot on terra firma. This time, in a letter he wrote to the Spanish sovereigns which was accompanied by a map he drew, he announced that he had reached a new hemisphere that was unknown to the ancients. South America had been found and the expression "New World" appeared. In 1493, Pietro Martir de Anghiera, who was in the service of the King of Spain and who was present at Columbus's reception at court after his first voyage, published all the discoveries that had been made. He called his work *De Orbe Novo* (Of the New World), as though he had a premonition of something else, whereas at this time Columbus still believed he had reached Asia.

Fig. 1. Christopher Columbus disembarks on Hispaniola. During his first voyage, after having landed at Guanahani (Bahamas), Columbus continued the exploration of the islands. He reached Cuba and then, on 6 December 1492, a large island which he baptized Hispaniola (the future Haiti), and which was then inhabited by the Tainos, an Arawak people. Being peaceful (unlike the Caribs, cannibals encountered in Cuba) and welcoming, they presented him with their golden jewels, even promising to show him where the mines were located. Faced with this welcome, Columbus immediately envisaged the seizure of this land, to have its riches exploited by its own natives and, "in exchange," to have them discover Western spiritual values by converting them to Christianity. (Engraving on wood, taken from C. Columbus, *De Insulis inventis,* published in Basle in 1493)

In the years that followed a succession of maritime voyages constantly discovered new islands and new continental lands: from 1497 to 1504 Amerigo Vespucci skirted the American coast a number of times and made many landings, from Florida to Brazil. In 1513, Francisco Nuñez de Balboa crossed the isthmus of Darien and reached the Pacific coast. In 1519, Magellan reached the Rio de la Plata and on 21 October crossed the strait that today bears his name. He baptized the ocean he penetrated as "Pacific" because of the unusual calmness of its waters.

Amerigo Vespucci died in 1512, probably unaware that the New World had borne his name for five years. Before then it was known as the "Western Indies" by the Spanish, while the Portuguese, after Cabral's voyages, called it the "Land of the True Cross" or the "Land of Parrots." The proposition to call the new lands "America" originated in 1507 from various geographers who were convinced that Vespucci was the true discoverer and who wanted to pay him a just homage. The name was quickly adopted by the majority of scholars and cartographers of the time, all the more readily because Balboa's discovery of the Pacific Ocean provided fresh proof that India and China were definitely elsewhere. The name of America was to be accepted by the whole of Europe from the seventeenth century onward, before being criticized in the nineteenth by various scholars who were to challenge—with some justification but no success—Amerigo Vespucci's role as "discoverer." The theory of French geologist Jules Marcou, that the name America was that given by the natives to a chain of mountains in Nicaragua, was discussed in a very learned manner at the Congress of Americanists in Paris in 1890 and then rejected. The Americanist Alphonse Pinart who, in his turn in 1891, tried to demonstrate that the name America came from a town that in ancient times was located on the coast of Venezuela, and called Ameracapana, found no followers either.

In Search of El Dorado

At the beginning of the sixteenth century, the continent—or at least its coastal fringe—had been discovered. Its interior beckoned; this time it was not courageous and (more or less) disinterested navigators or explorers who carried out the task but cynical, greedy, and brutish soldiers, driven only by the desire to find gold. In 1498, when he had reached the mouth of the Orinoco, Columbus thought he had found paradise on earth. When in 1524 Francisco Pizarro decided to leave Panama and to follow the Pacific coast southward as far as the rich kingdom of Peru—or Birú—of which he had heard from native chiefs, he could not have cared less about paradise. A single idea dominated his mind and led him to endure exhaustion, hunger, and thirst: reaching an empire whose cities were paved with gold. In 1527, moving from island to island and bay to bay, his little band reached the Tumbés region on the north coast of Peru, which at that time formed part of the *Tahuantinsuyu,* the empire of the Incas.

The bloody campaign in Peru ended in 1532 with the assassination of the last Inca ruler, Atahualpa, but before being strangled and still believing the promises of his conquerors, he had undertaken to pay a fabulous ransom to the Spaniards who were holding him prisoner: enough gold to fill to the height of a raised hand a room in his palace at Cajamarca 7 meters long and 5 wide. But the Incas gathered in far more from the whole empire: 70,000 loads of gold (each of them weighing an *arroba*, almost 12 kilos) did not reach Cajamarca and were supposed to have remained hidden in the region of Quito. The Spaniards then flew into a rage. Calicuchima, the military chief of royal blood, was burned alive, as were all those Indians who refused to reveal the hiding place.

A little later, an Indian captured by the Spaniards reported that to the east there ruled a sovereign called "El Dorado," the "Golden Man." Once a year, he covered his body with gold powder and went with his people to the edge of a lake, where he mounted a raft that was also laden with gold. On reaching the center of the lake, he threw the offerings into the water before immersing himself and then reemerging purified. This legend grew out of a mixture of tales from various countries that had been passed around and embellished a hundred times, and of a reality—the lake of Guatavita, a sacred site of the Muisca people (close to Bogotá in Colombia) where such a ceremony did indeed take place. The Spaniards came in ever greater numbers to Peru and shared or quarreled over the wealth of the Inca empire. It was for gold that in 1534 Sebastián de Benalcázar undertook an expedition to the north and reached the high plateaus of modern Colombia; for gold that Diego de Almagro in 1535 and then Pedro de Valdivia in 1540 rushed off to the south to conquer what was to become Chile; also for gold that Diego de Rojas, shortly afterward, crossed the cordillera of the Andes in search of the legendary "city of the Caesars" and reached the region of Tucumán in Argentina; and yet again for gold that in 1569 Jímenez de Quesada had a Muisca chief roasted in order to extract from him the secret of the treasure of Guatavita.

The treasures of the temples and idols loaded down the galleons that sailed to Spain, while insatiable adventurers continued the desperate search for El Dorado. In March 1541 Francisco Orellana and Gonzalo Pizarro, the brother of the conqueror of Peru, left Quito with a major expedition: 200 infantry and more than 4,000 Indians. By the time they crossed the Andes, hundreds of men had already died, but the adventurers continued to seek the marvelous city, went down immense rivers, and crossed the forest. They were in rags and tatters, haggard and devoured by fevers, and ceaselessly attacked by the Indians. Their meager reward was a few nuggets along the way. El Dorado did not exist. But Orellana, after 18 months of navigation, arrived on 24 August 1542 in the Gulf of Pará, where the river of the Amazons emerged into the Atlantic Ocean. The continent had been crossed.

Are They Really Human?

Who were the inhabitants of all these lands that were gradually explored and then exploited? What were the first reactions of the Europeans on discovering that the lands were occupied by beings who seemed, amazingly enough, to be very similar to themselves, apart from a few peculiarities? When in 1492 Columbus encountered the natives of Guanahani, he wrote to his friend Luis de Santángel, an officer at the Spanish court charged with keeping the accounts: "The people of this island and of all the other islands which I have found and of which I have information, all go naked, men and women, as their mothers bore them, although some of the women cover a single place with the leaf of a plant or with a net of cotton which they make for the purpose. They have no iron or steel or weapons, nor are they fitted to use them. This is not because they are not well built and of handsome stature."[1]

So these were indeed humans. Columbus did not doubt this for a single instant, even if, to his great surprise, they did not have the features one would expect of the Chinese (since he still believed he had landed in China). They were people with whom one might seek contact, to whom one could offer presents, to whom one might ascribe the faults and qualities of humans, and to whom one might even display a certain respect. In Haiti, that same year, the numerous and peaceful inhabitants gladly presented him with jewels.

During the second voyage, contacts were less easy. On returning to Guadeloupe and Martinique, Columbus discovered that the inhabitants were cannibals, and the natives of Haiti, so welcoming the year before, had massacred the 30 Spaniards who had remained there, probably because of the Spaniards' brutal conduct and repeated demands. Vespucci also encountered cannibals on the coast of Central America during his first voyage in 1497 (fig. 2). At the end of his third voyage in 1502, he wrote a detailed account, *Mundus Novus (New World)*, which contains numerous details about the life and customs of the Indians. It immediately was widely distributed. In 1504 he wrote a letter to his friend Piero Soderini, in which he says of the natives encountered on the coast of Honduras: "They are of medium stature, and very well proportioned. The color of their skins inclines to red, like the skin of a lion, and I believe that, if they were properly clothed, they would be white like ourselves" (quoted by Vignaud 1917: 337).

Finally, a few "specimens" of natives were brought back to Spain by the various expeditions. The first were presented to King Ferdinand by Columbus in 1493 on his return from the initial voyage. In 1498, Pinzon and Solis, members of Vespucci's first expedition, brought back to Spain 222 natives captured in Ity archipelago to be sold as slaves. But the problem of their true nature did not arise. They were indeed humans, but they were expected to submit, to hand over all the products at their disposal, and, especially, to convert to Christianity. As Columbus wrote at the end of his letter to Luis de Santángel, "As I have found no monsters, so I have had no report of any."

[1] Letter from Christopher Columbus to Luis de Santángel, doubtless written at the end of February 1493. From *The Voyages of Christopher Columbus,* trans. and ed. by Cecil Jane (London, 1930).

Fig. 2. A land peopled with monsters. When Columbus landed in Cuba, he learned with horror that the natives—Caribs—ate human flesh. "He also understood that far from there were men with one eye, and others with dogs' noses who ate men, and that when they took a man, they cut off his head and drank his blood and castrated him" (C. Columbus, *Journal de bord 1492–1493*, Paris, Imprimerie nationale, 1992, p. 101). He was to encounter them in Guadeloupe and Martinique during his second voyage. As for the half-human half-animal creatures, medieval legends are filled with them, and Columbus was obviously expecting to find some—dogs with human heads, or men with dog heads, a belief doubtless born, in this case, of a confusion between *Caniba* (or *Cariba*), the name of the people, and *can,* the word for dog in Spanish. (Above: "Savages' hullabaloo and cooking," from Theodor de Bry, 1590–1634, *History of America,* in thirteen parts, Frankfurt, 3rd part, fol. 179; below, fantastic creature with a human face, engraving published in Antwerp in 1557)

Why was there such an expectation of extraordinary creatures? It was because the writings and tales of the Middle Ages were full of descriptions of monsters occupying the unexplored countries of the Far East, and Columbus obviously thought he would encounter some. At the end of the fourteenth century or the very beginning of the fifteenth, *The Book of Marco Pol ... wherein is recounted the Wonders of the World* contained the tales of Marco Polo and various other travelers; one finds there descriptions of the court of the great Khan, the Holy Land, and the Indies, all illustrated with drawings of figures that were even more fantastic than the texts. Dragons and serpents, sea monsters of all kinds, and especially monstrous men—men with dogs' heads, men who had only a single eye, men with one foot. Bartolomé Benassar, in one of the most interesting books to arise from the frenzied writing activity triggered by the quincentenary, also recalls that John of Hollywood, in *Spherae Mundi*, described the Indians in 1498 as blue creatures with square heads; that Walter Raleigh mentions headless beings living in Amazonia; and that a number of travelers accepted the existence in South America of giants, which is a lesser deformity (Benassar 1991: 46–47). So Columbus was reassured after all, even though he wrote in the same letter: "There remain to the westward two provinces to which I have not gone. One of these provinces they call 'Avan' [Cuba], and there people are born with tails." So there were certainly monsters somewhere, but not in the places he had thus far visited.

Nevertheless, despite the unequivocal tales of the navigators and in spite of what they said about the "men" encountered over there, Europe wondered, or rather, as A. Laming-Emperaire wrote, pretended "to wonder whether these beings, so different both in their physical types and in their ways of life, were really human. A negative answer would have simplified many problems, since no moral law could then have prevented the plunder and massacre of non-human creatures, or their being reduced to slavery" (1980: 7).

Some individuals were already defending the people of the New World. In 1530, the orders given by Charles V were perfectly clear: "That nobody should dare reduce any Indian to slavery, either during a war or in times of peace; nor keep any Indian in slavery under the pretext of acquisition in just warfare, or of ransom or purchase or exchange, or for any other reason or pretext whatsoever, even if these are Indians whom the natives of these islands and continental lands themselves consider as slaves."

Father Bartolomé de Las Casas, who in 1519 accompanied the conquering expedition of Hernán Cortés to Mexico and took part in the annihilation of the Aztec empire, also defended the Indians' rights. But it was not until 1537 that a papal bull from Paul III solemnly recognized their human status: "The Indians, as veritable men . . . , can in no way be made slaves or deprived of their goods" (quoted by Todorov 1982: 23).

This would not prevent the 9 million inhabitants of Inca-period Peru in 1532 decreasing to no more than 1.3 million scarcely 30 years later. Around

1600 between 50 percent and 70 percent of the indigenous population of South America—the figures are difficult to estimate and vary from author to author—had disappeared thanks to massacres, epidemics, and forced labor.

Myths, Legends, and Fantasy

Since they were humans, they could only be descendants of Adam and Eve, given that—as stated in the Bible—there was a single creation of humankind. But then, since they had appeared like all the other people in the Old World, how did they reach the New? At the time of their discovery—that is, the sixteenth century—as Laming-Emperaire writes, "the concept of the world, linear and with no time-depth, was both Christian and dominated by an unqualified admiration for Classical antiquity" (1980: 13).

No human history could be imagined outside of these two reference points. Hence, on the one hand, the first explanations were based on the Bible, the revealed truth about the origins of humanity, and, on the other hand, on Greek and Latin writings. The hypotheses that found the most support were those based on the Bible. Since, apparently, the inhabitants of America had had no previous contact either with Europe to the east or with Asia to the west; and since, too—as the Pope himself had just confirmed—these were descendants of Adam and Eve, it could only have been through descent from Noah and his sons, the only survivors of the Flood. Thus, Noah's grandchildren must have landed in America in times past. Another hypothesis was that the survivors of a fleet of King Solomon had been cast onto these shores by a storm. Or alternatively, they were the descendants of the Canaanites, or one of the ten lost tribes of Israel, or survivors of the fleet of Alexander the Great. "Linking the Amerindian cultures to groups from ancient times whose traces had been lost was in perfect agreement with the vision of the world in that period. It would be extremely naive to laugh at it. Yet, in almost all cases the proof was based on childish arguments and superficial analogies (for example, the resemblance between the words 'Peru' and 'Ophir,' the fabled country where the descendants of Noah had settled). It is hard to understand how true scholars could have taken these seriously" (ibid.: 14).

According to these hypotheses—the only ones possible at the time—the "Indians" of America were, in the sixteenth and seventeenth centuries, successively considered to be descendants of the Hebrews, Egyptians, Assyrians, Phoenicians, Trojans, Greeks, Etruscans, Romans, and Scythians. A little later, the Tartars would be evoked, and then the Huns, Hindus, Chinese, Buddhists, Africans, Madagascans, Vikings, Gauls, Irish, Basques, and other peoples.

All these theories, which were based to a greater or lesser extent on an interpretation (with a dash of fantasy) of Christian texts or those of classical antiquity, would gradually be abandoned as the observations of travelers increased in number during the eighteenth century. Yet one man, the Spanish Jesuit José de Acosta, was alone among the thinkers and scholars of his time in displaying a surprising and somewhat premonitory intuition, albeit without deviating from biblical dogma. On the contrary, it was an in-depth reading of the Scriptures that led him, through rigorously logical reasoning, to formulate a very different hypothesis. In 1590, after a sixteen-year stay in America (from 1572 to 1587), he published his *Historia natural y moral de las Indias (The Natural and Moral History of the Indies)* for the benefit of the European cultural world. In it, he described the American universe, its inhabitants, its flora and fauna, and, especially, its origins, something that numerous other contemporary chroniclers had not done. The following passages from this work deserve to be quoted, despite their length:

> But seeing on the one side wee know for certaine that many years agoe there were men inhabiting in these parts, so likewise we cannot deny but the scripture doth teach vs clccrely that all men are come from the first man, without doubt we shall be forced to beleeve and confesse that men have passed hither from Europe, Asia, or Affricke, yet must wee discover by what means they could passe . . . for we intreat not of the mightie power of God, but only of that which is conformable vnto reason, and the order and disposition of humane things. [Book 1, chap. 16]

> I coniecture then, by the discourse I have made, that the new world, which we call Indies, is not altogether severed and disioyned from the other world; and to speake my opinion, I have long beleeved that the one and the other world are ioyned and continued one with another in some part, or at the least are very neere. [Book 1, chap. 20]

> We may easily inferre by these arguments and others like, that the first Indians went to inhabit the Indies more by land then by sea; or if there were any navigation, it was neither great nor difficult. [Book 1, chap. 21]

> And I beleeve . . . that the first men that entred, were rather savage men and hunters, then bredde vp in civill and well-governed Common-weales. [Book 1, chap. 24]

What an extraordinary prescience of the geographical proximity of Asia and America, which, even though they were not joined together in the north as Acosta supposed (the existence of the Bering Strait was still unknown at this time), were certainly united in times long ago (unimaginably long ago at this time), thus enabling people to pass from one continent to the other! And what a revolutionary hypothesis it was to ascribe an Asiatic origin to the Amerindians and to attribute to them a way of life that was at first "primitive" instead of making them the heirs of the highly developed civilizations of the classical ancient world!

Turning finally to our own period, we find that the hypotheses developed in the sixteenth and seventeenth centuries (apart from those of Joseph de Acosta) are far less strange than the ineradicable need for the fantastic which, even today, drives some people, and sometimes no mean experts, to propose highly eccentric ideas about the origins of the Amerindians. Laming-Emperaire observes that these pseudoscientific theories all display similar characteristics: "They present themselves as a struggle against official science, and emphasize the latter's stupidity, conservatism, dishonesty. . . . The propagators [of these theories] are the persecuted. . . . They consider themselves to be misunderstood geniuses" (1980: 9).

Moreover, one can call attention to the importance of symbolism here, through the deciphering of "unknown" scripts or the use of esoteric jargon that is hard to understand. The most famous of these theories is obviously the one that refers to Atlantis. It is also the oldest, since it appeared in the eighteenth century, in direct descent from the hypotheses based on the ancient texts. In two dialogues written in the fourth century B.C., the *Timaeus* and the *Critias,* the philosopher Plato, in just a few lines, mentions a people, the Atlanteans, whose life was exemplary and who inhabited a great island called Atlantis. Because they contravened the laws of life, their island was submerged beneath the waters. This mythical tale, which had more or less been forgotten, again became topical after the discovery of the New World. Around 1784 the Italian Carli announced that the inhabitants of America were quite simply the descendants of the Atlanteans: one merely had to compare the Inca monuments with the pyramids of Egypt and the similarities that existed between such things as weapons and tattoos on either side. Everybody seized on this hypothesis, from authentic scholars—anthropologists, linguists—to eccentrics. They passionately sought all possible connections—physical, ethnographic, or linguistic—between the Amerindians and the peoples of Europe and Africa because Plato had specified that Atlantis covered a surface equal to that of Asia and Libya combined and that it was close to Greece and Egypt.

Even the abbé Brasseur de Bourbourg (1814–1874), someone with a scientific mind who had devoted his life to the study of the American civilizations, late in life became an ardent supporter of Atlantis. The theme also became a subject for discussion during the first, very serious international congress of Americanists, held at Nancy in 1875. In 1932, human bones from the lake of Tacarigua in Venezuela were still presented as belonging to the Atlantean race. In a particularly comical episode, even earthworms and snails were called on for assistance: since it was obvious to some "biologists" that these species could not have arrived by sea to populate the New World, it became necessary to accept the existence of a land route, which could only be Atlantis. When in 1912 Wegener formulated his revolutionary theory of continental drift, according to which, for hundreds of millions of years, the continental blocks have slowly been moving away from each other, breaking up and reconstituting themselves in a different configuration, it was called a "great poet's dream." Certainly, true science is often as poetic as the craziest fabrications. Hence Atlantophilia enjoyed, and still enjoys, great success among sincere researchers as well as a certain number of dreamers. Numerous hypotheses have been put forward concerning the location of Atlantis, and indeed the Atlantic Ocean is not the only place that has been proposed. Traces of it have also been "detected," according to Laming-Emperaire, in the Caucasus, Persia, Siberia, Greenland, and Africa, especially the Sahara. "In North America, the members of the Rosicrucian Order and the theosophists still maintain that Atlantis was the origin of all human inventions.... In Brazil, in 1959, a book was translated from the German with the pretty title Os Filhos del Sol, 'The Sons of the Sun.' The theme of the book, which is presented as the result of scientific research, is the discovery in the Amazonian forests of traces that indisputably prove the existence of ancient Atlantean colonies in this region" (1980: 12).

Other equally crazy propositions have been put forward more recently that take over from—and even exceed in the audacity of their presuppositions—the theory of the Atlantophiles. The Mormons of the United States believe that the American civilizations were founded by the Hebrews, since Quetzalcoatl (the Aztecs' tribal divinity) and Jesus Christ were one and the same person. Although they do not exclude the Asiatic origin of the first peopling of America, which has now largely been proved (see chapter 2), it is with the high culture of the Maya and those of Egypt, Mesopotamia, and the Hebrews that they establish a parallel and demonstrate a relationship.

In 1970, the discovery of astonishing underwater rocky structures near the Bahamas got the controversy moving again. At the northwest point of the island of Bimini, at a few meters depth, two divers noted the existence of an alignment, more than 600 meters long, of enormous stone blocks. According to the discoverers, this was an ancient dyke, the work of an unknown civilization, inundated after an abrupt rise in the ocean level. The stones of the "wall" were allegedly different from the rock of the seabed and, moreover, rested on pillars. On the other hand, most scientists (including W. Harrison, the author of an article published in the very serious British scientific journal *Nature*) thought that this "paving" was of geological origin—that is, slabs joined together with a natural cement—and that its present appearance was due only to a succession of fractures triggered by earth movements and then marine erosion. In fact, it was nothing other than a phenomenon of beach rocks, quite common in this region. No geologist seriously defended the idea of a sudden collapse of the continent—there was only a slow upward movement of sea level over the course of the last 10 millennia, following the melting of the great Quaternary glaciers from about 10,000 years onward. The supporters of the theory of a sunken Atlantis are sticking to their guns, but nevertheless the geological hypothesis appears the more serious.

One of the most successful examples of scientific misappropriation is undoubtedly that of L. Pauwels and J. Bergier in their famous book *Le Matin des magiciens* (*The Morning of the Magicians*) (1960). In this case, one is not dealing with Hebrews, Phoenicians, or even the mythical Atlanteans but quite simply with extraterrestrials who, having attained a degree of knowledge that far surpasses that reached by wretched humankind, supposedly came from other planets a very long time ago—indeed, the authors unhesitatingly place this event several dozen, or even several hundreds of thousands of years ago. The proof of their visit is a jumble of things: the Easter Island statues, the Bolivian ruins of Tiwanaku, the geoglyphs of Nazca in the Peruvian desert, the Inca fortress of Sacsahuaman in Peru, to name but a few of their South American examples—in short, all monuments that are a little "strange" in form or size or whose creators, period of construction, or building technique constituted an enigma for a while and held the attention of archaeologists. The book is very clever in that it uses old chestnuts—the mysterious science of the Ancients, the innumerable myths about the Golden Age—but adapts them for modern tastes: knowledge of astronautics, nuclear physics, electronics, the whole contemporary scientific arsenal is marshaled into the service of the marvelous and the fantastic.

As a final example among these flights of fancy, one should mention a "paste for softening stones," which supposedly enabled the Incas to fit together their famous stone monuments—at Cuzco, Sacsahuaman, and Ollantaytambo—in which polygonal blocks (often of enormous size, certainly) have their sharp edges adjusted to each other with astonishing precision. But the prize for the most fantastic idea goes to Javier Cabrera, a Peruvian doctor who spent years amassing an impressive quantity of "Precolumbian" engraved cobbles from the Ica region, on which, according to him, there were depictions of such things as dinosaurs, highly advanced surgical operations such as heart transplants and even a brain transplant (a very advanced technique indeed!), and launches of intergalactic rockets. These "indisputably authentic" finds, supposed to be "60 million years old" in their time—1974—caused a great deal of ink to flow, especially from the pen of Robert Charroux (1974), France's specialist in forgotten worlds. The following year, after an official investigation carried out by the Peruvian museum authorities, the perpetrator of the deception confessed all—he was a peasant of the region who had found this excellent way of earning a bit of money by pleasing the good doctor and who derived his inspiration from cheap comic strips (and even from the educational supplements in Lima's daily papers!).

It is not the intention here to challenge all these incredible propositions—they were already dismantled and refuted in 1975, with great rigor and humor, by Jean-Pierre Adam. P. Ostoya (1962) put it best: "Authentic science, with its increasingly abstract apparatus, is becoming harder for many people to assimilate. It demands of us a certain mental asceticism, the renunciation of easy food for the mind, and it is difficult to maintain this rigor unflaggingly. Moreover, the joys it offers us in compensation are a little severe. No wonder, then, that the old dreams seek their vengeance."

CURIOUS TRAVELERS AND THE BIRTH OF A DISCIPLINE

Despite the astonishing premonitions of Joseph de Acosta, the intellectual context at the end of the eighteenth century was still prescientific and almost completely irrational. Yet at this time there was growing curiosity concerning this new world and its occupants. A century later, this somewhat disorganized curiosity—first on the part of a few diplomats, churchmen on ecclesiastical missions, or simple travelers who had arrived in America more or less by chance—had been imperceptibly transformed into a more rational quest. People sought to answer more precisely formulated questions: among them, the origin of the "Indians" and the antiquity of their presence. Travels multiplied, often organized by scientific societies (an innovation) with the aim of gaining knowledge about the far-off lands, which were little known or completely unknown. Accounts of travels, geographical descriptions, and debates about the existence of races—their characteristics, origin, migrations, and diffusions—were now the preferred themes.

Once again, it is in the small but very dense book by A. Laming-Emperaire (1980) that one finds the clearest summary of these first questions and of the first attempts at explanations that might answer them, based on the knowledge then existing of the biological sciences, paleontology, and archaeology—in other words, not much knowledge at all! She reminds us that the first person to display any curiosity about the indigenous peoples and to wonder about their origin was doubtless the Spaniard Antonio de Ulloa. This sailor and mathematician was sent by the king of Spain in 1734 to take part in the French expedition organized by the Academy of Sciences, and led by La Condamine, to measure the Earth's arc of the meridian; he was in Quito in 1735 and then, in the following years, for various reasons made a number of visits to South America, especially to Peru and Chile. It is in his *Noticias secretas de América* (Secret news of America), a kind of report on the political, military, and social situation in these countries, written after these expeditions with Jorge Juan and intended for the Spanish Crown, that one finds this famous sentence: "When you have seen one Indian, from whatever region, you have seen them all, from the point of view of color and general appearance" (cited by Laming-Emperaire 1980: 23).

In a second book published in 1772, Ulloa also made numerous, well-informed observations on the "antiquities of the Indians," including remains of buildings and temples, implements, and idols. "One has no certainty as to the creator of these memorable works [he is speaking of the ruins of Pachacámac in Peru]; in general one believes them to be the Incas, and there is some evidence for this; but this is contradicted by the fact that, when they conquered the region, the cult of the god Pachacámac was already being practiced and his temple was already built" (1772: 280–93).

Of course, there was as yet no question of imagining a "prehistory"—that was inconceivable at this time—but Ulloa was doubtless the first person to foresee the historical depth of the Peruvian past, which hitherto had been totally ignored, since the monuments and objects Europeans had discovered continued to be attributed, without the slightest differentiation, only to the Incas, the last and short-lived (they barely lasted two centuries) sovereigns of this country. The few travelers who preceded him in Peru—Father Louis Feuillée, mathematician and botanist, in 1707; Amédée-François Frezier, "king's engineer," in 1711—had opened ancient tombs and brought back objects, especially ceramics, to France, but none of them had truly posed the problem of their antiquity. The botanist Joseph Dombey, who made a long sojourn there after Ulloa (from 1778 to 1785), amassed an important collection and quantities of notes.

Between 1798 and 1804, the German naturalist Alexander von Humboldt, perhaps the most universal mind of his age—he was a mineralogist, geologist, botanist, geographer, and occasionally archaeologist—embarked for South America accompanied by the French doctor and botanist Aimé Bonpland. The expedition was mounted at the request of Louis-Antoine de Bougainville, the French navigator and explorer, who was then 70 years old but whose past exploits had fascinated von Humboldt during his youth. On 5 June 1798 the two friends boarded the corvette *Pizarro* bound for Havana. For five years, in the course of several voyages, Humboldt and Bonpland traveled through half of the American continent, from Venezuela to Colombia and then Ecuador, Peru, and, finally, Mexico. It was in Peru, at Cajamarca, that for the first time they had the chance to examine the remains of indigenous civilizations and to wonder about their antiquity. From then on, they took an increasing interest in the traces of the past, whether real or supposed:

We found in the possession of the Indians of the Río Negro some of those green stones, known by the name of "Amazon stones," because the natives pretend, according to an ancient tradition, that they come from the country "of the women without husbands." . . . But this is not the work of the Indians of our days, the natives of the Orinoco and the Amazon, whom we find in the last degree of barbarism [*sic*], who could have pierced such hard substances and given them the forms of animals and fruits. Such works, like the perforated and sculptured emeralds found in the Cordilleras of New Grenada and Quito, are vestiges of anterior civilization. (Humboldt and Bonpland 1961: 293–94)

In 1804, during another voyage, they discovered even more imposing remains in Mexico and, being very impressed, decided from then on to study them systematically This was the origin of the famous archaeological collections brought back by the two travelers and given to the Berlin museums. The whole of their published work constitutes an enormous monument, and its first part (Humboldt and Bonpland 1810), the best known, is the first rational book on the ancient American civilizations, a basic work that would subsequently be used by generations of Americanists. In contrast to Ulloa, Humboldt emphasized the diversity of Amerindian human types, a diversity that he believed to be caused more by the influence of the environment than by the multiplicity of their origins.

About 20 years later, between 1826 and 1834, Alcide d'Orbigny in his turn visited the greater part of South America: Uruguay, Argentina, Chile, Bolivia, and Peru, not counting a brief stop in Brazil. His goal was to gather geographical, geological, zoological, climatological, and ethnographic information. The voyage of Humboldt and Bonpland had aroused considerable and widespread interest, but the southern part of South America remained poorly known. The end of the wars of independence in Latin America henceforth made voyages and systematic explorations far easier. In Paris, there was a desire to verify a mass of information, some of which appeared incredible and also, generally, to renew knowledge of the nature of these regions. At the same time, however, there was no desire—since France had now undergone the Restoration—to display too conspicuously any recognition of the new nations that had emerged from revolutionary movements. So it was not a team that was entrusted with carrying out all this research but, more discreetly, a single man. The Natural History Museum in Paris chose Alcide d'Orbigny, whose intelligence and knowledge were well recognized and who, before his departure, took the project so seriously and conscientiously that he went to Brongniart, Cuvier, and Geoffroy Saint-Hilaire to acquire extra training in paleontology. After 8 years of travel and investigations of all kinds, he returned to France and set about writing up his results, a task that was to take him 14 years. O. Baulny (1968) notes: "The work undertaken was certainly enormous: 160 mammals, 860 birds, 115 reptiles, 166 fish, 980 mollusks, 5,000 insects and crustaceans, 3,000 plants, not to mention the notes on ethnography, paleontology and geology; geological and geographical maps; and, in the historical part of the Voyage, for each important locality, a historical and climatological study! And this is not even a complete list, because it does not include a particular study which, moreover, was greeted favorably by the general public: L'Homme américain (American Man)."

This was in fact part of the *Voyage* that was published separately in 1839, in which d'Orbigny attempted a synthesis of everything that was then known about the South American Indians in the domains of anthropology, linguistics, and ethnography. In it, one finds a critical examination of the historical sources—the accounts of the "chroniclers" of the Conquest—a study of the native civilizations and archaeological data, and a study of the Indian races indicating the areas of distribution of the principal human groups, among which he distinguishes three great races. As Paul Rivet was to write later,

> Three great races can be distinguished, according to d'Orbigny, from all of his observations: the Ando-Peruvian, with three branches . . . , the Pampan race with three branches . . . , the Brazilio-Guaranian race. As a naturalist, he gives the diagnosis of each of these races and of their branches.
>
> It is remarkable that after a century, this classification still remains classic in its broad outline. . . . This remarkable durability of d'Orbigny's ethnological work is the finest praise that one can give to the naturalist's penetrating eye. (Rivet, cited by Baulny 1968)

D'Orbigny, like Humboldt, was struck by the heterogeneity of the Amerindian types rather than by their resemblances. As for his *Voyage dans l'Amérique méridionale* (Voyage to southern America), published between 1835 and 1845, this monumental natural history in nine volumes deals almost exclusively with geography, floras, and faunas; American people of the past or present are scarcely mentioned in it, except incidentally.

The voyage of HMS *Beagle*, which took place in the same period (from 1831 to 1836), was commanded by Captain Robert FitzRoy, whose government entrusted him with a scientific expedition around the world and, more especially, with the exploration of the coasts of South America. The young Charles Darwin took part in this expedition as its naturalist and, on his return, published (in 1839) his account of the voyage, the *Narrative of the Surveying Voyages of HMS 'Adventure' and 'Beagle,'* between 1826 and 1836. In this work, which had immediate and considerable success, one finds abundant, detailed observations on the geology, botany, zoology, and paleontology of the regions visited but also an extremely lively description of the native populations of Tierra del Fuego whom Darwin had encountered—although not without disdain for "these abject and miserable creatures" (fig. 3). Darwin asks himself about their origin (1875: 18): "Whilst beholding these savages, one asks, whence have they come? What could have tempted, or what change compelled a tribe of men to leave the fine regions of the north, to travel down the Cordillera or backbone of America, to invent and build canoes, which are not used by the tribes of Chile, Peru, and Brazil, and then to enter on one of the most inhospitable countries within the limits of the globe?"

But obviously it was the Andean regions—Peru and, to a lesser degree, Bolivia—rich in remains of "high cultures" that attracted the greatest number of travelers. In contrast to the naturalists who were curious about everything, they took a particular interest in the indigenous populations and in the evidence that was still visible of their past—monuments such as Chavín, Pachacámac, Tiwanaku, the Inca ruins of Cuzco. The *Antigüedades Peruanas*

Fig. 3. "Native of Tierra del Fuego of the Tekeenica tribe." This unflattering portrait was produced by Conrad Martens, official artist on the *Beagle* expedition (1831–1836) in which Charles Darwin took part. The members of the expedition, and Darwin himself, were struck by the natives' extreme penury, by the malformations of their bodies (caused by the fact that they lived in very low huts and spent most of the time crouched in their canoes), and by their (very real) state of dirtiness. They called them "satires upon mankind . . . , miserable lords of this miserable land"; Darwin, who wondered from where they had come and how they got there, even added: "I believe in this extreme part of South America, man exists in a lower state of improvement than in any other part of the world." (*Narrative of the Surveying Voyages of HMS "Adventure" and "Beagle," between 1826 and 1836*, London, 1839)

Fig. 4. An amateur-collector's cabinet at the end of the nineteenth century. In 1877 the French "traveler" Paul Marcoy met Sir James Spencer in Peru, an "odd individual" who had withdrawn there from the world and had gradually amassed an impressive collection. Marcoy's description gives some idea of this extraordinary bric-a-brac and at the same time reflects the degree of ignorance at that time concerning the origin of the Amerindian cultures: "In a vast room lit from above by daylight there were grouped . . . Peruvian works of art intended for all manner of uses. . . . Obsidian axes, sandstone and porphyry clubs, metal spears and slings [sic] . . . , offensive and defensive weapons of all kinds, garments and fabrics of every sort . . . , costumes of emperors and empresses . . . , there was nothing lacking in this admirable collection. On shelves of huarango wood carved with a knife by some Red-Skin, he had arranged in hierarchical order all the gods of the Quechua Olympus, derived from the Aztec, itself stemming from the Hindu. . . . Two carved, hollowed-out beds of basalt supported centuries-old mummies so well preserved as to reduce to despair those who worked on the corpses of the time of Rameses. . . . These people wrapped in animal-gut, painted with the colours of life and health, were of such striking realism that one would have believed that blood was still circulating beneath their parchment-like skin." (From P. Marcoy, "Voyage dans la région du Titicaca" (Voyage in the region of Titicaca), *Le Tour du Monde,* Hachette, Paris, 1877)

(Peruvian antiquities) of Eduardo de Rivero and Johan-Jakob von Tschudi, who visited Peru between 1838 and 1842, appeared in 1851. In 1865, in Paris, the *Lettre sur les antiquités de Tiaguanaco et l'origine présumable de cette ancienne civilisation du Haut-Pérou* (Letter on the antiquities of Tiwanaku and the presumable origin of this high civilization of High-Peru) was published, in which Léonce Angrand set out his theory about the Toltec origin of Tiwanaku. France's vice-consul in Lima from 1834 to 1838, he traveled around the country and brought back an impressive collection of objects and drawings of sites and monuments. The second half of the nineteenth century was finally to see a succession of numerous scholarly explorations,

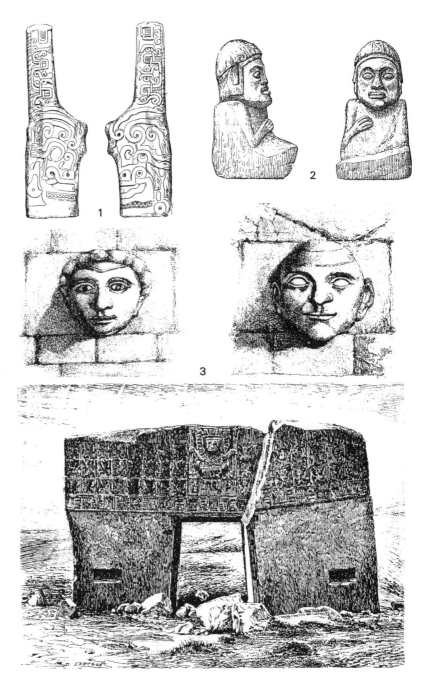

Fig. 5. The first recordings of archaeological sites and monuments. 1. The Lanzón, principal idol in the temple of Chavín de Huantar (Peru). 2. Statue found in the region of Tiwanaku (Bolivia). 3. Heads decorating the exterior wall of the temple of Pashash (Peru); note the obvious Eurocentrism of these depictions. 4. The Gate of the Sun at Tiwanaku (Bolivia). Despite a few distortions or interpretations, the 1,100 engravings that illustrate the volume by Wiener constitute one of the most enormous and complete iconographic catalogues from nineteenth-century Peru. (From C. Wiener, *Pérou et Bolivie. Récit de voyage,* Hachette, Paris, 1880, pp. 179, 449, 613)

generally led by Europeans or North Americans. They cannot all be cited here, but among the most important are those of the American Ephraim Squier to the southern United States, Central America, Peru, and Bolivia (1842–1851); the Italian Antonio Raimondi to Peru (1850–1877); the Swiss Adolph Bandelier to Mexico, Peru, and Bolivia (1870–1888); the Frenchman Charles Wiener to Peru and Bolivia (1875–1877) (fig. 5); and the German Ernst von Middendorf to Peru (1876–1888). All combined scientific curiosity with a taste for risks and a lot of romanticism, resulting in a certain lack of rigor in their descriptions. None of them seriously tackled the problem of the origin of the Amerindians and the antiquity of their presence in these lands. Some time before, however, another scholar had been preoccupied with this topic, and he came close to the subject of the present book: the prehistory in its currently accepted sense, that is, the history of the most ancient populations of South America.

A Misunderstood Botanist: Wilhelm Peter Lund

During the summer of 1830—a month after the "July revolution"—Wilhelm Peter Lund, of Danish nationality, arrived in Paris. Unconcerned with politics, he took lodgings and immediately got down to writing a scientific report with the somewhat unromantic title *Lettre sur les habitudes de quelques fourmis du Brésil* (Letter on the habits of some ants of Brazil), which he hoped to have published in the *Annales de sciences naturelles*.[2] He had just spent several months in that country, where he was a passionate observer of the habits of termites and giant ants, after those of the sloth and the black vulture. At this time, Paris was considered the center of scientific thought: it had an abundance of libraries and museums, and internationally recognized and appreciated journals of the highest standard were published there. He therefore decided that this was where he would publish his treatise, which was aimed at reappraising everything known about these formidable creatures that he saw pillage, reduce to powder, or devour everything in their path. He was soon being invited to the soirées given by Baron Cuvier where, in the midst of a fantastic accumulation of specimens of animals, fossils, and mineral samples, there were a number of scientific celebrities then in Paris. He was to make the acquaintance of Alexander von Humboldt, freshly returned from a voyage, this time to Russia. Naturally, they discussed zoology, paleontology, and especially the history of evolution, a field in which Cuvier's theory on natural cataclysms, set out in his *Le Règne animal* (The animal kingdom), had at that time almost the power of law.

Strongly influenced by this encounter, and by his conversations with his Danish colleagues and with his childhood friend Peter Christian Kierkegaard, the philosopher's brother, whom he met again on his return to Denmark and who tried unceasingly to convince him of the primacy of God over nature, Lund continued to evoke Brazil nostalgically. Finally he could stand it

[2]On Lund's life and work, one can profitably read—although it is in no way a scientific work—the highly fictionalized account by the Danish writer Henrik Stangerup, *Lagoa Santa* (Paris, Mazarine, 1955), from which I have extracted several details.

no longer, and on 1 November 1832 he set sail once again. This time he settled close to Rio and first threw himself into botanical observation. He was already contemplating the writing of a vast treatise of natural science, which he wanted to call the Creative Plan and in which he would at last set out his views on evolution: the whole of nature leads toward individualization, in increasingly perfect forms, and this in three successive stages—mineral, vegetable, and finally animal, the final outcome of which is humankind. "We thus see that Nature makes its way step by step to its goal: that of tearing the individual from the soil. Man, the fruit of this ultimate effort, is thus freed: we enter the kingdom of liberty" (quoted by Stangerup 1985: 105).

He would henceforth devote all his energy to reconstituting the history of humankind which, according to theologians whose only known truth was the Bible, was 4004 years old. To this end, he was to explore the still unknown regions of Brazil and was also to become as famous as (or even more famous than) Charles Darwin, who had just completed a voyage along the coasts of southern America and who was the talk of Rio. This is how, in October 1834, after a long and tiring voyage of several months, he and a friend arrived at the village of San Antônio de Curvelo in the heart of Minas Gerais. By chance he made the acquaintance of Peter Claussen, a landowner and a kind of local potentate, who was also Danish and, moreover, an amateur naturalist and a member of several learned societies of geology and paleontology. The region was rich in natural cavities, or *lapas*, hollowed into the limestone cliffs; these caves and rockshelters had been systematically exploited since the beginning of the century for extraction of saltpeter (used as fertilizer), and it had long been known that many fossil bones were to be found there. Claussen immediately showed Lund some bones collected from the back of the caves located on his property. From then on, there was no holding Lund back: these remains, which had to date to the Flood, were the first of their kind to be found in a tropical country. How did they get there, when they belonged to animal species from cold countries? After a sudden cooling of the climate, a massive migration, a gigantic earthquake? Claussen and Lund set off for the little town of Lagoa Santa, crossed the village of Caéta, reached Ouro Prieto, the capital of the province, continued their walk across the campo, and finally arrived at the entrance of an immense cave, where a succession of underground chambers and corridors were decorated with fabulous draperies of translucent calcite. Its name was Lapa Nova do Maquiné. Here, Lund observed, beneath a limestone crust that was broken in many places—Peter Claussen had already passed that way—a layer of red earth containing bones. One day when he was able to return alone, without Claussen to follow and keep an eye on him, he carried on his exploration of the cave and reached a deep chamber, which apparently no one had ever entered before and where the protective layer of limestone was still intact. He was to spend whole days in there, breaking this crust and extracting from their matrix of earth a series of bones that proved to be those of fossil species of antelope and of *Megatherium,* a giant edentate. Lund's conviction grew even stronger: these remains could only have accumulated here following a cataclysm on a world scale, involving, successively, an earthquake, a gigantic tidal wave, the melting of the poles, and a shift in the ecliptic. Once calm returned to the Earth, God re-created the plant and animal species, but not all of them, and they were not necessarily identical. As for humans, they did not yet enter the picture, because Lund did not imagine for an instant that people could have existed before the great Flood.

During this time, gossip was well under way in the region. Naturally, Claussen and Lund were searching for treasure—diamonds, pearls, and nuggets hidden in the cave long ago by an Indian chief. They were looked on with respect and envy and were treated with the greatest consideration. Lund had tremendous difficulty in putting right the inhabitants of Curvelo—until the day when he found the entrance of Maquiné Cave blocked with enormous rocks and was threatened with a rifle by the landowner. Both he and his assistant draftsman had to leave the village. He now had to find other caves and enough fossil bones to find the proof that his theory of re-creation was correct. Lund and Brandt, his draftsman, visited dozens of caves, almost always without result, before finding themselves at Lagoa Santa again, where they resumed their research. Among other caves—they were to see more than a hundred—they explored Lapa da Cerca Grande, rich not only in fossils but also in rock paintings depicting animals "of primitive race," Lapa do Baú, and Lapa da Serra das Abelhas, where Lund undertook the calculation of the age of the Earth. According to his estimate, this cave contained the remains of 7 or 8 million animals dating back to the postdiluvian period, that is, to the period of re-creation. It must have taken at least 5,000 years for them to accumulate. Since the antediluvian era must have had more or less the same duration, the Earth must be about 12,000 years old. QED.

At Lagoa Santa, in the midst of the cases containing the thousands of bones he had collected, now reconstituted and classified, Lund also resumed the writing of his history of the antediluvian world, *Aperçu du règne animal au Brésil avant le dernier cataclysme* (Outline of the animal kingdom in Brazil before the last cataclysm). In it, he claimed that mammals were predominant at that time, that the species were different from those of today, and that humans did not yet exist—that a universal cataclysm caused the mammals to disappear and that the world was then re-created, this time including a superior species, the human species. During this time, while he was already experiencing the first attacks—unbearable pains and dizziness—of the insanity that would finally engulf him, he became famous in his homeland. His herbaria and botanical observations earned the admiration of the Danish scientific community, and he was awarded a decoration by his sovereign. His renown spread throughout Europe, and a number of distinguished scientists told him how much they admired him—but as a botanist, not as a paleontologist.

It is 1840. The harvest of fossils continued at Lapa do Sumidouro, one of the richest caves he had visited. Then, in the middle of the bones of prehistoric (that is, "antediluvian") animals, he discovered what were indisputably human remains: several skulls and some scattered bones, in the midst of remains of *Megatherium* and of the giant feline *Smilodon* (see fig. 7). The bones were broken, and their appearance was similar to that of the animal bones. Lund thought that these human remains, which could only be postdiluvian, were mixed with those of the animals only because the limestone crust was not sufficiently solid or impenetrable. At the end of 1844, Lund ceased his excavations. He wanted to return to Europe in order to think and write in comfort, far away from this exhausting climate and the harassments of Peter Claussen who, in the meantime, had taken credit for the discoveries. Claussen claimed he was the only man who had excavated the caves and collected remains of fossil animals and that he had sold his collections to different European museums, including that of Paris. He merely admitted having collaborated for a moment with a Danish doctor who was passing through the region. The last report Lund wrote before his departure from Brazil is called *Observations sur les ossements fossiles humains découverts dans certaines cavernes du Brésil* (Observations on the fossil human bones discovered in certain caves of Brazil). In it he concluded that South America was occupied a very long time ago by humans of identical appearance to present-day people and who must therefore have arrived in America after a migration from the Old World. From this moment on, and after having in 1845 sent Christian VIII, king of Denmark, his enormous collection of fossils, Lund carried out no further fieldwork and wrote no more reports. However, as we shall see, he continued to take part from afar in several scientific debates, most notably the one around 1850 that stirred up the scientific community regarding the origin of the shell mounds, or *sambaquis,* on the Atlantic coast of Brazil. However, he gradually sank into madness, occasionally wracked with pain, affected by nightmares, and pursued by thousands of ants and snakes that tracked him, surrounded him, gnawed him. He died on 25 May 1880 without having left Lagoa Santa.

How was Lund's discovery of this "Lagoa Santa Man" amid the remains of large Quaternary animals received by the scientific circles of the time? Those who knew about it accorded it little importance and thought, as Lund himself had suggested at one time, that the bones were remains from several periods—ancient animals, recent human—that had been disturbed and mixed up by the waters flowing in the caves. The problem of a possible contemporaneity of humans and fossil animal species was at that time far from resolved in Europe. As Laming-Emperaire observes: "The years 1840–1850 were not very far from the time when the myth of the flood was used to explain geological phenomena, and moreover high water-levels, which really did leave their mark on the walls of numerous caves, could help support this interpretation" (1979: 55). It was not until the twentieth century, and even the 1920s, that paleontological and archaeological research began again in this part of Central Brazil that is so rich in remains.

The Origin of the Sambaquis

During his long Brazilian sojourn, Lund was not only interested in the ante-diluvian "Lagoa Santa Man" and in the now-famous rock paintings that adorn the walls of the shelter of Cerca Grande and which he was doubtless the first European to have observed. As Ella Hoch and André Prous (1985) remind us, he also took part in a debate that was then stirring up the European scientific community concerning the origin of the numerous accumulations of mollusk shells scattered along the coast of Denmark. In 1847, a Danish commission was set up to determine whether these were natural accumulations or if they had been built by humans. One of its members who favored human activity as the explanation wrote to Lund. Lund gave him his full support and informed him, in his reply sent in 1852, that in Brazil, too, along almost the whole of the littoral, there are comparable accumulations located, like those of Denmark, at a certain distance from the present shoreline. Also as in Denmark, one finds bones of vertebrates, fragments of charcoal, and worked stone tools mixed with the shells. The two authors add that, paradoxically, although Lund's opinion very quickly helped convince the European scientists that the Kjökkenmöddings were of human origin, it was only acknowledged much later in Brazil, where it was not until the 1870s that a similar explanation for the *sambaquis* was proposed and finally accepted.

Did Humans Originate in America?

In 1906, Argentine paleontologist Florentino Ameghino published a report on a series of fossils in the very serious *Anales* of the Buenos Aires National Museum, fossils to which he had given names that clearly revealed the theory he claimed to support: *Homunculus patagonicus, Anthropos perfectus,* and so forth. His view was that humans had appeared in South America and had evolved in situ, giving rise to a whole lineage that subsequently spread throughout the world at the start of the Pleistocene.

Ameghino was born in 1854. At first a modest schoolteacher, he then taught himself geology, anthropology, and paleontology, to the extent that he soon became Argentina's official paleontologist. On 28 July 1875, the date that Jorge Fernández (1982: 78) suggests should be considered as the day of the official birth of Argentine archaeology, the Argentine Scientific Society gathered for his birthday. He presented it with a series of objects ("fossil" bones, "worked" implements) which, he claimed, demonstrated the existence of a fossil human on the Argentine pampa. The society, impressed, awarded him with a diploma of honor ("as a powerful incentive to pursue his research" (quoted by Fernández 1982: 79); sure enough, Ameghino, then aged 25, was to redouble his efforts. Despite the doubts expressed by a few scientists, including the highly respected naturalist and paleontologist Hermann Burmeister, he continued his excavations, extending them into Uruguay. He also traveled to Belgium, England, Italy, and especially France, where he visited the recently discovered prehistoric site of Chelles and where he began to publish. His articles and his assertions rapidly caused a great fuss in the European scientific world where, curiously, nobody cast doubt on his discoveries. The idea of a fossil human did not shock anybody in France, where there was also talk of a "Tertiary Man." All of Ameghino's discoveries were based on the same postulate: not only was humankind very ancient in South America, it originated there. More specifically, humans could only have appeared in a single place and at a single moment, and this was on the Argentine pampa toward the middle of the Tertiary era. "Man must have had a beginning and a point of departure," he wrote in 1881 in his most important work, *La antigüedad del Hombre en la Plata* (The antiquity of man in La Plata), which was published in Paris: "Since no bones of humans of Tertiary age have been found in the other regions of the Earth, we conclude that the origin and the center of dispersal of Man was the southern half of South America, where his fossil remains from the Tertiary period occur in abundance."

His research continued during the following years, and in the first years of the twentieth century he drew up a genealogical tree of the human species and published—afterward, because it was only after thinking up the transitional forms that he sought them in the field—various "fossil" bone pieces: an atlas and a femur found at Monte Hermoso (several years apart and by different people, but he considered them to be from the same individual), a fragment of cranial vault unearthed during work on the port of Buenos Aires, a skull discovered accidentally by the edge of a stream. According to him, all this material was unearthed in the Miocene terrains of the Tertiary, so the entire human species originated in South America from a homunculus of the Upper Eocene, *Homunculus patagonicus*. There followed a whole lineage of prehominids, *Tetraprothomo* (of which the *Pithecanthropus* that had just been found in Java in 1892 was merely a descendant), *Triprothomo, Diprothomo,* and finally *Prothomo*, which immediately preceded the genus *Homo*, successively represented by *Homo caputinclinatus, H. Sinemento, H. Cubensi*s, and then *H. Pampaeus*, the latter of Pliocene age. Born on the pampa, humans then passed into North America by means of an uplifting of the isthmus of Panama, which joined the two parts of the continent. They then reached Asia via the Bering Strait and constituted the Mongol race, while another branch, using a bridge linking America with Europe at the very beginning of the Pleistocene, was gradually transformed, giving birth to the white race. "Heidelberg Man," discovered in 1907 near Mauer in Germany, and which Ameghino baptized *Pseudhomo*, represented a lateral branch of *Tetraprothomo*.

As one can imagine, this fine structure immediately aroused a very lively controversy, and many people were highly skeptical. In 1910, one year before his death, Ameghino presented his *H. pampaeus* to the International Congress of Americanists, meeting at Buenos Aires. At the same time, he presented the stone tool industry it was supposed to have produced and on which he had already published the year before—an industry "of broken stones, the simplest one can imagine," made up of cobbles split lengthwise. A young North American anthropologist of Czech origin, Alès Hrdlička, reacted particularly virulently after this presentation. Henceforth, he set out to demonstrate the baseless nature of Ameghino's theories and undertook a trip to Argentina in order to prove that Ameghino was mistaken in attributing to the Tertiary the terrains that had yielded the "fossils." In the United States in 1912, Hrdlička and W. H. Holmes published *Early Man in South America*, which aimed to demonstrate the absurdity of Ameghino's theories. Even in Argentina, sharp criticisms were put forward, a good example being the little book by Felix F. Outes and Carlos Bruch (published in 1951 but containing texts written in 1910), professors at the University of La Plata. Bruch was also the head of the zoology section of the university's museum:

> The discovery of Tetraprothomo and of Diprothomo platense, which according to Doctor Florentino Ameghino are two new representatives of the hominid family, deserves a special mention. . . .
>
> The existence of Tetraprothomo was judged DOUBTFUL by the majority of the scientific world: specialists are certain that the FEMUR MUST HAVE BELONGED to a CARNIVOROUS mammal; as for the atlas, the virtually unanimous opinion is that it is from a MAN suffering from CERTAIN ANOMALIES which, if correct, would confirm the doubts that exist about its provenance, since the coexistence of a true human and the ancient fauna of Monte Hermoso is logically impossible. . . .
>
> Specialists have equal reservations about Dyprothomo platensis, because they object above all to the ORIENTATION given to the piece, since its position, which in their eyes is DEFECTIVE, DETERMINES all the characteristics that are considered typical, and which DISAPPEAR as soon as the skull fragment is PLACED in the POSITION they judge to be CORRECT. (1951: 39)

Unfortunately for Ameghino, these are indeed Quaternary terrains, not Tertiary. Some bones are merely those of small present-day monkeys, types of sapajou. The skullcap of *Diprothomo* and the atlas of *Tetraprothomo* come from totally modern humans, similar to the contemporary natives (the femur was misorientated by Ameghino). The femur of *Tetraprothomo* is that of a small carnivore. Finally (but this would not be discovered until later), the implements of worked stone were only a few centuries old at most, being remains abandoned by the indigenous tribes of the historical period.

Homo pampaeus never existed except in the imaginative and somewhat disordered mind of Ameghino.

Yet Argentina's "Tertiary Man" was resilient. Ameghino died in 1911, more convinced than ever of its existence. In 1912, however, after the severe but well-founded criticisms of Hrdlička had spread widely through the scientific community, the Frenchman M. Vignaud wrote, in his preface to Henri Beuchat's *Manuel d'archéologie américaine* (Manual of American archaeology) (the first of its kind):

> Far from believing that there is evidence allowing one to think that America was the cradle of the humana genus, as a few authors used to believe and as is still claimed by Mr. Ameghino [Carlos Ameghino, Florentino's younger brother], one must declare clearly that the theory of an indigenous origin of American man raises two formidable objections which nothing has been able to shake.
>
> The first is the absence of fossils of any species of anthropoid ape, which excludes the possibility that man evolved in situ.
>
> The second is the lack of authentic evidence that the human bones found at certain points in the New World are not those of individuals who lived in historic times and belonged to the same races as exist today. (1912: xv)

But Carlos Ameghino did take up the torch, and between 1913 and 1919 he published several notes and articles about "new evidence," that is, various objects—a polished diorite ball, fossil bone fragments with worked stone points stuck in them, various worked stone tools—that supposedly came from Miocene terrains. In 1919, the Swede Eric Boman, who was carrying out archaeological research in Argentina, reported all this in Paris's *Journal de la Société des Américanistes* and displayed profound reservations about the matter:

> At a time when Florentino Ameghino's *Diprothomo* and *Tetraprothomo* have been definitively rejected by all anthropologists, traces of human industry have just been discovered in a Tertiary layer [the "Chapalmalean" stage, supposedly of Miocene age] on the coast of the province of Buenos. . . .
>
> In the face of such extraordinary facts, one might imagine a possible deception but, as far as I am concerned, I have not been able to find any evidence to support that hypothesis. . . .
>
> For me, although one can admit the possibility of the existence of Tertiary Man in the Pampas, the main difficulty in accepting the Tertiary origin of the objects that I have just listed is as follows: without exception, all the objects unearthed from the Chapalmalean layer of Miramar bear a remarkable resemblance to the similar objects that are found everywhere on the surface and in the upper layers of the Pampa and Patagonia. (Boman 1919: 657–64)

This final doubt does him great credit, because it was realized a little later that the objects were far younger than had been thought. Until about 1930, various specialists tried to demonstrate that these chronological attributions were false, while others stubbornly defended them. In 1927, Alfredo Castellanos, of the Museum of Natural History in Buenos Aires, was still able to write: "I have already shown that the problem of the existence of fossil man in South America is very complicated. One cannot accept the phylogenetic tree of Ameghino, nor the enormous age he assigns to the sediments, but it is also not possible to support his opponents' idea that nothing was in situ, that the remains are not fossil or belong to the natives of protohistoric times, or that all the layers are Pleistocene" (1927: 3).

On the basis of two molars found at the foot of a cliff, again in the region of Miramar on the Atlantic coast, this learned paleontologist created, "on a sounder basis than those of Ameghino," a new species, *Homo chapadmalensis,* which he attributed to the middle or upper Miocene (ibid.). In 1929, at the end of a note on a piece of mandible, he persisted: "The purpose of these lines is to make known a new find concerning fossil man, by observing the most noteworthy features which allow one to consider these remains as belonging to Homo sapiens, and to declare on the basis of these new clues that the existence of this species is far older in South America than in Europe" (1929: 7).

He was to repeat these sentiments until 1934. However, as Schobinger concludes in a work of synthesis (1982: 89), fatigue set in and the problem progressively sank into oblivion, as in all cases where public opinion is polarized for many years. Schobinger adds: "There then began [in Argentina] a calmer period of research; above all because researchers preferred remote regions that were difficult to reach, but less dangerous to interpret.... From 1930 onwards, and for several years, there would be no further interest in 'archaeolithic' or 'prehistoric archaeology,' as they were then known" (ibid.: 89–90).

A Scientific Archaeology

Hence it was only at the end of the nineteenth century that there existed a true Americanist archaeological science. Certainly, "Americanism" already existed. The First International Congress of Americanists met at Nancy in 1875, and, as we have seen, archaeological and especially ethnographic expeditions had multiplied. But the hunt for antiquities often remained disorganized until two German geologists, Wilhelm Reiss and Alphons Stübel, undertook excavations in the necropolis of Ancón in Peru that were of far greater extent than the "holes" dug by even their most serious predecessors. Published in Berlin, their report, *Das Totenfeld von Ancón in Perú (The Graveyard of Ancón, in Peru)* (1880–1887), constitutes the first example of an archaeological monograph on South America and also the first publication of intensive excavations.

At the close of the nineteenth century, South American archaeology finally had a solid basis. The field was ready for a methodical and fully scientific approach, practiced by professionals, of the kind that was to be inaugurated by the excavations of the German Max Uhle, the first person to base his or her reasoning and interpretations on the systematic recording of data and the stratigraphic position of objects. He was also the first to try and follow this by placing them in chronological order. Uhle carried out research in Bolivia in 1891 and published, in collaboration with Stübel, *Die Ruinenstaette von Tiahuanaco* (*The Ruins of Tiwanaku*) (1892), in which for the first time a chronological sequence was proposed for the cultures of the high Peruvian-Bolivian plateau. He then worked in Peru, at Pachacámac, where his excavations are rightly considered the first scientific excavations to be carried out in America (Uhle 1903), and at Moche, Chincha, Ica, and various other coastal sites. However, this work was always devoted entirely to the relatively recent periods of the Peruvian past. In 1904, he undertook new excavations at Ancón (where Reiss and Stübel had already worked), but this time he studied shell mounds, to which he ascribed an age of about 2,000 years and which he believed had been accumulated by "primitive fisherfolk" (Uhle 1910). This time he was dealing with prehistory, in today's sense of the term. From 1912 onward, Uhle lived in Chile and excavated on the north coast, where he brought to light the prehistoric cultures of Arica and Tacna (1919). Uhle, who died in 1944, was the true pioneer of South American prehistory.

From these few portraits, or "spotlights," on the infancy of prehistoric research in South America, one cannot, of course, derive a complete and exact picture of the genesis of a discipline—this genesis required a total of a hundred years, like that of the discipline of prehistory in Europe, give or take a few years. It is not the aim of this book to tell this story in detail; this has already been done very well by A. Laming-Emperaire (1980), J. Fernández (1982), and J. Alcina Franch (1985). The purpose here is merely to show, by means of a few examples purposely chosen from before the 1930s, the moment when the prehistory of South America—having gradually forged its implements and developed its set of problems—became a fully fledged discipline and to provide the historical and scientific context and the political and social climate in which a local scientific community of prehistorians was gradually constituted. Research in South America sometimes lagged behind prehistoric research in Europe, although South America closely followed Europe's trials and errors and its discoveries; but sometimes researchers in South America were astonishingly advanced, as shown by the intuitions of W. P. Lund concerning "Lagoa Santa Man" or the *sambaquis*.

2

THE FIRST OCCUPANTS

W HEN DID PEOPLE REACH THE DIFFERENT REGIONS OF THIS IMMENSE subcontinent, and how did they come to settle there? The problem is crucial because it is connected to the more general problem of the first peopling of the whole of America, a question that is still far from resolved. It is also at the heart of a controversy that splits the community of Americanist prehistorians into two opposing camps, each of which maintains an extremely clear-cut position but neither of which ever manages to convince the other side completely. There is a "conservative" school that refuses to accept an antiquity greater than 12,000 or 13,000 years for the arrival of humans. And there are the self-declared "radicals" who, with equal intolerance, advocate a far older American population, which arrived about 40,000 years ago, if not more, but certainly earlier than 20,000 years ago. Debates on this topic always arouse passions and, while stopping short of downright dishonesty, often display a certain amount of distortion, even deliberate omission, of facts or arguments that might support the opposite view.

THE OPPOSING THEORIES

Let me attempt to summarize the genesis and the different phases of what often resembles combat more than decorous scientific discussion. In both cases, the "weapons" are the archaeological data, supported (or contradicted) by those of geology and climatology. Naturally, everyone employs these same data: a small number of sites that some consider very ancient and whose antiquity is ferociously denied by others. Curiously, these controversial sites are almost all in the south, located in Mexico, Central America, and, especially, South America, while for the moment the United States and Canada have only three that really provide a solid basis for discussion. This complicates matters because, while most specialists agree that the initial population must have come from Siberia and acknowledge the primarily Asiatic origin of the Amerindians, it follows that human occupation should be more ancient in North America than in South America since people had to cross the former to reach the latter. Have the traces of these first occupants disappeared from North America for geological or climatic reasons?

Some have insinuated that less rigor is displayed in excavation methods and that there is less fuss over the validity of data, especially absolute dates, in South America and Europe.[1] This argument borders on arrogance; but one must accept that, whereas the conservative North American theories are based on dozens of relatively recent Paleoindian/Clovis sites and dozens, if not hundreds, of C14 dates, the defenders of the opposing theory, whatever their nationality, still have at their disposal a mere handful of sites scattered throughout an immense continent with sometimes a single date for each of them.

Genesis of the Controversy

At the beginning of the twentieth century, Argentinian paleontologist F. Ameghino claimed to have discovered remnants of a Tertiary-era man (see chapter 1). During the 1910 International Congress of Americanists held at Buenos Aires, Ameghino and his hypotheses were rapidly and mercilessly demolished by W. H. Holmes and Aleš Hrdlička. Hrdlička, an anthropologist of Czech origin, from 1900 onward headed the anthropology section of the Bureau of American Ethnology at the Smithsonian Institution, then the main center for the study of the indigenous populations of North America. Holmes and Hrdlička, who considered themselves the champions of a veritable "New Archaeology" before the expression was coined by a later archaeologist, faced the "fanciful" hypotheses then in vogue regarding the origin of the Amerindians. But it was especially in an article published in 1912 that Hrdlička, on the basis of the exterior physical traits observed in Amerindian populations (for example, skin color and hirsuteness), tried to demonstrate the fundamental racial unity of the original Americans (Hrdlička 1912). In his view, and despite undeniable differences of detail that he attributed to the influence of the environment or genetic variation, the "American Indians" all belonged to the same type and represented a single human branch of Mongoloid origin. In order to support his hypothesis, Hrdlička reappraised all the fossil human remains that had then been discovered in America, studying their osteological characteristics and measuring the cephalic index of the skulls. His categorical conclusion was that all these fossils were anatomically modern. This confirmed his certainty that the Americans were recent and came from a single Mongoloid stock. Hence America was populated in a relatively recent period (four or five millennia ago at most) by one or several human groups that came from Asia via the region of the Bering Straits. Hrdlička's authority and prestige were such that, during the 1920s, his propositions acquired the strength of dogma.

[1]One article by the "conservative" Lynch is entitled—with no circumlocution—"El Hombre de la edad glacial en Suramérica: una perspectiva europea" (Ice Age man in South America: a European perspective) (Lynch 1990b).

However, one new fact turned up to cause trouble: in 1926, at Folsom in ✶ New Mexico, a team of paleontologists from the Colorado Natural History Museum unearthed a fragment of a projectile point of worked stone between the ribs of a large bison skeleton, of a fossil species considered to have been extinct for thousands of years. This unquestionable association of a humanly made object and the bones of an animal that disappeared long ago was of enormous importance: it proved that the human presence in America was much more ancient than had been hitherto believed, even though, when confronted with this evidence, Hrdlička began by suggesting that the animals with which the points were associated had perhaps not disappeared quite so long ago. It turned out to be difficult to convince anthropologists and archaeologists: most of them believed that this association was accidental and that the objects of worked stone were far more recent and thus intrusive among the bison bones. However, Alfred Vincent Kidder, one of the few who had doubts, declared (albeit confidentially) after a visit to the Folsom site that the arrival of humans in America doubtless "took place at least fifteen or twenty thousand years ago" (Kidder 1927: 5). In the years that followed, excavations continued, and finally another bifacial point was discovered, again in association with bones of a fossil bison. The contemporaneity of the two was at last accepted by various eminent specialists, who were urgently called in to examine the latest find in situ. In all, after three years of research, 19 points of the same type—since named "Folsom points"—and 23 skeletons of fossil bison were discovered at this site, always in association and contained within sediments of Pleistocene age (see Wormington 1957: 23–29). However, it was not until W. Libby developed the C14 dating method in the 1950s that these discoveries could be dated to between 11,000 and 10,000 years ago. The antiquity of humans in America was extended back by six millennia. The "type fossil" of these sites, where discoveries had multiplied since 1926 in the southwestern United States, was thus the Folsom point, a lanceolate projectile with edges that are finely retouched bifacially and whose concave base is thinned by the removal—on each face and along the point's axis—of an elongated flake that creates a longitudinal "fluting": hence the name of "fluted point" that is still given to these pieces. A few years later, between 1932 and 1937 and again in New Mexico, the discovery was made, in undisputable association with the bones of a mammoth this time, of bifacial points of a type slightly different from those of Folsom. Longer and a little thicker, they also had a fluting on both faces, rarely on only one, but shorter than that on the Folsom points. These "Clovis points" (from the eponymous site) belonged to levels that would later be dated by C14 in various sites, to around 11,500 B.P.; they were thus a little older than Folsom points and considered to be their most probable "ancestors." Thus from 1950 onward the lower limit of the peopling of America that was accepted more or less willingly by the conservatives was fixed at 11,500, or 12,000 B.P. at most.

In opposition to the conservatives arose—albeit somewhat later, in the 1950s, when the first sites were discovered that were then thought to be older—a "radical" school proposing that people reached America, and particularly South America, far earlier, perhaps as long ago as 30,000 years. In the meantime, America (both North and South) had seen the gradual establishment of a true science of prehistory, while every year (or almost) brought fresh technical advances or new discoveries. In 1957, O. Menghin, the Argentinian archaeologist of Austrian origin, in his book *Urgeschichte Amerikas* (*Prehistory of America*), for the first time put forward the hypothesis of a cultural stage in South America that predated the Paleoindian cultural horizon that was represented in North America by the Clovis and Folsom points and which he called "Protolithic." In his view, this stage was characterized in lithic assemblages by the absence of bifacial projectile points and was derived from the Lower and Middle Palaeolithic of Eurasia.[2] This position was taken up again in 1964 by A. Krieger, who proposed for this stage the term "Pre-projectile point" (Krieger 1964). However, it should be stressed that, in Krieger's view, this unfortunate name was to be applied only to a technical stage, with no chronological connotation—but apparently not everyone understood this. In the same line of thought, P. Bosch-Gimpera, the Mexican archaeologist of Spanish origin, in the early 1960s accepted the idea of an American Lower Palaeolithic. In 1966, in a work that still serves as an important reference, Gordon Willey likewise accepted the existence of a South American Early Lithic stage. These pioneers were criticized severely in their time, but one must acknowledge that their hypotheses sprang more from an act of faith than from true scientific knowledge, since the archaeological data on which they relied were for the most part highly questionable, as we shall see. In fact, most of the data are rejected today.

What Is the Situation at Present?

After the discoveries at Folsom and Clovis and the C14 dates that were obtained, one might think that, since the limit of a few millennia fixed by Hrdlička and his successors had been exceeded, research would now see its results and its ensuing hypotheses able to range freely through time. But nothing of the kind happened. The date of 12,000 B.P., forced on grudging specialists in the 1930s by irrefutable evidence, became a *terminus ante quem*, a kind of checkpoint beyond which many of them refused to acknowledge the slightest human presence in America.

The date of 12,000 B.P. in North America, and more particularly in the Southwest and the Great Plains, marks the beginning of the Paleoindian period, which corresponds to a way of life based on the hunting of Pleistocene megafauna: mammoth, mastodon, horse, and camelid in the first phases and especially bison later. The hunters were highly specialized and mobile, organized into small bands at first, then bigger groups for the great

[2]In 1947, the French ethnologist Paul Rivet was already admitting—albeit without any discussion or arguments—the existence of an American Paleolithic that perhaps extended back to the end of the Pleistocene.

bison hunts later in time. This Paleoindian phase ended around 8000 B.P., at the same time as most of the great Pleistocene mammals disappeared. I am dwelling on this period, on its type fossils—the Clovis and Folsom points—and on the means of subsistence that they characterize, because we shall meet them again in South America, where the places they were discovered and their various vicissitudes are the subject of interminable controversies that always involve the same theme: was there a pre-Clovis peopling of South America or, in a more general way, one that was earlier than the Paleoindian of North America? The conservatives' answer is a categorical no. They include geologists, paleontologists, and a large number of the North American prehistorians who work in North America. However, the title of standard-bearer can be accorded to Thomas Lynch, who has worked in both North and South America (which perhaps explains his position).

The arguments of the steadfast conservatives are as follows: first, none of the human remains found in the Americas are ancient, or at least earlier than about 10,000 years. If humans were present before this time, how is it that none of the sites supposed to be older have yielded any trace of them, whereas human remains dating to around 10,000 B.P. are rare, certainly, but do exist? As for the "ancient" sites, none meet the minimal scientific demands: a clear stratigraphy, objects or structures (hearths and so forth) of indisputably human origin, and multiple dates that are fully controlled and well associated with remains of human origin. According to the conservatives, the remains are either lithic material found on the surface and consequently impossible to date in any certain way; or the objects are contained within a sedimentary stratum that is itself well dated to the Pleistocene, but they were accidentally introduced into it through disturbances of various kinds (water flow, slippage, collapse); or the sediment and the remains of human origin are definitely associated, but the dates do not have sufficient guarantees; or, in the worst cases, the "objects" discovered and the "structures" observed are in no way the result of human activity. In different papers Lynch (1974, 1978, 1983, 1990a, b, 1991) has engaged in a merciless and detailed review of the "ancient" sites.

In the camp of those holding the opposite theory, several names stand out: Alan Bryan and Ruth Gruhn, North American archaeologists who work especially in South America; the geographer G. Carter; and the Latin-American archaeologists J. L. Lorenzo (Mexico) and J. Schobinger (Argentina). But the prize for audacity unquestionably goes to Richard (Scotty) MacNeish. In 1976, he proposed the following scenario: at some point at least earlier than 20,000 B.P. and doubtless closer to 50,000 B.P. or even 70,000 B.P., people arrived from Asia by taking the continental bridge that then occupied the position of the present Bering Strait. The human groups then began their advance southward "at a very slow rate" (1976: 317). They possessed no specialized toolkit of worked stone and mostly used fairly crude implements (worked cobbles or rudimentary bifaces), that is, an assortment bearing some resemblance to that of Europe's Lower and Middle Palaeolithic hunters. About 20,000 years ago, and doubtless even earlier, they reached South America after crossing the isthmus of Panama. Certainly the traces of their passage are very rare, but this is hardly surprising. The population during this period, which MacNeish calls "Stage I," must have been very small, and the geological contexts have subsequently undergone major disruptions and various contaminations. There then came a "Stage II" lasting from 40,000 to 25,000 B.P. in North America and from 25,000 to 15,000 B.P. in South America. People were now a little better equipped with tools made from big stone flakes and bone points, but MacNeish observes that "the paucity of sites certainly hints at very small populations and slow population growth" (ibid.: 320).

"Stage III," from 25,000 to 13,000 B.P. in North America and from 15,000 to 11,000 B.P. in South America, corresponds to specialized groups hunting the large Pleistocene fauna and possessing an evolved lithic toolkit, including "fine leaf-shaped bifacial projectile points as well as blades and . . . skillfully made flint burins" (ibid.). MacNeish even went so far as to compare this stage with the beginning of the European Upper Palaeolithic (Aurignacian and Solutrean). However, there is little material evidence to support this fine reconstruction.

A. Bryan, another fervent defender of a great antiquity for the peopling of America, offered his first theoretical propositions in the 1960s, when he outlined a model of the peopling and cultural development of the American continent, placing its start in the Pleistocene: "A small human group first entered the New World via the Bering Straits some time during the Late Pleistocene or possibly the latter part of the Middle Pleistocene" (1965: 88).

He may have intended to say Paleolithic rather than Pleistocene, because the Middle Pleistocene dates from 700,000 to 130,000 B.P. Be that as it may, this was a daring proposition at a time when the few dates known for America, already hotly disputed, did not exceed 30,000 years. In a series of more recent publications, Bryan and Gruhn have taken up this thesis, "enriched" with new data from excavations. This is how they ended an article published in 1990 (though written in 1984): "The year 1984 should see the final collapse of the 50 years old model of earliest American man as a specialized big game hunter carrying fluted points across the Bering Straits no earlier than 13,000 years ago" (1989: 81). One admires their optimism.

I have chosen to illustrate the thesis of a very ancient peopling of South America through the work of MacNeish and Bryan because they are not only the most convinced defenders of this idea, but they also have developed conceptual models to support their hypotheses. Still, it is astonishing that the sequence so boldly outlined by MacNeish and the chronology he put forward were based overall on such flimsy data—surface finds (Rio

Pedregal in Venezuela), uncontrolled dates (Californian skeletons), doubtful associations (Muaco in Venezuela), sometimes surprising typological determinations ("Paccaicasa" toolkit in Peru)—admittedly, almost the only evidence that was available when he published his articles. Besides, since then, most of the sites or layers cited in support of his hypotheses have disappeared from the archaeological literature.

Naturally, the archaeologists who have obtained a date earlier than 12,000 B.P. in their sites have since grown in number, because few Americanist prehistorians who have obtained a very early date in the course of their excavations have seriously questioned it. Nevertheless, it is noticeable that the most optimistic of the advocates of great antiquity have rarely suggested that people were present in America more than 100,000 years ago. Two exceptions are the defenders of the Calico site in California, who have put forward dates of more than 200,000 years, dates that have been rejected even by Bryan, and, more recently, a Franco-Brazilian mission that claimed to have discovered traces of human occupation in a cave of the Bahía region dating back to 300,000 years. The span of dates that are the subject of serious debate is from 60,000 to 12,000 B.P.

The debate appears hopeless. With each new site-candidate for great antiquity, the response is predictable: some accept the site, others do not. The diehard skeptics remain unmoved. The clearest result, as noted by David Meltzer in 1989, is that the "Clovis barrier" remains erect. Perhaps it is far less solid now, but it still bristles with thorns: "Fundamental to all that follows is the conviction that there is *no* convincing evidence in sub-Laurentide America for *any* human presence prior to the appearance of Clovis, which is to say 11,500–11,000 years ago" (West 1996: 539). Further: "There will probably be those who will continue to seek earlier, and perhaps more exotic, origins for the beginnings of America, but the array of evidence presented in this volume would seem to render that an uncommonly fruitless task" (ibid.: 553).

Yet, in the final decade of the twentieth century, the body of evidence provided by "ancient" sites—that is, earlier than 12,000 B.P.—began to look impressive. Given the nature of the controversy, the personalities of the adversaries, and the ambiguity of the archaeological data in many cases, it is certain that none of the sites concerned can be accepted without critical examination. Further, it is true that after detailed evaluation, some sites seem to require elimination. However, some are acceptable, while others at least inspire a certain amount of confidence. Since each of the opposing theories uses the same data, it is necessary to review them briefly here and to summarize the current arguments.

The Early Sites of North America

Although the North American sites lie outside the geographical framework of this book, a brief reference to them is indispensable in this context. In the

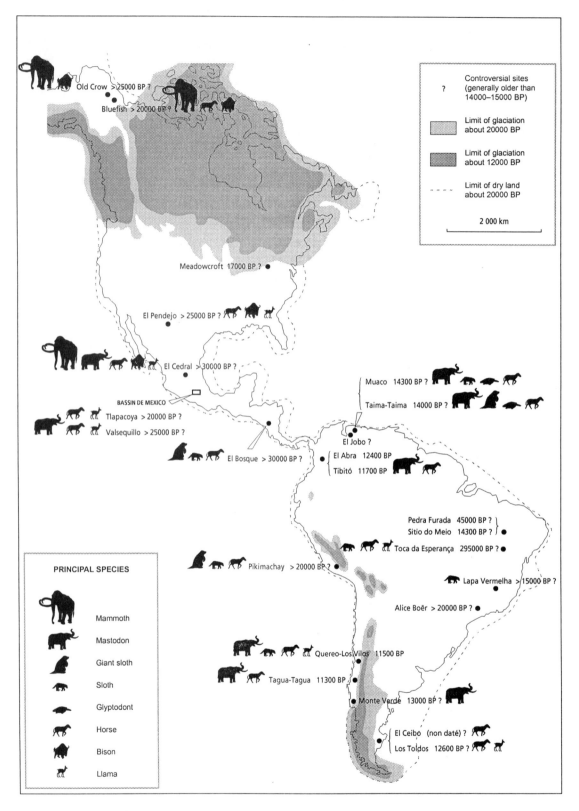

Fig. 6 American sites earlier than 11,000 B.P.

Canadian Yukon, the open-air Old Crow site, excavated by R. Bonnichsen and his team, contained an impressive assemblage of bones of fossil fauna, predominantly bison and mammoths, and mostly contained in sedimentary deposits that correspond to the Wisconsin (America's final Quaternary glaciation, equivalent to the European Würm). Several of these bone fragments have been dated, and the C14 ages range between 43,000 and 22,000 B.P. (Bonnichsen 1978; Morlan 1979, 1983). The traces of removals and fractures observed on numerous specimens led the researchers to take a detailed look at them and to try and reproduce them by experimentation in order to determine whether they were of human or natural origin. The interpretation of the results of these experiments, which pointed to human intervention carried out before the bones became mineralized, led the site's discoverers to postulate a first occupation of the site by people between 40,000 and 25,000 B.P. (Bonnichsen 1979; Irving 1987), but this hypothesis remains highly controversial (Nelson et al. 1986; Sorg 1985). For the record, one should mention the famous worked caribou tibia (a "deflesher," used in prehistoric and historic times for hideworking) from the same site, which was long considered to be associated with pieces made of mammoth bone. Recently dated by C14 to about 1350 B.P., this relatively modern object is thus intrusive in the older layers, unless it invalidates the body of "associated" pieces.

The data obtained not far from there, in the little Bluefish Caves, by J. Cinq-Mars and R. Morlan, seem to be more convincing. They recovered in loess deposits thousands of mammoth and horse bone fragments that (like those of Old Crow) bear the marks of being worked and of traces of percussion, producing cores and flakes analogous to implements of worked stone. These bone pieces, dated to between 20,000 and 13,000 B.P., were associated with undisputable lithic tools. An apparently worked mammoth tibia even yielded a date of 23,500 B.P. (Cinq-Mars 1990; Morlan and Cinq-Mars 1989; Morlan 1983).

Farther south, south of Lake Erie in Pennsylvania, the Meadowcroft Shelter, excavated by a team led by J. Adovasio, was apparently occupied by people around 17,000 B.P. (Adovasio et al. 1983; Adovasio et al. 1990). The stratigraphy and the numerous dates obtained for this site's lower occupation layer were called into question for a long time, but the discoverers recently subjected them to a detailed revision aimed at eliminating all ambiguity concerning the possibility of contamination by nearby coal sources of the dated samples, which might have made them look older (Tankersley and Munson 1992). This verification has led them to reaffirm unequivocally the definite occupation of the site by people around 14,000 B.P. and perhaps as early as 16,000 B.P. The first anthropic layers of the shelter also contained unambiguous objects of worked stone (knapping waste and flake tools). Meadowcroft has yielded the longest occupation sequence in the northeast United States. (Its later occupation, undisputed this time, continues up to the dawn of the historical period.) No other site has produced so many dates

(52, including 13 from the controversial deep level alone). In Adovasio's view, Meadowcroft represents the best evidence for pre-Clovis occupation in the entire hemisphere.

Finally, there are the initial results of excavations at Pendejo Cave in southern New Mexico. Bones of Pleistocene fauna, including fossil bison, camelid, and horse, associated with lithic implements made on flakes, have been dated here to between 12,000 and more than 50,000 B.P. (Orogrande, McGregor, and North Mesa complexes); and "a bone projectile point carved from the femur of a small animal, that was driven well into a horse phalange" is claimed to be more than 35,000 years old (MacNeish 1996: 171–200). Naturally, MacNeish, the primary investigator, believes that these data demolish the "Clovis barrier."

Thus, at present, only two sites in Canada and the United States—Bluefish and Meadowcroft—have achieved a fairly broad (though not unanimous) consensus.

The Early Sites of Mexico and Central America

In northern Mexico (San Luis Potosí), the open-air site of El Cedral (or Rancho La Amapola), still under excavation, contains a fossiliferous level that has yielded remains of mammoth, mastodon, and fossil horse and camelid, as well as a circular hearth structure surrounded by proboscidian tarsal bones, which has been dated to 31,850 ± 1600 B.P. In another part of the site, other hearths have been discovered, four of which, associated with fragments of burned bones from small animals, are dated to between 28,000 and 21,000 B.P. Hearth No. 1 has yielded a date of 37,694 ± 1963 B.P., which is astonishing, and indeed needs to be checked, as the excavators themselves emphasize. Above, other levels are dated to between 15,000 and 8000 B.P. The tools are few in number: a chalcedony discoid sidescraper of a type that is likewise very surprising for its supposed age (around 33,000 B.P.), and cores, flakes, and undiagnostic limestone debris. According to the archaeologists L. Mirambell and J. L. Lorenzo, the evidence for human occupation at El Cedral is sparse but undisputable (Lorenzo and Mirambell 1986a; Mirambell 1994). Everything is based on the dates which, if reliable—and naturally the conservatives doubt this—make El Cedral the oldest occupied site in Mexico.

In the Basin of Mexico, at a place called Tlapacoya 1 located on the shore of the former Pleistocene lake of Chalco, these same specialists have unearthed from within the lake sediments some remains dating back to more than 20,000 years. In their view, the remains correspond to the temporary camp of a small group of hunters: a hearth with a structured edge containing two small obsidian flakes (whereas this rock is not found naturally in the vicinity), some flakes or blades of rocks of local origin, and a mass of cervid bone fragments, the whole dating to at least 20,000 years ago (24,000 ± 4000

Fig. 7. Large Pleistocene fauna. The main fossil species of South America: the first South American hunter-gatherers exploited the Pleistocene megafauna, whose extinction began around 8000 B.C. and was to last for about a millennium. The biggest prey animals (*Haplomastodon* and *Cuvieronius*) resembled a smaller version of present-day elephants. The edentates, peculiar to America, are represented by animals (*Megatherium, Scelidotherium, Glossotherium, Mylodon*) that, apart from in size, resembled the present-day sloths. Impressive but harmless, they fed on stalks and leaves, which they tore off with their long claws as they stood up on their hind legs and supported themselves on their thick tails. The glyptodons (*Glyptodon, Doedicurus*), a kind of armadillo as big as a car and with formidable armor, were also somewhat peaceful grass browsers, although one of them, *Doedicurus,* had a powerful weapon at the end of its tail that enabled it to defend itself against carnivores. The latter, of more modest size, were nonetheless dangerous. *Smilodon* was endowed with gigantic upper canines, curved sabers that allowed it to slash its prey. Only the horses (*Equus, Hippidion*) and the camelids (*Palaeolama*) were comparable with their present-day counterparts.

B.P. and 24,000 ± 500 B.P.) (Lorenzo and Mirambell 1986b); another hearth dated to 21,700 ± 500 B.P.; and finally some associated heaps of bones containing, among other species, bear, equids, and fossil camelids. For MacNeish (1976), Tlapacoya illustrates "Stage II" (along with Old Crow in Canada). Although naturally subject to criticism—for example, the obsidian objects were supposedly transported by rodents, those in local rocks are supposedly not worked, and even the structure of the circular hearth is allegedly due to burrowing animals (!) (Waters 1985)—this site appears to be one of the most definite proofs of an ancient peopling of Mexico. In their monograph on the site, Lorenzo and Mirambell (1986: 220) point out that even C. Vance Haynes, one of the most ardent conservatives of the United States, does not dispute the early dates. Yet Lynch and others continue to reject them.

In Nicaragua, the site of El Bosque, whose study and publication remain far from complete, is more doubtful despite the international reputation it has already acquired. Fossil fauna (horse and edentate) and bone implements associated with rudimentary stone tools have been dated here, according to Gruhn (1978), to between 32,000 and 22,000 B.P., but some researchers such as Haynes suggest that the "tools" are merely geofacts and not humanly made objects.

One could add to this short list the names of two Mexican sites of even more uncertain age—Caulapan (21,000 B.P.?) and Valsequillo-Hueyatlaco (35,000–24,000 B.P.?)—yet MacNeish (1976: 319) did not hesitate to make them representatives of his "Stage II" despite the serious doubts they raise.

The Early Sites of South America

About 10 sites here have yielded dates earlier than 12,000 B.P. For our purposes, it is necessary to examine them in more detail than those above.

At present, Brazil is unquestionably making the big news. The sites that are presented as being the oldest have been discovered in the arid northeast, around São Raimundo Nonato (Piauí) by N. Guidon and a Franco-Brazilian team who have been studying them since 1978. The most famous, the Toca (rockshelter) do Boqueirão da Pedra Furada, contained a succession of layers more than 5 meters thick that were excavated over an area of 400 square meters. The deepest layer was dated by C14 to more than 50,000 years ago. The early occupation of the shelter then continued at regular intervals, spread through a whole series of dates (a total of 32), until about 14,000 B.P. These lowest layers, grouped by the archaeologists into a Pedra Furada phase (>45,000 to 14,000 B.P.), contained the remains of 86 "hearths" (charcoal and ash) and several lithic objects, knapping waste but also "tools"—worked cobbles, denticulates, and rudimentary sidescrapers made from rocks (quartz and quartzite) that are different from that which makes up this (sandstone) shelter's walls. After a hiatus in the sequence that, according to the excavators, corresponds to a temporary abandonment of the area, the Pedra Furada

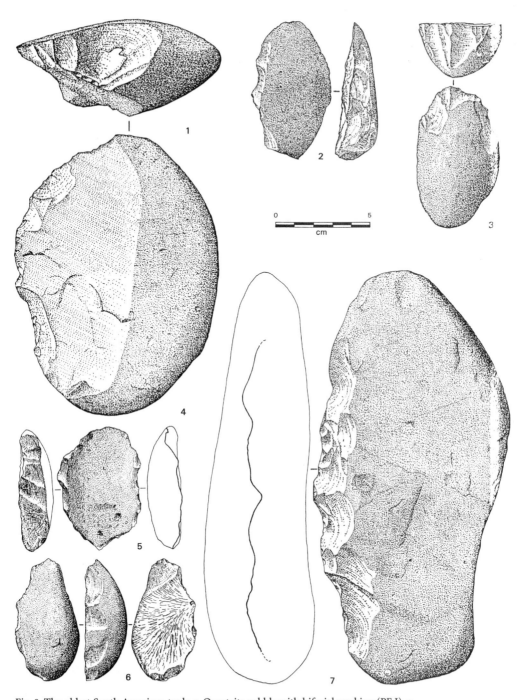

Fig. 8. The oldest South American tools. 1, Quartzite cobble with bifacial working (PF I). 2. Denticulate on a portion of quartz cobble (PF II). 3. Scraper on portion of quartz cobble (PF II). 4. Double transverse sidescraper on a quartz cobble (PF II). 5. Denticulate on a portion of quartz cobble (PF II). 6. Quartzite cobble with unifacial working (PF II). These objects, of which the North American "conservative" school continues to deny the human origin, come from the Pleistocene levels (Pedra Furada phases I and II) of the Brazilian site of Boqueirão da Pedra Furada (Piauí). The typological identifications were drawn up by the archaeologist responsible for the excavation and the study of the material.

phase is followed by another occupation phase, the Serra Talhada (about 12,000 to 6000 B.P.). This latter phase is likewise characterized by the presence of numerous hearths that this time comprise an edging of stones and by the appearance of better worked tools (sidescrapers, "limaces," and fine scrapers on flakes) made from new raw materials (chalcedony, siltite). In the same region, other shelters—Sitio do Meio, Baixão do Perna—were occupied around 14,000 B.P., according to N. Guidon (Guidon 1984, 1986, 1989; Delibrias and Guidon 1986). These dates, and especially those of surprising antiquity obtained at Pedra Furada, have obviously not won unanimous acceptance. The successive discoveries in the Piauí shelters have often been occasion for great media fanfare but with contradictory effect. The general public learned from the French or Brazilian press that the American people dated back 50,000 years or more, accepting this with little question. After all, what are 50,000 years in relation to the time span of world prehistory? The scientific community, on the other hand, reacted with suspicion and hostility, since dissemination of knowledge by press release is rather alien to the usual parameters of scientific discourse. Yet this almost visceral rejection by the specialists, particularly in North America, was accompanied by arguments that are worth examining (Lynch 1990a, 1991; Meltzer et al. 1994). Since materials like flint are present close to the site and easy to work (far easier than quartz or quartzite), why were they only used from 12,000 B.P. onward during the Serra Talhada phase, coinciding with the appearance, alongside the summarily worked cobble tools (the only lithics present in the preceding phase), of a well-made toolkit comprising sidescrapers, knives, and scrapers? Could it not be because the older "tools" of quartz and quartzite are nothing more than naturally broken cobbles in which humans played no part? As for the "hearths" of this Pedra Furada phase, which consist of fairly extensive patches of charcoal and ashes though mostly without any visible structures, could they not rather be residues of natural fires carried into the shelter by the wind? Could not part of the shelter's fill be due to water flow? To this the excavation team and its defenders have responded, quite fiercely (Guidon and Pessis 1996) or more subtly (Guidon and Arnaud 1991; Parenti et al. 1996), that the objects made from cobbles in the lowest layers are indeed tools made by humans (as proved by the recurrent technical characteristics observed on hundreds of specimens) and not geofacts; that no one questions similar pieces of comparable manufacture from later layers; that the hearths of the same layers are indeed of anthropic origin because it is impossible for the ash and charcoal to have been carried into the shelter by wind or water; that the thermoluminescence measurements taken of several stones surrounding the hearths have revealed temperatures (> 450 degrees) that are not compatible with the hypothesis of spontaneous natural fires (Parenti et al. 1990); that, besides, around these hearths were numerous "worked" stone objects, and a study of the "microwear" on these has been undertaken, which will evidently confirm their anthropic origin.

In fact, neither of these two positions has yet succeeded in convincing all the prehistorians in America. However, a masterly doctoral thesis, submitted in 1993 by F. Parenti, who has been in charge of the site's excavation since 1988, brings in stratigraphic sections well correlated with a series of C14 dates, combined with rigorous analysis of lithic material and structures that are considered to be of human construction. Even if one maintains a certain amount of doubt, it no longer appears possible to reject the discoveries made in Piauí. But not surprisingly, three archaeologists published an article in 1994 in which they took the position that the "tools" of the oldest phase were simple cobbles that for almost 40,000 years sustained the impact of other cobbles fallen, like them, from the top of the cliff (Meltzer et al. 1994). Pedra Furada remains the most controversial place in American prehistory. If a Pleistocene occupation is established and accepted one day, the entire model of the peopling of America will have to be substantially revised.

The excavations of the Boqueirão da Pedra Furada have been completed. The team is working in a different sector of the region of São Raimundo Nonato where, in a limestone environment this time—the rockshelters of Janela da Barra do Antonião and Cima do Pilão, to mention only the most important—an abundant fauna of the Upper Pleistocene has been recovered (whereas bones are totally absent from the sites with an acid sandstone substratum such as Pedra Furada and other nearby shelters). According to paleontologist C. Guérin, this fauna "from the paleocological point of view seems to characterize a savannah landscape, bushy in places, and interrupted by forest zones, with a climate that was far more humid than at present" (1991: 571).

One can still hope that, in the near future, the Piauí region, so fabulously rich in sites of all ages, will finally yield the miracle site: one with an association of Pleistocene fauna, human-made tools and structures, C14 dates earlier than 12,000 B.P., and for finality the human occupants' remains. For my part, let me state clearly that while I favor the possibility of such an ancient human occupation, neither am I completely convinced by the "proof" that has thus far been furnished.

A little farther south, the Lapa (cave of) Vermelha IV (Minas Gerais), excavated first by A. Laming-Emperaire from 1971 to 1976 (1979), then by A. Prous (1986, 1995), has yielded, in its 14-meter-thick fill, scattered charcoal dated, at the bottom, to 25,000 and 22,000 B.P. and, in an intermediate sedimentary series, to between 15,000 and 10,000 B.P. A scraper, a quartz flake, and a few doubtful limestone fragments, and some claws and coprolites of a fossil edentate may testify to a joint presence of humans and Pleistocene fauna between 20,000 and 14,500 B.P. But the excavator himself remains very cautious. It certainly appears possible that the association, at a depth of 9 meters, of these few remains and charcoal particles may be the result of accidental intrusions and disturbances, since this is the fill of an almost vertical "chimney" less than 2 meters wide. The association of anthropic remains and bones of extinct fauna is more convincing in the layers dated to between 12,000 and 11,000 B.P.

Finally, there is Alice Boër (São Paulo), an open-air site located on a riverside terrace, where Maria Beltrão claims to have discovered at the bottom of layer III, dating to more than 14,000 years ago, some fine flake tools and a bifacial barbed and stemmed point. Even lower, in layer V, she claims a few tools made from flakes or blocks that are more than 20,000 and perhaps even 40,000 years old (Beltrão 1974; Beltrão et al. 1982; Bryan and Beltrão 1978). But this lower layer V has, in reality, never been dated, and the anthropic nature of its toolkit appears highly dubious to many specialists. Layer III was initially dated to 14,000 B.P., a figure that the dating laboratory suggested should be treated with the greatest caution. More recently, some burned flint objects from this layer were redated by thermoluminscence (TL), yielding TL ages of between 11,000 and 2000 B.P. (Beltrão et al. 1982). Although in this same article Beltrão continues to reaffirm an antiquity of more than 20,000 years for lower layer V, it is hard to understand the basis for her views.

In Venezuela, near Coro (Falcón) in the north of the country, I. Rouse and J. Cruxent in the early 1960s located in the valley of the Rio Pedregal and more particularly in the region of El Jobo about 50 sites containing—mostly on the surface—a great abundance of worked lithic material (Rouse and Cruxent 1963). In 1959–60 they excavated the site of Muaco, which consists of a series of archaeological deposits 2.5 meters thick covering a slope of late glacial age. At the base of these deposits, they unearthed some fossil remains of mastodon, glyptodon (a big fossil edentate), and horse. Some of these bones were burned; others seemed to have been intentionally broken. The burned bones were then dated by C14 to between 16,000 and 14,000 B.P. With the fauna were a few objects of worked stone, including big hammer-grinders, a "knife," and a lanceolate bifacial point.

Finally, 3 kilometers from there, in 1962 J. Cruxent and A. Krieger discovered at Taima-Taima another site similar to the previous one (originally, during the Pleistocene, a pool or a quagmire due to the presence of an artesian spring). First excavated by J. Cruxent, with somewhat confused results and with C14 dates obtained from fossil fauna spanning a period between 14,000 and 12,000 B.P., which were immediately called into question, the site was investigated again in 1976 by A. Bryan and R. Gruhn (Bryan 1979) in order to clarify matters. Their investigation yielded the following stratigraphy: at the base, a stratum of compact, hard, sterile sand of Tertiary age, covered here and there by a kind of natural cobble pavement, then by a gray layer of sandy clay (Unit 1). In this level, they discovered bones of mastodon, glyptodon, and horse, but especially the skeleton of a young mastodon, lying on its left side. Several portions of the skeleton had clearly been moved and others were missing, but some parts were still semiarticulated, especially the rib cage, of which two ribs "display butchering marks made with a sharp knife." The animal's pelvis was also in connection. A fragment of a lanceolate bifacial point still lay in the pelvic cavity, while several more crudely worked stone objects lay close to the skeleton. Finally, remains of cut branches discovered near the skeleton and thought to come from the animal's stomach have been dated to between 14,000 and 13,000 B.P. A sterile paleosol (Unit II), then a level of organic alluvial sand (Unit III, dated to between 10,290 ± 90 and 9650 ± 80 B.P.), and finally a stratum of sterile colluvial sand (Unit IV) seal in this fossiliferous level. In Bryan's eyes, Unit 1, whose C14 age varies between 14,000 and 13,000 years, represents "one of the best dated kill-sites in America" (ibid.: 53).

But not everybody shares this opinion. Lynch's view, and that of the majority of the conservatives, is that the association of the bones and stone objects is merely accidental, the latter having sunk into a soil saturated with water before being deposited next to the bones. Yet, when one really thinks about it, how is it that each time an undisputable worked tool—a fragment of bifacial point, knife, or scraper—ended up in direct contact with faunal remains? How is it that an intermediate level, which Bryan calls Disconformity I/II, located higher than Unit I and separated from it by a sterile palaeosol, also contains fossil Pleistocene fauna, different from that of Unit I (no mastodon but some horse and edentate)? How is it that several bone fragments in Unit I are burned and display butchering marks? In reality, what embarrasses those who doubt the antiquity of the fauna-toolkit association is the presence in the latter of a bifacial arrowhead. The presence around 13,000 B.P. of a point of this type in South America calls into question both the timing and the entire model of the peopling of America proposed by the supporters of a short chronology. It is true that at Muaco, a site with similar conditions (a terrain saturated with water), Rouse and Cruxent themselves had declared that the bifacial point found with the fauna might be more recent and could have sunk into the muddy soil (Rouse and Cruxent 1963: 537); certainly, at Muaco there were also indisputably recent fragments of glass mixed with this fossil fauna (Cruxent 1970: 224). However, the stratigraphy of Taima-Taima appears clearer, and the risks of an intrusion of this kind seem far less probable. It thus appears that the data provided by this site are acceptable, which is also the view of South American specialists G. Ardila and G. Politis (1989: 12–16), who recently reviewed them and who could hardly be suspected of bias.

In Colombia, in the Sábana of Bogotá (a former Pleistocene lake) at an altitude of 2600 meters, between 1967 and 1969 G. Correal and T. Van der Hammen unearthed occupation layers dating to more than 11,000 years in several shelters at the foot of enormous sandstone blocks close to the lake. At El Abra, level C3, dated to between 12,400 and 11,210 B.P., contained a small number of flakes quite crudely retouched into scrapers or denticulates—an industry that the discoverers termed the "Abriense" or "Edge-trimmed Tool" tradition—and unidentifiable faunal remains. The first date was called into question, and the discoverers themselves remained very cautious, acknowledging that the period of the first human occupation of the rockshelters of El Abra was still obscure. Lynch (1990a: 17) once again believes that the cultural assemblage of level C3 is far more recent (no more than 7000 B.P.).

At Tibitó, an open-air site excavated by the same team in 1980, identical lithic material was associated with bones, some of them burned, of mastodon and fossil horse, as well as of fox, cervid, and birds (present-day species), which have yielded a date of 11,740 ± 110 B.P. (Correal 1981). This time it was not the date that troubled the conservatives nor the nature of the fauna but the lithic material, a "meager industry of a few flakes and two possible scrapers," according to Lynch (1990b: 17), that was, as at El Abra, devoid of bifacial points. Whether the latter are an indispensable marker for identifying the first authentic South Americans, the association of mastodon and horse remains with lithic objects at this site appears indisputable.

We now turn to Peru where, in the course of an ambitious program of research undertaken in 1966 in the inter-Andean basin of Ayacucho, R. MacNeish and his team discovered and excavated (from 1969 to 1972) the cave of Pikimachay. Like other shelters or caves studied by the same team, it yielded a series of stratified levels dating to between 9000 and 6000 B.P., but unlike the other sites of the region it also contained layers that were apparently older. Beneath a layer of rubble produced by the collapse of the cave's ceiling (perhaps following an earthquake) and at the base of the levels dated to 9000 B.P., the excavators discovered several deeper layers. First, they encountered a poorly defined layer that contained several bone fragments of fossil camelid and horse, and about 60 lithic objects, which MacNeish baptized the "Huanta" phase but which could not be dated. Lower down, they discovered two layers containing abundant remains of fossil fauna (edentates, horse, camelid) and more than a thousand lithic objects, including 212 tools, big bifaces, and rudimentary scrapers or denticulates; these layers, dating to 14,000 to 13,000 B.P., are grouped together in the Ayacucho phase. Finally, over a very small surface, a series of four lower levels contained bones of big edentates, horse, cervid, and a big carnivore, as well as 74 lithic "tools"— hammerstones, choppers, flakes crudely shaped into tranchets, denticulates or push-planes, as well as a bone "point." Charcoal was absent from these levels, and dating of the bones gave results around 20,000 B.P. (MacNeish et al. 1981: 19–56, 1983: 3–5). According to MacNeish, who considered this first Paccaicasa phase the type-occupation of his "Stage," a small group of hunters had been occupying the cave occasionally between 25,000 and 15,000 B.P., tracking the giant sloths and then butchering and consuming them.

This interpretation, although accepted without question by some like Bryan and Gruhn (1989: 85–86), nevertheless raises a number of problems. First, the limits proposed for this first phase are actually based on more recent C14 dates, none of which are greater than 20,650 B.P. but whose margin of statistical uncertainty, often more than a thousand years, seems to have been used to make them "older"; the chronological bracket suggested by the entire set of dates would rather indicate a time span between 20,000 and 15,000 B.P. Moreover, all these early dates were obtained—in the absence of charcoal—on bones of fossil edentate, a material of uncertain reliability. With regard to these edentate remains, Lynch (1983: 93) also wonders whether the carcasses might not be present at the site without having been brought there by humans and perhaps even long before people reached the area; however, there is no evidence to prove this. I find the cultural arguments more convincing: a review of the material from the Paccaicasa levels led several specialists to cast very considerable doubt on the lithic objects that were claimed to be "worked." For the most part, these are chipped and more or less unshaped fragments of volcanic tuff (the rock in which the cave occurs). It is indeed probable that these are fragments fallen from the wall, being a material that is very poorly suited to being worked and to obtaining a cutting edge (Lynch 1983; Cardich 1980; Fladmark 1979; Lavallée 1985). Four pieces shaped in rocks from outside could quite easily have slipped down from the upper layers at the time of the massive collapse of the roof, which occurred after the Huanta phase. Conversely, the following occupation, represented by the Ayacucho phase, seems to be fairly undeniable: the lithic toolkit, which is in any case far more abundant, is this time unquestionably worked, and more than half of it consists of materials that are not of local origin. This cave thus contains evidence of a human occupation going back not to 20,000 B.P. or more but more definitely to 14,000 or 13,000 B.P.

Next I must address a site that has become famous both for the wealth of its cultural material and for the long polemic it raised, which has only just ended. In southern Chile, at Monte Verde (province of Llanquihué), the remains of an open-air habitation site dated to about 12,500 B.P. (level MV6, between 11,990 ± 250 and 12,650 ± 130 B.P.), buried in a peat bog (which protected them) were unearthed and studied by T. Dillehay from 1978 to 1985 (Dillehay 1984, 1986). Monte Verde has been the subject of an enormous, exhaustive publication (Dillehay 1989; Dillehay et al. 1997) that is worthy of the archaeological treasure it yielded: the remains of a dozen huts, made of a framework of thin trunks covered with mastodon hide; bowl-shaped hearths dug into the floor, and, close to one of them, a child's footprint! The excavators also found mortars and numerous implements of wood (shafts, pointed sticks, and handles, one of which still had a stone scraper held in it), ivory, or bone; remains of roots, seeds, and fruits (representing almost 70 species); and more than 600 lithic objects. The lithics included apparently utilized cobbles or natural fragments, choppers and chopping tools, hammered stone spheroids, and four bifacial pieces (a biface, doubtless a preform of a point; two small fragments of bifacial points; and one almost entire specimen, lanceolate and finely worked in basalt). Finally, one very spectacular find was that of the remains of six or seven mastodons, scattered in the vicinity of camp, with several bones bearing traces of butchery and incisions. But the problem for some is that all this is more than 12,000 years old. Writing in 1991, Lynch did not believe it, nor did others who took a more conservative view (none of whom visited the site, with the exception of J. Bird, who had the bad luck to make a rapid inspection of the work in 1979, just at the time when a sterile level was being exposed, and who declared on his return that he had seen no cultural evidence). In their view the "artifacts" in wood and bone were doubtful, as were the remains of dwellings and hearths, and the projectile points were intrusive. Moreover, the association of the remains with the dated materials was uncertain (Lynch 1991). In 1996, West dismissed these discoveries, asserting that the "Monte Verde II assemblage is extraordinarily heterogeneous, consisting largely of elements not clearly identifiable as artifactual. The relevance of the dating is therefore unclear" (1996: 540).

Perhaps it was the exceptional nature of the find itself that aroused such incredulity. This example of an open-air habitation site dating back 12,000 or 13,000 years is the only one of its kind at present. It has good preservation of the dwelling structures, the remains of the hunted prey (and what prey: at least six mastodons!), and a rich set of tools made of perishable materials that are rarely preserved in prehistoric sites. The site is enough to excite the imagination, so vast is the scope for paleoethnological interpretation offered by these remains. The evidence was enough to cause the hitherto ultraconservative Haynes to state: "It's pretty hard to disregard the evidence from Monte Verde (Chile). It's overwhelming. They have structures, they have hides, they have footprints, they have sophisticated tools, and they have some of the crudest tools I've ever seen. That makes me look back at Taima-Taima (Venezuela). When it comes to the bifacial points, well, the closest thing to it is the Monte Verde material" (quoted by K. Ross, *Mammoth Trumpet* 8, January 1992, p. 5).

The impressive site monograph appeared in 1997. Just before this, in January of the same year, a delegation of specialists, including the biggest skeptics representing bodies such as the Smithsonian Institution, finally visited the site and yielded to the facts. No, there was no trace whatsoever of any disturbance in the layers or of any possible contamination of the dated materials; yes, the camp of Monte Verde was definitely occupied more than 12,000 years ago; and, yes, its occupants possessed bifacial projectile points. Even better, a "possible" (as Dillehay himself put it) deep occupation layer, detected 2 meters lower and dated to around 33,000 B.P., was considered favorably by this same delegation, although some legitimate doubt remains. In this regard three possible features containing charcoal specks in association with several fractured stones are not enough to be totally convincing (Dillehay 1989:18).

The implications of this acknowledgment are enormous: by breaking down the "Clovis barrier," the conservative school has to reconsider its theory about the arrival of people in America—which could certainly have taken place 20,000 years ago—and, at the same time, revise its attitude toward Meadowcroft, Taima-Taima (in fact, Monte Verde's projectile point is morphologically very similar to those unearthed in the latter site), and even Tlapacoya.

Finally, I should mention the deep levels of two shelters located in the far south. In Argentinian Patagonia (province of Santa Cruz), at the shelter of Los Toldos 3, beneath some layers (10 and 9) dated to 9/8000 B.P. and containing hearths, fossil fauna, and a fine industry with bifacial points (see chapter 3), A. Cardich distinguished a lower level (11) containing an identical fauna but also lithic material made up only of big, partially retouched flakes, which was first dated to 12,600 B.P. (Cardich et al. 1973; Cardich 1978) and recently dated more reliably to 12,125 B.P. Not far from there, at El Ceibo, a lower level (12) also yielded modern and fossil fauna (horse) and lithic material that is similar to that from layer 11 at Los Toldos, but it has not yet been dated (Cardich et al. 1981–82). Here, too, there is no unanimity. In Lynch's view (1990b), level 11 at Los Toldos does not really exist but was artificially separated from the upper layers, and the antiquity of the date obtained comes from the fact that the charcoal fragments used for the analysis, collected from the bottom of the layer, were brought into the shelter by animals before its use by humans. It is true that this layer 11 does not contain hearths, unlike the more recent occupation levels. However, it is curious to note the extent to which animals are called on for help and accused of every misdeed when people are trying to challenge "awkward" dates (remember the big hearth of Tlapacoya, built by rodents!), whereas in later periods they seem to stay quiet.

A Very Provisional Conclusion

Hence a total of about 20 sites testify, in the eyes of the radicals, to a human presence in America before 12,000 B.P.: 4 in Canada and the United States, 4 or 5 in Mexico and Central America, but more—a dozen or so—in South America. As we have seen, there is no increase in the age of these sites from the south to the north, as the "logic" of a population coming via the far north would suggest. One can understand the bitter controversy that all of these sites have aroused, but nevertheless the revision carried out leads one to adopt an opinion, positive or negative.

In limiting ourselves to South America, therefore, several data win our approval. Leaving aside all geographical and national considerations, the sites of Taima-Taima (Venezuela), Tibitó (Colombia) (the age of El Abra remains more doubtful), and Los Toldos (Argentina) seem to have been excavated, studied, and interpreted with all necessary rigor. The same can be said for El Ceibo (Argentina) and Lapa Vermelha (Brazil), but in the former the controversial layer is undated, and in the latter the excavator himself has ex-

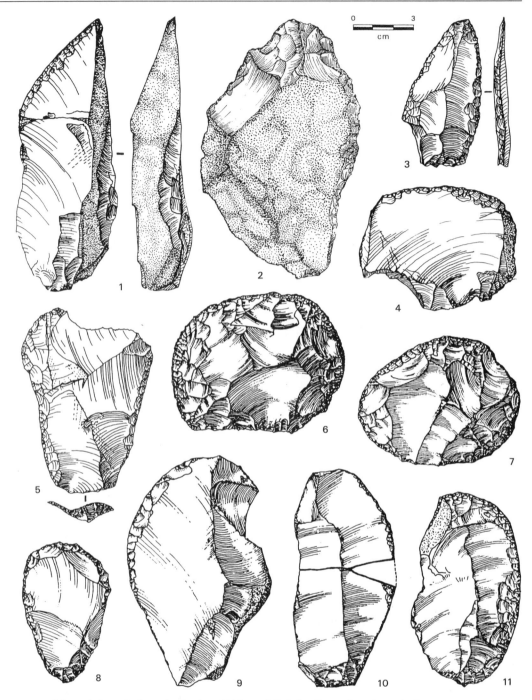

Fig. 9. Flake tools from the lower levels of Los Toldos and El Ceibo (Santa Cruz, Argentina).
Level 11 of Los Toldos: 1. Naturally backed knife, with a partially retouched cutting edge. 2.
Retouched flake. 3. Convergent sidescraper. 4. Transverse sidescraper. 5. Double sidescraper.
Level 12 of El Ceibo: 6, 7. Circular sidescrapers, with unifacial covering retouch. 8.
Endscraper. 9–11. Simple convex sidescrapers. Cardich considers this industry to be typical
of the "pre-projectile" phase, but Lynch believes it to belong to the Toldense complex, from
which it was artificially isolated (see fig. 15).

pressed reservations about the antiquity of a human presence. The age of
the Piauí sites (Brazil) other than Pedra Furada, such as Sitio do Meio and
Baixão do Perna, does not appear suspect. There remain the doubtful case
of Muaco and the truly "problematic sites": Alice Boër (Brazil), Pikimachay
(Peru), and, of course, Pedra Furada (Brazil). It seems the first two must be
rejected (that is, of course, where their earliest occupation evidence is concerned), while the third is and continues to be the subject of a polemic,
which the long-awaited publication of Parenti's work should soon bring to
an end. As for Monte Verde, it constitutes the one and only pre-Clovis site
that has passed its "final exam."

If one compares the ages of these various sites, one notices that those that
inspire the most confidence—that is, they all meet the minimal conditions
set out at the start of this chapter: associations of real tools with dated charcoal or fauna, clear stratigraphy, existence of real archaeological floors—are
dated to between 14,000 and 11,500 B.P. As for those that are still prudently
put to one side, while the existence of older layers in them may remain controversial, there is no doubt that humans occupied two of them from about
14/13,000 B.P. (beginning of the Ayacucho phase at Pikimachay: 14,150 ± 180
B.P.; beginning of the Serra Talhada phase at Pedra Furada: 14,300 ± 210
B.P.).

Doubtless, my selection is open to criticism because it is inevitably somewhat subjective. How could it be otherwise? If the objection were made that
I have not actually seen most of these sites, I would respond that the same
goes for the vast majority of the contradictors. We all make our judgments
from publications, graphics, drawings, and photographs (the latter being
supposedly more reliable), and from results of analyses, since archaeologists—as an old cliché has it—destroy the subject of their study. But some
accounts are more complete, some documents more convincing than others. Finally, since this is above all a matter of "conviction," I should state
clearly that the reasoning of the conservatives is often no more convincing
than that of their adversaries. In any case, one very clear fact emerges from
all their demonstrations: the sharp dividing line between what is valid in
their view and what is not. Anything before 12,000 years ago is generally
condemned without right of appeal, the only exception for the moment being the case of Monte Verde. For dates between 12,000 and 11,000 B.P., opinions are more divided, although tremendous reservations are usually expressed. Finally, after 11,000 B.P., a site is rarely called into question, regardless
of the quality of the archaeological work carried out there. Yet one could say
a great deal about certain excavations that have yielded far more recent data
yet which nobody bothers to question.

Why is there this difference in treatment? If one definitively rejects the
work of certain archaeologists, then all the results of their excavations, of
whatever antiquity, should be called into question. But if their scientific
qualities are acknowledged, then the antiquity of their discoveries, as long as

they meet the demands of science, should in no way detract from their validity. The fact is that, along with the question of age, another criterion, likewise highly subjective, is taken into account by the conservatives to reject
the supposed antiquity of the controversial sites: the appearance of the lithic
industry discovered in them, and in which projectile points are almost always absent (except at Taima-Taima and Monte Verde). As we have seen, in
the opinion of the conservatives, the first humans to reach America 12,000
years ago could only have been hunters who were already very highly specialized and equipped in particular with an elaborate lithic toolkit, including carefully developed projectile points for hunting the large Pleistocene
fauna. They consider it impossible that people could have lived from hunting, even supplemented by gathering (wild plants, shells) if the only technical equipment they possessed was a crudely worked stone toolkit (which in
general is what the "ancient" sites have yielded) that did not include any
sharp points adapted to the game of the time, which comprised some fairly
large animals.

As we saw at the beginning of this chapter, the North American archaeologist Alex D. Krieger tried in the 1960s to answer this objection. Forgetting
the extreme prudence of many of his colleagues yet still maintaining the
strictest objectivity, he drew up a model of the history of the prehistoric
peopling of America based on a series of well-defined concepts. Focusing on
the initial stages of the peopling of America, he created the concept of a
"Pre-projectile point" stage which, as the name implies, characterizes the
cultures, sites, or lithic assemblages devoid of such objects (Krieger 1964).
This was an unfortunate choice of name, because it suggested that lithic
assemblages without points were earlier than those that had them, whereas
Krieger, from the start, specified that in his view this was a technical "stage,"
which sometimes could even occur quite late, and not a "period." Yet, as
noted earlier, this is how the concept was generally interpreted. In 1966,
Gordon Willey wrote: "Although the earliest radiocarbon dates on secure
evidences of man's presence in the western hemisphere fall in the vicinity of
10,000 B.C. (before Christ), there are other signs that suggest that his arrival
in the Americas was much earlier. . . . The evidences for such an early appearance . . . come from a great many localities in both North and South
America. The art factual materials in question are difficult to characterize in
general terms . . . perhaps their most significant aspect is negative: the assemblages of tools with which we are concerned here do not include bifacially flaked projectile points or knives" (Willey 1966: 29).

At the time Krieger published his text and Willey, shortly afterward, produced his manual, only a few surface sites were known in South America—
in Peru, Brazil, Chile, and Argentina—in which sometimes very large quantities of crudely worked lithic material (and without points) had been
collected, devoid of any stratigraphic context and, moreover, mostly without any dating. So the data were far from satisfying the minimal scientific

requirements. The only "proof" of a relative antiquity was, in a few cases, the presence of remains of Pleistocene fauna. But the existence in one part of a territory of a lithic assemblage devoid of points in no way proves that it belongs to a technological stage in which the points did not exist. For one thing, even if projectile points constituted indispensable weapons, they could never have been numerically the most important objects in a human group's technical equipment, which must have been dominated by all kinds of implements for cutting, scraping, or multiple functions; hence an assemblage "without points" may simply be the truncated sample of far more diverse equipment. For another thing, the manufacture of a point implies a whole sequence of technical operations and therefore the development of an entire series of intermediate products, from the initial block of raw material to the rough, then the pre-form before the final retouch. If these intermediate stages were broken or for some reason abandoned before the work was finished, they would bear no resemblance at all to the point they should have become. In fact, when it was noticed, a few years later—after studies of knapping techniques had developed—that most of the crude "tools" found on the surface in all probability merely represented an initial trimming of the blocks of raw material or unfinished roughs of far more elaborate objects (in some cases, fine projectile points, as found in other sites not far away) and that these objects could therefore be far more recent, the concept of a "Pre-projectile point" industry underwent a distinct decline in popularity. In two extreme cases of sites considered by their discoverer—somewhat hastily—to be "very ancient," it was even possible to demonstrate that, in one case, the artifacts were the products of a recent crushing, as the site was close to a modern quarry (Manantial in Ecuador). In the other case, the remains were blocks or flat nodules broken by passing carts or donkeys (Lanning 1973:26), the site being located along an ancient caravan route (Chuqui in Chile)! Better and more convincing candidates were needed—if possible, levels with a lithic industry without points but in a stratigraphy and, if possible, beneath layers with points to prove their earlier date or, failing that, some lithic assemblages without points but well associated with remains of Pleistocene fauna and well dated. We now have examples of levels like this (Sitio do Meio and Baixão do Perna, Pikimachay in its Ayacucho phase, and Los Toldos). Moreover, in most cases these sites have not simply yielded lithic material but other remains of different kinds (structured hearths or features, food remains) that show that people stayed in these places and that, consequently, one must find here a representative sample of their toolkits and their weaponry and not only the partial samples of a fraction of their daily activities. But it is a fact: none of these levels or sites contained lithic objects—tools or weapons—that were bifacially worked and carefully retouched; none of them have yielded a single projectile point.

One final example provides a good illustration of the passions that surround *Homo americanus* and which sometimes seem to lead to a few mistakes. In 1987, Beltrão announced the discovery in the Toca da Esperança, a cave in the Brazilian state of Bahía, of extremely fossilized faunal remains associated with an apparently worked quartzite cobble (Beltrão and Danon 1987). "Associated" bone fragments were dated (in France) by the 230Th/234U method (Uranium/Thorium, since this was far beyond the possibilities of C14), and the result obtained was astounding: between 200,000 and 350,000 years! This sensational news was soon relayed by a French team led by H. Lumley, which carried out new excavations (Lumley et al. 1987, 1988). Numerous bones and worked lithic "pieces" were once again unearthed in the deepest layer (IV), sealed in at the top by a thick carbonate crust. Among the fauna could be identified three kinds of big fossil edentates; fossil armadillo, horse, and camelid; and a small cervid, peccary, and agouti. The new dates spanned a period from 295,000 to 204,000 years ago. The discoverers were categorical: "The discoveries made in the Toca da Esperança enable one to push back considerably the antiquity of the first human presence in America" (Lumley et al. 1987: 939).

The news was surprising, even to the most convinced of the "radicals." Pushing back the arrival of humans in America to 300,000 years ago poses problems that are far more difficult than accepting an arrival only 60,000, 50,000, 15,000, or 12,000 years ago. Beyond any speculation, the results announced so ostentatiously invite a number of remarks (Lavallée 1989): the cave forms part of a karstic system which, in the course of time, underwent some intense episodes of water flow; layer IV, which only survives in fragments on a very pronounced slope, is in reality a totally destroyed level. The fauna contained in this layer comprises fossil forms whose age oscillates (judging by other South American sites with analogous assemblages) between 20,000 and 13,000 and even 10,000 B.P., as well as species that still exist today. The assemblage thus suggests a relatively recent and perhaps even heterogeneous fauna (a mixture of faunas of different ages and not in situ). The "worked" lithic material on quartzite cobbles of fluviatile origin has been subjected only to a succinct analysis; a "microwear analysis," in particular, was not based on any experimentation but only on the examination of photographs at various magnifications. In sum, the contemporaneity of the fauna and the industry, if actual, has not been demonstrated and may never be. All of this reminds one of Lagoa Santa and the finds made there by Lund (see chapter 1). The fever has now passed. Who still believes in the possibility of a human presence in Brazil 300,000 years ago? It would appear that not even the site's discoverers do.

Let us end this section with a few highly provisional conclusions. There no longer appears to be any use in clinging to the buffer date of 12,000 B.P. Today it seems difficult to deny that people were in South America more than 15,000 years ago. Even if one were to persist in rejecting the archaeological data that suggest this, the fact that people were settled—this time indisputably and undisputed—at the southern extremity of the continent in Patagonia and as far as Tierra del Fuego around 11,000 B.P. (see chapter 3) should suffice as a demonstration. South America, and indeed the whole of America, was certainly not populated over an extremely short time span, although some researchers stubbornly continue to claim this. As small groups of people penetrated a continent empty of humans but rich in various resources, natural refugia, game, and flora, their advance southward must have occurred only under pressure following the arrival of other groups in the territory where they had settled. This was a slow migration, with an irregular rhythm and numerous detours. Logic suggests that it must have started at least 30,000 years ago.

WHERE DID THEY COME FROM?

Since most prehistorians agree that the first occupants of America came from the northwest, that is, from Siberia, the answer to the question "Where did they come from?" requires that we examine the geographical and climatic conditions of the far north of Asia and America at the end of the Pleistocene, because the possibilities for the human groups arriving and advancing were, as we shall see, directly linked to the successive modifications undergone by this environment for 100,000 years. I have neither the intention nor the competence to go into detail about the climatic phenomena nor to present the various methods that have led to their reconstruction. I shall limit myself to summarizing them and to pointing out that, here again, there are multiple hypotheses and various routes have been proposed, depending on whether one accepts the great antiquity of humans in America.

Land Routes or Water Routes?

Most prehistorians consider the arrival of people in America via the Bering region to be the most probable—whatever the date of this arrival—followed by an advance through the interior of the land along the eastern side of the Rocky Mountains. In order to explain this advance, this classical position requires the hypothesis of the "Ice-free Corridor" or "Yukon-Alberta Corridor" that supposedly existed during certain periods between the two enormous ice caps that then occupied the north of America. Just like a large part of Europe and Asia, the territories of Canada and the northern United States were covered by ice several times during the Pleistocene, that is, approximately between 2 million and 10,000 years ago. During this long period (only the end of which concerns us here), the alternation of cold phases and more temperate periods resulted in the advance or retreat of the glacial masses and, correspondingly, a fall or rise in the ocean level. Hence since during the coldest periods an enormous mass of water was held back in the form of ice in the Arctic regions, the ocean level was (depending on the hypotheses) between 100 and 120 meters lower than at present. The floor of the Chukchi and Bering seas had emerged, uniting eastern Siberia and Alaska in a land bridge that was over 1,000 kilometers wide—Beringia, a vast stretch of steppe and tundra that was not covered by ice. On the Asiatic side, numerous regions likewise remained free from ice, from the Urals to the Sea of Japan. If one takes into account only the last 100,000 years, which in America correspond to the last Pleistocene glaciation, the Wisconsin, more or less contemporaneous with the European Würm, the Beringian isthmus existed several times and for several thousand years: at least between 75,000 and 60,000 B.P.; around 32,000 B.P.; between 25/23,000 and 15/13,000 B.P. during the glacial maximum of the Upper Wisconsin; and finally perhaps one last time around 11,500 B.P. during the final cold phase of the Pleistocene. Conversely, during the periods of relative warming, and in particular during the Mid-Wisconsin between about 60,000 and 30,000 B.P., the ocean level rose because of the partial melting of the glaciers and separated Asia from America. Theoretically, therefore, there must have been two possible periods for a terrestrial passage from Asia to America: before 60,000 B.P. and then much later, between about 30/25,000 and 15/12,000 B.P. Naturally, there is no unanimity among authors on this chronological scheme, and some even think that, far from having represented an episodic phenomenon, the Beringian isthmus might have existed almost continuously from 80/70,000 to 14,000 B.P. (Hopkins et al. 1982; West 1996) and perhaps to as late as about 11,000 B.P. (Elias et al. 1992). I shall say no more about hypotheses that I am in no position to discuss, let alone confirm or invalidate, since my intention is simply to show that the schemes developed by specialists as numerous as they are competent and eminent can differ widely and that these divergences have serious consequences for the interpretation of the entry of humans into America.

Moreover, the situation is even more complex. When Beringia existed and humans could theoretically pass from Asia to America without getting their feet wet, the north of the American continent was at the same time covered by an enormous continental glacier, formed by the fusion of the two masses of the Laurentide ice sheet and the glacier of the Rockies. These ice sheets, 2 to 3 kilometers thick, created an almost impassable barrier. Conversely, when the volume and extent of these glaciers diminished because of a warming of the climate, a "corridor" opened up between the two, a strip of land east of the Rockies not covered by ice and stretching from the Yukon to the northern United States more or less following the trace of the present Mackenzie Valley. But Beringia was then submerged, replaced by a wide arm of the sea.

This model is still too simple to be totally correct—notably because the climatic fluctuations of the Pleistocene are still far from known with any precision. First determined from the study of the moraines left by the glaciers, which enabled their advances and retreats to be located and dated, their study was henceforth based more on the isotopic analysis of planctonic foraminifera, which apparently provide more reliable elements of evaluation for the average temperature of the oceans. However, the dates proposed for the opening and closing of the "corridor," and even for the major climatic oscillations, vary from author to author. Hence, beyond a scenario that is general enough to remain undisputed, any detailed reconstructions—of the utmost importance for our needs—are uncertain, and several questions still remain unanswered. At the glacial maximum, were the two ice sheets of the Rockies and the Laurentides coalescent, or did they form two distinct masses, thus letting the famous "corridor" survive, if not permanently then at least for much longer periods than is generally believed? Moreover, during the periods of warming, when the ocean separated the two continents, were the 90 kilometers of the Bering Strait more impassable than the 100 or so that separated Asia from Australia at this same period? Yet Australia was populated at least 50,000 years ago.

Although the theory of the "Ice-free Corridor" has not lost all of its supporters—indeed they remain very numerous—it has been somewhat undermined by the acceptance of Monte Verde and its age (12,500 B.P.), because it now becomes difficult to explain the presence of people in southern Chile at this date if they had to use the famous corridor, which was blocked by ice till about 12,000 B.P. Hence there has been (for example, at the 63rd Annual Meeting of the Society for American Archaeology in 1998) a reemergence of an alternative theory that had been put forward in the 1980s by the Canadian archaeologist K. Fladmark (1982, 1983); he believes that the two continental glaciers must indeed have been coalescent during the coldest periods, thus making difficult, if not impossible, any movement between Beringia and the lands to the south that were free of ice; so a third route could have been followed, the coastal route. With regard to the "corridor," which could theoretically (because no material proof of its existence has ever been found, and no archaeological evidence either) have been followed before and after the glacial maxima, he points out in addition that "bounded at east and west by massive glaciers, any narrow early-stage corridor must have been an extremely unpleasant area to occupy. . . . Certainly any surviving biota in the corridor must have been only a pale and impoverished reflection of the rich plant and animal communities usually inferred for Beringia, if any life at all existed in the area until well into deglaciation. Thus it seems conceivable that the "Ice-free Corridor" offered little or no inducement for human population . . . until the ice-sheets had substantially withdrawn, perhaps as late as 10–11,000 years ago" (Fladmark 1982: 1114).

On the other hand, the modern, very ragged appearance of this coastline, especially in British Columbia, was less pronounced at the time of the glacial maxima. The lowering of the sea level then uncovered a coastal strip that was wider than at present, and relatively free of ice thanks to the mild influence of the ocean, in which promontories and islands could have formed a chain of possible refugia stretching from Beringia to the south of the ice cap. "Mollusca, fish, sea-mammals and waterfowl would have provided a continuous, rich food supply along the entire coast, and even major land mammals such as caribou may have reached some of the refugia. Any people possessing a simple watercraft would have had little difficulty in traveling between the chain of ice-free 'islands,' just as modern Eskimo coped with the coastline of Greenland" (ibid.: 1116).

In his view the idea that people reached America by the coast is as acceptable as, if not more than, that of the continental corridor. In addition, this hypothesis removes the necessity of the Beringian land bridge, and the arrival of humans is no longer dependent on a modification in sea level. However, Fladmark remains very prudent, considering it merely a possibility, and that as yet "there is still no empirically satisfactory evidence of human occupations older than 12–15,000 B.P." (ibid.: 1117).

So the theory of the "coastal route" has just resurfaced, inaugurating the post–Monte Verde era. Carol Mandryk, a paleoenvironmental specialist, has presented it forcefully, defending the hypothesis of a human penetration either via the northwest coast or far earlier: "The implications of non-accessibility of the corridor prior to 12,000 years ago are that archaeological sites south of the borders of the ice sheets dating prior to 12,000 years ago are either (1) evidence of migration prior to the establishment of the environmental barrier or (2) remains left by people who arrived in the New World via some other route—for example, the coastal or interior British Columbia route" (*Mammoth Trumpet*, 13 March 1998, p. 6). In the same article she states that "recent research in the Queen Charlotte Islands has led to the discovery of uplifted terraces with associated archaeological remains that may represent some of the earliest evidence for human occupation on the Northwest Coast" (ibid.: 2). Farther south, in the small Daisy Cave site on San Miguel Island in the Santa Barbara Channel off California, Jon Erlandson has discovered vestiges from a human group with a maritime specialization dating to more than 10,000 years (10,390 ± 130 B.P., though a date of 15,780 ± 120 B.P. has been cautiously advanced). This site currently represents the most ancient human occupation known on the North American Pacific coast (Erlandson et al. 1996a, b). The islands of the Santa Barbara Channel do not seem to have been connected to the mainland even at the lowest sea level during the Pleistocene, leading Erlandson to suggest that the Daisy Cave occupants arrived by sea. In the next chapter I will discuss several coastal strata yet more ancient in Ecuador and Peru where archaeologists have also suggested the possibility of a maritime arrival by means of small craft.

In carrying this reasoning as far as it will go, one reaches the conclusion that people could have arrived during the warm periods—that is, in the Mid-Wisconsin (between 60,000 and 30,000–25,000 B.P.)—having advanced along the string of Aleutian Islands. The problem remains that the use of this route is based on speculations that are difficult to support since any material evidence that may have existed is now submerged off the continent. As can be seen, none of the hypotheses put forward have achieved unanimity but, in any case, neither geology nor climatology has yet brought the slightest proof that it was impossible for humans to have penetrated America well before 12,000 B.P. The only point on which everybody is agreed, more or less, is that after this date their arrival and advance southward faced no further difficulties.

THE ORIGIN OF THE PRINCIPAL MIGRATIONS

Without exception, the Indians of all the provinces of the New World share the following characteristics. They all have black eyes. . . . A second common characteristic of all Indians is their hair. It has five properties. It is black, thick, and straight . . . it seldom grays and, if it does, only among the very aged, and . . . it seldom falls out, result-ing in baldness.
—*B. Cobo,* Historia del Nuevo Mundo, *1613–1653, Book 11,*
chap. 3

Which Eurasian groups could have originated the people who first advanced eastward through an immense and unknown territory? The problem pre-sents itself differently, depending on whether one accepts an ancient or re-cent first arrival.

Where the first hypothesis is concerned, one has to take into consider-ation the data from eastern Asia that are earlier than 30,000 B.P., correspond-ing to the Mid-Wisconsin. It is known that, in the Old World, this period saw important biological and cultural changes: appearance of *Homo sapiens sapiens,* advances in techniques such as bone industry, systematization of social relations, and enlargement of the exploited territory. People reached Australia, Japan, and eastern Siberia (Lena-Aldan). This was a time both of cultural affirmation and of population expansion into hitherto unoccupied territories. It could well have seen people reach America, too. Between 45,000 and 10,000 B.P., the Siberian climate fluctuated widely, but even at the maxi-mum of the last glaciation (c. 25,000 to 10,000 B.P.) corresponding to the late Wisconsin, the major part of Siberia and the far east of present-day Rus-sia remained ice-free. According to one source, "In northeastern Siberia, (or western Beringia) there have been no natural obstacles . . . to prevent human migration toward North America during the last 25,000 years" (Kuzmin and Orlova 1998:29).

Unfortunately, the prehistory of eastern Asia is still quite poorly known for this period. No origin or filiation has yet been established, or even pro-posed, for the American "Pre-projectile point" industries, with choppers and flakes, that are older than 12,000 B.P. and that still have no equivalent in eastern Siberia. In Japan—close to the former location of Beringia (via the Kuril Islands and Kamchatka) and occupied by populations that came from China at an unknown date but in any case earlier than 35,000 B.P. before a rise in sea level separated it from the continent—several sites in the south, dating to between 35,000 and 20,000 B.P., contained industries of cobbles and flakes. One site on the island of Hokkaido, the northernmost of the archipelago, is dated to 18,000 B.P. (Leroi-Gourhan 1991); other recently discovered sites might be older but are still controversial (Reynolds 1986). Consequently, one hardly needs to add that the meager results from these comparative studies merely reinforce the conservatives' convictions concerning the recent arrival of humans in America.

Certainly, the only resemblances or filiations that have been more or less attested between the prehistoric cultures of Siberia and North America date to the very end of the Pleistocene, between 15,000 and 12,000 B.P. A few sites in Siberia have yielded lithic assemblages that could be the origin of the toolkits of the American Paleoindian period, which begins around 12,000 years ago. The most solid comparisons have been established with the Upper Palaeolithic layers of the Siberian sites of Djuktai (c. 24,600 to 10,300 B.P.: Kuzmin and Orlova: 1998:39) and Uschki (in Kamchatka; ibid.: 19) whose lithic toolkit includes leaf-shaped points or bifacial projectile points comparable to the first American bifacial points from Clovis, although none of the Siberian points feature the typical basal fluting of the Paleoindian points.

Moreover, archaeology is not the only discipline capable of maintaining the discussion; other debates have recently been begun that concern factors other than the appearance of the tools or the hearths. Other approaches also have something to say about the process of the peopling of the American continent.

An Asian origin for the Amerindians is generally accepted, but numerous questions remain. Apart from the date of arrival, there is the question of whether there was one wave of migration or several in succession. Did people come from a single region, or must one accept several origins, as suggested by the polymorphism of the cultures, past and present, and of the present-day languages? Finally, was the Asian contribution the only one, or must one accept the hypothesis of contributions from other parts of the world?

A hypothesis that is already quite old—that of multiple contributions from different parts of the world—was defended by the anthropologist P. Rivet in 1924 and set out in his book *Les Origines de l'homme américain* (*The Origins of American Man*), published in 1943, which has remained a classic though now dated. In Rivet's view, the principal and oldest peopling of America did indeed come from Siberia via Bering, probably several times and in different periods; the languages and cultures of the "emigrants" subsequently evolved separately through the ages.[3] But this evolution alone cannot explain the profound differences that one sees today, which he attributed to the arrival of non-Asiatic ethnic elements. Among these, he

[3]Rivet's theories are particularly well set out and analyzed in the book by A. Laming-Emperaire *Le Problème des origines américaines* (The problem of American origins), completed and edited in 1980, after the author's death.

distinguished Australian, Melanesian, and Polynesian elements, the first attested by the predominance of blood group O, common to the Amerindians and the Australians; by ethnography (for example, use of mantles of hide, spiral plaiting, bark boats); and especially by the linguistic similarities observed between the languages of the tribes of the extreme south (Tehuelches and Onas of the historical period) and the Australian languages. As A. Laming-Emperaire writes: "The arguments [used by Rivet] are astonishingly poor, and it is somewhat difficult to understand how some of them could have been put forward" (1980: 47).

Nevertheless, they led Rivet to an audacious conclusion: since it is scarcely possible to envisage an Australian migration from the north, one has to accept the idea of a passage via the South Pacific and the fringes of the Antarctic during the postglacial. This hypothesis had been formulated a few years earlier by the Portuguese anthropologist A. A. Mendês Correa (1925). This theory of an Australian migration has now been generally abandoned. Where the Melanesian elements are concerned, they, too, are to be found in anthropology, pathology (diseases common to America and Oceania), culture (including use of the blowpipe, the spearthrower, the bow, the sling, the hammock, wooden seats, reed boats, the conch shell, panpipes), and finally language (affinity between the Hoka group, which stretches from California to Colombia and the group of Malayo-Polynesian languages). Rivet concluded that the Melanesian migrations came via the Pacific 4,000 or 5,000 years ago. Finally, several Polynesian elements are supposedly present in America (cultivation of the sweet potato,[4] use of the Polynesian oven, and stone axes, which in both regions are called toki). In Rivet's eyes, the introduction of words, even more than that of objects, implied regular contacts. He therefore thought that the Polynesians, who were excellent navigators, had reached the American coast on various occasions. This proposition is the only one which, today, has retained some validity, because several Indian traditions in Colombia, Ecuador, and Peru make reference to the arrival of foreigners on the Pacific coast. On the other hand, it seems possible and even probable that around the mid-fifteenth century, the Inca sovereign of Peru, Tupac Yupanqui, organized an expedition to islands to the west and brought back dark-faced prisoners. However, all these are relatively recent contributions.

While the Asiatic origin of the first arrivals is demonstrated more clearly every day,[5] it seems nevertheless that several successive migrations need to be envisaged. This view is the result of the intervention in the debate, over the past ten years, of three disciplines that are related not to the earth sciences and archaeology but to the life sciences and the humanities: linguistics, physical anthropology (with the study of dental features and hematology), and finally molecular biology, with genetic analysis. However, far from speaking with a single voice, the specialists in each of these disciplines present for the moment the spectacle of an extraordinary variety of often contradic-

[4]The sweet potato is actually of American origin, as is shown by the discovery of sweet potato remains at Huaynuma, a preceramic site on the coast of Peru, in a level dated to about 4000 B.P. (see chapter 4).

[5]There is now a broad consensus on this topic. Nevertheless, mention should be made of a surprising and relatively recent hypothesis. In 1963, the North American researcher Greenman claimed to have demonstrated that, at the end of the Pleistocene or the very beginning of the Holocene, contacts took place between northern Europe and America via the Atlantic, contacts that could be the origin of North America's Paleoindian culture. Without taking into account the immense chronological gap, he based this theory on similarities between the cultures of the European Upper Palaeolithic and those of present-day Eskimo. The methodological foundations of this theory were very feeble, and it was rapidly rejected by all specialists. A full summary and pertinent critique can be found in A. Laming-Emperaire (1980).

tory hypotheses, which makes it difficult to form an opinion. The summary given here, therefore, can only be very schematic (and unquestionably incomplete).

During the 1980s, J. Greenberg observed the current extreme diversity of indigenous languages spoken in the whole of the American continent—hundreds of languages, among which he identified three families. Basing his conclusions on the supposed rapidity of their diversification, he proposed that humans arrived in three distinct waves, the first of which (Amerind language family) reached America around 15,000 B.P. (Greenberg 1987; Greenberg et al. 1986). Yet in 1996, in an article in the book edited by West, he retracted this first chronological hypothesis and fell into line with West, proposing that the first arrival took place no more than 12,000 years ago (West 1996: 553). However, other linguists have also put forward very different hypotheses on the basis of the same approach. J. Nichols, for example, estimates that the initial peopling of America took place earlier than 22,000 B.P. and in any case before the last glacial maximum (Nichols 1990; Gibbons 1998: 1306).

There is also dental evidence worth considering. C. G. Turner II, a specialist in human dentition, explains that dental traits "indicate that all Native Americans are more closely related to northeastern Asians such as Chinese and Japanese than they are to Europeans and that the ancestral origin of east Siberian and Native American populations was likely in eastern Asia" (Turner 1988:114). He argues that a differentiation between two main groups he calls Sinodonts (North China, Mongolia, and eastern Siberia) and Sundadonts (southeastern Asia and all Europeans) would have occurred in Asia between 22,000 and 20,000 years ago. Turner further distinguishes three groups among the American Sinodonts: Aleut-Eskimo, Na-Dene, and Amerind, differentiated largely prior to their installation in America. The Paleoindians, ancestors of the Amerinds, would have been the first, initiating migration toward the east via Beringia and then Alaska. This migration must have been between 14,000 and 12,000 years ago (ibid.: 115).

Without going into detail, the first migration would also have been associated with the Paleoindian Clovis culture, which matches Greenberg's formula. We are back at a late date for the peopling of America, not prior to Clovis. Yet Meltzer has rightly noted that the scheme proposed by Turner is based on the study of dental material (200,000 teeth!), proving only that individuals belonged to the middle Holocene, if not later. He states that "fossil teeth can provide a direct record of the age and features of the first Americans, *provided those teeth come from sites occupied by the first Americans*"—which is not the case (my emphasis). The dates and events proposed by Turner thus become inferences, "a process that makes them dependent on troublesome assumptions, and always requiring archaeological verification" (Meltzer 1993: 163–64).

Hematology is another avenue. Blood groups are part of the hereditary patrimony (genotype) that is not modified by environment and can therefore be a direct attestation of a biological relationship. We now know that, unlike the modern European, African, and Asiatic populations, in which individuals of groups A, B, AB, and O coexist (with variable frequencies), all the Amerindians who are not of mixed blood belong to group O, except for one tribe on the northwest coast of the United States in which group A is predominant. Almost all the Amerindians (over 99 percent) also have a positive Rhesus factor. Finally, the Diego factor, discovered in 1955 in the blood of an Indian tribe of the same name in Venezuela, is strongly represented in Amerindians, from northwest North America to Brazil; it is frequent in the indigenous populations of eastern Asia, whereas it does not exist either among the Europeans or among the Africans. The final contribution of the relatively recent discipline of hematology is the discovery of the HLA system and research into it among America's increasingly rare populations that are not yet of mixed blood. This has revealed a certain homogeneity and, at the same time, a strong resemblance to the Mongols. All these studies have enabled specialists to define the Amerindians' blood quite precisely and to shed light on the history of their migrations. Not only has the Asiatic origin of most of them been confirmed, but above all, according to J. Bernard, the first migrations could date back to about 50,000 years ago, insofar as the Asiatic, European, and African hemoglobins are not found in the blood of Amerindians, except in cases of mixed blood. In his view, this means that "the first migrations took place before the mutations responsible for the presence of abnormal hemoglobins in the blood of Asiatics." He adds that "of the Asiatic populations living today, the closest to the present-day Amerindians are to be found either in eastern Siberia or in the north of Japan. The Amerindians' blood groups, like their morphology, link them with the oldest populations of Asia, and enable us to attach them to this primitive Asiatic branch which had scarcely begun its differentiation towards the Mongoloid at the time when it reached America" (Bernard 1983: 57–58). Thus the hematologists estimate that the first crossovers from Asia to America took place about 50,000 years ago, rather than 20,000, which seems to them extremely short (ibid.: 58).

We next reach the infinitely small, the human genetic heritage as recorded in DNA. This is the most recent approach, and therefore, as is normal, opinions are still the most divided here. To summarize the situation quite simply, suffice it to say that the demonstration is based on the genetic analysis of the present-day Amerindian populations of North and South America, of the archaeological human remains from different periods, and finally of the present-day Asiatic, African, and European groups. To put it quite synthetically: on the basis of modifications observed in the genetic stock of the various groups studied and by calculating the time supposed to be necessary for these modifications to occur, the different teams of biologists acknowledge that all the Amerindian individuals examined who are not of mixed blood carry one of the four varieties of mtDNA (DNA carried by the mitochondria and which is passed down by the mother) that also exist among Asians but are absent among Europeans and Africans. Moreover, as A. Gibbons puts it: "The frequency of the variants is much higher in Native American populations than in Asians, indicating that all American Indians . . . are descended from a small number of 'founding mothers' from Asia" (1993: 312).

But beyond this global account, opinions diverge on the problem of defining the possible number of migrations and especially on proposing a timetable for the arrival of humans in America. Here I shall attempt a brief review, which is in no way meant to be exhaustive.

One team led by the geneticist L. L. Cavalli-Sforza has found, within the Amerindian populations, the three (and not four) groups identified by the linguist Greenberg. The team has even found remarkable agreement between this hypothesis and the results of the genetic analysis (Cavalli-Sforza 1991).

Another research program, in which T. G. Schurr, D. C. Wallace, and A. Torroni, among others, have been collaborating for ten years, has become convinced that there were "five founding Asian mtDNAs," which were then grouped into "four lineages, each characterized by a different rare Asian mtDNA marker" (Wallace and Torroni 1992: 407). In 1983, this team specified that "the initial migration occurred between 17,000 and 34,000 years before present" (Torroni et al. 1993: 591), dates which a short time later were pushed back to between 42,000 and 21,000 B.P. (as reported by Gibbons 1993: 313). In an article published in 1994, the data provided by the Brazilian site of Pedra Furada were even accepted explicitly (Parenti and Torroni 1994). That same year, the group summarized its conclusions as follows (with dates that were again different): "We estimate that if the Amerinds [the first group to arrive] entered the New World as a single group, that entry occurred approximately 22,000–29,000 B.P. This estimate carries a large but indeterminate error. The mtDNA data are thus at present equivocal with respect to the most likely times of entry of the Amerinds in the New World mentioned above but favor the 'early' entry hypothesis" (Torroni et al. 1994: 1158). They even pushed the degree of precision as far as proposing an arrival "between 22,414 and 29,545 B.P." (ibid.: 1161).

In the view of D. A. Merriwether and his colleagues, however, there was a single wave of migration from Asia; going even further, they claimed that Mongolia was the closest point to the place of origin of the first Americans (Merriwether et al. 1996; Powledge and Rose 1996).

A Japanese team assumes that the peopling of America took place through four principal waves of migration, the first of which arrived between 21,000 and 14,000 B.P. For these researchers, the ancestors of the populations studied supposedly left Siberia more than 70,000 years ago.

Genetics is clearly the scientific discipline that, for the moment, is developing the most varied and most complicated scenarios, because the study of DNA's "molecular clock" is a very new discipline. Today, dozens if not hundreds of researchers have taken up the study of this fabulous time machine, but very few are as yet in agreement on the results. Estimates on genetic divergence are indeed only estimates, and it is important to realize that they are not inevitably equivalent to migratory events. Nevertheless, almost all of the researchers maintain the hypothesis of several successive migrations, and many are pushing back the arrival of humans in America to before 12,000 B.P.

For the present, physical and biological anthropology has brought the most convincing proof of the Asiatic origin of the Amerindians, but since the dates are so varied, one can only conclude quite severely, like Meltzer: "If the geneticists want to convince anthropologists to take their dates seriously, they will have to 'get their house in order' (quoted in Gibbons 1993: 313). In other words, it is important to wait. Which leaves on one side, the supporters of a recent arrival of people in America and, on the other, those of an arrival long before the Clovis horizon.

The Invisible Early Man

We still know very little about the physical appearance of the first Americans. If, for a land-crossing of Beringia, one accepts two moments in the past, an early one before 60,000 B.P. and the other between 30,000 and 15,000–12,000 B.P., not forgetting the hypothesis of a coastal route accessible during the intervening period, one certainly has to wonder about the physical appearance of the first Americans. Before 60,000 B.P., archaic *Homo sapiens* could have penetrated America, but no evidence has yet been found in eastern Asia nor in America. While there are increasingly numerous clues indicating that humans were definitely in America 25,000 or 30,000 years ago or more, it is curious that nobody has discovered their remains, and so their physical appearance is still totally unknown. The oldest human fossils discovered are scarcely more than 10,000 years old; all are of *Homo sapiens sapiens,* and all belong to the Mongoloid variety. This means that America is the only continent where the presence of humans is attested for a long time only by the implements they used and by the animals they ate but not by their own remains. Yet the discovery in the supposedly earliest sites of skeletons indisputably associated with cultural remains, which would perhaps—in view of their supposed antiquity—display archaic morphological characteristics, would constitute a most convincing argument. Maybe the first Americans did not bury their dead or preferred to burn them or leave them exposed in the open air. But, Lynch asks, how is it that none of these sites have yielded the slightest fragment of them, even where the conditions of preservation were optimal? He adds with some irony: "Early man was probably not a cannibal, and he may not have been buried, but he surely lost teeth" (1990: 13).

This is indeed one of the major arguments used by the conservatives against the radicals. Yet in the 1970s, sensational dates of 40,000, 48,000, and even 70,000 years had been published for North American skulls or human skeletal fragments found in various parts of California—for example, Sunnyvale, La Jolla, Santa Rosa, Taber, and Del Mar. Remains were taken from their museum drawers in order to test a new dating method that had just been discovered: amino acid racemization. Unfortunately, the method was still highly experimental, and new analyses carried out since then, with the classic method of C14 but using refined techniques (AMS), produced far younger ages: none of these bones were more than 10,000 years old; some were only 2,000 or 3,000 years old, the oldest barely 6,000 years old. Only one of these recently reexamined fossil humans has had its age confirmed: "Midland Man"—actually a woman of about 30—unearthed in 1953 by an amateur in Texas, is about 11,000 years old (11,600 ± 800 B.P., a date obtained by the Uranium-Thorium method), which makes it the oldest dated human in all of America. However, it is not earlier than the fateful date of 12,000 B.P.

In South America, supposedly ancient remains are even rarer or more doubtful. Besides, as Lynch inevitably observes (refusing to let slip the slightest possible argument), they have an annoying tendency to disappear, turning out to be lost when one tries to date them with these new techniques. For example, the human bones that a tomb robber accidentally unearthed at Garzón (Colombia) in 1956, at the same time as bone remains of giant sloth and a mastodon molar, have disappeared, and it has never been possible to study them. An archaic-looking skullcap discovered at Lagoa Santa and published by A. Bryan in 1978 has been "lost." Also in Brazil, A. Laming-Emperaire discovered in the site of Lapa Vermelha IV, already mentioned, a few long bones and a mandible of a child in levels dating to more than 9,000 years ago, the very ones that also contained worked quartz flakes. As we have seen, this site's very complicated stratigraphy leaves a lot of doubt about the antiquity of its sparse remains. In the 1950s, another skull was much talked about: the Otavalo skull (Ecuador), a chance discovery (unearthed by a dynamite explosion on a construction site!), was studied by D. Davies and dated by three different methods (racemization, thermoluminescence, and C14) to between 30,000 and 20,000 B.P. But the new analyses carried out since then, this time on bone collagen (taking into account the fact that this skull was covered by a thick layer of natural carbonates—aragonite—which could have distorted the previous analyses), did indeed produce far younger and less spectacular dates, within a time span from the fourth to the seventh centuries A.D. Other Ecuadorian skulls, from Punín, do not appear to be more than 3,000 years old.

In fact, the only fossil human remains from South America that are well dated all come from sites occupied later than 12,000 B.P. (see chapter 3). While their age is not disputed, they do not really tell us anything about the physical appearance of the very first South Americans. They are, in order of increasing antiquity: the remains unearthed in Chilean Patagonia by J. Bird in 1936, in the cave of Palli Aike, dating to 8640 B.P.; those from the burials of Tequendama (Colombia) excavated by Correal, the oldest of which may date to 9000 B.P.; the skeletons of Santana do Riacho (excavations by Prous) dating to between 9400 and 7900 B.P. and the female skeleton of Barra do Antonião (excavations by the Piauí mission in Brazil) of 9670 B.P.; and the skeleton of Paiján Man, discovered by Chauchat in the desert of northern Peru, dating to 10,200 B.P., which makes it the oldest South American known at present. According to their discoverers, the skulls of all these skeletons display more or less marked resemblances with those from the region of Lagoa Santa (Brazil), which were used to define the "race" of the same name.

It was in the nineteenth century around Lagoa Santa, a little locality in Minas Gerais (Central Brazil) which has already been mentioned in connection with the work of W. P. Lund, that human bones were discovered. The bones were mixed with remains of the great quaternary fauna in the fill of several caves. At the time it was impossible to interpret these discoveries correctly (see chapter 1), but several decades later, when the contemporaneity of humans and certain fossil animal species was demonstrated in Europe, "Lagoa Santa Man" became famous. Several missions came in succession to the site in the 1920s and 1930s, and, "without any scientific preparation and with no program, people set about completing the emptying of the caves and shelters that Lund had begun. The collections recovered by pickaxe and dynamite, devoid of all scientific value, were scattered among amateurs or sold abroad" (Laming-Emperaire et al. 1975: 3).

Other, more serious research programs were carried out in the 1950s. An abundance of human bone material was collected, although the contemporaneity of people and fossil fauna could not be definitively verified or disproved. In addition, the pillage of the caves continued. It is only recently that a certain number of burials have been discovered in the well-dated levels of a few caves or shelters, confirming that the race of Lagoa Santa, probably present in the region by 10,000 B.P. at the end of the Pleistocene (skeletons found in the cave of Sumidouro by Lund and that of Confins by Walter), survived until far into the Holocene. Moreover, its distribution was not limited to the eponymous region since, outside of Brazil, its remains have been identified in various parts of the South American continent (Colombia, Peru, southern Chile) (one can find a description of some of these burials in chapter 3). The main morphological characteristics of this race are as follows: a relatively gracile physique, with bones that are not very robust; average or small stature; dolichocephalic skull (elongated and narrow) or hyperdolichocephalic; a broad, curved forehead and a prognathous face, broad and short, with high eye-sockets.

After a detailed review of the data known at that time, A. Laming-Emperaire wrote: "For more than a century, physical anthropology has been working on the problem of American origins, without managing to find a definitive solution. The paleontological data are very poor, both on the Asian side and on the American. . . . The definite data that are based on physical anthropology amount to almost nothing: the presence of humans in America in the Wisconsin, and a coexistence with big quaternary animals; these humans were already Homo sapiens and dolichocephalic, while brachycephalics only appeared during the Postglacial" (1980: 38).

The few discoveries and studies made more recently have in no way invalidated these lines written almost twenty years ago. No human fossil of a different type has been discovered and, above all, none of them date back the 12,000 years that are necessary to merit the much sought-after title of "pre-Clovis."

3

THE TIME OF THE HUNTERS

T HE DATE OF 12,000 B.P. IS GENERALLY ACCEPTED AS THE LIMIT OF AB-
solute credibility. Yet, in several cases, dated remains of unimpeach-
able authenticity display only qualitative differences with their older but still
unacceptable neighbors. Conversely, one must acknowledge that after the
approximate date of 12,000 B.P., the known sites are suddenly far more numerous and richer in data. Since it is necessary to divide time and define
limits, we should also note that from 12,000 until about 8000 B.P.—a date
that also marks a new threshold—one sees major and rapid changes both in
the natural environment and in human lifeways and technology.

From the diversification of the natural resources exploited by humans
and the development of the lithic toolkit to the layout of dwellings, the un-
doubted progress in technology also owed a great deal to the profound
changes in the natural environment at the end of the Pleistocene. This was a
turning point, sandwiched between the end of the last glacial episode and
the arrival of present-day environmental and climatic conditions.

A CHANGING ENVIRONMENT, NEW LANDSCAPES

Although the current landscapes of South America have changed relatively
little over the past 10,000 years (that is, since the beginning of the Holocene),
they are, on the other hand, very different from those at the end of the Pleistocene. Between 14,000 and 10,000 B.P. changes occurred that had the biggest effect on the final quaternary environment. The slower changes persisted until 8000 B.P. and beyond. I shall only mention a few of them here,
selected from those that had a direct influence on human occupation.

At all times the isthmus of Panama has been an obligatory passage between North and South America, the only migration route used by both
animals and people in prehistoric times (except for a possible maritime route,
for which, however, there is no evidence—see chapter 2). The coastal plain

was then considerably wider than today, because the ocean level was 100 meters lower. A drier climate, a more open environment, a temperate vegetation in which savanna and forest alternated—all things contributed to make up a natural setting that was very different from the lush forests, bathed in stifling humidity, that characterize these regions today. It was only after around 13,000 B.P. that the forest gradually invaded the lowlands while, on both sides, the ocean slowly encroached on the land until it transformed the isthmus into a narrow bottleneck that was very inhospitable for people.

In South America, even at the height of the last cold phase, the glaciers by no means covered the whole Cordillera. The tongues of ice only descended a few hundred meters lower than today, and the icefields never formed a continuous barrier as in North America. In the north, where the altitude is largely offset by latitude, the Venezuelan, Colombian, and Ecuadorian Andes only comprised a few ice-covered peaks and secondary chains, separated by basins and plateaus with a more temperate climate. The Central Andes of Peru were the only ones to be covered with ice, from 8 to 15 degrees south latitude, and above 4,000 meters, but to the south the Andes of Bolivia, northwest Argentina, and northern Chile remained ice-free except for a few isolated massifs above 4,500 meters. It was only even farther south, beyond approximately 30 degrees south latitude, that a vast glacier covered the entire mountain chain, from 3,500 to 3,200 meters, as far as Tierra del Fuego (which, at the time, was not separated from the continent), and then disappeared into the Pacific Ocean. On the Atlantic side, this glacier covered southern Patagonia as far as 51 degrees south latitude. During this period, the high plateaus and inter-Andean basins had open landscapes, most of the time bereft of trees and, depending on latitude and altitude, covered with prairies, savannas, deserts, or tundras. The eastern piedmont of the Cordillera was probably also covered with savanna and comprised only wooded enclaves; even Amazonia was not the inextricable jungle we know today and was probably an alternation of islands of forest and drier expanses. However, after 14,000 B.P., the glaciers began to retreat, as everywhere else in the world, albeit with a certain chronological time-lag. After a brief and final outbreak of cold around 11/10,000 B.P. (Late Glacial), the warming that had already started became widespread and gradually resulted in the installation of present-day conditions. In the northern Andes, in the highlands where there was a cold, humid climate, the *páramos* developed, with their characteristic vegetation of big plants with whitish hairy leaves—the *frailejones* ("monks")—while the eastern piedmont and the lowlands that follow it to the east were progressively invaded by the tropical forest. In the Central Andes, the deglaciation also freed vast expanses of high plateaus, where a climate that was less humid than in the north encouraged the spread of the puna's vast carpets of gramineae. Even farther south, the rapid warming led to the expansion of the high-altitude deserts (the dry puna of the Atacama and southern Bolivia). The immense expanses of eastern South America, from

Brazil to Patagonia, underwent a similar evolution. A covering of woodland gradually spread in eastern Brazil, which until then had been occupied by savanna or semiarid steppes, while in the Argentine pampa and Patagonia, there occurred a notable amelioration in the climate, which had previously been humid and cold.

Along the Atlantic and Pacific coasts, during the glacial maximum, the sea level was around 100 meters lower than today. As a consequence, the Pacific coastal plains, for example, that of northern Peru, were doubtless twice as wide as today. To the east, along the coasts of Brazil and Argentina, the continental plateau emerged everywhere, which occurs today at less than 100 meters depth: the Falkland Islands (Malvinas) were joined to the continent, as was Tierra del Fuego in the extreme south. After about 12,000 B.P. sea level began to rise, mainly due to the slow thaw of the polar ice caps (eustasy). This slow thaw was observable on a global scale, but there were also more localized causes for a rise in sea level such as seismic activity that was especially important along the Pacific coast.

When the ocean waters rose, littoral zones were gradually submerged, isthmuses narrowed, and arms of the sea were created; but it is important to remember that, while the melting of the continental glaciers of the Andean Cordillera was rapid (a few decades or a few centuries), that of the icecap lasted for several thousand years. Hence, whereas the Andean glaciers had everywhere reached their present limits by 10,000 years ago, the level of the Pacific was still 50 meters lower than today. In the extreme south, the Magellan Straits that separate the continent from Tierra del Fuego probably opened only around 10,000 B.P. This slow rise of the waters was to continue for millennia: until 6000 B.P. the ocean level was to rise, depending on the region, until it exceeded the present level by 2 to 4 meters. This "transgression" was certainly offset in part by the slow rise of the continental masses liberated from the weight of the glaciers (isostasy), but as a consequence, along the lowland coasts, it led to the submersion of all human occupation sites earlier than 6000 B.P. and located on the shore, the existence of which we can only now imagine.

As for the whole of the prehistoric population—whether it occupied the littoral regions or the interior—one can imagine the impact that such major modifications had on the choice of migration routes and settlement areas, as well as on the way in which a territory was exploited, even if the changes obviously could not be detected at the scale of a generation, let alone that of a human lifespan. However, this climatic history of South America has by no means been fully studied; while the major episodes have been identified and dated, the local variations remain very poorly known for the most part. For that reason, one can also judge how incomplete and uncertain the best archaeological reconstructions may be for periods earlier than 8000 B.P., the time when environmental conditions became relatively stabilized and more or less like those we know today. This applies not only to "population maps"

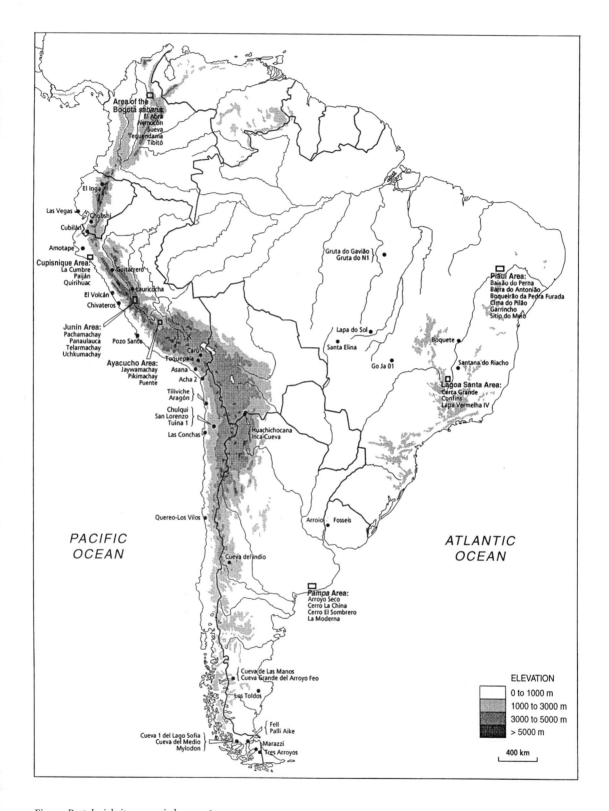

Fig. 10. Postglacial sites occupied 9000–6000 B.C.

but also to "chrono-cultural sequences," since landscapes were in the process of being modified radically, and hitherto inhabitable lands became inhospitable, while new and vast spaces were opening up. But one general fact appears more or less certain: after 10,000 B.P. ecological diversity became infinitely greater than before, and it is not impossible that the combined effects of the melting of the ice, the subsequent change in sea-level, and the formation of new plant communities brought about major displacements of both human and animal populations. According to Dillehay, this vast movement doubtless took place on a continental scale and from north to south, toward the great grassy plains of the east and extreme south, the Argentine pampa and the Patagonian steppe. This expansion supposedly led not only to a diversification of human groups, which were increasingly specialized both economically and technologically, but also to the rapid diffusion of certain technological features (Dillehay et al. 1992: 182).

THE LAST GREAT HUNTS OF THE PLEISTOCENE

Extinction or Extermination?

After 12,000 B.P., when this new phase of South American prehistory begins, at the start one sees few changes in the way of life of the human groups; they were apparently still few in number and scattered through immense territories. Even though hundreds of kilometers often separated them from each other, there were similarities in their ways of life, especially in the exploitation of natural food resources and, above all, in the exploited fauna.

At present we know of about 30 sites, scattered all over the immense territory of South America, that were occupied between 12,000 and 10,000 B.P., and the list grows every year. A few had already been occupied for a millennium or two, or even more (see chapter 2), while the others were new sites, occupied after the natural environment had undergone the main transformations outlined above. In most cases, the bone remains found in the dwellings or in the butchering areas belong to genera or species that have disappeared today and which are grouped for convenience under the term "Pleistocene megafauna." In South America, they are mostly large herbivores: equids that were quite similar to the horse we know today (*Equus, Hippidion*), camelids that were also little different from the present types (*Palaeolama, Lama gracilis*), and more rarely the proboscidians (*Haplomastodon, Cuvieronius*), but especially a few bizarre beasts that were closer to the notion we generally have of prehistoric animals: big edentates, morphologically close to the present-day sloths and armadillos but as big as an elephant. They include monsters with a carapace more than 3 meters long (*Glyptodon, Doedicurus clavicaudatus*), the latter equipped, at the end of its tail, with a big ball bristling with spikes, a formidable mass of weapons that it must have used as did medieval warriors. There were giant sloths (*Mylodon* in Patagonia, *Megatherium, Scelidotherium, Eremotherium*). *Megatherium,* the biggest of all, measured up to 6 meters high and probably weighed almost 3 tons. All these animals were on the menu of prehistoric people, whether they were hunted or tracked to their lair or whether, as sometimes seems to have been the case, only their decaying carcasses were recovered. More rarely, one also finds a few remains of felids and canids. Some of these were formidable, like the *Smilodon* with its enormous and very sharp upper canines, bigger than a modern lion's. This monstrous animal was obviously not a prey taken by humans—rather, it was the opposite. But others, more modest in size, were occasionally hunted and eaten, like the little fox *Dusycion*.

After about 11,000 B.P., a fairly general phenomenon took place in all the regions that were then occupied (or, more exactly, in those for which we have data): the gradual disappearance of this Pleistocene fauna. Faunal remains become much rarer in sites until they disappear almost completely around 9000 B.P. The causes of this "rapid" disappearance (which nevertheless remains at the scale of a millennium) are still poorly understood, and several hypotheses have been put forward that are difficult to prove. Some evoke natural events, such as climatic changes and the subsequent modifications in the natural environment, while others suggest catastrophic episodes such as volcanic eruptions that affected vast regions. Others point to human activities, accusing prehistoric people of having hunted both indiscriminately and too efficiently, which scarcely acknowledges that they might have had the slightest capacity for optimal exploitation of their territory and intelligent management of its resources. In the Old World in this same period, one sees the blossoming of the highly specialized cultures of the Upper Palaeolithic and especially, in western Europe, that of the Magdalenian. This flowering corresponds with a spectacular diversification of toolkits and weaponry and a systematic and rational management of an environment in which there also lived some big fossil species that would likewise soon disappear. Yet nobody would dream of accusing the Magdalenians of having exterminated the mammoths and bringing about the disappearance of the species.

Where the American continent is concerned, it is noteworthy that the "overkill theory" (of an extermination by humans) was first formulated by one of the most dogged defenders of a recent arrival by humans in America: in the 1960s and 1970s, Paul Martin published a series of incisive articles on what he called the "*Blitzkrieg*" model, the consequence, in his opinion, of the sudden and catastrophic arrival on the North American plains around 11,000 B.P. of hunters from Siberia, armed with the notorious and terribly efficient projectile points called "Clovis points" described in the previous chapter (Martin 1967; Mosimann and Martin 1975). The "model" was quickly extended to the whole of America, creating a surrealistic mix of warlike vocabulary with mathematical flights of fancy:

Possible values for the model include an average frontal depth of 160 kilometers, an average population density of 0.4 person per square kilometer on the front and of 0.04 person per square kilometer behind the front, and an average rate of frontal advance of 16 kilometers per year. For the first two centuries the maximum rate of growth may have equaled the historic maximum of 3.4 percent annually. . . . The model generates a population sufficiently large to overkill a biomass of Pleistocene large animals averaging 9 metric tons per square kilometer (50 animal units per section) or 2.3 x 10 to the 8 metric tons in the hemisphere. It requires that on the front one person destroy one animal unit (450 kilograms) per week, or 26 percent of the biomass of an average section in 1 year in any one region. (Martin 1973: 973)

One could extend this quotation. The whole of the text is aimed at demonstrating that the extinction of the megafauna, as seen in this way, may have required no more than ten years. This estimate is claimed to "explain" both why the animals did not have time to acquire defensive reflexes and why archaeologists have been able to discover so few killing sites, insofar as "extinction would occur within a decade. There was insufficient time for the fauna to learn defensive behaviors, or for more than a few kill sites to be buried and preserved for the archaeologist" (ibid.: 973). I should admit straightaway that the logic of this demonstration escapes me completely. Moreover, other estimates that are doubtless closer to reality, and that are based on observations made among present-day or recent hunter-gatherers, tend to indicate that the annual rate of increase of America's first "invaders" was probably much lower, and the speed of their advance much slower, than Martin maintains.

Let us return to a view that is probably closer to the facts. It is hard to imagine how the extinction of more than 30 types of big mammals (in the two Americas) could have happened so fast. In fact, several centuries, if not a few millennia, seem a far more reasonable time span to envisage for such a process. Moreover, the hypothesis of an abrupt disappearance loses much of its force if one accepts that South America had already been occupied for several thousand years by relatively large populations—and which did not live exclusively from hunting—even if they were still thinly scattered. In reality, the extinction of the Pleistocene megafauna certainly owes more to climatic changes than to human interference, no matter how deadly. On the coast of Peru, it was doubtless the increasing aridity; in the northern Andes of Colombia and Ecuador, it was the expansion of the forest zones and, generally speaking, the disappearance of the great open spaces of the "savanna" type that constituted the favorite habitat of these big animals. This does not rule out the possibility, at a local scale, of abrupt episodes like the first great postglacial volcanic eruptions that took place around 9000 B.P. in the region of the Magellan Straits, traces of which are preserved in various sites in the form of easily dated ash layers. A cycle of intense volcanic activity can certainly have brought about the disappearance of several species more rapidly than elsewhere (for example, following a contamination of the waters by toxic elements). Other causes that have been invoked—though only as secondary causes—are possible attacks of parasitic diseases or competition with newly appeared animal species. All causes are equally dependent, to differing degrees, on modifications of the natural environment.

It is true that one must add to the list of these phenomena, which were responsible for an ecological balance that had become precarious, the actions of humans who, not content with killing a good number of these animals, disturbed their habitat and their habits. In any event, the extinction of the great fauna can only have been very gradual, apart from a few exceptional cases. Besides, not all the species disappeared at the same time: around 9600 B.P. a giant sloth was still living in Brazil (cave of Lapa Vermelha IV), and the American horse was perhaps still being hunted around 9600 B.P. The American horse may also have continued to be hunted in the Peruvian Andes (shelter of Uchkumachay). This animal then disappeared completely, and a different species, although similar, was not to reappear in America until the sixteenth century A.D., as a not insignificant auxiliary of the European conquest. The hypothesis of a very late survival of the mylodon in Patagonia, which for a while was claimed on the basis of a date of 5360 B.P. obtained in the Mylodon Cave, has now been abandoned. On the other hand, this animal certainly coexisted with humans until around 9500 B.P.

While the megafauna grew rarer, other species that already existed or were new but doubtless less fragile because of their smaller size, survived and multiplied: camelids (vicuña and guanaco) in the Andean mountains and the steppes of Patagonia and, throughout the continent, various species of cervids and numerous rodents, some of imposing size. Imagine a guinea pig weighing more than 50 kilos, with paws like a dog's—this is the *capibara* of Brazil, the biggest living rodent known, and a much valued prey of the prehistoric hunter. Finally, there are numerous birds, and an extremely abundant marine fauna (whales, seals and sea lions, fish and mollusks). All these animals were identical to those we know today, and their remains are found in the sites, mixed with those of the last great fossil species with which they coexisted until the latter's complete disappearance.

After about 9000 B.P., apart from the exceptions mentioned, the sites only contain remains of present-day species. Finally, one must point out that some sites that were apparently occupied from the beginning of the period that concerns us here contained no remains of fossil fauna, even in their deepest occupation levels. This is the case at the Colombian sites of El Abra and Tequendama, occupied, respectively, since 12,400 ± 160 B.P. and 10,920 ± 160 B.P., as well as at Quirihuac and Guitarrero in Peru, the earliest occupation of which occurred between 12,500 and 11,000 B.P.

NEW PREY, NEW WEAPONS

Was this modification of the animal inventory, these profound upheavals that affected the environment, to be accompanied by one or more technological mutations aimed at finding new solutions to new problems or simply at increasing the efficiency of existing equipment? Hitherto, as we have seen, such equipment comprised crudely worked stone objects, or even objects with almost nonexistent working—split cobbles, flakes with little or no retouch—obtained by percussion with a hard hammer (cobble). Their often very rough appearance explains why their nature is often still disputed, when no other element (for example, their association with faunal remains or the proximity of a hearth) can confirm their anthropic origin. More finely worked flake tools were very rare, and working with soft hammers (wood or antler) and retouch by pressure were unknown, as was bifacial working. In only two places on the subcontinent, Taima-Taima in Venezuela and Monte Verde in Chile (see chapter 2), have fragments of bifacial projectile points been found that are earlier than 12,000 B.P.: in both cases, they are very elongated lanceolate points, of a type baptized "El Jobo" (after the Venezuelan site where they were first identified, as surface finds). Their presence in two places so far from each other but both located close to the ocean has led Dillehay to imagine a north-south human migration along the coasts (Dillehay 1997: 808–9). However, the points found at Taima-Taima and Monte Verde remain unique for their antiquity. For all the supporters of an earlier human occupation of America—who need to explain how the great Pleistocene animals could have been killed with very rudimentary weaponry— the hunters mostly used weapons of wood (sharpened sticks, hardened by fire, and clubs) or of bone (bone points that could be fixed to shafts, or spearpoints). The sites have very rarely conserved traces of these, and most of the time they are ambiguous (for example, the bone "points" of Pikimachay or from the New Mexican cave of El Pendejo—see chapter 2), but the example of the camp of Monte Verde, which remains unique for the moment, and the rich and diversified technological equipment it has yielded, demonstrate that the hunters' toolkit and weaponry before 12,000 B.P. were by no means limited to the lithic industry, which is merely the mineral skeleton of a far richer panoply.

However, after about 11,000 B.P., and on a fairly widespread basis, lithic assemblages began to include more finely worked tools, both unifacial and bifacial, and especially projectile points of various shapes: triangular with or without a stem, leaf-shaped of various sizes, and the most original of all, the type called "fish tail," whose peculiarity was to arouse numerous questions. But things are not quite so simple, because these points did not appear everywhere at the same time and sometimes did not appear at all. In this same period, the Pleistocene fauna gradually disappeared but at different moments depending on the region in question. From one end of the continent to the other, the known sites (which are also far more numerous than those of the preceding period) display the whole range of possible combinations: in some places, some megafauna hunters henceforth armed with projectile points and others not; elsewhere, hunters—some of whom also possessed points and others not—of a fauna that was already of modern type. In short, it is a complex panorama. Leaving aside all the surface finds or those bereft of context, let us now examine these projectile points, their possible origin, and their association with well-dated faunal assemblages.

A Fishy Tale

One of the arguments used most often by the conservatives to assign the arrival of humans in South America to a relatively recent period is a worked stone projectile point of a particular kind, known as a "fish tail" point. More or less oval in shape, and measuring between 4 and 6.5 centimeters, it was first shaped by percussion and then retouched with pressure flaking. Its proximal end has a narrowing that forms a broad stem whose shape certainly evokes a fish's tail. Points of this type have been found in various parts of the continent, from Ecuador in the north to as far south as Patagonia.

Their morphology, their geographical distribution, and their age require some comment. First, the technique involved: most of them display, on one or both faces, and from the base of the stem, the scar (of varying length) of a slender, vertical flake removal. This fluting, which may involve one or both sides of the piece, seems to have had a double use: it facilitated the insertion of the point into a shaft of split wood or reed, by reducing the thickness of its base and, at the same time, reducing the weapon's total thickness at the point of insertion, which could only facilitate its penetration of the prey. As for its production, it clearly required a perfect knowledge of the material being worked and of its mechanical reactions to applied force (in this specific case, pressure and not percussion), as well as great dexterity that could only be the fruit of a long apprenticeship. Next, the geographical aspect: if one adds to the few discoveries that were stratified, or in association with well-dated remains, the numerous surface finds of (undated) isolated points, in northern Colombia (Bahía Gloria), on the north coast of Peru (Piura, La Cumbre), in the northern Andes of Venezuela (La Hundición), in eastern Brazil, in Uruguay (Laguna Mirim, Itapiranga, Cabo Polonios, Rincón del Bonete, and Arroyo Pintos), in Argentina (Cerro Sombrero, La Crucesita, Villa del Dique) and Chile (Piedra del Aguila)—and I am doubtless forgetting some—then one sees that this type of point is represented, albeit by an extremely small number of examples, in almost all parts of the continent. One must also remember that similar points have also been found in Central America in Panama, Costa Rica, and Honduras, but always on the surface and hence impossible to date. Finally, the chronological aspect: in the few cases where it has been possible to date them, their age lies between

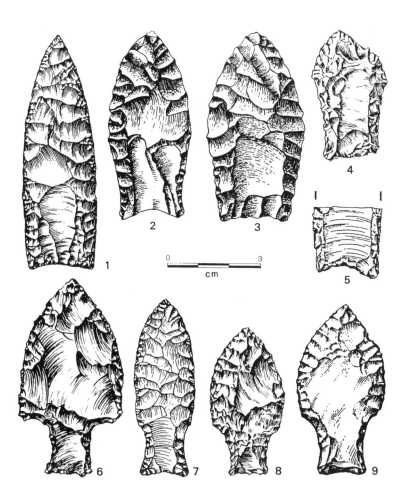

Fig. 11. Points with a proximal fluting. 1. Clovis point (USA), considered the archetype of the Central and South American points. 2, 3. Fluted points of Central America (Guatemala and Costa Rica, surface). "Fish tail" points of South America: 4, 5. El Inga (Ecuador). 6. Piura (Peru, surface). 7. Uruguay (surface). 8, 9. Fell's Cave, lower level (Chile). As can be seen, these points display different shapes from one region to another, and the only link is the presence, on one or more faces, of a proximal fluting of varying size. It seems that, while the diffusion of a technical "trick" like this within preexisting populations is highly probable, fluted points cannot be the "type fossil" that testifies to some migration or other from North to South America.

11,000 and 8000 B.P.: between 9000 and 8000 B.P. in Ecuador (El Inga); be-tween 11,000 and 10,000 B.P. in Peru (Chicama Valley) where several speci-mens have been collected on the surface but in clear association with Paiján points (Chaucat 1998: 115, 156); between 11,000 and about 8500 B.P. in Chil-ean Patagonia (Fell's Cave and Palli Aike); and around 10,700 B.P. in Argen-

tina (Cerro La China). In other words, those found in the south and the far
south are older than those found in the north.

For various reasons—technological originality, difficulty of manufacture,
geographical distribution, and age—the most widespread opinion among
the conservatives is that the "fish tail" points of South America are directly
derived from the Clovis points of North America, where they characterize
the Llano Paleoindian tradition between 12,000 and 11,000 B.P. Lynch (1978,
1983, 1990a, b) sees the appearance of this type of point as evidence left by
the bison hunters of North America who were the first people to inhabit
South America. Others have a more subtle view, like J. Schobinger (1988)
who, while accepting the idea of an older human presence in South America,
also believes in the sudden adoption of new techniques, such as that of bifacial working, that came from North America. Still others, including Bryan
(1991), go even further. Finding it difficult to believe that such a peculiar
technical feature as basal fluting could have been invented, several centuries
apart, in places as far from each other as the Great Plains of the United States
and Patagonia, Bryan thinks that it certainly originated in North America
but that its adoption in South America was not the direct result of a human
migration, but rather of the propagation of a technical "trick" among preexisting South American populations who already possessed bifacial weapons
"invented" locally, that is, El Jobo points. This hypothesis has the merit of
explaining why, despite a common general appearance caused by the presence of one or two flutings, the South American "fish tail" points actually
display a fairly wide variety of shapes, depending on the region concerned.
The basal narrowing that earned them this epithet is especially characteristic of the points found in the extreme south. In defending this view, Bryan
intends not only to demonstrate that people had already been there for a
long time, but also that the bifacial technique and projectile points were
invented independently in South America.

The latter proposal seemed poorly supported until recently, but the discovery of two fragments of points at Monte Verde obviously raises some
doubt. What appears to be the most probable scenario is indeed a North
American origin of bifacial points with basal fluting (or "fluted" points) and
their rapid diffusion among preexisting populations, most of which had hitherto used a lithic toolkit of simple technology (tools from blocks or big flakes,
shaped by percussion and unifacially worked). The diversity of the environments and the exploited resources would explain the fact that the South
American points are not exact replicas of the North American Clovis points
and that various shapes—triangular, leaf-shaped, stemmed—were very rapidly differentiated, depending on such things as the region, the nature of the
prey, the materials available, and the hunting techniques.

It is still impossible to be certain about this, and the numerous books or
articles published in the early 1990s (for the 500th anniversary of Columbus's
voyage) that wanted to be "clarifications" or "syntheses" clearly reflect the

limits of the interpretations put forward. Hence, while opting for a North American origin of the Clovis features (fluted points), Dillehay in 1992 did not rule out the hypothesis of an independent invention of the "fish tail" forms in the extreme south of South America (Dillehay et al. 1992)—an object lesson in how to reach a conclusion that does not upset anybody.

HABITATS, HABITS

While hitherto it was difficult, and even impossible, to use the few sites and the relatively scarce material remains they have yielded to reconstruct the way of life of the first hunters before 12,000 B.P. (apart from the exceptional finds of Monte Verde), the panorama subsequently has become somewhat clearer. In the first place, the relative abundance of the known sites—several dozen—henceforth allows one to sketch the outline of a few big cultural areas, within which the ways of life and the technical solutions adopted follow original trajectories that point to a variety of adaptive strategies that depend on the environments and the resources that they procure. Moreover, the enrichment and diversification of the range of tools and weapons also help to produce more precise reconstructions. It then becomes possible to leave the arid terrain of lithic typology and try to discover—through the tools but also far beyond them—the people themselves, their way of life, their way of occupying the environment and using it to their advantage. The notion of "industrial facies" finally gives way to the far more human one of "culture," of which technological equipment provides only an impoverished reflection.

A Well-Stocked Toolbox

The lithic panoplies, which had hitherto been fairly undifferentiated, now became enriched with several types of specialized tools. New techniques of analysis (microwear studies, identification of organic microremains on the implements) enable us today to establish their function: unifacial or bifacial knives, numerous flake tools that are often finely retouched—sidescrapers, scrapers, denticulates, awls, burins—for butchering game; scraping, currying, and fitting together hides; cutting up bones, and splitting wood or bark. The weapons include projectile points, of course, varying widely in shape and size, but also spears and bolas, a cluster of two or three stone balls attached to the end of a leather strap. When thrown spinning at the legs of the animal being pursued, it immobilized it. This implement thus constituted an extremely efficient hunting weapon for open spaces such as the high plateaus of the Andes or the pampas and steppes of the southern regions, where bolas were still being used recently by the last Indians to hunt the ostriches and guanacos of Patagonia.

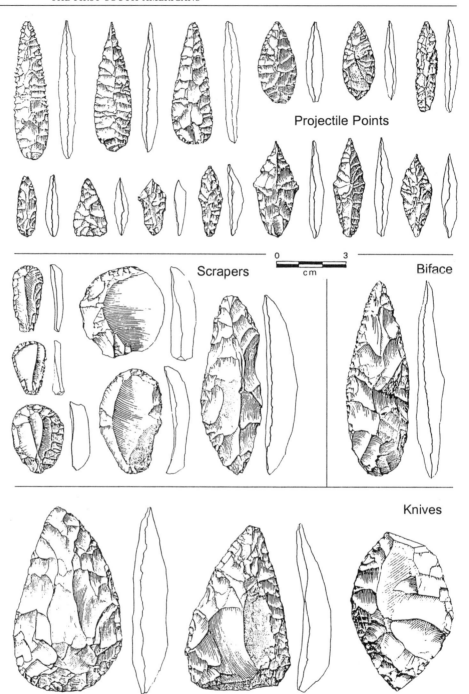

Fig. 12. Projectile points. Scrapers. Biface. Knives.
The "toolbox" of the hunter-gatherers of the Central Andes, between 7000 and 2000 B.C.
Projectile points of various sizes for arming darts (thrown with an atlatl) or javelins,
scrapers and unifaces—or "limaces"—for cleaning animal skins, big bifacial points that
may have been fixed at the end of a spear, and knives of various sizes, worked unifacially or
bifacially—these all constitute a basic toolkit, to which they also often added notched flakes
or denticulates and, very rarely, burins. All the objects illustrated come from the shelter of
Telarmachay (Junín, Peru).

Thus, with the exception of the occupants of the Colombian high plateau who, as we shall see later, seem to have continued deliberately to shun the innovations adopted everywhere else, the use of projectile points spread widely and very rapidly. Their adoption doubtless contributed to the disappearance of the big fauna, but these points also must have profoundly modified the techniques of stalking, chasing, and killing game. Without projectile weapons, the animal had to be approached very closely and lured to a place from which it could not escape. It is probably no accident that the open-air sites where remains of very large prey have been found, especially mastodons—be they sites dating to the end of the previous period (Taima-Taima and Tlapacoya in Mexico) or sites dated to shortly after 12,000 B.P. (Quereo and Tagua-Tagua in Chile, La Moderna in Argentina)—were at that time marine, riverside or lakeside beaches, or marshes: all places where the animals, driven and terrified, were doubtless trapped and relatively easy to kill. Conversely, in the cases where the remains of big fauna have been found inside a natural refuge, mixed with other anthropic traces such as remains of hearths, tools, or lithic waste, it seems more logical to imagine that only some parts of the prey—the easiest parts to transport and the most "profitable" in terms of consumable quantity—were carried there. For each of these two categories of site, one would like to know the number and the detailed anatomical identification of the bone fragments discovered. As this has never been done in a systematic manner, my explanation remains hypothetical.

From the moment when the hunters possessed weapons that could be thrown from a distance, like stone-tipped darts, and also from the moment when the prey (henceforth mostly present-day species) was of smaller size, things were different. First of all, it became possible to reach prey on the move; possible to do it in the very heart of a herd without it being necessary to isolate the selected animals beforehand; possible, finally, during a collective hunting expedition to kill several animals simultaneously, since killing the prey could henceforth be an individual act and not, as was the case for the big fossil species, an activity requiring the participation of several hunters around the same animal.

We still need to know what these tools and these weapons really looked like, and how they were handled, because, with a few rare exceptions, only the nonperishable parts—that is, those made of stone—have been discovered in the sites. Yet we know, thanks to the rare specimens found, that various tools must have been hafted most of the time: in the Peruvian cave of Guitarrero, a scraper was found wrapped in a piece of leather and tied up with string, which must have made it easier to grip and also protected the user's hand; several Andean sites have also yielded fragments of sawn bone tubes with carefully regularized edges, whose shiny surface indicated prolonged handling and which could well have been handles for knives or scrapers. The projectile points (bifacial stone points) were naturally inserted into a shaft of plant material (wood or reed), fragments of which are sometimes

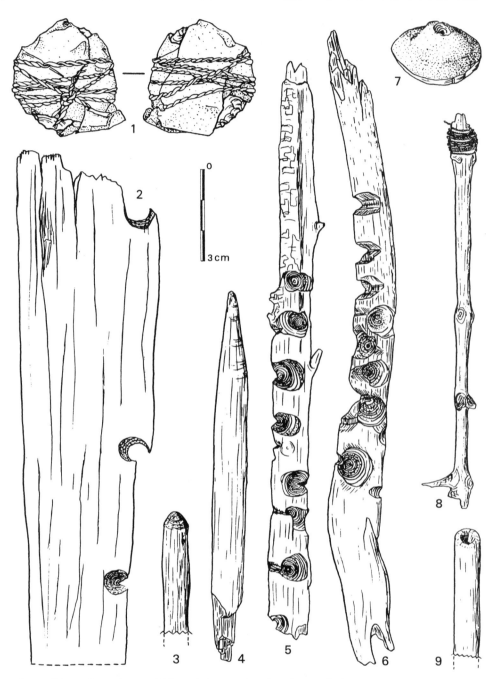

0

3 cm

Fig. 13. Objects of organic material from Guitarrero Cave (Peru). 1. Worked stone scraper wrapped in hide and bound with a string of plant fibers. 2, 5, 6. (Passive) pieces of fire drills, in soft wood. 3. (Active) piece of a fire drill, in hard wood. 4. Sharpened stick (spear?). 7. Fragment of gourd (vessel lid?). 8. Branch tied with string. 9. Probable proximal fragment of a wooden arrowshaft, the cavity at the end being for the hook of an atlatl. It is very rare to find objects of this kind in prehistoric sites in caves or shelters at altitude, where they have generally been destroyed by humidity and other natural agents.

preserved. The points were generally fixed to the shaft by a reinforcing bind-
ing of tendons or plant fibers, and often also—as shown by traces found on
the proximal parts of numerous points—by some kind of mastic (bitumen
or resin). It is more difficult to determine the type of throwing implement
used. Numerous experimental studies with contradictory results have shown
that neither the shape, nor the volume, nor the weight of the stone points
enables one to identify the "launcher" (Van Buren 1974; Lavallée et al. 1985:
181–83). Ten thousand years ago, the bow was unknown in South America
and even throughout America. In Europe, the first known bows date to the
end of the Upper Palaeolithic (10,000/9000 B.P.), but this implement was
apparently introduced to America much later. In fact, the first known North
American bows do not seem to be older than the fourth millennium. In South
America, some remains of a bow are thought to have been identified on the
northern coast of Chile, where some long, thin pieces of wood were found
inside mummies belonging to the Chinchorro culture (around 7800 B.P.)
(Bittmann and Munizaga 1979). However, their identification remains uncertain, and I shall return to them in relation to the very special burials peculiar to this culture (see chapter 4). In the absence of any unquestionable
remains, archaeologists have therefore tried to deduce the use of the bow
from the size of the projectile points, laying down the principle that its use
demanded lighter arrows, and thus smaller points, than darts thrown by
atlatl or a fortiori by hand. One can certainly see—though much later, after
about 5000 B.P.—a fairly widespread diminution in the size of projectile
points, especially in the Andean region, but nevertheless this does not necessarily constitute an irrefutable proof of the bow's introduction.

It is therefore highly probable that, from the appearance of the first worked
stone points until about 5000 B.P., only the atlatl was used. This is a straight
rod of wood or bone, equipped with a hook or stop at one end that enables
darts to be thrown with greater speed at the same time that it increases the
precision of the shot. Its use is well attested in Eurasia during the Upper
Palaeolithic and in North America since more than 9,000 years ago. In South
America, several intact or fragmentary specimens have been found in contexts dating to 7000 B.P. or older, especially on the Peruvian coast. In contrast to the bow, the manufacture of which presupposes the existence of
trees providing long, straight, and supple poles, an atlatl can be made from a
much shorter branch. Its length can vary from a meter or more to about 30
centimeters, without this being prejudicial to its efficacy. In other words, it
could have been made and used in virtually all the environments and all the
climates that then existed in South America.

Finally, among the hunting implements, we should not forget traps, snares,
or nooses with which small game was captured; the spears or harpoons used
for fishing in rivers; and doubtless the light darts, of wood or bone, used to
hit birds, similar to those still frequently employed by the natives of the
Amazon forest.

A Balanced Diet

In almost all regions, we have evidence that the natural plant resources were used very early, alongside the animal resources that were more specific to different environments, coastal or terrestrial, highland or lowland, forested or not. In many sites pestles and mortars have been discovered. Far from proving, as has long been claimed, early agricultural practices, these were simply used for breaking, crushing, or grinding the innumerable nuts, berries, seeds, tubers, or stems available from the natural environment, depending on the circumstances and the seasons. Moreover, plant materials were not all used for food. The stems or bark, having been softened and shredded, were sometimes turned into straps and cords, baskets and bags, and lines and nets for fishing.

Of course, all this rich paraphernalia, all the resources offered by the environment, were neither identical nor present everywhere. Since the number of sites known prevents my enumerating the particularities of each one, I have chosen to linger over a few of them, selected from the most representative (and the richest in data) within each of the main types of natural environment: Andean mountains, arid Pacific littoral, tropical lowlands of the northeast, plains and plateaus of the center and east, and finally the steppes and oceanic regions of the extreme south.

The Hunter-Gatherers of the Cordillera

No sooner have I chosen this way of dividing things up (obviously as arbitrary as any other) and written this title, than the first difficulty already arises, because the Andean Cordillera alone includes an extreme variety of natural environments. This colossal mountain system (the world's second after the Himalayas) stretches over almost 8,500 kilometers. Because of its latitudinal extent and the variety of its landscapes and climates, it presents a multiplicity of highly contrasting ecological facets.

We have already seen that the climatic oscillations of the final Pleistocene caused several changes of landscape in the Andean mountains, albeit of moderate extent. Despite the altitude and a mostly severe climate, the Andes never constituted an obstacle to human settlement and movements, which perhaps explains why, together with the eastern edge of the Brazilian plateau, they were the region of South America that was occupied the earliest.[1] The *sábana* of Bogotá (Colombia), the altitude of which does not exceed 2,800 meters, was occupied shortly before 12,000 B.P. In the Central Andes—despite being the most affected by the last glaciation because of their higher altitudes—people were already present in the sheltered and relatively dry intramontane basin of Ayacucho around 14,000 B.P. (see chapter 2). Conversely, all lands located above 4,000 meters in the Central Andes and 3,000 meters in the northern Andes were still uninhabitable at this time.

[1]The antiquity of this peopling can be seen, in the groups that today occupy the highest regions (between 4,000 and 4,500 meters on the high plateaus of Peru, Bolivia, and northern Chile), in a physiological adaptation to the environment and notably in a modification of the respiratory and circulatory systems: thoracic capacity several liters greater than normal, a more developed heart, a higher number of red blood corpuscles (7 or 8 million instead of about 4.5). At 5,000 meters, the quantity of oxygen is only half that at sea level.

The warming that became noticeable after 11,000 B.P. led to the wide-spread and relatively rapid retreat of the glaciers but also to a fresh outbreak of pluviosity and, consequently, the development and altitudinal rise of forest cover. This was the case in Colombia, where some doubtless quite small groups of hunters continued to frequent the few natural shelters that had already been used before: Unit D at El Abra, between 9325 ± 100 and 7250 ± 100 B.P.; Unit 3 of Tibitó, around 11,000 B.P.; and they also occupied new sites, close to the previous ones: Sueva, between 11,000 and 10,000 B.P. (?), Tequendama, 10,920 ± 260 B.P., Checua 8200 ± 110 B.P. The range of game they exploited henceforth exclusively comprised present-day species, mostly cervids (*Odocoileus* and *Mazama*) and rodents (*Sigmodon* and *Cavia*). At Tibitó, the mastodons and horses disappeared: the gradual diminution of the great herbaceous expanses at high altitude and their replacement by forest no doubt contributed to their becoming rare and then their disappearance.

It remains more difficult to qualify and describe these hunters' way of life. The discoverers of the sites think that, as in the past, they were short-lived seasonal occupations. In fact, the only change that can be seen in the lithic assemblages is the appearance, alongside the vaguely retouched flakes of Abriense type, of a few more elaborate pieces made out of nonlocal rocks,[2] including a few objects that were apparently retouched with pressure flaking—a few flakes, a limace, one or two fine bifacial knives (but still no projectile points)—a small and disparate assemblage that the discoverers have baptized the "Tequendamiense" complex (Correal 1979, 1981; Correal and Van der Hammen 1977; Groot 1995; Van der Hammen 1992; Van der Hammen and Correal 1978). Elsewhere in Colombia, research carried out in the middle valley of the Magdalena has led only to the discovery of lithic assemblages that sometimes include bifacial projectile points of unknown age, apart from a level at La Palestina dating to 10,400 ± 90 B.P. (which is bereft of points) (López Castaño 1995). Clearly, Colombia remains a promising terrain, but one that has been very little explored.

In the Ecuadorian Andes, which are likewise very poorly known, only three sites illustrate the period from 12,000 to 8000 B.P. Of the three—the open-air sites of El Inga and Cubilán and the cave of Chobshi—only the first poses a real problem. Excavated by R. Bell and W. Mayer-Oakes in the 1960s by artificial layers, it apparently consists of a vast knapping workshop, with a confused stratigraphy, but they obtained more than 80,000 worked objects made of a very fine smoked obsidian, including tools on finely shaped flakes retouched by pressure, and, especially, some bifacial "fish tail" points. In fact it was the presence of these points that led the discoverers—despite C14 dates that are more recent—to ascribe an antiquity of 9,000 years or more to the site (Bell 1965; Mayer-Oakes 1986b). As for the other two sites, which are more "classic," Cubilán is a probable open-air camp, dating to between 10,300 ± 170 and 9100 ± 120 B.P., while Chobshi is a cave settlement dating to be-

[2]This leads certain specialists to suggest that, for their hunting expeditions into the highlands, people arrived supplied with good-quality equipment (eventually including projectile points) which they took with them afterward; all they left in the places where they camped was a rapidly worked makeshift toolkit used for butchering the game they killed and which they abandoned just as rapidly. This is an attractive hypothesis, but it remains to be proven insofar as no contemporary Colombian site has yet yielded, in a chronologically well-defined stratigraphic context, a single bifacial point.

tween 8615 ± 90 and 7537 ± 295 B.P.; both seem to correspond to very short stays. At the former, the quality of the excavations has made it possible for a few paleoethnological observations to be made. The lithic material is of high quality—flake tools and bifacial points of jasper and chalcedony—but there are no faunal remains (Temme 1982). At the latter, the fauna is well represented by remains of cervids, rodents, and birds (present-day species). The lithic toolkit is diversified and fairly similar, but the excavation by trenches and by artificial levels does not allow any interpretation (Lynch 1989; Lynch and Pollock 1981). The highlands of Ecuador are of moderate altitude and have climatic conditions that are greatly tempered by latitude; it is very probable that the rock outcrops here conceal numerous natural shelters, and once again prehistorians need to take a closer interest in them.

In the Basins and on the High Plateaus of Peru

The Central Andes of Peru provide a slightly more lively picture in this period. First, and as in Colombia, the midaltitude sites that were already used in the previous period (Ayacucho Basin) were frequented more and more intensively. The environmental modifications at the start of the postglacial seem to have played a much less decisive role there than at higher altitudes. At Ayacucho, the Puente (c. 11,000–9000 B.P.) and Jaywa (c. 9000–7800 B.P.) phases defined at the caves of Pikimachay, Puente, and Jaywamachay, corresponded to seasonal occupations (MacNeish et al. 1980–83): the camps set up by "microbands"(?) in different "microenvironments" were supposedly each associated with a season and a preferred subsistence strategy (gathering of berries and wild seeds during the wet season, hunting of cervids and camelids in the dry season), completed in both cases by the tracking or trapping of birds and "microfauna." The lithic industry, which is abundant and diversified (albeit without "microlith"), includes a rich toolkit on flakes, with bifacial diamond-shaped or leaf-shaped projectile points (of the Ayampitin type, which is found, in this period, throughout the Andean area and even beyond to the east) and numerous implements for crushing or grinding, which point to the rather systematic exploitation of wild plants.

This evocation of an early and regular use of plant resources leads me to bring up Guitarrero Cave, located in the heart of the northern Andes of Peru. Dominated by the impressive summits of the White Cordillera (6,870 meters at Huascarán), the valley of the Santa—known as Callejon de Huaylas in its central, intra-Cordilleran portion—is of relatively moderate altitude (between 3,000 and 2,000 meters) and today constitutes one of the most beautiful and most welcoming landscapes of the country. The cave opens on the side of the valley's eastern flank at 2,580 meters altitude and has yielded one of the longest sequences of Peruvian prehistory—12,560 ± 560 to 2315 ± 125 B.P.—and also, above all, evidence of the very early manipulation of a few plant species (Lynch 1980; Lynch et al. 1985). The first occupants of

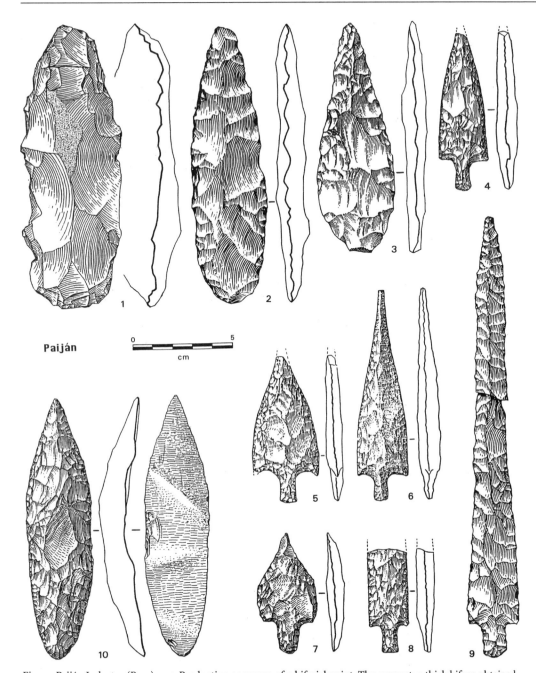

Paiján

0 — 5
cm

Fig. 14. Paiján Industry (Peru). 1–4. Production sequence of a bifacial point. The support, a thick biface obtained with a stone hammer (1), is then shaped and thinned with a "soft" (wood) hammer to make a symmetrical leaf-shaped piece known as a "rough" (2, 3), which is finally retouched with pressure flaking to create the stem and shape the distal extremity into a sharp point (4). 5–9. Various kinds of finished points, including the longest known (9), which was found broken, doubtless because of its fragility. 10. Another characteristic Paijanian tool, the uniface, a big elongated plano-convex sidescraper, similar to the "limaces" of the European Palaeolithic.

Guitarrero had a "classic" behavior for the period. As at Ayacucho, they hunted the big herbivores that were present in the region (mostly cervids, since the big Pleistocene fauna had apparently disappeared from the region), killed or trapped small game (rodents and birds), and used a toolkit that was no less classic, made on flakes (sidescrapers, scrapers), or bifacial pieces (triangular or leaf-shaped projectile points). However, by 9/8000 B.P. (Complex IId: 8800 to 8200 B.P.) the occupation layers start to yield plant remains that the botanists who analyzed them believe to be cultivated. The first to appear are beans (*Phasaeolus lunatus*, a bit later *P. vulgaris*), then pimentos (*Capsicum chinense*) and gourds (*Cucurbita* sp.) (Kaplan 1980; Smith 1980). In South America at present, the beans of Guitarrero represent the oldest known evidence for domesticated plants, and hence of horticultural practices. We shall see (in chapter 4) the problems that these discoveries create concerning the domestication of plant species and the appearance of agriculture in South America. Guitarrero is also the only place where, because of the excellent conditions of conservation, it has also been possible to recuperate elements that are normally lacking in the Cordillera's sites, including numerous fragments of various strings or straps of plant material; a piece of (cultivated?) gourd, doubtless used as a vessel; several wooden fire drills, used intensively; and a scraper wrapped in hide.

Nevertheless, it was at high altitude that prehistoric human settlement underwent its most sudden expansion. On the high plateaus, recently liberated from the ice, which extend beyond 4,000 meters, the expanses of uncovered moraines were promptly colonized by a herbaceous vegetation, doubtless quite similar to that of the present-day *páramos* of Colombia. The expansion of these vast pastures encouraged the proliferation of big herds of herbivorous ungulates—cervids (*Odocoileus virginianus* and *Hippocamelus antisensis*) and camelids (vicuña *Lama vicugna*, and guanaco *L. guanicoe*). It was then that hunters began to occupy the natural shelters of the Peruvian puna, between 4,000 and 4,500 meters and even sometimes higher. Concentrated on the high plateaus of Central Peru, the caves or rockshelters of Lauricocha (4,100 meters), Pachamachay (4,250 meters), Uchkumachay (4,050 meters), Panaulauca (4,050 meters), and Telarmachay (4,420 meters) were intensively used—as soon as the last tongues of ice had retreated (between 10,000 and 9000 B.P.)—by hunters of cervids and camelids who gradually specialized in hunting the latter, doubtless because of their more gregarious and territorially more stable behavior (Cardich 1964; Kaulicke 1981; Lavallée et al. 1985; Rick 1980). The excavations carried out by J. Rick at Pachamachay and my own work at Telarmachay brought to light the existence of an often very elaborate arrangement of the domestic living space: low stone walls or walls of flexible materials (hides, rushes) held up by poles (materialized by lines of postholes), delimiting a protected occupation area in which there were structured hearths of various types and specialized activity areas (for butchery, cooking tasks, stone knapping, skinworking). However, this in no way proves that the occupations were permanent, and in fact they still seem to have remained seasonal. The different studies carried out at Telarmachay have even enabled us to reconstruct a cycle of movements within the high plateau that doubtless implies a rotation between different winter and summer habitats located at a slightly different altitude, in accordance with the annual cycle of precipitation and the consequent movements of the animal populations (Lavallée 1997). In all these camps, the "toolbox" was more or less the same: a very diversified and well made assemblage of flake tools dominated by scrapers, probable evidence of a very important utilization of animal hides; abundant bifacial leaf-shaped, pentagonal, or diamond-shaped points, which must have been for reed-shafted darts thrown with an atlatl; and abundant hammers or grindstones that were often used for breaking bones—the microtraces left encrusted on their surface demonstrate this. A fine bone industry includes, alongside "classic" objects such as points and awls, spatulas that often display traces of red ocher, and big sidescrapers made on camelid scapulas, likewise used for hideworking (as shown by microwear studies). Other implements in animal materials include some that were used to retouch stone tools (by pressure) and cervid antlers used for knapping blocks of stone (by percussion). The true grinding implements (mortars and pestles) are far rarer than in the sites at moderate altitude, although the puna contains a surprising quantity of usable plants, from a range of tubers to the fruits of the cactus, not forgetting a great variety of edible berries, and medicinal herbs that have probably been known for a very long time.

Dry Puna and Salt Puna of the Southern Andes

The Andes of the far north of Chile are both extraordinarily beautiful and extremely harsh. From an arid steppe, scattered with intensely blue lakes or immense salt marshes inhabited by pink flamingoes, there arise cliffs of pinkish ignimbrites or black flows of basalt, landscapes of violent contrasts that are dominated by the ice-covered peaks of the volcanoes, surmounted by a little plume of smoke (because these volcanoes are still active). This apparently uninhabitable environment was nevertheless occupied—though admittedly the climatic conditions were doubtless a little less dry at the time— by the beginning of the Holocene. Evidence for this is to be found in the shelters of Tuina (10,820 ± 630 B.P.), San Lorenzo (10,400 ± 130 B.P.), and Chulqui (9590 ± 90 B.P.), located in the heart of the Atacama Desert—the most arid desert in the world—at an average altitude of 3,000 meters and occupied, between 10,000 and 9000 B.P., by vicuña hunters. Once again, the technological equipment is classic: a diversified toolkit on flakes, and bifacial projectile points, though here they are triangular and not leaf-shaped as in Peru. However, the excavations carried out in these different sites were too limited in their extent (mostly they were simple test-pits) to permit any kind of paleoethnological interpretation (Nuñez 1983; Nuñez and Santoro 1988).

Not far from there, on the high plateaus of northwest Argentina that are scarcely more inviting, the first known human settlements are similar and contemporaneous. However, at Inca-Cueva and Huachichocana, both occupied from 9500/9000 B.P., the cultural inventory is richer. In shelter No. 4 of the Quebrada Inca-Cueva—a miraculous little paradise, with an almost pleasant climate and profuse vegetation, nested in a gash in the puna and edged on both banks with impressive scree-slopes of red sandstone filled with numerous natural shelters—C. Aschero unearthed in the deepest occupation level (9230 ± 70 B.P.) lithic material that is more or less similar to that of Tuina, alongside bone remains of rodents and, especially, traces of various structures (postholes, refuse pits filled with plant remains, hearths) (Aschero 1979). As for the cave of Huachichocana, occupied around 9620 ± 130 B.P., its principal originality resides in the fact that this first occupation level yielded, alongside a technological paraphernalia that could be called banal for the period (leaf-shaped and triangular bifacial points, various flake tools), numerous organic remains—fragments of objects in wood or basketry and plant remains. According to A. Fernández-Distel (1986), the latter include cultivated plants—beans, pimentos, and, even more surprising, maize (which would thus be the oldest cultivated corn in America, but its authenticity is far from being accepted by all archaeologists—see chapter 4).

Finally, let me mention the exceptional site of Asana, located at 3,430 meters altitude in the basin of the Rio Osmore, in southern Peru, discovered and excavated by M. Aldenderfer (1989, 1990, 1998). First, it is significant because it is an open-air camp, whereas all the Peruvian, Chilean, and Argentine sites just cited are cave or rockshelter settlements, and because it yielded an occupation sequence that is almost six millennia long, the most complete sequence known in this mountainous part of southern Peru. Hitherto we only knew of a few rare sites, which have been studied somewhat summarily and which have provided a single date: the shelter of Carú (8190 ± 130 B.P.) and, especially, the cave of Toquepala, whose fame rested on the presence of rock paintings that were attributed—perhaps a bit hastily?—to its first occupants (c. 9500 B.P.) and which today have been irreparably pillaged. The occupation of Asana began around 10,000 B.P. (9820 ± 150 B.P.), that is, almost at the same time as that of the Ecuadorian camp of Cubilán. Unlike the latter site, this one would continue to be occupied almost without interruption until about 4000 B.P. Another noteworthy fact is that the excavations, carried out over wide areas, have led to the discovery of remains of habitations that in the oldest levels consist of circular structures delimited by lines of postholes and containing hearths. Among the lithic material obtained from the early levels, which includes bifacial projectile points and various flake tools, there is a marked abundance of scrapers, associated (as at Telarmachay) with a great quantity of red ocher and used for hideworking, again as at Telarmachay.

All the data just summarized thus suggest, throughout the Andean mountains, from the humid *páramos* of Colombia to the arid punas of southern Peru and northern Chile, a seasonal exploitation of the territory that was suited to the various subsistence systems then in place—whether it be the hunting of big herbivores, the trapping of small game, or plant collecting—with a particular emphasis always placed on the intensive exploitation of animal materials. Moreover, the practice of an annual cycle of nomadism seems to be well established. Albeit limited in scale, it was clearly aimed at an optimal exploitation of the different accessible resources within a radius of no more than a few dozen kilometers. However, a more ambitious theory had been proposed in the 1960s and 1970s by Lanning (1967) and then by Lynch (1971). Having noted a certain similarity between the coastal and Andean lithic assemblages (from, respectively, the central Cordillera and the central coast of Peru), they tried to demonstrate that a "transhumance" of greater extent—linking the coast and the high regions—had been undertaken by the Andean hunters, who had followed the seasonal migrations of the herds of wild camelids and cervids down to the coastal valleys with pastures that were still green while the puna underwent its annual period of dryness. At the time when this undoubtedly attractive theory was put forward, there were few known sites in the highlands and the way they were used was poorly defined, as was the behavior of the animal populations that were exploited. In reality, the pastures of the high plateau did not dry out during the southern winter (June to November) to the extent that the animal populations were forced to migrate. These animals have now been well studied, and their territorial behavior is very stable. Finally, the typological resemblances noted between the coastal and Andean lithic industries were based above all on the presence, in both cases, of leaf-shaped points (of the Ayampitin type)—but it is now known that these are present more or less everywhere from Venezuela to the south of Argentina and are not characteristic of any cultural area in particular. The only well-attested examples of long-distance relations between coast and interior are in arid northern Chile, where they suggest the arrival on the coast, at the beginning of the Holocene, of populations from the highlands.

It should also be noted that the sites cited here as examples are located either in the middle of the vast open spaces of the very high lands (from Colombia to northern Chile) or in relatively broad basins or valleys such as that of Ayacucho or the valley of the Callejon de Huaylas in Peru. No early settlement has yet been detected in the innumerable deep little valleys or gorges—known as *quebradas*—that cut into the high plateaus. It seems that, contrary to what one might imagine, the sectors at highest altitude constituted a privileged habitat, insofar as they represented (unlike the narrow valleys) a huge reservoir of easily exploitable fauna. Conversely, these same transverse valleys were obligatory passages to the Amazonian piedmont as well as the littoral plain. This is not simply an attractive working hypothesis, because the existence of contacts with the Pacific coast by 7000 B.P. is established by the presence of seashells in various high-altitude sites. As for the relations with the eastern forest piedmont, we shall see in the next chapter how important these probably were for the "invention" of Andean agriculture.

One last remark: none of these high-altitude sites contained the slightest remains of a Pleistocene animal species. Only the little shelter of Uchkumachay, in Peru, excavated by P. Kaulicke (1981) yielded in its deepest (undated) level a few fragments of horse bones (*Parahipparion*) and a big fossil cervid (*Agalmaceros blicki*), remains that might indicate either an earlier occupation than that of the neighboring sites (this is not very probable because of the climatic conditions of the period) or a fairly long survival of these two species in the Central Andes.

From Savanna to Desert, along the Pacific

Although we are beginning to get to know the dwellings of the hunter-gatherers in the mountainous regions where the jagged relief offers numerous natural shelters, and their way of managing the tasks they carried out there, it is far more difficult to reconstruct (and locate) them in the open areas bereft of such shelters. This certainly applies, among other areas, to the Pacific coast, whether it be the subdesert littoral of Ecuador or the desert coast of Peru and northern Chile. Prehistoric sites of the period 12,000 to 8000 B.P. are not very numerous here, mainly for the simple reason that most of the camps set up along the shore were covered by water during the slow postglacial rise in sea level. The only sites to escape submersion were those set well back from the shore or in locations high enough to avoid the rising waters.

On the south coast of Ecuador, a single site is known at present, but the data it provided—thanks to the quality of the investigation—make it both a very rich source of information and an example. It was in the semidesert peninsula of Santa Elena that K. Stothert (1988) unearthed the remains of the camp of Las Vegas 80, located about 4 kilometers from the bay of Santa Elena and occupied, by 10,000 B.P., by a population that lived mainly on maritime resources. During the Early Las Vegas phase (9800 to 8000 B.P.), in an environment quite similar to the one existing on the peninsula until recently (before its massive deforestation)—semiarid savannas alternating with zones of denser vegetation and, along the coast, thick mangrove formations—a small human group (25–50 people according to Stothert) settled quasi-permanently. They hunted cervids, peccaries, and foxes in the surrounding savanna; gathered wild plants that were edible (cactus *Opuntia*, fruits of the *algarrobo*) or useful in other ways (various rushes or woods); and especially fished and collected the shells that were found in profusion in the nearby mangrove. These resources were easily accessible throughout the year within a radius of a few kilometers around the camp, which led Stothert to think that Las Vegas must have been permanently occupied, since nothing forced the population to abandon the camp temporarily, except to maintain episodic contact with the groups who lived in 30 other locations on the peninsula. Its inhabitants apparently lived in circular huts covered with rushes fixed onto a framework of wooden poles that left very visible impressions in the ground. Few changes seem to have affected this way of life over the course of time, apart from the increasing importance accorded to the collecting of mollusks at the expense of hunting—and, among these mollusks, a higher proportion of open-water species, reflecting a steadily growing appropriation of the aquatic environment. During a later phase (Late Las Vegas) it is not impossible that the occupants of Las Vegas learned to cultivate a few plants, including gourds and perhaps maize, though the evidence is inconclusive.

Until about 8000 B.P., this judicious and diversified exploitation of the environment only utilized very simple technical equipment that was as unspecialized at the beginning as at the end of the occupation: quartzite flakes with little or no retouch, cobbles for crushing or grinding, a few bone spatulas and points, shells turned into vessels or spoons, but no perfected fishing equipment, no bifacial lithic tools, and no projectile points. It is true that numerous utensils made of perishable materials, like basketry, matting, nets, and wooden objects and weapons, must have disappeared totally, as was the case in the Cordillera sites (apart from Guitarrero), leaving only an extremely impoverished impression of the technical paraphernalia that was used.

An almost similar littoral adaptation, and one perhaps slightly older but far less dense (or studied less extensively?), has also been discovered in the extreme north of the Peruvian desert close to Talara at the foot of the hills of Amotape in an analogous environment (although slightly less arid than today?). Here J. Richardson (1978) located and baptized the "Amotape" complex, the remains of a dozen small camps dating to between 11,200 ± 115 and 8125 ± 80 B.P. As at Las Vegas, the remains unearthed consist of food refuse—especially mangrove shells and remains of small mammals and birds—and undifferentiated lithic implements made from quartzite flakes. And, as in all the other cases of sites that have only yielded an industry of flakes or cobbles, Richardson imagines the existence of a whole range of equipment of wood or bone that has disappeared today, which the rudimentary lithic objects discovered merely served to manufacture.

However, it is farther south in the Peruvian desert, in the Cupisnique region, that C. Chauchat (1992), in some 20 years of intensive research, has unearthed and described with great precision the industrial and cultural complex of the Paijanian (after a modern village around which numerous diagnostic tools were collected), dating approximately to between 11,000 and 8000 B.P. (10,720–7940 B.P.). Dozens of open-air sites—among which it has been possible to distinguish quarries, workshop sites, and camps—have been located in this desert that is even more arid than in the north, even if it was less dry then than today. The flora was poor and sparse, the fauna rare, and the biggest animal was a little sand fox; cervids only appeared sporadically. Conversely, small rodents, lizards, and snails abounded. In this environment, which was not totally arid but not very welcoming either, small groups of very mobile hunter-gatherers moved around between the first foothills of the Cordillera and the littoral. At the time the littoral was 15 kilometers farther away, because although the sea level had already undergone a rapid rise, it was still considerably lower than today (about 50 meters). The people lived from fishing, as shown by the refuse found close to the camps, mostly made up of the remains of salt-water fish, but also including small desert species, which they hunted, trapped, or collected. They doubtless also gathered—like their contemporaries at Las Vegas and Amotape—the succulent berries of the *algarrobo* (*Prosopis* sp.). However, their toolkit—unlike the one at those sites—comprised some very well worked pieces, retouched with pressure flaking, on flakes (unifaces of the limace type—Levallois points on which the periphery has been retouched to form two convex sides converging at the ends, becs or chisel burins, notched pieces, and denticulates) and bifacials. The latter included long, narrow-stemmed points with a very sharp distal end, known as "Paiján" points, that are unique in America. According to Chauchat, these points with their often extremely fine end were sometimes more than 10 centimeters long and were probably used for harpooning big fish (up to 80 centimeters). Finally, the oldest human remains to be discovered so far in Peru, and even in all of South America, have been unearthed in this region: "Paiján Man," whose grave will be described later, was buried in 10,200 ± 180 B.P.

Despite the geographical connotation of its name, the Paijanian has been recognized over a very large portion of the Peruvian coastal desert. Slightly south of the region studied by Chauchat, where it has mostly been illustrated by surface sites, it has also been identified in a rockshelter that remains unique for the moment: discovered and excavated by P. Ossa in 1968 (1973), the shelter of Quirihuac, at the foot of an enormous block of granite that came down from the nearby Andean mountains, was also the first Paijanian site to be dated (12,795 ± 350 B.P.). In Chauchat's view, the surprising antiquity of this date, 2,000 years older than the earliest date obtained for the open-air sites of Cupisnique, is due to the fact that it was obtained through analysis of bone apatite and not of the collagen, which had disappeared. Farther south, the Paijanian has recently been identified by D. Bonavia at El Volcán, in the valley of Huarmey. It is also present north of Lima, 600 kilometers south of Cupisnique, where the lithic assemblages detected by Lanning in the 1960s, on the surface of the *lomas* of the Ancón region—which he called the "Lúz" complex (Lanning 1965)—are none other than Paijanian, with the characteristic big, elongated points. Even farther south, in the Ica region, similar points found on the surface of the desert of Pozo Santo represent, for the moment, the southernmost appearance of the

Paijanian (Bonavia and Chauchat 1990: 399–412). Finally, one should mention the famous site of Cerro Chivateros, very close to Lima, which its discoverers, E. Lanning and T. Patterson, interpreted—because of the very crude appearance of the thousands of big "bifaces," flakes, and denticulates that strew the hillside—as evidence for an occupation dating back to the Pleistocene, during which these big tools were used for cutting wood, since they supposed the region was forested at the time. The research by Chauchat and others (Fung et al. 1972) has established once and for all that these are quarries where one finds objects representing every stage of manufacture of the big bifacial points of the Paiján type, and the date obtained at Chivateros—10,430 ± 160 B.P.—"fits" the Paijanian's chronological sequence perfectly well. There remained the problem of determining the origin of these peculiar points: the discovery in 1992 of Paiján points and a "fish tail" point associated in the same site in the Cupisnique region, and all made in situ with local materials, suggested to Chauchat that the Paijanian's origin, hitherto poorly understood, had to be sought in the fluted-points "horizon" that is peculiar to the American continent.

Finally, one question remained unanswered for a long time: did the Paijanians coexist with, or even hunt, the great Pleistocene fauna? It is true that in the sector of the Cupisnique desert that is called "Pampa de los Fósiles," numerous paleontological remains can be found beneath the present ground surface, including those of a giant edentate (*Scelidodon*). Farther south, at La Cumbre (a surface site) in the Moche valley, P. Ossa (1978) had found mastodon ribs "associated" with typical Paijanian tools. In Chauchat's view, after a detailed revision of the data, things appear quite clear: the association found by Ossa at La Cumbre is purely theoretical. "The Paijanians evolved in an environment in the process of rapid desertification, an environment in crisis that was in the process of causing, or had just caused, the extinction of this great Pleistocene fauna" (1998: 346), and the Paijanians apparently played no role in this.

Continuing our descent along the Pacific coast, we now arrive in the extreme south of Peru where, close to Ilo, the shell mound of El Anillo, or Ring Site (thus called because of its annular shape), could correspond to a very ancient settlement of a human community that lived, according to its discoverers, on the ocean's resources throughout the year: this site, according to D. Sandweiss, was occupied from the ninth millennium (10,575 ± 105 B.P.). However, this date was obtained for a basal level that is very poor in remains, while the occupation was to become especially significant between 7000 and 5000 B.P. (see chapter 4). Even more curiously, the deep levels of this shell mound have not yielded the slightest remains of a tool or fishing implement. Yet the discoverers considered it to be "the earliest known maritime settlement in the Andes and the earliest shell midden in the New World" (Sandweiss et al. 1989: 48). So it is regrettable that they decided to excavate it in five pits of a meter square, and four "columns" of 25 centimeters! Today the site has disappeared, destroyed by the industrial exploitation of its shells, carried out by bulldozer.

More recently, a team of North American archaeologists reopened and enlarged the test pits at Quebrada Jaguay (Arequipa), originally made more than 60 years earlier by Frédérie Engel. They obtained a new series of dates, the oldest of which, 11,105 ± 260 B.P., would then have marked the oldest known human occupation in the arid extreme south of Peru (Sandweiss et al. 1998). Unfortunately, the cultural material they collected was poor: lithic debitage but no bifaces. In Quebrada Tacahuay south of Ilo, several cuts in the course of road maintenance exposed a level below the supposed anthropic traces, though less convincing than in the preceding case, which has been dated to 10,770 ± 150 (Keefer et al. 1998).

Slightly to the south, on the Tacna littoral, our own excavations, still under way and very partially published, have also unearthed deep occupation levels in shell mounds that are comparable, albeit a little more recent: 9830 ± 140, 8820 ± 80, and 8020 ± 65 B.P., for different settlements detected in Quebrada de los Burros (Lavallée et al. 1999). Contrary to the Ring Site, Quebrada Jaguay, and Quebrada Tacahuay, fishing implements and an abundant lithic industry have been discovered. Faunal remains on the earliest level include fish bones and crustacean shells, marine mollusks, and terrestrial remains (camelid guanaco and cervid). The occupations appear to have been seasonal here. But the excavation, done by layer-stripping, of the occupation levels has brought to light veritable installations comprising specialized activity areas and numerous features such as hearths, postholes, and concentrations of lithic debris.

However, it was on the coast of the extreme north of Chile, where the beaches, alternating with abrupt cliffs, border the most arid desert in the world (the Atacama), that the most eloquent evidence has been discovered for the existence of numerous very early fishing communities. The climatic conditions are even more constraining here, the transverse valleys much rarer, the *lomas* zones far poorer, and dependence on the ocean much greater, than in the more northerly regions. However, some of the oldest known human settlements are relatively far from the shore, at any rate farther than in Ecuador and Peru. Although the important camp of Tiliviche 1b (Tarapacá) is located nearly 40 kilometers from the ocean, almost in the first foothills of the Andes, with an occupation beginning between 9500 and 9000 B.P., all of the garbage dumps linked to its habitations contained a very high proportion of waste or marine origin, mixed with remains of terrestrial fauna and wild plants (Nuñez 1989). The importance of the remains of fish, marine mammals, and mollusks, like the presence of shell hooks and cords of plant fibers (remains of lines or nets?), point to very close relations with the littoral. On the other hand, the lithic toolkit has nothing to do with that of the coastal camps of Ecuador and north Peru, not even with that of the Paijanian. It includes a large variety of bifacial projectile points—the terrestrial hunting weapon par excellence—and a diversified and well-worked toolkit on flakes, in short, a "toolbox" that is more Andean than coastal in nature. Close by, the camp of Aragón is comparable and of similar age (8860 ± 230 B.P.). It also contained abundant food remains of marine fauna. Generally, therefore, it appears that in this part of the Chilean littoral, a system of seasonal movements, of greater extent than that observed in the Central Andes, was practiced in regular fashion, in an environment whose facets were even more distinct. A little farther south than the above sites, close to Antofagasta, the site of Quebrada Las Conchas—or La Chimba 13—was doubtless also occupied around 10,000 B.P. (Llagostera 1979, 1992, and pers. comm.).

Continuing our descent southward along the Pacific coast, we reach the littoral fringes of central and south-central Chile, approximately between the present cities of Santiago and Valdivia, where the desert has gradually given way to different landscapes and to a temperate climate that becomes increasingly humid and cool as one goes farther south. Two other sites have also become quite famous because of their great age. Quereo–Los Vilos (Coquimbo) is a stratified site located on a marine terrace, in which a deep level has been dated to about 11,500 B.P. The lithic toolkit was almost entirely made up of unretouched but "utilized" flakes, and the fauna comprised both Pleistocene species (mastodon, horse, big edentates, fossil camelid, and cervid) and present-day species (felids, canids, rodents, and birds) (Nuñez 1983). Tagua-Tagua (O'Higgins), even farther south, is a famous fossiliferous site, located on the edge of an ancient dried-out lagoon. Known to paleontologists since the nineteenth century, it has yielded remains of human occupation dating to about 11,300 B.P. (level 1), including worked lithic material (cores, flakes that are retouched or not) and both fossil (mastodon, horse) and present-day fauna (cervid).

Several bones bear traces of butchery. According to J. Montané, who excavated it in 1967–68, this was a kill-site located on the edge of an expanse of water that could have played the role of a trap (yet again . . .) (Montané 1968). In contrast to Monte Verde, which is "a bit" (just a millennium) older but which apparently represents a single episode, the occupation of Quereo–Los Vilos continued, with the initial occupation being succeeded by another that Nuñez calls "paleoindian" (Level II: between 11,000 and 9370 ± 180 B.P.). It is poorly defined, and one can only say that its hunted game still includes a few Pleistocene species, especially horse, mastodon, and giant edentates. However, the toolkit does not include the slightest bifacial object, comprising only—as before—flakes that are unretouched but which bear traces of use. Should one imagine, as in the other cases evoked previously, a toolkit of wood and bone that has disappeared today? Or should one suppose that somewhere in the vicinity one or more complementary sites remain to be discovered that contain a better stocked toolkit? This is by no means certain. The hunting site of Tagua-Tagua, which contains evidence for a relatively short utilization (two to three centuries?), would only be reoccupied much later, around 6000 B.P. and in a very different economic context.

Finally, between 40 and 55 degrees south latitude, the continental coastal fringe gives way to the labyrinth of the Magellan Channels. At this extraordinarily narrow extremity of the continent where the Andes disperse into the Pacific Ocean in a multitude of jagged islets, no trace of coastal occupation earlier than 6000 B.P. has been discovered. The great glacier that covered the southern Cordillera, after a last important advance between 15,000 and 13,000 B.P., began a marked retreat and around 10,000 B.P. more or less reached its present-day limits (which nevertheless make the current ensemble of glaciers the biggest in the Southern Hemisphere). The vast expanses located in the same latitudes on the Atlantic side were, as we shall see, already inhabited in this period, indeed apparently quite densely. But in the region of the Magellan Channels, only three sites are as yet known that were occupied by humans between 12,000 and 8000 B.P. One is the famous Mylodon Cave, or Eberhardt Cave after one of its discoverers in 1896; another is Cueva del Medio, discovered in 1985 by H. Nami (1987a, b); and the third is the Cueva 1 del Lago Sofía, excavated by A. Prieto (1991). These are not really coastal sites, strictly speaking, but large natural shelters, close to each other, located in the pre-Cordillera, several kilometers from the present shore. They were used by terrestrial hunters who apparently maintained very few economic relations with the nearby ocean. The first of these sites owed its notoriety to the discovery, by E. Nordenskjöld in 1899, of excrement and hide fragments of a giant sloth, the mylodon (*Mylodon* sp.), in the deepest level, and to the controversy that followed as to whether this animal was hunted by humans or if people arrived only after this creature had disappeared. The most recent studies and verifications carried out in Mylodon Cave, and especially the discoveries of mylodon remains in the Cueva del Medio, which, in this case, were clearly associated (according to Nami) with anthropic remains as well as with remains of another fossil species, the horse (*Hippidion*), tend to demonstrate the contemporaneity of humans and mylodon during the oldest occupation phase (12,000–9500 B.P.). This does not necessarily mean that the latter was the former's prey, since its presence could be due "as much to natural as to cultural causes" (Nami and Menegaz 1991: 126); nevertheless, it proves that certain species of the Pleistocene megafauna survived quite a long time, at any rate beyond the Pleistocene-Holocene limit that was hitherto considered as marking the end of their extinction. Another important fact was observed in the Cueva del Medio: the presence, in the oldest occupation level, in the midst of abundant lithic material, of several "fish tail" points analogous to those of the contemporaneous levels of Fell's Cave in Chilean Patagonia. In the Cueva 1 del Lago Sofía, on the other hand, the basal sediment contained a few bone fragments of mylodon, but no traces of any human occupation at this time. Human occupation began (as in the Cueva del Milodon) only a bit later (11,570 ± 60 B.P.) with a first anthropic level that had no mylodon remains but contained the remains of the horse *Hippidion* and a small number of unifacially retouched flakes. And no bifacial points.

Amazonia Incognita

Turning back again, we now have to return for a moment to an immense territory that also represents an immense gap in our knowledge, despite a few recent discoveries that are particularly interesting because of their very singularity: the Amazon Basin and its outskirts. Where the study of the process of the prehistoric peopling of South America is concerned, Amazonia is certainly and unquestionably a fascinating region, both for the problems it poses to the geographer, the climatologist, and the archaeologist, and for our state of ignorance about its first penetration by people. It has been the victim of stubborn prejudices that saw it as a hostile environment, covered for all time by an impenetrable forest and particularly unwelcoming to humans; hence it has not really attracted the attention of archaeologists until fairly recently. Research in this region is indeed very difficult. Vast parts of the territory are regularly flooded, others are covered with a dense and tangled vegetation, and yet others cannot be reached except by negotiating often dangerous rivers. Because of its climate—the region is saturated with humidity that causes rapid rotting—vestiges of plant material are poorly preserved; stone is a raw material that is either rare or deeply buried.

All this explains why the simple inventory of the few traces and sites that have been discovered can only provide an approximate idea, even a misleading one, of prehistoric reality. In fact, the immense forest that we know today has existed in its present form for three or four millennia at the most. The most recent studies suggest that, during the last cold phase of the final Pleistocene, the forest only covered certain sectors that remained humid, and which formed something like islands of woodland separated by vast dry or quasi-arid expanses (Colinvaux 1989a, b). Conversely, during the phases of warming, especially after about 10,000 B.P. (following the general postglacial warming), the forest once again gained ground, forming links between the "refuges" that had hitherto remained isolated. With regard to this "refuges theory" (their number and location remain vague, and vary from author to author), A. Marcel d'Ans wrote: "One can accept that the primitive Amazonian populations of hunter-gatherers, in order to survive periods of drought, must have had to cluster in the forest refuges, while broad corridors into the tropical plain were available for the nonforest peoples to penetrate" (1982). Between 6000 and 5000 B.P., the Amazonian region underwent a further period of intense drought, which caused a marked regression of the forest in favor of expanses of savanna, as well as natural fires that affected immense areas. Moreover, the reality of these great dry episodes punctuated with gigantic fires has just been confirmed for Guyana (Tardy, in Vacher et al. 1998).

In the period that concerns us here (10,000 to 8000 B.P.), the forest cover must have been dense. Thus extremely few very early sites have been detected, and most are located on the edge of the great forest, not at its heart.

In the State of Pará, two caves of the Serra Norte were supposedly occupied shortly before 8000 B.P. The remains discovered at Gruta do Gavião and Gruta do N1, whose occupation, dated by radiocarbon, extends from 8140 ± 130 to 2900 ± 90 B.P., have made it possible to define the Carajás preceramic complex, characterized by the presence of an industry of quartz and amethyst flakes, but lacking projectile points. The worked stone objects were associated with bones of small mammals and especially of aquatic fauna—fish, shells, and turtles. In the Mato Grosso, where several other more recent sites have been discovered, a few sites appear promising: the Lapa do Sol, which has yielded a worked stone industry comprising broken cobbles and flakes, seems to have been occupied around 9000 B.P.; and, especially, the painted rockshelter of Santa Elina where the excavations (still under way) have brought to light, beneath a succession of occupations dated to between 6040 and 2350 B.P., a deep level containing bones of fossil giant sloth (*Glossotherium*) and plaquettes and retouched lithic flakes, the whole thing dating to 10,120 ± 60 B.P. Indeed, the occupation of this site could be even older because a lower level that still contains fossil fauna and lithic material has been reached but not yet dated (Delibrias and Fontugne 1992; Vilhena Vialou et al. 1995).

Finally, the most exciting recent discovery is that of a human occupation dating back more than 10,000 years, this time in the very heart of the great forest, between Manaus and Belém. Near Monte Alegre, in the Caverna da Pedra Pintada, A. C. Roosevelt has unearthed unquestionable remains of human occupation dating to between 11,200 and 10,500 B.P. Published in *Science* (Roosevelt et al. 1996: 373–84) (but also in all top newspapers of the United States in a very polemical fashion), the announcement obviously aroused distrust and rejection—as was to be expected—on a priori grounds among the North American conservatives: the dates were supposedly too early. Why too early? Simply because they did not fit the "Clovis first" theory (this was still the pre–Monte Verde era). Today, the struggle seems pointless and, besides, the most interesting aspect of the finds made at Pedra Pintada is perhaps not their age but rather the way of life and the technological knowledge to which they testify. Until very recently, there was a deeply rooted notion that the natural resources of the Amazonian forest—both game and plants—were too rare at this time to guarantee the survival of "primitive" groups of hunter-gatherers before the "invention" of agriculture in burned-off areas. But the faunal remains found in the lower level of Pedra Pintada prove not only that the hunting inventory was very rich (it includes fish, rodents, turtles, snakes, and birds, alongside bigger herbivores) but also that its occupants exploited a range of wild plants. One last particular: the lithic equipment is very well made from fine-grained rocks, and includes varied flake tools (sidescrapers, awls, limaces), and bifacial projectile points—the latter are triangular and carefully retouched and have a stem. They are thus very different from the points of the Clovis hunters, whom some claim to be their ancestors.

These recent discoveries are filled with promise. But although they are still too rare and scattered, and do not allow us to define with any precision how the Amazonian territory was first populated and by whom, they do seem to demonstrate that "the existence of a distinct culture tradition contemporary with the Clovis tradition but more than 5000 miles to the south does not fit the notion that the North American big-game hunters were the sole source of migration into South America" (Roosevelt et al. 1996: 381). Clearly, people were already in this immense, humid, tropical environment, even if not all specialists recognize it as yet.

On the Plateaus of the Atlantic Side

Fortunately, central and south Brazil are better known. Indeed, it will be recalled that, thanks to the work carried out by Lund at Lagoa Santa between 1834 and 1844, this country was among the first in South America to undergo an "archaeological" investigation. However, research entrusted to professionals only began here in the 1950s. At the same time, under pressure from a few local people who were indignant at the accelerating pillage of the most famous sites in Minas Gerais, foreign missions also multiplied. One must make special mention here of the work of the French researchers José Emperaire and Annette Laming-Emperaire, who carried out ten years of almost uninterrupted research in the south of the country (1954–1966). Their work was continued despite José Emperaire's accidental death in 1958 on a site in remote Patagonia. Their university teaching helped to train an entire generation of Brazilian archaeologists, and they were responsible for the discovery and study of several sites. Their work ended in 1977 with Annette Laming-Emperaire's death in Brazil.[3]

The end of the Pleistocene saw profound environmental modifications in the interior of Central Brazil (Ab'Saber 1977; Coltrinari 1992). Between 12,000 and 9000 B.P., there was a marked increase of humidity in a still cool climate. Then, after about 9000 B.P., increasingly warm conditions culminated in the Climatic Optimum between 8000 and 4000 B.P. This gradual change, punctuated by minor oscillations, brought a major increase in plant cover. The *caatinga* ("white forest" in the Tupi language), an expanse of cactus and thorn trees that takes on a grayish appearance in the dry season, retreated and gave way to the *cerrado,* a savanna with trees, sometimes in quite dense stands. The modifications of the climate and vegetation brought about changes in fauna: terrestrial or aquatic mollusks multiplied—and we shall see the importance they took on in the diet of prehistoric groups—while the expansion of dense vegetation led to large animals becoming rare in the sectors in question. All of this explains why, in several regions, fishing and plant collecting increased in importance and why hunting only remained predominant in the more open areas.

Since I cannot and do not wish to go into detail here about the numerous "traditions" that have been defined here and there or the chronological se-

[3]Since the death of A. Laming-Emperaire, the Mission Archéologique Française has continued its work under the directorship of A. Prous, within the Federal University of Minas Gerais at Belo Horizonte. The paragraphs concerning Brazil owe a great deal to the book he wrote about Brazilian archaeology (Prous 1992).

quences peculiar to each archaeologist and each sector studied, I shall simply mention three major regions where research has been particularly concentrated: the Nordeste, domain of the *caatinga,* and the Goiás and the Planalto of Minas Gerais, domains of the *cerrado.*

In the preceding chapter I presented at some length the sensational and still controversial discoveries made in the Piauí, in the first of these regions. After 12,000 B.P., the human occupation—of which this time nobody disputes the reality—displays some new features: the occupations at the start of the Holocene unearthed in the shelters of Toca do Sitio do Meio (8800 ± 60 B.P.), Toca do Baixão da Perna (9540 ± 170 B.P.), Toca da Barra do Antonião (9670 ± 140 B.P.), Toca da Cima do Pilão (10,390 ± 80 B.P.), and finally the Toca do Boqueirão da Pedra Furada (10,400 ± 180 B.P.), grouped into a Serra Talhada phase (c. 10,000 to 6000 B.P.), present numerous hearths, often built with stone blocks, and their lithic industry indicates a new typological richness. Although local quartz and quartzite cobbles continued to be used, nonlocal fine-quality raw materials (chert, chalcedony) were now worked, and flakes were finely retouched (by pressure) into sidescrapers, becs, limaces, scrapers, and denticulates. It should be noted, however, that no bifacial projectile point appears in the inventory, whereas the "toolbox" contains more or less all the types of objects present in numerous contemporary sites in South America. As for the kind of game that was exploited, most of the sites have a very acid sediment and have not preserved any bones. Only the Toca da Barra do Antonião and Toca da Cima do Pilão, which are located in a karst, not a sandstone context, have yielded both anthropic remains and important assemblages of megafauna (though not in direct association), which poses the problem of a possible exploitation of the latter by humans.

In the Goiás, P. I. Schmitz and A. Barbosa in their turn defined a Paranaiba phase for the same period (c. 11,000 to 9000 B.P.), with quite similar cultural characteristics. In the GO JA 01 shelter—an unromantic name that simply means Goiás Jazida (site) 01—the lithic industry of the lower level (9060 ± 65 B.P.), fairly similar to that of the Piauí, is associated with the remains of a present-day fauna: a few cervids, but especially armadillos, rodents, lizards, and a whole series of medium-sized or small species, whose presence doubtless reflects the growing scarcity of big animals, as well as the gathering of eggs, the capture of small fish, and the systematic collection of terrestrial mollusks and palm nuts (Schmitz 1987). Similar material was unearthed in the GO NI 49 shelter, 100 kilometers farther north (Barbosa et al. 1976).

On the Central Planalto, the recent excavations carried out by A. Prous in several shelters of the Peruaçu Valley (Minas Gerais) and especially that of Boquete have brought to light the same cultural characteristics, broadly speaking: the first Holocene levels (c. 12,000 to 10,000 B.P.) contain a fine lithic industry made of quartzite and flint, and faunal remains that belong to the same species as in the Goiás (Prous 1991). The lithic industry seems to become impoverished subsequently (Serranopolis phase) while, in the diet, terrestrial mollusks and fruits take on a growing importance, as in the Goiás. In the same region, the Lapa do Dragão yielded comparable material, though its age (11,000 ± 300 to 10,000 ± 255 B.P.) is less certain (Prous et al. 1984).

As for the region of Lagoa Santa, so rich in caves and shelters known since the nineteenth century and in rock art (a domain that is not covered in this book) and which is considered one of the meccas of South American prehistory, it has only—paradoxically enough—yielded data that are fragmentary and mostly derisory in view of its fame. Pillaged by dozens of amateurs who were both active and incompetent (see chapter 1) and exploited as quarries, its limestone massifs no longer offer any possibility of scientific investigation, apart from the improbable discovery of an intact site. Yet this is what happened in 1971, with the discovery of the shelter of Lapa Vermelha IV, whose study, albeit disappointing in many ways (see chapter 2), nevertheless had the merit of revealing the probable great antiquity of a human presence. However, W. Hurt and O. Blasi (1969) defined a Cerca Grande complex (c. 10,000 to 9000 B.P.) for the region, characterized by a lithic industry on small, rarely retouched crystal flakes. Two quartz bifacial projectile points were also found in these levels (the oldest in Central Brazil, if they are not intrusive) and, equally unexpected, ax blades in semipolished hardstone, likewise the oldest in Brazil (apart from the still-unpublished discovery of a polished ax blade in the Piauí, which probably dates to around 9000 B.P.).

Of course, the few sites that I have just briefly reviewed are not the only ones that have yielded evidence of an earlier human occupation between 12,000 and 8000 B.P., although elsewhere the evidence is more tenuous or less solidly dated, or incompletely published. Examples of such sites include the shelter of Pilão (Bahía) excavated by A. Bryan and R. Gruhn (1993), where the lithic industry was sparse but the fauna was abundant and varied (9650 ± 90 to 8790 ± 80 B.P.); and the shelter of Gentio II (Minas Gerais), excavated by O. Dias (10,190 ±120 to 8620 ±110 B.P.), which is of extra interest because it yielded burned remains of human bones.

As the above descriptions have doubtless shown, the pronounced local particularism of the archaeologists who work in Brazil means that they have tried to outdo each other in multiplying "phases," "traditions," and other "complexes," and hence made it a singularly complicated task to acquire a global grasp of the cultural evolution. However, Schmitz (1987, 1990) has proposed the creation of a vast Itaparica tradition (c. 11,000 to 8000 B.P.) that would incorporate all of the cultural manifestations of the early Holocene that have been identified on the Central Brazilian plateau, from the Nordeste to the south of Minas Gerais. It is certainly true that the data yielded by the sites cited earlier display some very strong similarities: existence of a well-made flake industry but absence (except at Lagoa Santa) of bifacial projectile points and, generally speaking, ignorance of the bifacial working of stone; temporary occupation of natural shelters, probably linked to the markedly seasonal character of the natural plant resources, which seem to have been intensively gathered at this time; equally intensive exploitation of various small animal species, and especially of terrestrial mollusks; and general absence of remains of megafauna (except in the Piauí where their direct association with the human occupation remains to be confirmed).

Hunters of the Prairies and Southern Steppes

The savannas and trees of the Brazilian *cerrado* gradually give way, in the south of the country, to the vast humid, grassy plains that, from the Tropic of Capricorn to approximately 40 degrees south latitude, constitute the pampa, today the domain of immense cattle herds, but formerly that of the Pleistocene megafauna that was to be replaced, little by little, by herds of cervids and guanacos. Very little is known about the prehistoric past of its northern part, which corresponds to the extreme south of Brazil, to part of Paraguay, and to Uruguay. Several assemblages of worked lithics have been collected as surface finds in numerous regions, but it has not been possible to date them with any certainty. Excavations are still very rare, and the absence of detailed publications makes it difficult to assess them: in the region of Arroio do Fosseis (Rio Grande do Sul), the deep level (today liable to flooding) of an alluvial terrace of the Rio Uruguay has yielded lithic material to the Brazilian archaeologist E. Miller—cores and unretouched flakes of basalt, and remains of fossil fauna, including a bone of the giant edentate *Glossotherium,* which was dated to 12,770 ± 220 B.P. Despite the doubts that remain about the human origin of the lithic objects, this site represents the oldest human occupation of the region during a first phase, the Ibicuí, followed by a Uruguai phase (c. 11,500 to 9000 B.P.) which is scarcely better defined (Miller 1987). At the Uruguay-Argentina frontier, a Franco-Brazilian program of salvage archaeology carried out between 1976 and 1978 in the region of Salto Grande brought other landmarks: a C14 date of about 12,000 B.P., remains of hearths, a few worked flakes of chalcedony, and a few cobble hammers. Hence, despite the rarity and frequent insufficiency of the data, it seems that humans were present in the region from at least 12,000 B.P. In fact, this appears very logical, insofar as a great deal of rigorous research has recently been carried out, this time in the Argentinian part of the pampa, south of Buenos Aires. This research has identified several open-air camps, workshops, or dwellings in shelters, all produced by hunters of the great Pleistocene game. At La Moderna, an open-air site excavated by G. Politis, by 12,000 B.P. the hunters were taking advantage of a marsh (now dried out) to drive and bring to bay a very large fossil armadillo, the glyptodon *Doedicurus clavicaudatus,* an epithet that refers to the terrible studded mace at the end of its tail (Politis 1984; Politis and Gutiérrez 1998). However, in this kill-site, relatively "classic" for the period and analogous to the Chilean sites of Quereo and Tagua-Tagua, no other weapon or tool has been found apart from quartz flakes and splinters, derisory objects for killing a mass

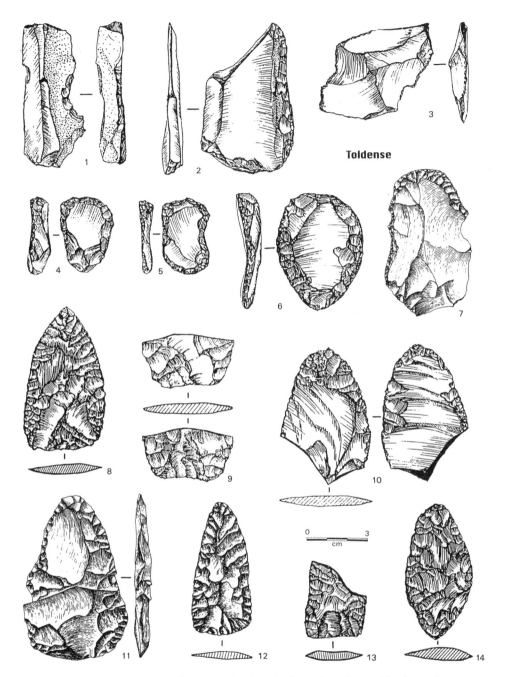

Toldense

Fig. 15. Characteristic tools of the Toldense complex, from levels 9 and 10 of Los Toldos (Argentine Patagonia). 1. Notched piece. 2. Sidescraper. 3. Atypical scraper. 4–7. Scrapers. 8, 10, 12. Subtriangular points. 9, 13. Bases of bifacial points. 11. Bifacial point. 14. Leaf-shaped point. Some specialists think that this assemblage should not be dissociated from the big retouched flakes that are considered by others to be characteristic of a "pre-projectile" phase (bereft of bifacially worked objects) depicted in fig. 9.

that was 3 meters long and with such terrible protection. Once again, therefore, this leads one to suppose that all complementary equipment has either disappeared or been carried away by the hunters after the carcass was butchered. In the same region, at Arroyo Seco, a stratified open-air site, the deepest level contained a mixture of fossil (horse and giant sloth) and present-day fauna (cervid and guanaco) accompanied by unifacially retouched quartzite flakes (but still no projectile points). The excavations are not yet finished, but already the dates (on collagen) obtained from horse and edentate bones are somewhat surprising: 8890 ± 90 and 7320 ± 50 B.P. which, if correct, would mean that certain species did indeed survive quite far into the Holocene. Finally, not far from there, at Cerro La China, excavated by N. Flegenheimer, the remains of fossil fauna are limited to those of a big armadillo *Eutatus,* albeit less impressive than that of La Moderna. But the real interest of the site lies elsewhere: it comprises both a dwelling in a shelter and, in the vicinity, two open-air workshops. The shelter contained armadillo remains and a rich assemblage of lithic implements, both unifacial and bifacial including—at last!—some "fish tail" bifacial points (level dated to $10,790 \pm 120$ B.P.). In one of the workshops, these same points were associated with abundant flakes resulting from bifacial working (waste from point manufacture?); in the second (dated to $10,610 \pm 180$ B.P.), there was other knapping debris but no points. This is one of the very few sites (together with Fell's Cave, farther south) where "fish tail" points have been found stratified and well dated. I should also add that, at the top of the nearby Cerro El Sombrero, numerous intact or fragmentary points of the same type doubtless point to the existence of a place, contemporaneous with the previous assemblage, where the points were manufactured (Flegenheimer 1987). In Politis's view, these different sites correspond to places where small groups of very mobile hunters camped for short periods as they moved between the Atlantic coastal plain and the first foothills of the Cordillera. However, no discovery has yet confirmed the identity of these hunters of the pampa and of those who, in the same period, occupied the Andean piedmont where just one site, the Cueva de los Indios, has yielded evidence that is confused and undiagnostic.

The endless prairies of the pampa imperceptibly give way, under the influence of a climate that is increasingly dry and cold as one descends southward, to the interminable open and semiarid steppes of Patagonia, almost flattened by an immense sky and swept by winds of extreme violence that erode, uproot, and bend to the ground the few trees and bushes. In this enormous territory, which was even more vast in this period, when a large part of the continental platform was still above water, humans were also present by 12,000 B.P., as were the great fauna. No doubt to take refuge from this haunting wind, humans systematically occupied the slightest natural shelters hollowed into the flank of the deep valleys (*cañadones*), dug by the rivers that originate in the melting of the Andean glaciers. The Rio Colorado,

Rio Neuquen, Rio Negro (which marks the limit between the pampa and Patagonia), Chubut, Santa Cruz—all these are lazy rivers today but formerly had raging and headstrong courses that over the millennia cut deeply into the thick sedimentary deposits of the Patagonian plateau.

The oldest known site is a group of caves located on the estancia Los Toldos in the province of Santa Cruz, the southernmost of continental Argentinian Patagonia. In 1951, test-pits dug by Menghin had identified a cultural complex (undated at that time) that he baptized "Toldense"; he estimated its age as about 10,000 years. Subsequently, systematic excavations carried out from 1972 by Cardich (1977, 1984; Cardich et al. 1973) in cave No. 3 made it possible to fix the Toldense at between about 11,000 and 8700 B.P. (levels 10 and 9), above a level 11 that was the subject of dispute till recently (see chapter 2). Since then, C. Gradin and A. Aguerre have worked in various sites where—although bearing a different name, the Rio Pinturas I tradition—the Toldense represents the oldest human occupation (Cueva de Las Manos: 9320 B.P.; Cueva Grande del Arroyo Feo: 9330 B.P.) (Gradin et al. 1976, 1979). These sites have helped better define the complex's age and cultural content. The Toldense is distinguished above all by its lithic industry, the characteristic pieces of which are well-made triangular bifacial points with a convex base, very slender and made with pressure flaking, accompanied by a toolkit on flakes that is more "banal" (for example, sidescrapers, scrapers, denticulates) but still well made, and a few bone implements (awls, retouchers) (fig. 15). In short, all this is quite normal for the period, except that the "fish tail" points, present farther north and south, are absent. The Toldense people mostly hunted camelids (fossil *Lama gracilis* and present-day *L. guanicoe*); birds, including the American ostrich or ñandú (*Rhea americana*) and the tinamou, a kind of big partridge; a few rodents; and the Pleistocene horse (*Hippidion* sp.)—this is one of the last pieces of evidence for that species.

Let us continue our descent southward, to the northern shore of the present Magellan Straits (which, it will be recalled, probably did not yet exist). Here, in the midst of an arid steppe bristling with hundreds of little volcanic cones, one finds what is doubtless the most famous prehistoric site of South America, Fell's Cave, discovered by Bird in 1936 at the end of his long journey in the Magellan Channels (see chapter 5). Subsequently, numerous archaeologists succeeded him there—first, the owner of the site, J. Fell, who had known the cave since his childhood and had put together, with great discrimination, a very fine collection of lithic industry; after him came the French archaeologists J. Emperaire and A. Laming-Emperaire in 1953; Fell again in 1958; A. Laming-Emperaire and H. Reichlen (following the accidental death of J. Emperaire) in 1959; Bird again; a new French expedition in 1968; Bird and Nuñez in 1969; and finally Bird once again in 1972. Undoubtedly, no other prehistoric site in South America has been visited and scrutinized as much as this one, and one wonders what can possibly remain today, in this key site for American prehistory, of the blocks that were scrupulously left as evidence by each of the excavators, and then picked at by the next. In any case, the syntheses of the data contributed by all these studies, with their sometimes contradictory results—was the mylodon contemporaneous with humans or not? (it seems it was) and hunted by them? (it seems not)—have made it possible to establish that the cave had been occupied from at least 11,000 B.P. by hunters of fossil horse, guanaco, ñandú, and various other smaller animals (all present-day species). During the first phase of their occupation (11,000 ± 170 and 10,080 ± 160 B.P.), they used a well-made lithic toolkit comprising diversified flake tools and bifacial projectile points of a somewhat peculiar shape that reminded Bird, their discoverer, of a fish's tail (fig. 10), for it was here that this type of projectile point was first reported, described, and dated. After a period of abandonment, apparently caused by an episode of strong seismic activity and volcanic eruptions around 9000 B.P. that affected a vast portion of Patagonia, and traces of which can be observed in other sites in the form of ash layers, occupation of Fell's Cave resumed after 9000 B.P., in a techno-economic context of astonishing poverty: a reduced panoply of simple flake tools, no bifacial points, and sparse faunal remains dominated by small species. Perhaps this reflects a period during which the cave and its surroundings constituted an unfavorable habitat? After this interruption, a denser utilization resumes, this time characterized by the presence of subtriangular points similar to those of the Toldense. During this period the Pleistocene animal species were definitively absent from the range of game exploited and the present-day species abundantly represented.

At the end of this long journey, we have at last arrived at the farthest extremity of the American continent, in Tierra del Fuego. "Uttermost part of the earth," "limit of the world"—there have been plenty of descriptions of this curled-up extremity of the immensity of America, the "Tail of the Dragon" as the cartographers of the fifteenth century had nicknamed it. Without the slightest doubt, this *finis terrae* was reached by humans more than 10,000 years ago. This fact alone should suffice to end the interminable controversy about the first peopling of the Americas. At the time, the Big Island was not yet separate. Although the glaciers had already liberated most of the Patagonian south, the sea level was doubtless several dozen meters lower than today, and the Magellan Straits, uniting the Pacific and Atlantic oceans, had not yet opened. A chain of glacial lakes occupied this location, cut by arcs of moraines that constituted terrestrial bridges that were easy to cross. Hence small bands of hunters simply had to skirt round the lakes and, perhaps, the last tongues of ice. They probably had no difficulty in crossing these bridges and penetrating farther southward, across the game-rich steppes of western Tierra del Fuego that were the direct prolongation of those of Patagonia. This would explain the almost identical age of the sites located on the continental shore of the Straits and in what was to become, between

10,000 and 9000 B.P., the island of Tierra del Fuego. Between 10,500 and 10,300 B.P.,[4] a group of these hunters occupied (apparently briefly) a small rockshelter located 20 kilometers from the Atlantic coast, Tres Arroyos (also called Cerro de los Onas) (Massone 1987). They brought there, and consumed, guanacos, a few foxes, and some birds, and they occasionally completed their meal with a shellfish despite the distance separating them from the shore. However, the few tools discovered in the shelter by Massone—a few flake tools (knives, sidescrapers, and scrapers) but no bifacial points—remain insufficient to obtain any precise idea of their way of life. A little later, around 9500 B.P., another group settled beneath a big erratic block deposited by the glaciers not far from the Bahía Inútil, on the west coast this time. In this shelter of Marazzi, which provided limited protection against the terrible westerly wind—I know this personally, having taken part in the excavations directed by A. Laming-Emperaire—the fauna and lithic tools discovered indicate once again that this was a sporadic occupation by terrestrial hunters (Laming-Emperaire et al. 1972). In contrast to the oldest continental sites, these first human settlements in Tierra del Fuego have yielded no remains of Pleistocene fossil animals.

DEATH AND THE DEAD

As pointed out at the end of the previous chapter, ancient human remains (dating 12,000–8/7000 years ago) are still extremely rare in South America (and, indeed, in North America), and specimens earlier than 12,000 B.P. that could at last win the approval of the most deeply entrenched conservatives are still lacking. Among the material that has been unearthed, many specimens are merely pieces of bone, even isolated fragments found scattered inside archaeological or paleontological fills—for example, the fragment of human parietal bone discovered in the Toca do Garrincho (Piauí, Brazil), in a fossiliferous level of Pleistocene age, which has not yet been precisely dated. Also in Brazil, a portion of the skull of an adolescent female of the Lagoa Santa race, found in the sedimentary fill of the cave of Lapa Vermelha IV (Minas Gerais) at the boundary of the Pleistocene and Holocene levels, could date, in Prous's opinion, to between 15,300 and 10,200 B.P. (dates obtained from scattered charcoal). The site's extremely indistinct stratigraphy, however, casts doubt on this chronological attribution—especially as remains of the same individual, clearly transported by running water, are scattered in the same level but at different depths (Prous 1992: 131). One should also mention the better-dated discovery of an almost complete female skeleton made at Janela da Barra do Antonião (Piauí), dating to 9670 ± 140 B.P. (Peyre 1993).

However, none of these human remains provide evidence of intentional burial. Fortunately, other sites in caves or shelters in various parts of the continent have yielded burials that are more or less intact but that bear wit-

[4]An older C14 date of 11,880 ± 250 B.P. has recently been obtained for a hearth in the lower occupation level Vb. At first rejected by the site's discoverers because it contradicted the date of 10,420 B.P. obtained previously for this same level, its validity in fact seems to be confirmed by the presence, between level Vb and the overlying level Va, of a layer of volcanic ash that proves an eruption took place in 12,480 BP. This evidence, if confirmed, would lead one to envisage an arrival by people in Tierra del Fuego even earlier than hitherto believed (Massone 1991).

ness, without any possible doubt, to the existence of funerary rites; these differ from region to region and are sometimes complex. I shall describe only a few of the most elaborate and those that are most firmly fixed chronologically. However, they cannot teach us much about beliefs, except to confirm that the fact that their inhabitants buried bodies, tried to preserve them from destruction, and adorned them or deposited a set of selected objects or implements next to them, which is strong evidence for the existence of a belief in survival in a mythical next world.

Pits in the Desert

At the same time that he was studying the Paijanian camps and work-sites in the desert of northern Peru, Chauchat noticed a "line of small bones eroding out on the surface" (1992: 155). In fact, these were fragments of a human pelvis and right foot, protected only by a fine crust of superficial clay. Two burials were thus located and then studied. The first tomb contained the bones of an adolescent of about 13 years of age, lying on the left side in a flexed position, the knees raised to the chest, the arms bent, and the hands joined at face level, a position that almost evoked a peaceful sleep. The body had no objects with it except for a perforated fish vertebra, found at the level of the lower part of the spine, which the discoverers interpreted as a possible button or pendant.

In immediate proximity to this adolescent's body was that of an adult about 25 years old, probably a male, also lying in a flexed position but on his right side: "The body had been deposited on a layer of ashes and embers that were hot enough to have slightly reddened the sediment beneath. . . . On his chest one observed a second layer of ash, thinner with a bit of reddened sand. . . . Finally, the long bones of the upper part of the body display brown traces in the form of transverse stripes that strongly evoke the imprint of some kind of crude fabric or matting" (ibid.: 160).

The C14 analysis of the charcoal beneath the second burial yielded the date of 10,200 ± 180 B.P., which makes these the oldest human remains known at present in South America. However, it was not possible to demonstrate that the two burials were contemporaneous.

The Children of the Peruvian Puna

In the cave of Lauricocha, the first preceramic site discovered and excavated on the Peruvian puna, Cardich (1964) exhumed, in cave L-2, the remains of 11 human skeletons that constitute the biggest funerary assemblage unearthed in the highlands of the Central Andes. The skeletons were either inside the cave or buried within the exterior talus. Several of them, poorly preserved, were reduced to "simple groups of bones." However, among the best preserved—inside the cave—three belonged to children buried in the sterile layer below the archaeological fill. One of these (No. 9) was a child of one to two, bent in a fetal position in a pit dug at the foot of a slab jutting out of the rock wall. Cardich mentions the presence around the body of a few stone flakes, a piece of red ocher near the head, and half-burned fragments of animal bone. A second burial (No. 10), marked by three stones, contained the very deteriorated remains of a child of 12, "accompanied" by seven lithic tools, five bone tools, a fragment of yellow ocher, a turquoise bead, and various fragments of burned bone. Finally, the third burial (No. 11) corresponded to a completely fragmented skeleton, bereft of its long bones, of a child of about two, entirely covered with crystals of iron oxide; near it were a bifacial point and a bone bead. Cardich attributed these three burials to the cave's oldest occupation level, dating to 9525 B.P., but the stratigraphic description suggests a date closer to 8000 B.P.

Also on the high plateau of Central Peru, but farther south, in a pit dug at the back of the shelter of Telarmachay, I directed excavations in 1980 that unearthed the skeleton of a child aged between five and six months (although its small size first suggested a neonate) belonging to occupation phase VI (7200–6800 B.P.) (Lavallée et al. 1985). The body was resting in a little oval depression demarcated by five stone slabs and blocks set in an arc. Red ocher—with which it had probably been covered when buried—impregnated all the bones and the surrounding sediment. It was difficult to reconstitute the body's original position because of the skeleton's very bad condition, but it seemed to be resting on its back, its head turned to the west. On the body, under the chin, had been deposited a long necklace of 99 discoid white shell beads, while at the pelvic level and on the lower limbs lay a pile of 18 rectangular pendants of polished bone, with a circular perforation. There is no direct evidence for their function, but one may suppose that, since they were superimposed with no apparent order, albeit all orientated the same way, they were originally sewn or threaded on some perishable material. On the basis of (admittedly fragile) ethnographic comparisons, it could be a carrying-belt like those adorned with identical pendants still used by the women of several tribes of Peruvian Amazonia.

Hence the bodies of children seem to have been the object of particular care, since they were accompanied in both cases by ornaments, isolated beads, necklaces, or pendants. The meaning of the crystals of iron oxide at Lauricocha remains obscure, but it is not impossible that they have the same meaning as the ocher at Telarmachay, where its presence in abundance suggests some nontechnical use (it is known that ocher was used in abundance in the working of hides, since it prevented them from hardening and protected them from attacks by worms and insects). Here it was perhaps used for ritual purposes, even if it was just the simple desire to preserve a body from decomposition. Ocher was also present at Lauricocha, although Cardich only mentions a few fragments of it; nevertheless, these were very probably deposited close to the bodies on purpose. In this site, on the other hand, one can express some doubt about the status of "offering" that Cardich attributed to the few lithic objects and, especially, to the burned bone fragments, which are more likely present by chance, accidentally incorporated in the fill of the burial pits.

Two Women Who Died 7,000 Years Ago

At Telarmarchay, close to the child's body, there were also two other burials of adults that, without doubt, were chronologically associated with it. In the first, the skeleton of a woman lay in an elliptical pit dug at the back of the shelter, almost at the foot of the rock wall. Orientated east-west, with the head to the west (like the child), the body had been deposited in a flexed position on its stomach. In fact, the skeleton's very compressed layout, the position of its arms and legs bent beneath the ribs, and finally the detachment of the femoral heads from the cotyloid cavities all suggest a forced flexion, maintained with bonds. The feet, crossed under the pelvis, had their phalanges curled up in an unnatural position. The body must certainly have been bound and then inserted into some kind of container of hide or basketwork (of which nothing survived), closed at one end, which caused this compression of the feet during transportation or deposition of the body. Around the skeleton were several stone flakes and tools, and a few fragments of burned bone that were doubtless included, as at Lauricocha, quite fortuitously when the pit was filled. The most interesting aspect of this burial, which was unaccompanied by any kind of offering, lies elsewhere: this woman, more than 50 years old, displayed a pathological condition (arthritis) in the right elbow which resulted—according to the anthropological analysis—from a probable "functional excess" or repetitive strain injury (Guillén, ibid.: 426).

In the other case, there were just the very dislocated pieces of a second skeleton, also female and about 20, whose original position—orientation, forced flexion—must have been the same as in the first case. However, the interesting aspect of this burial lies not so much in the bones but rather in the material found nearby, in indisputable association with them. At the level of the proximal part of the femur was a big ball of red ocher enclosing 11 worked stone tools (6 scrapers, 2 small bifaces, 1 bifacial point, 2 retouched flakes); 1 small, highly polished ovoid cobble; and 6 bone implements (2 awls, 3 smoothers, 1 fragment of pointed diaphysis). These objects had their active part heavily impregnated with ocher. Under this pocket of ocher, wedged between the femur and the tibia, was a series of thin, elongated pieces of bone (ribs of a very young camelid and bird long-bones) laid out parallel to each other, which, from the traces that remain on them, seem originally to have been joined together into a kind of comb. The association of scrapers (on which microwear analysis has revealed polishes characteristic of hideworking), of bone tools with polished ends impregnated with ocher, and finally of the ball of ocher itself is extraordinarily suggestive: is one not dealing here with a kind of "toolkit," an assemblage of implements that are different but all designed for the same task, that is, hideworking? Was this woman not buried here with the implements of her daily work, doubtless held in a bag (of perishable material and now disappeared) that also contained the indispensable ocher powder and which she carried attached at her waist? While this skeleton is too fragmentary to have permitted an osteopathological examination (all the upper part, disturbed by recent vandalism, was missing), did not the older woman buried nearby display a lesion of the elbow that could well be the result of a repetitive and labored movement of the right arm, tirelessly scraping or smoothing the hides of the killed animals whose remains were, at the time, extremely abundant in the shelter?

The Necropolis of Santana do Riacho

Leaving the Andean region for the plateaus of eastern Brazil, it was in the "big shelter" of Santana do Riacho, mentioned above, that one of the most important "cemeteries" known in South American prehistory was unearthed (Prous 1980–81). The intensive excavations carried out in this site certainly showed that, in this natural refuge of imposing size (80 meters in length), more than 40 individuals (minimal figure) had been buried between about 9500 and 4500 B.P., but only the most ancient burials concern us here (between 9460 and 7900 B.P.). Luckily, these were the least disturbed by natural agents (roots, termites, and snakes). The primary burials, by far the most numerous, are in circular or oval pits, in which the bodies (of adults, children, and sometimes fetuses, all belonging to the Lagoa Santa race) were deposited in a flexed position, the skeleton's head sometimes resting on a kind of "pillow stone." Moreover, it seems certain that several bodies were not buried whole. Sometimes the skull is missing, or a limb, or several limbs; two heads and some feet, found in isolation, "could be the counterpart of this ritual," but it has not yet been possible to ascribe them to their original bodies. Necklaces of seeds, palm nuts, and various lithic objects sometimes accompany the bodies. Finally, fragments of string found in several burials suggest that the corpses must have been wrapped up in hammocks of woven plant fibers, sometimes doubled with tapa (bark cloth), before being buried.

What conclusions can be drawn from all that has just been said—certainly far too briefly—in this chapter? Above all, one obvious observation: the extraordinary diversity of the strategies developed, and of the techniques employed, by people in order to adapt to and take advantage of natural environments that were themselves extremely diverse and in the process of changing. This diversity is sometimes accompanied by some particularly effective technological "tricks": the Paiján point in Peru, whose tapering shape made it a perfect fish harpoon; the *boleadora* in Patagonia for stopping very mobile game at a distance and in full movement, game that would doubtless be missed by a spear thrown by an atlatl. But equally, this diversity is only partially reflected in the variety of the sets of implements that were made and used in the four corners of the continent, and it does not always seem "logical" to our eyes. In the same period, one can find astonishingly similar "toolkits" in different environments—in the cold and humid highlands of the Andes, in the dry and warm Nordeste of Brazil, in the cold dry steppes of Patagonia—whereas neither the landscapes nor the natural resources were the same. Conversely, these sets of tools sometimes appear curiously different in environments that closely resembled each other: why should one find a highly differentiated and very well developed lithic toolkit in the Andes of Ecuador, Peru, and Chile, and nothing of the kind in the high plateaus of Colombia, a very similar environment? Why the same toolkit (more or less) in the Nordeste of Brazil (Piauí sites) and the Andes (sites of the Junín puna), while not far from there, on the plateaus of Central Brazil (Minas Gerais), people seem to have made and used only a "rudimentary" toolkit of flakes, which was close to what was being used in the same period in the Andes of Colombia? These are questions to which, for the present, we have no satisfactory answer.

As for hunting, it is noteworthy that, even when only present-day species were being exploited, specialized hunting of one or more species seems to have been rare; it was only on the high plateaus of Peru and in the steppes of Patagonia that people rapidly turned to specialized hunting of the large herbivores (guanacos and vicuñas in Peru, guanacos in Patagonia), whereas everywhere else it was the "minor fauna" (such as small mammals, birds, and reptiles), obtained by hunting or, more likely, trapping that doubtless played a more important role in the economy than has generally been suspected.

One fact is even more striking: the presence of projectile points in the sites, which thus implies the practice of bifacial working of stone implements, scarcely seems to be linked—during the period under consideration (between 12,000 and 8000 B.P.)—in any way to the nature of the game exploited (big fossil species or smaller present-day species), any more than it is to environmental characteristics (warm or cold climate, open spaces, or more enclosed milieus). On the other hand, the survival of the Pleistocene animal species, whether the biggest (giant sloths and armadillos, mylodon) or the medium-sized ones (paleolama, horse), seems to be directly linked to the presence of the most open spaces, some of which still remain so (Patagonian pampa and steppe), while their growing rarity and then their disappearance were more rapid in the environments which, at this time, underwent a notable increase in plant cover, and notably in forest. In any case, in this period, there never seem to have existed any hunters who specialized in hunting the great Pleistocene game, or at least what was left of it. Instead, it appears that the groups of hunters carried out a type of hunting that was undifferentiated but which, from time to time, took advantage of the presence of the last great Pleistocene animals, especially when these were trapped by the environment (at bay on a riverbank or bogged down in a marsh). This brings us back to the earlier remark concerning whether these hunters possessed effective projectile weapons. In the face of the "poverty" of the lithic industry encountered in various places (El Abra and Tequendama in Colombia, the Cerca Grande complex in Brazil, La Moderna in Argentina), it will be recalled that several specialists have suggested that their occupants were equipped during their hunting expeditions with good quality weapons—eventually including missiles with worked stone points. They then brought back these materials with them, leaving behind only a makeshift toolkit, rapidly made and not very developed, that was used for cutting up the killed game in situ and then as quickly abandoned. But then, this should only have been noticed on the kill-and butchery sites, that is, mostly in open-air sites like La Moderna. Conversely, well-established habitation sites of equivalent age, like Tequendama, should have contained material evidence of the existence of more sophisticated tools and more effective weapons—but this is not the case. In addition, there is still the problem of all the sites that are apparently even older that contained remains of exclusively Pleistocene fauna but no projectile points (Tagua-Tagua, Quereo, Tibitó). Only Taima-Taima in Venezuela, and Monte Verde in Chile, have yielded a few points or fragments of points. This leads me to accept—somewhat through force of circumstances or for want of anything better—the idea that, at this time, in South America, there coexisted two distinct great technological traditions: one of these did not know the projectile point and, generally speaking, the bifacial working of stone and made up for this with equipment of wood and bone (now disappeared); it was the heir of the first waves of population to reach South America. The other adopted and modified (or independently invented?) a tradition of bifacial points that were brought in by the more recent migrations. This latter hypothesis is not entirely satisfactory, and, in the present state of our knowledge, proof is lacking. Consequently, this opinion may need to be revised. The prehistorian must (should?) eschew all dogmatism.

4

THE ANDEAN BOOM

A FTER ABOUT 8000 B.P., SOUTH AMERICA'S CULTURAL DEVELOPMENT took on a new rhythm. While most of the continent was occupied by hunter-gatherers or fisher-gatherers, still organized in relatively small, mobile groups who perpetuated the practice of a hunting economy, some privileged regions underwent the first manipulations of plant species and, more rarely, animal species, which were to lead to the gradual emergence of a farming economy, although the ways of life that were based on hunting or fishing did not disappear completely. At an earlier date than elsewhere (though after the period covered in this chapter), this development was to result in the establishment of elaborate social organizations, the appearance of monumental architecture, the building of centers of population that evolved, little by little, into an urban model, and finally the predominance of agriculture and/or stock herding (see chapters 6 and 7).

The collection of innovations included in this South American "Neolithic" is explicable both by the changes undergone by the environment in the postglacial, described in the preceding chapter, and by the existence in a few regions of particularly favorable biotopes. The region called the Central Andean area—the desert or subdesert coast, the Cordillera, and its eastern forested piedmont, from southern Ecuador to northern Chile (from approximately the 2nd to the 20th degree south latitude)—has some ecological characteristics that clearly played a decisive role:

—the richest marine biomass of the western hemisphere;
—a coastal desert that is only habitable at the mouths of little rivers that come down from the Andes, each of which forms an isolated oasis;
—the concentration of the few animal species suited to domestication in a biotope located beyond the upper threshold of agriculture; and
—the existence, in the mid-altitude inter-Andean valleys on the one hand and in the regions of tropical forest on the other, of various wild plant species that are edible and of great nutritional value.

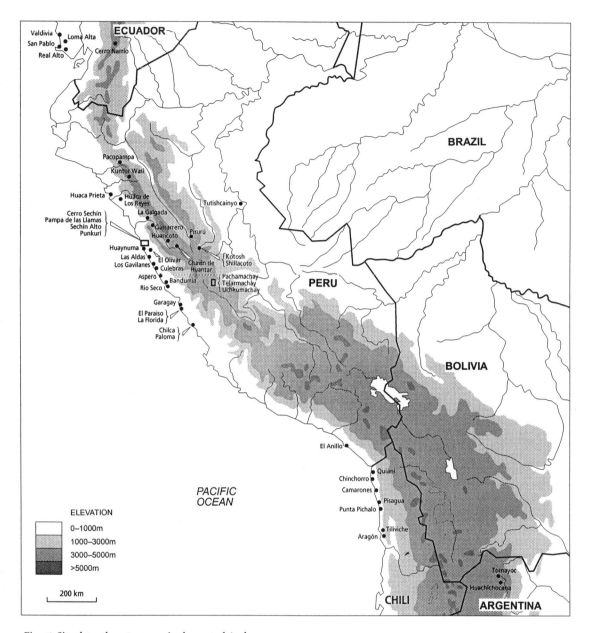

Fig. 16. Sites later than 6000 B.C. in the central Andean area.

These various elements (and others of lesser importance) go a long way toward explaining the originality and the diversity of the adaptive strategies that were employed by Andean people. Hence, from the seventh millennium B.C. onward, and perhaps even earlier, the ocean's natural richness enabled relatively stable populations to settle at certain points on the coast, even though cultivated plants do not seem to have played an important role in the economy at this time. In the preceding chapter, I looked at two of the earliest examples, at two points in the Central Andean littoral that are ex-

Fig. 17. Sites later than 6000 B.C. in the Piauí area.

tremely far from each other (Las Vegas in Ecuador and the Ring Site in Peru). I shall now examine some others in Chile and on the central Peruvian coast that are a little more recent. Along this interminable coastal desert, agriculture was only to become predominant some 2,000 or 3,000 years later. Conversely, in the broad inter-Andean valleys and basins, where the first experiments in horticulture doubtless took place by 8000 B.P., and on the high plateaus above 4,000 meters where around 6000 B.P. camelids were to be domesticated, a long time was still to pass before a farming and herding economy came to support a demographic increase and a social organization that were equivalent to those known much earlier on the littoral.

Yet, as always, nothing is simple and, in this chapter, I shall evoke the contradictory hypotheses, the differences in interpretation, and the disagreements that sometimes turn into polemics—American archaeology is certainly not lacking in those—between two extremes that can be given the following names, which are obviously simplified: on the one side, the supporters of the "oceanic" theory (who assign priority and prevalence to the exploitation of marine resources) and, on the other, supporters of "gardening" (priority and prevalence to plant domestication and then agriculture). As usual, the truth must lie somewhere between these two extreme positions.

A GENEROUS OCEAN

The Pacific's coastal waters which, from northern Peru to northern Chile, bathe an extremely arid desert, are among the richest in the world. Thanks to the existence of the Humboldt Current, or Peruvian Current, which, through the combined action of the trade winds and the Coriolis force, diverts the masses of surface waters from south to north and slightly deflects them toward the open sea—deep waters rise to the surface along the coast, waters of a temperature that is several degrees lower than is normally found in these latitudes. These cold waters bring to the surface great quantities of phosphates, nitrates, and other elements that provide profuse nourishment for a superabundance of marine microflora, the first link in a prodigious food chain: billions of tiny herbivorous animals and little fish are, in their turn, the prey of bigger creatures. Whales, seals, sea lions, fishes of all sizes, and crustaceans and mollusks that are often twice the size of the European species are found in profusion (or, to be more precise, were still found in profusion a few decades ago) off the sandy shores, in the sheltered coves, and in the cavity of every rock; such abundance also supports thousands of birds. The action of this same Humboldt Current, combined with that of the winds and the presence of an enormous mountain barrier very close to the coast (an average of 50 kilometers), is likewise the cause of the very special climate that is found over most of the western facade of the north Chilean and Peruvian Andes. In one of the world's most arid deserts, despite an astonishingly low average temperature (from 18 to 22 degrees Celsius), rainfall is virtually nonexistent, except once or twice per decade when the warm Equatorial Current—called "El Niño" because its effects are generally felt around Christmas—comes close to the continent, bringing warm waters from the north along the Ecuadorian and north Peruvian coast. During half of the year (the southern summer, from December to May), when the air from the open sea becomes cold on contact with the cool waters that bathe the coast, the littoral plain remains drowned in a very dense fog, a mass of humidity that comes from the ocean. Pushed by the wind and blocked by the barrier of the Andes, the fog condenses into fine droplets that remain in suspension and never (or almost never) manage to turn into anything other than a fine drizzle, the *garúa* of Peru, the *camanchaca* of Chile. Conversely, during the other half of the year, when the wind weakens and the movement of the masses of water slows down, the cloud cover disappears, giving way to sunny skies.

These very peculiar climatic conditions (which readers will forgive me for having set out in some detail) mean that, despite the air's degree of humidity, the presence of water—whether surface or underground—has considerable importance for plant life on the coast. For more than 3,000 kilometers, the coastal desert of Peru and northern Chile is interrupted by about 60 transverse water courses, of which slightly less than half have a permanent flow. The valleys of these rivers all form oases, rich in terrestrial flora and fauna, around their mouths and for several kilometers upstream. Finally, in northern Peru and away from the fluvial valleys, a few zones with xerophytic vegetation and a few stands of trees owe their existence to the proximity of the water table.

The coastal fringe also features a very peculiar phenomenon that is directly linked to the presence of the winter, that of the *lomas*, spontaneous and intermittent plant formations that develop during the southern winter on the flanks of the desert hills a few kilometers from the shore and between 200 and 1,000 meters altitude. The humidity condenses on the leaves and trunks of the highest plants and concentrates at their base as well as on the surrounding soil, which is then carpeted with herbaceae and gramineae. These "fog oases," which live on next to nothing, during their brief period of luxuriance accommodate a range of animals and birds, from thousands of snails to cervids, foxes, and various rodents. Among the plants, one also finds several edible rhizomes or tubers.

One can thus see that the Pacific Ocean, so rich in resources, was able to guarantee a varied and superabundant food supply to the prehistoric populations throughout the year. One also certainly finds that semipermanent camps were established here very early, behind the beaches or on the rocky promontories that dominate the ocean, with most of their locations combining the proximity of the beach and that of a river mouth. The *lomas*'s resources were only seasonal, so the *lomas* were never chosen by prehistoric people for anything other than small camps that were occupied sporadically during a hunting expedition or an outing to gather plant foods.

Settling Down Early

Following the pioneering research carried out on the coast of Peru in the 1960s by E. P. Lanning (1963, 1965, 1967), in 1975 M. Moseley published a very detailed study of the prehistoric occupation of the Ancón-Chillón region, on the central coast to the north of Lima, between 5000 and 3500 B.P. His hypothesis, which is summarized in his title, *The Maritime Foundations of Andean Civilization*, is both provocative and seductive: the ocean was supposedly the major factor in the early explosion of the coastal societies, which were able to become sedentary so quickly precisely because of the abundance and stability of the resources it offered and the calorific contribution these represented, and all this well before true agriculture appeared. The idea appeared revolutionary because, at this time—despite the fact that the Peruvian archaeologist R. Fung had already put forward this hypothesis three years earlier, in an article that unfortunately remained unpublished for too long (Fung 1982)—traditional opinion was that there could be no sedentism, demographic increase, or any kind of complex socioeconomic development without agriculture. The Near Eastern "model," developed by V. Gordon Childe in 1930 and further developed and enriched by the innovative hypotheses of R. J. Braidwood about the nuclear areas and the appearance of agriculture, by the comparative research of K. Flannery in the Near East and Mexico, and by others, still constituted the unavoidable point of reference, even though the idea of a Neolithic revolution had been abandoned in favor of a concept that was certainly closer to reality: that of highly complex processes and of a very slow maturation over thousands of years.[1] Hence in America the axiom was that only in maize cultivation could there have been an economic basis indispensable to the establishment of elaborate socioeconomic systems.

Since the publication of Moseley's work, archaeological discoveries have multiplied on the coast, from Ecuador to Chile, and hypotheses have become diversified and especially full of nuances, thanks to research by R. Feldman and J. Quilter in Peru (Feldman 1992; Quilter 1992), A. Llagostera in Chile (1992), and K. Stothert in Ecuador (1992), among others. Moseley (1992b) acknowledged that "the MFAC hypothesis," as he calls it, was purely inductive when he formulated it. Since then it has been discussed, criticized, rectified, and tested, thanks to the recent discovery of sites such as Paloma, as well as advances in methods of excavating, collecting, and analyzing evidence, especially organic materials. Gradually, archaeological data turned up that confirmed its relevance. One of the most interesting facts unearthed recently is that, contrary to Moseley's 1975 proposal, the most substantial food supply did not apparently come from the shellfish and large fish but

[1] We now know that, even in the Near East and especially in Stria and Palestine, the appearance of permanent villages was earlier than that of agriculture.

from the small ones. Anchovy shoals (Engraulis ringens) with millions of members abound along the coast and ensure that Peru is still one of the foremost fishing nations in the world. Being easy to collect with nets throughout the year, they could, in the period that concerns us here, be dried, preserved whole, or crushed into flour, thus constituting a particularly useful food reserve to mitigate, for example, the episodic but catastrophic effects of a Niño (or, more exactly, an ENSO phenomenon, El Niño Southern Oscillation).

The First Fishing Villages

In 1975, the age of the earliest stable coastal settlements then known in Peru and Chile was no more than 4500 B.P. The few earlier dates known at that time were from nonpermanent settlements of hunter-fisher-gatherers, like the camps in the region of Talara and Paiján on the north coast and the more recent ones of the *lomas* of Ancón. Since then, others have been discovered that are even more ancient but which reveal a way of life that was more or less analogous—like Tiliviche, La Chimba 13 (Quebrada Las Conchas) in northern Chile, and Quebrada de los Burros in extreme southern Peru (see chapter 3). Moseley thought that the early occupants of the littoral, who had hitherto been terrestrial hunters, had suddenly "discovered," around 4500 B.P., the advantages of a more stable coastal settlement and the profits of fishing, following the impoverishment of terrestrial resources, itself the consequence of a climatic change that had brought about increasing aridity. As Moseley himself recognized, this does not say very much for the early occupants of the littoral plain and their capacity for adaptation: "They [this explanation] proceeded from the unstated premise that if the continent's first colonists were hunter-gatherers, then their descendants would perforce scrounge around the hyperarid landscape of the barren coast for millennia before discovering that there was considerably more to eat in the sea" (1992b: 13).

It is now known that the sudden "appearance" of coastal camps around 5000 B.P. is only due to the effects of the postglacial variations in ocean level, which then gradually rose following the melting of the icecaps, thus submerging any earlier settlements. Around 5000 B.P., when the water level had stabilized more or less at its present height, the sites closest to the shore would henceforth be preserved, while the traces of the older ones—which very probably existed—disappeared beneath the waters. The settlements that were some distance inshore obviously had nothing to fear from the oscillations in sea level, and some of those mentioned previously (unknown at the time when Moseley was developing his hypothesis) are dated to 8,000 years ago or more.

In the extreme south of Ecuador, the village of Las Vegas, mentioned in the preceding chapter (Stothert 1988), had its densest occupation between

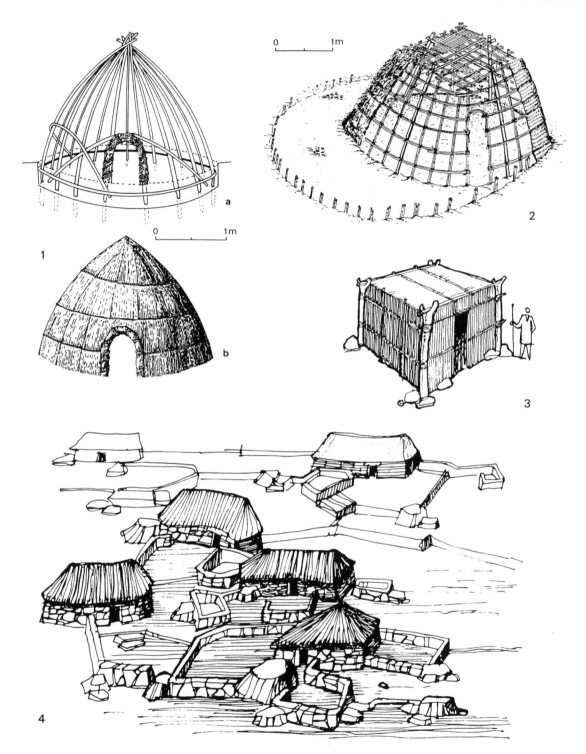

Fig. 18. Peru's first houses and first villages. 1. Reconstruction of a hut in the preceramic village of Chilca (Peru); the remains of this structure were discovered, collapsed in situ and almost intact, covered by a layer of sandy sediment. 2. Hypothetical reconstruction of a hut in the village of Paloma (Peru). 3, 4. Hypothetical reconstructions of a final preceramic dwelling on the coast and of one of the first Andean highland villages; whereas the coastal houses are always built of plant materials (wood and rushes), in the highlands construction was of stone (for the bases and low walls) and turfs of earth or peat (for the house walls).

8000 and 6500 B.P. (Late Las Vegas phase), and the fruits of the sea represent about 50 percent of its food. However, whereas in the first phases of occupation, subsistence seems to have been based essentially on the collecting of mangrove shellfish and terrestrial hunting, it later turned more toward the gathering of plants, mostly wild species, although a few were probably cultivated from then on (*Cucurbitaceae* and perhaps a primitive maize). The village's population apparently increased, the area covered by the traces of dwellings and food refuse became more extensive. This late phase also features a large cemetery, where the remains of 192 individuals were unearthed, the biggest collection of skeletons of this antiquity known in America. One of the burials has achieved a certain notoriety: it is a primary double burial, that of a man and a woman, both aged between 20 and 25, who were interred together. The man's right hand was placed on the woman's waist and his right leg lay over her pelvis. The woman lay on her side, her legs folded and her left arm above her head. Stones were then laid on the bodies of this couple, who have been called the "lovers of Sumpa" (Stothert 1988: 133–40).

A better example of the first true fishing villages is that of Paloma, about 15 kilometers north of the Chilca valley on Peru's central coast. Located around 4 kilometers from the present shore and close to a zone of *lomas*, its traces cover 15 hectares. Three occupation phases have been brought to light at this site, excellently excavated by a North American team led by R. Benfer (Benfer 1984, 1986, 1990; Quilter 1989; Reitz 1988). During the first, between 7800 and 7000 B.P., Paloma was no more than a seasonal camp, but after 7000 and until about 4800 B.P., this spot became a fully sedentary settlement whose occupants lived in 100 small hemispherical houses with a framework made of big reeds covered with bundles of grass or rushes and which had a slightly hollowed inner floor. Almost 1,000 burials wrapped in mats of woven reeds have been discovered in pits dug inside these houses, the bodies lying on their sides, their legs bent, and their hands protecting their face or pelvis. The detailed study of 200 of these skeletons, together with that of the accumulations of refuse next to the habitation areas, has enabled archaeologists to determine the nature of their food: it mainly comprised small fish, anchovies, and sardines, as well as a smaller quantity of marine mammals and shellfish. A very careful paleopathological study has also shown that the men had frequent bony lesions in the ear area, apparently caused by repeated dives into cold water. Certainly, the plant resources, especially those of the nearby *lomas*, were also exploited but mostly for nonalimentary uses (fuel). Even quite late, when horticulture was being practiced, it was only to contribute a minor complement to a diet that still remained of marine origin, which seems to have agreed with the village's occupants: a gradual increase in the height of the adults was recorded through time, as well as a decrease in infant mortality. Compared with the inhabitants of Las Vegas, those of Paloma were on average several centimeters bigger, from which Benfer (1990: 300) deduced that they must have been better nourished and their children in better health. Finally, some individuals, some families(?)—groups of individuals found buried in the same dwelling—clearly ate more and better than others. As Moseley (1992a: 103) remarked, this proves that at Paloma all the inhabitants were not equal. The village was abandoned around 4800 B.P. for reasons that are unclear but which, according to Benfer, might be linked to the general rise in ocean level, which brought about the depletion or disappearance of certain mollusk beds and drove the population to move its dwelling place and to modify its alimentary habits by according a greater importance to cultivated plant resources.

The village of Chilca (5500–4500 B.P.)—later than Paloma and in the same region—was likewise located a few kilometers behind the beach. It reflects an analogous way of life, although the cultivation of gourds and beans was practiced there from the start. But, as at Paloma, it was always secondary. According to Engel (1966), the village, with conical huts of rushes on a framework of wooden poles tied together at the top, could have housed several dozen families.

Finally, in extreme southern Peru, the shellfish-gathering camp of El Anillo, mentioned in the preceding chapter, enjoyed its most important occupation between 7000 and 5000 B.P. This is when the enormous ring of shells and various kinds of organic refuse was gradually formed. Twenty-six meters in diameter and 3 to 8 meters high, it constitutes the visible part of the site, or rather, constituted, because the site has now disappeared. In the center of the heap, a vast depression is probably the negative reflection of a domestic space around which all kinds of refuse, thrown outside the dwellings, accumulated through time. Yet, for at least five millennia (eight according to Sandweiss), this site reveals the presence of a population living exclusively from fishing, doubtless carried out with lines and nets (Sandweiss et al. 1989).

However, it was again extreme northern Chile, which had been frequented by groups of fisher-gatherers for almost 2,000 years (see chapter 3) that at this time had the densest human occupation (or merely the best studied so far?). Following the first settlements of "maritime gatherers" (El Anillo, Quebrada Las Conchas), several large shell mounds, traces of sedentary fishing camps—including Camarones 14 (Schiappacasse and Niemeyer 1984), Pisagua, Quiani, Chinchorro, and Punta Pichalo (Bird 1943, 1946)—that occur along the shore to the south of Arica, have led to the definition of the Camarones complex (c. 7800 to 5600 B.P.). The complex is characterized by the use of nets and, an innovation, of hooks—the latter were either simple, cut out of a big mussel-shell, *Choromytilus* (hence the name of "Shell fishhook Culture," which was first given to this complex by Bird), or composite (a tapered weight of stone, bone, or shell to which a bone barb was fixed)—and finally that of harpoons with a detachable end, armed with a worked stone point and a bone barb. The occupants of these camps caught fish of all sizes, hunted sea lions, cut up the whales that came aground on the beach, and collected mollusks (Llagostera 1992: 91–97). In the same period (7850 B.P.) the occupants of Tiliviche and Aragón, two settlements close in latitude but located 40 kilometers inland (and already occupied for almost 2,000 years—see chapter 3), also began to use similar harpoons, and their refuse heaps reflect the increasing importance of the sea's products, mollusks and especially fish. The Camarones complex seems to have extended as far as the central coast of Peru where, a little later, the fishing village of Chilca (5500–4500 B.P.) has also yielded shell hooks. A bit later in Chile, but in an economic context that had stayed more or less the same, the Quiani complex (c. 5600–3200 B.P.) differed from the preceding one through the use of hooks that were mostly made of curved cactus spines. These two complexes, in reality, are no more than the successive phases of what is also called the "Chinchorro" tradition, defined on the basis of its extraordinary treatment of the dead.

Hence, for at least 8,000 years, permanent villages existed along the Pacific, doubtless within a social organization that was already relatively well developed thanks to the intensive exploitation of the marine environment, whereas the role of plant foods in the diet was always of secondary importance, albeit increasing through time. In the examples mentioned, the technical equipment is much the same: the lithic toolkit is most often rudimentary, projectile points are rare, and hooks are numerous. The hook is doubtless the most significant, if not the most important, object in this technical gear. It appears very early and, in Peru as in Chile, thanks to the hook the littoral people attained a new techno-economic dimension; they could henceforth capture open-water species, whereas their predecessors were, through force of circumstance, limited to exploiting the intertidal zone or the rocky parts of the littoral. Remains of nets only become numerous after cotton replaced the other materials used hitherto for their manufacture, that is, not before about 5000 B.P.; however, stone net-weights, calabash floats, and even a few fragments of nets made of plant fibers of other species (rushes, reeds), found in various sites in Chile and Peru, show that they existed earlier. Finally, the use of light craft, doubtless of reeds or sea-mammal hide, which would enable people to move around at some distance from the coast and to fish for open-water species with rod and line, seems obvious, although this has not yet been proven archaeologically.

In this period, plant products, which were nevertheless necessary, were essentially used for technical purposes. Although the ocean could offer food for thousands of people, it did not provide the fuel for cooking, nor the fibers and floaters for the lines and nets, nor the shafts for the harpoons, nor the clothes or the materials needed for the construction of dwellings. Despite everything, it was the land from which people demanded the infrastructure that was indispensable to fruitful fishing.

The World's Oldest Mummies

In 1917, the German archaeologist Max Uhle was the first to work in the Arica region, on the edge of the Atacama desert, and to describe the remains of an ancient community of fishers that he baptized "Chinchorro," from the

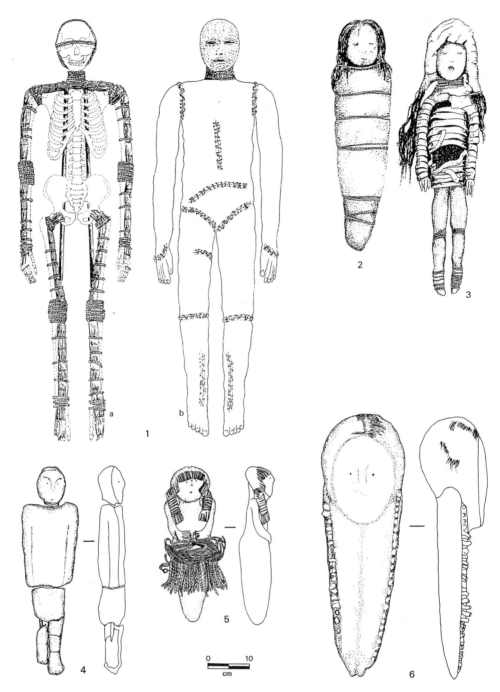

Fig. 19. Chinchorro Culture (Chile). 1. "Complex" mummies. a. Internal preparation, showing how the joints were bound with cords and the body stiffened with wooden poles. b. External preparation, showing how the skin was subsequently readjusted and sewn after a padding of plants or earth had been inserted between the skin and the skeleton in order to restore the body's shape. 2, 3. Mummies of children, prepared like those of the adults. 4–6. Figurines—or "substitutes" of unfired clay; X rays of one of them (4) revealed that the head contained a bird skull, while another (6) was modeled on a dolphin jaw.

name of the nearby beach (and which also denotes the type of net used by the local fishers). During his excavations, close to the refuse heaps and the traces of habitation, he unearthed numerous, very curious mummies (Uhle 1922). At this time, obviously, no absolute dating method was known, and no one could suspect the antiquity of these finds. The research by J. Bird (1943) in the 1940s and especially the recent work by the paleopathologist M. Allison (1985), who has studied more than 1,500 mummies, have made it possible to specify their age: the oldest correspond to the Camarones cultural complex (c. 7800–5600 B.P.), the most recent—and also the most numerous—to the Quiani complex (c. 5600–3200 B.P.). And the oldest of them, recently dated to slightly more than 7810 ± 180 B.P., is thus more than 2,000 years earlier than the oldest mummies known in Egypt.

In contrast to the relative simplicity of their daily life, their funerary practices were extraordinarily elaborate and very spectacular. Of course, there are numerous cases where they limited themselves to placing the body in a pit dug into the sand, with no particular preparation—the intense dryness subsequently ensured its desiccation and conservation. But in many cases, the body first underwent an extremely complicated preparation (fig. 19). All the internal organs were first removed, both viscera and brain, the latter extracted through the occipital hole; the skin was slit open and the main muscles removed by means of stone or shell tools or sharpened pelican beaks (metal would appear in the region only much later, around 2800 B.P.). The interior of the body was then dried by means of embers and warm ashes, with which the cavities were filled. Next, the corpse was reinforced and stiffened with an elongated piece of wood[2] attached along the vertebral column in order to remove all its flexibility. The kneecaps and elbow joints were rasped and filed down, which made the limbs rigid; the limbs were then tightly wrapped with cords, as was the neck. The prepared and dried body was finally "reconstructed": the limbs were wrapped with mats of woven rushes, and the cavities were stuffed with tufts of wool, feathers or earth, grass, and shells. In order to restore some appearance of life, the body was coated with a layer of clay, in a kind of modeling, while the face, which was likewise covered with clay, was sculpted into a mask with eyes and mouth indicated by holes. The skin (which had doubtless been preserved in seawater during this process) was then adjusted and sewn back onto the whole body, like a glove. As a finishing touch, the hair was fixed back onto the skull, and the body was painted red or black, depending on the period. Finally, the mummy was buried, not far from the dwellings, together with other older mummies. The inhabitants sometimes used this occasion to repair the latter in order to keep them in "good condition," reinforcing any bonds that had come loose or had broken, applying a fresh layer of clay, replacing any pieces of skin that had disappeared or been damaged here and there with pieces of ostrich or sea-lion skin.

These extremely refined techniques of preparation and conservation are unique in America, and doubtless in the world, and their meaning is hard to

[2]It was pieces of wood like this that were interpreted by their discoverers as the oldest specimens of bows known in America (Bittmann and Munizaga 1979) (see chapter 3). However, these identifications appear doubtful in the eyes of many who believe the bow is only definitely present in South America around 2500 B.P.

grasp. The complexity of the processes used and the care accorded to the longest possible conservation of the dead bodies certainly point to elaborate rituals and a very rich spiritual life. According to Llagostera, the predominance of children's bodies (often newborn infants) among the mummies in relation to adults and the use of "mummy-statuettes"—substitutes modeled in clay or bone—suggest not a simple veneration of the dead but rather a more extensive cult in which these "'ritual artifacts' must have formed part of a broader cultic conception; perhaps as symbols or propitiatory messages to the natural or supernatural forces of the cosmic environment" (1989: 63). Until about 3700 B.P. the descendants of the Chinchorro continued to practice this artificial mummification, before abandoning it and contenting themselves, like the other littoral populations of the time, with burying the bodies in a flexed position in the burning sand of the desert, which took care of conserving them all by itself.

I should not end this section about life on the littoral and the economic importance of the resources provided by the ocean without mentioning—as I pointed out at the start—that several specialists, including some of the foremost, categorically reject Moseley's MFAC theory. In their opinion, only agriculture can account for true sedentism and explain the subsequent emergence of "civilization" along the Pacific coast, especially in the central Andean area. The severest criticisms have been put forward by Osborn, Wilson, Raymond, and, more recently, Bonavia (1982, 1993–95). In fact, Osborn went so far as to call Moseley's proposals "fairy tales." In his view (1977), the marine resources, and especially the mollusks, could not ensure a sufficient dietary contribution; for Wilson (1981), they were too uncertain; and for Raymond (1981), the theory greatly underestimated the plant resources. Suffice it to note here that, when the first of these articles was written, the excavations at Las Vegas in Ecuador, Paloma in Peru, Camarones 14 and Quebrada Las Conchas in Chile, among others, had not yet been published. Isotopic analyses, which enable one to use a fragment of human bone to determine the relative importance of animal and plant proteins in the diet and which showed, for example, at Paloma (Benfer 1990), the predominance of marine foods, were not yet in use. Consequently, an inductive hypothesis (as was acknowledged by Moseley himself) was met with premature criticisms and decisive but hasty conclusions. Once again, a proposition needs to be validated or rejected by testing it against the facts and not on the basis of arguments of principle, which are inevitably decided upon beforehand.

THE FIRST HORTICULTURALISTS

Whereas on the ocean shore large villages housed a growing sedentary population, seminomadic bands of hunters continued—as they had for dozens of centuries—to occupy the natural refuges of the Cordillera. Their way of life, their array of implements, and their prey remained astonishingly stable, whether on the high plateau of Colombia, in the Cordilleran valleys and basins, or on the punas of Peru and northern Chile. However, it is the Cordillera and not the coast that has produced the oldest remains of cultivated plants, all discovered in Peru. Of course, these remains bear little resemblance to the plants we know today, and their fruits or ears are generally far smaller. For example, the first cultivated maize cobs in Peru (at Guitarrero) measure only 4 to 6 centimeters instead of the 15 centimeters or more of the present-day cobs.

Very Old Beans

I have already mentioned Guitarrero several times—without any doubt one of the richest sites studied in the Peruvian Andes, notably because of its dry conditions, which enabled organic materials to be preserved. This explains how Lynch (1980) was fortunate enough to be able to recover several kinds of objects that normally are lacking in the cave sites of the Andes: wooden utensils, pieces of basketry, remains of various ropes, and, especially, remains of edible plants. In this shelter that was occupied by hunters (see chapter 3), these remains are present almost from the start, and, what is even more astonishing, according to specialists they are cultivated plants. The layers that make up Complex II contained pimento (*Capsicum chinense*) (Complex IIa: 10,600–10,000 B.P.) and two kinds of beans, *Phaseolus lunatus* (Complex IId: 8800–8200 B.P.) and *P. Vulgaris* (Complex IIe: 7700 B.P.), all of them plants that do not exist in a wild form in this region. These are the oldest cultivated plants ever found in America. A little later, around 6000 B.P., gourds (*Cucurbita* sp.) and calabashes (*Lagenaria* sp.) appear. Finally, remains of maize cobs (*Zea mays*), primitive but already domesticated, come from Complex III, dated, according to Lynch, to about 7700 B.P. (1980: 306). Another region of Peru where remains of plants cultivated very early have been retrieved from caves and shelters is the Ayacucho Basin, where gourds and calabashes were also cultivated early (Piki phase: c. 7700–6300 B.P.) and where maize is recorded a little later, certainly later than at Guitarrero (Chihua phase: c. 6300–5000 B.P.) (MacNeish et al. 1980–83). These elements point to a very precocious manipulation of certain species and, from around 7000 B.P., the existence of already well-developed horticultural practices if not of true agriculture, although, in all the sites mentioned previously, the bulk of the diet continued to be provided by hunting, trapping, and the gathering of edible wild plants. Moreover, the dispersal of these innovations was not limited to the Peruvian Andes, since maize was possibly also cultivated in Ecuador, at Las Vegas, by 7000 B.P. and in northern Chile, at Tiliviche, around 6900 B.P. Other finds of even earlier dates have been claimed, but they are very controversial and may come from contexts of disturbed stratigraphy, so they still require confirmation.

Plant domestication seems to have been earlier in the highlands than on the coast of Peru, where cultivated species appear in the fishing villages only around 5500 B.P. On the other hand, they were far more numerous here, as was stressed by Bonavia (1993–95: 94). From the start, various fruits (peanut, *Arachis hypogaea*; pacay, *Inga Feuillei*; guava, *Psidium guajaba*: lucuma, *Pouteria lucuma*), manioc (*Manihot esculenta*), cotton (*Gossypium barbadense*) around 5000 B.P., and, from 4500 B.P. onward, the beans and pimento just mentioned and the sweet potato (*Hipomoea batatas*), to cite only the most important species. One still sees a notable hiatus between the first appearance of a species that is domesticated or on the way to domestication in the Cordillera and its reappearance, now in a fully domesticated form, in the coastal oases. If our current knowledge does not preclude the possibility of cultivated plants being discovered one day in earlier coastal sites, there seems little likelihood of this chronological difference being filled completely or reversed, especially as excavations have been far more numerous on the coast than in the highlands and the conditions of preservation of organic materials are incomparably better there.

With regard to the Andean species, one curious fact remains. Some, which undoubtedly originated in the mountains, were very probably cultivated quite early: for example, various tubers such as the potato (*Solanum tuberosum*), the Andean plant par excellence, of which there are about 5,000 varieties today, some of them able to grow up to 4,100 meters altitude; or quinoa (*Chenopodium quinoa*), widely cultivated today above 3,000 meters. Yet no archaeological trace of these two plants has yet been discovered in a domestic form in the highlands, and the most ancient cultivated potatoes come from a coastal site, Huaynuma (Bonavia 1993), where they are no more than 4,000 years old, which clearly implies an even earlier domestication that doubtless began in the Cordillera. "Cultivated" remains of quinoa were recorded by MacNeish in the "Piki" layers (7700–6300 B.P.) of the Ayacucho sites; but their domestic status is far from proved, and in its wild form *Chenopodium* is scarcely more than a "weed."

Chance or Necessity?

Since it appears to be confirmed for the moment that agricultural practices in the Cordillera are the earliest, the problem to be solved is that of their geographical origin—and this has been and continues to be a bone of contention. As Bonavia reminds us (1991: 128), there are three main hypotheses on this topic. According to the first, this origin is to be found in Mexico, from where agriculture then diffused northward into the present southern United States and also southward where it reached the Andean zone. The second hypothesis, put forward in 1952 by C. Sauer and adopted by Lathrap (1971), proposed a great center of domestication in the tropical lowlands. The third, which seems to be confirmed by archaeological data at present,

sees the great midaltitude inter-Andean basins as a primary center of domestication and then of diffusion, independent of the Mexican center. The
first hypothesis—the earliest to be put forward—is hard to support today
when one considers the range of North and South American cultigens, which
are rather different; conversely, debate still rages about maize (see chapter
6). The other two hypotheses are both based on solid arguments. In Lathrap's
view, the origin lies in a forest zone, specifically the Amazon. Basing his arguments on the fact that several of the earliest species to be cultivated in the
Andes—especially beans, pimento, maize, and peanuts—are plants that originated in a humid tropical environment, he maintains that they were first
manipulated in the eastern piedmont of the Andes at the beginning of the
Holocene, during a relatively cool and dry climatic phase in which plant
cover was far less dense than today and which favored human settlement in
what was then no more than savanna. Subsequently, a warmer climate, the
return of heavy rainfall, and the concomitant increase in forest supposedly
forced the human groups to seek other lands to settle. Traveling up the great
rivers, they reached the Cordillera, where they introduced the nascent practice of agriculture. It is an attractive theory, but it remains impossible to
demonstrate because none of the (very rare) archaeological sites in the tropical forest have yet yielded the slightest evidence in support of it. Hence the
third hypothesis, which sees the midaltitude Andean regions as the "cradle"
of South American agriculture, remains the best attested for the moment,
though it does not exclude the possibility that multiple centers of domestication may have existed (Bonavia and Grobman 1978; Pickersgill 1972;
Pickersgill and Heiser 1978).

In fact, the truth must lie in the two hypotheses' area of overlap. While
several plants certainly originated in a humid tropical environment, others
grow wild in the highlands, and the inter-Andean valleys and basins offer
soil and climate conditions that are very favorable to a diversification and
multiplication of varieties. Human movements also certainly played their
role, which is why Lynch (1973) postulates that a determining factor in the
transfer, diversification, and amelioration of species, making them more
suited to agriculture, may have been the practice by the Andean hunter-
gatherer groups of a system of seasonal migrations. Such movements were
indeed carried out very early, taking advantage of the whole range of seasonally complementary ecological facets offered by the Andean mountains.
Hence the Andean populations must have transferred certain plants from
one ecological milieu to another, whether purposely or not (seeds can be
transported accidentally on clothing or in feces). This migration system would
also have made it impossible for them always to harvest the wild plants of a
particular place at the optimal time, that is, when the plants had fully rip-
ened. For example, if what he calls "nonoptimal harvests" are carried out
too late, "men will select accidentally, but with tremendous efficacy, for varieties that do not disperse their seeds properly. This single factor, which is

virtually certain to be effective wherever men were migratory, may be of great importance in the history of domestication" (Lynch 1973: 1256). I should also note that animals, especially birds, can also be responsible for the accidental transportation of seeds from one ecological zone to another.

The theories of Lathrap and Lynch are not the only ones that have been developed to explain the origins of agriculture in America, and, moreover, they do not claim to explain agriculture but only the conditions and circumstances that favored domestication—that is, the fact that from a certain period onward (which varies according to region) plant species were deliberately planted in anticipation of a harvest. As J. Cauvin (1992: 266) has stressed with regard to the Near East, while the selection of the characteristics that resulted morphologically in the emergence of new, so-called domestic species may have been unconscious, the actual cultivation of plants can only have been done consciously. Here again, the answers to this question "why?" vary from author to author, and the problem is far from solved. Without going into details, which are beyond my competence, let me simply say that, for the moment, none of the "models" that have been proposed—climatic changes (Willey, Wright), demographic growth (Binford), even overpopulation (Cohen)—have provided a satisfactory explanation for the appearance of agriculture in the Andean area. In particular, it is doubtful whether the Andean region, even in its most favorable "ecological niches," experienced a veritable demographic saturation at this time. In the view of Cauvin (who always refers to the Near East, but a certain parallelism appears self-evident here), after millennia of hunting and gathering, it was humans who were to be modified. Plants followed later: "In order for people to begin exploiting their environment, and especially plants, differently, they first had to 'perceive' this environment, and themselves, differently" (ibid.: 266).

In the Andean case, one can imagine that, while a few "domestic" species certainly appeared earlier in the highlands as a consequence of manipulation and a nondeliberate selection, "true" agriculture was indeed born on the coast, taking advantage of the preliminary evolution of the sociotechnical environment, thanks above all to the early sedentism that was made possible by the exploitation of the marine riches. On the coast, the appearance of agriculture this time implied an intelligent choice in which the exploitation of the chosen species was indissociable from the development of techniques that made possible not only their exploitation but also the survival of the population based on that exploitation.

Finally, there is one plant that I have not yet dealt with, although its domestication and utilization profoundly modified and enriched the material universe of Andean people: cotton. The cotton cultivated in South America (*Gossypium barbadense*) is different from that of the Old World, although it may be the product of a very early crossbreeding between a wild species that had formerly reached America after its seeds accidentally crossed the Atlantic and a wild species originating in America (Pickersgill and Heiser 1978: 153). The first traces of cultivated cotton come from the coast of Peru, where they date to between 5,000 and 4,500 years ago, and its "appearance" in the sites has been considered sufficiently important for archaeologists to distinguish a "preceramic period without cotton" from a period "with cotton." Cotton would henceforth replace the other plant fibers (cactus, rushes, reeds), which were more fragile and breakable, in the fabrication of fishing nets and lines and would also replace hides in the production of clothing. First used with the same techniques that were employed previously—weaving, intertwining (fig. 28)—it was soon to be woven on a loom, another technological innovation that, in the Andean area, would later undergo an extraordinary expansion (see chapter 6). Moreover, as Pickersgill and Heiser (1978) have observed, in contrast to the Old World where the first plants cultivated in the Near East were exclusively for alimentary use, among the earliest cultigens of America there are two species of technical use: calabashes and cotton. These authors conclude as follows in a daring summary that brings us back to the start of this chapter: "While the early Near Eastern farmer may have been eating bread in the sweat of his face, his New World counterpart had probably gone fishing" (ibid.: 159).

PROVIDENTIAL ANIMALS

While people in the midaltitude valleys and basins were engaged—consciously or not—in manipulations of various plants, those living in the high plateaus of the puna were still hunters. Apart from tubers, the austere environment of the Andean steppe does not really offer any wild plant resources capable of constituting an important complement to the diet, and the few plants that people were starting to cultivate at lower altitudes cannot be acclimatized to an altitude higher than 3,500 meters. In these regions, a different process took place, one involving the domestication of a few animal species, very few in fact: the guinea pig (so named by sixteenth-century Spaniards who had never seen any) but especially the camelids of the genus *Lama*. The latter would very soon play a role of the first rank in Andean cultural development, doubtless a greater role than the far more numerous species domesticated in the Old World, precisely because they originated in the highlands located beyond the upper limit of agriculture and because their domestication was to be the origin of a form of pastoral civilization that had no equivalent elsewhere.

What Bones Tell Us

The recognition of the first domestications is essentially based on the analysis of the bone remains recovered from sites. The specialized knowledge nec-

Fig. 20. The llama and the vicuña. "These animals are not found in the old continent, but belong uniquely to the new; . . . they seem to be attached to the mountain chain that stretches from New Spain to the Magellanic lands; they inhabit the highest regions of the terrestrial globe, and in order to live they appear to need to breathe sharper and lighter air than that of our highest mountains. . . . Their flesh is good to eat, their coat is a fine wool that wears extremely well. . . . They spit in the face of those who insult them, and it is alleged that this saliva which they spit in anger is so bitter and caustic that it raises blisters on the skin. . . . Vicuñas resemble llamas facially, but they are smaller, their legs are shorter, and their muzzle more compact. . . . They go about in herds, and run very nimbly; they are shy; and as soon as they see somebody, they flee, driving their young before them" (G. L. de Buffon, *Oeuvres Complètes*, D. Pillot, Paris, 1830, t. 17, "*Mammifères*," 4, pp. 405–13 and pl. 83)

essary for the identification of the species, age, and sex of the animals, from their bones alone, constitutes a special discipline: archaeozoology.

At present, there are four species of Andean camelid: two domestic (the llama, *Lama glama*, and the alpaca, *Lama pacos*) and two wild (the vicuña, *Lama vicugna*, and the guanaco, *Lama guanicoe*; fig. 20). Let us rapidly examine the criteria used by the archaeozoologists to distinguish wild forms from domestic forms (these criteria are enumerated, with references, in Lavallée 1990):

(a) Criteria relating to animal morphology:
—morphology of the skull, which makes it possible to highlight the differences between species, especially between the vicuña and the guanaco;
—width of the astragalus and height of the calcaneum and dimensions of the first phalange, which make it possible to distinguish between "big" individuals (like the llama) and "small" ones (like the alpaca);
—aspect of the articular surfaces, which when studied on thin sections of the bones of the extremities and examined in polarizing light, makes it possible to distinguish domestic from nondomestic animals;
—morphology and dental structure, which make it possible to distinguish "alpaca-type" incisors from those of "vicuña-type," on the one hand, and, on the other, those of "guanaco/llama-type," the two not being distinguishable from each other.
(b) Criteria relating to the composition of a site's faunal assemblage:
—relative representation of camelids and noncamelids (especially, the proportion in relation to cervids);
—age structure in the camelid bone remains (in particular, the proportion of remains of fetuses or newborn animals, with a very high proportion being considered evidence of the presence of domestic animals).

These are the criteria used most often, but there are others relating to other parts of the body, like the characteristics of the fibers of the fleece or more recently developed analytical techniques like the study of blood polymorphism or the DNA sequence. The effectiveness of these new avenues of research has not yet been fully demonstrated, and the results are only just emerging or remain unpublished.

From Hunting to Domestication

Since the start of the occupation of the high plateaus about 10,000 years ago, the two species of wild camelids, the vicuña and the guanaco, together with a fairly big cervid that lived in the highlands (the Taruca or Andean deer, *Hippocamelus antisensis*), constituted the favorite prey of Andean hunters who hunted them in almost equivalent proportions (see chapter 3). But in certain regions a clear evolution rapidly took place. Hence, in the shelter of

Fig. 21. Camelid herd. Among the numerous assemblages of rock paintings in northern Chile, especially in the valley of the Río Loa, those of Taira are both the most important and the most beautiful. Executed in a very naturalistic style, the paintings—whose outline was first engraved and then filled with red or yellow coloring—depict groups of camelids that at times are associated with human silhouettes that sometimes seem to be holding a sling or a bow. In the absence of any archaeological context, these paintings are impossible to date. However, the presence of the bow suggests a relatively late date (not before the first millennium b.c.), and hence a period when the camelids were fully domesticated. Thus these depictions may be linked to the traffic of caravans, well attested at this time, rather than to hunting practices.

Telarmachay, at almost 4,500 meters altitude on the Junín puna in central Peru, the remains of camelids quickly became predominant in the faunal refuse. They represented 65 percent of the game at the start of the occupation around 9000 b.p. (versus 34 percent for cervids), but progressed to 78 percent between 7200 and 6800 b.p., then to 86 percent around 6000 b.p., and finally reached almost 89 percent around 4500 b.p. The number of cervids killed declined in inverse proportion. A similar phenomenon can be seen in other nearby sites, such as the cave of Pachamachay or the little shelter of Uchkumachay, both likewise located above 4,000 meters.

How can figures like these be interpreted? In the eyes of archaeozoologist J. Wheeler, who carried out the faunal analysis of Telarmachay, this constant and regular evolution over five millennia points to two processes (Wheeler 1984; Wheeler in Lavallée et al. 1985). First, between 9000 and 6500/6000 b.p. there was a gradual change from the undifferentiated exploitation of cervids and camelids to an increasingly specialized hunting of the camelids. This change does not seem to reflect any growing rarity of the former in relation to the latter, insofar as the puna does not undergo any notable climatic disturbance at this time. In reality, this change could be explained by the behavior of the camelids, which has been studied in present-day populations of vicuñas and guanacos, doubtless very close to their prehistoric ancestors. Vicuñas and guanacos live in small family groups—one male and four to ten females. They move around inside a defined territory, which remains stable from one year to the next and which they defend against intrusion by other groups. Hence, provided they can moderate the toll taken by hunting and protect the females and young animals, hunters find here a sure and regular source of food, in contrast to what the cervids represented, with their less gregarious and less stable behavior.

There then followed a period, between 6500/6000 and 4000 B.P., during which the predominance of the camelids was henceforth assured among the animals killed, and they show an abrupt increase of very young individuals, or stillborn young, even fetuses. Their proportion increased from less than 40 percent at the start (the "normal" rate in a wild population) to 57 percent and then, between 5500 and 4000 B.P., to the astonishing figure of 73 percent. In Wheeler's view, such a choice, which was totally antieconomical on the part of the hunters—indeed it is hard to imagine them systematically killing the youngest members of a herd that had to ensure their annual subsistence—can only reflect the faults in the control exercised by people over camelids, which were doubtless shut up in enclosures some of the time. The growing mortality of newborn individuals recorded between 6000 and 4000 B.P. was apparently due not to ill-considered killing but to bacillary attacks that were directly linked to the overcrowding of the animals in inevitably dirty and muddy enclosures. Wheeler's conclusion is that this is a by-product—or, rather, a contrary effect—of domestication. Moreover, her analysis is confirmed by the presence among the bone remains of typical alpaca incisors (different from those of guanacos and vicuñas) around 6000 B.P. and then, a little later, bone remains of llama, the second domestic species known. Finally, herding is fully established after 4500 B.P.

This transition from hunting to domestication of the camelids is fundamental in the Andean cultural trajectory because the two species thus "created" by people would quickly be destined to play a prime role in society. Their economic contribution was to be manifold and varied: first, as a source of raw materials (meat, leather, bone, tendons, wool, and even excrement, used as fuel)—the prehistoric hunters were already making the most of these; then, in the later agro-pastoral societies, as participants in economic and social life (beasts of burden, trade goods, symbol of social status and wealth); finally, as elements in rituals (whole animals for sacrifice and offerings of sebum, wool, fetuses, and bezoar-stones).

The demonstration of the process of domestication, which for the moment has only been observed in the shelter of Telarmachay, has not been accepted by everyone. Hence, in the nearby cave of Pachamachay, the same very appreciable increase in the number of camelids, at the expense of cervids, has been recorded but interpreted differently. In J. Rick's view, these were always wild vicuñas, and an economy of pure predation was practiced until around 3500 B.P., when the domestic species appeared along with a pastoral economy, both of them "imported" from outside (Rick 1980: 265). In fact, this does not matter much, because it is quite possible, after all, that experiments tried out successfully in one place, consciously or not, were not tried out elsewhere, even in a neighboring region. "Pure" hunters and first herders may very well have coexisted for centuries, mutually enriching their knowledge of the animals.

All of this leads to the question: why did Andean people domesticate the camelids? At Telarmachay, those who gradually achieved this transformation were nonsedentary hunters, and they remained so even when they had become herders. Telarmachay was still occupied seasonally, between December and March (which is proved by the presence in the site of newborn animals, since female camelids always give birth at this time of year). A system of rotation between different winter and summer habitations, following the seasonal migrations of the wild herds, continued to be practiced with domestic herds and, even later, in a fully agricultural context. This is a typical Andean way of life, and one that is still practiced today, a perfect example of cultural adaptation to the ecosystem of the puna.

Another question also needs to be asked: in relation to hunting, what kind of innovation was really represented by the domestication of these camelids? Certainly, the control of animal reproduction and the creation of new species constitute fundamental changes at the biological level. However, the way of life implied by the nascent domestication of the camelids became so well integrated with the ancestral behavior of the hunters that they merged into one. The seasonal rhythm of the sojourns remained immutable; the herders killed the animals, butchered them, prepared them, and ate them, using the same techniques and the same implements, in a shelter inhabited for millennia by their hunting ancestors. Very probably, the social and economic (production/distribution) relations of the human groups had changed, especially with the use of the llama as beast of burden, which facilitated contacts and exchanges sometimes over very long distances. However, archaeology yields few clues to all this.

In the face of this undeniable continuity, one can thus wonder why—when on these high plateaus of the puna there was a solid and stable subsistence system based on making rational use of wild fauna—people gradually abandoned it for the constraints inherent to pastoral life. It would seem that one can eliminate the hypothesis of pressure from the natural environment (climatic fluctuation and/or increasing rarity of the wild fauna), at least in a restrictive form. Indeed, it appears that domestication was doubtless not premeditated, and people's main concern remained that of an optimal exploitation of the stock of wild animals. But as hunting grew increasingly intensive and selective, it brought a profound knowledge of animal behavior. This knowledge, together with the behavior itself which favored keeping the animals in a restricted space, was doubtless the origin of a kind of commensalism in which animals and people lived almost in symbiosis, without the freedom of the former and the availability of the latter being hampered. The beneficial effects of this association and of human action (even unconscious) on the animals' life-cycle—through selection of animals to kill, the protection of the females, the elimination of aggressive or sick individuals, the control of reproduction, and the supervision of births—were clearly noticed quite quickly. The means of re-creating them were memorized and repeated from generation to generation, and people rapidly took advantage of their results.

In the Andes of northern Chile and northwest Argentina, the presence of llamas and alpacas is not really confirmed before about 3000 B.P.[3] (fig. 21). One of the problems that remains to be solved is that of determining whether the appearance of domestic camelids in these regions was the consequence of migratory movement or of contacts that transferred pastoral practices from the punas of the central Andes, or whether there existed other independent centers of domestication. Before the results of the excavations at Telarmachay were published in 1985, E. Wing (1977) had already suggested that the domestication of the camelids must have begun at high altitude, where these animals were always abundant. Vast regions like the Altiplano of Bolivia still need to be explored.

As for the guinea pig (*Cavia porcellus*), its economic importance was, and remained, infinitely inferior, although this prolific little animal, with its tasty flesh, very quickly became the habitual commensal of the Andean peasant, whose dwelling it cleaned both gluttonously and efficiently before it ended its days grilled on feast days. Curiously, the first evidence of its domestication was not discovered in the central Andes, where it existed in a wild state, and still does so, but in Colombia, where it has become rare. In various sites of the *sábana* of Bogotá (see chapters 2 and 3)—Tequendama, Sueva, El Abra, Nemocón—this animal, which had been present but rare in the faunal record since 11/10,000 B.P., became much more common after 9500/8000 B.P. and then very abundant after 2500 B.P. According to G. Ijzereef (1978), it was hunted (or rather, trapped) for a long time and then rapidly became a favorite food of the hunters who gradually "tamed" it. But it was not domesticated until after 2500 B.P., a time when one can see both an increase in the size of individuals and modifications in the morphology of their skeleton, which were presumably due to the animals being confined in enclosures or inside the dwellings.

To conclude these few pages on one of the most prodigious leaps forward that prehistoric America has ever known, and one that also caused the most

[3]In the shelter of Tomayoc (puna of Jujuy, Argentina), recently found by a French mission (unpublished), two alpaca incisors have been identified in a level dated to 1530 B.C. However, there is still much to do in order to demonstrate that pastoral practices were in use in extreme northwestern Argentina in the second millennium B.C.

radical transformation of human behavior—as also happened in the few other parts of the world that experienced this slow but decisive evolution that was the "Neolithic"—let us return for a moment to its irreversible aspect. Subsequently, the Andean area and other regions of South America would see the blossoming of brilliant civilizations, with a much more accomplished socioeconomic organization and with much more refined artistic products than those of the first "Neolithic" populations. But all these civilizations disappeared one day, after a period of splendor and influence that was sometimes long (almost 1,000 years) but more often brief (200 or 300 years). In contrast, "Neolithization" made people, who had hitherto lived as predators on nature, into manipulators of this nature and the producers of their own food. No population that has attained this stage ever returns to its previous way of life. And what about the modifications that were stamped onto the natural environment? As J. Guilaine says, "What can one say of the metamorphosis of a space, every part of which was to carry the imprint of human labor?" (1992: 164).

The domestication of plants and animals was followed by that of the landscape. Henceforth, every oasis on the Peruvian coast was crisscrossed by irrigation networks of ever increasing extent and complexity. The slopes of the Andean mountains would gradually be transformed—and far earlier than is generally imagined—into gigantic staircases of *sandenes*, the tiers of terraces that enabled people to cultivate slopes that had hitherto been unusable, if not inaccessible. And what about the new social behavior that was adopted at this time? The appearance of permanent villages and the territorial anchoring of food resources, be they fields or herds, created new ways of life, a new perception of daily space that would never be forgotten, and new relationships between the members of a community. Social divisions appeared. Henceforth, in Ecuador and Peru, there were those who produced food and those who were fed so that they could devote their time to other tasks (see chapter 6). Hunting societies that were (apparently) egalitarian would survive only in the regions located away from the Andean center— that is, in most of South America—which was to undergo a slower development. Unusual economic plans were sometimes developed which, in the land closest to the Andean area, largely relied on borrowing. Elsewhere, it took several more centuries before one saw the diffusion of agricultural techniques and the use of pottery. Some populations would encounter them or adopt them only after the always devastating invasion of the Europeans.

5

THE OTHER SIDE OF THE CORDILLERA

W HILE THE ANDEAN AREA WAS UNDERGOING THIS EXTRAORDINARY boom, what was happening to the east, in the immense Amazonian Basin, on the plateaus of Brazil, and along the Atlantic littoral? What became of the guanaco hunters who lived on the steppes of Patagonia and Tierra del Fuego? Down there, the former life continued almost unchanged in relation to the preceding period, except for alterations that were directly linked to the gradual modifications of the environment and the general increase in the density of human occupation, which encouraged regionalism but also stimulated contacts, trade, and borrowings. On the one hand, there is no question here of describing in detail all the aspects of this occupation in each of the innumerable facets of the South American environment; on the other hand, where large portions of the territory are concerned, archaeological data continue to be virtually nonexistent.

This certainly applies to most of the great Amazonian forest and the expanses of savanna that border it to the north and south. Yet we have recently learned that a good part of the Amazonian territory was certainly occupied, and had been so for a long time, but only a few rare ancient sites have been studied. The only ones known are, in the Mato Grosso, the Lapa do Sol and the shelter of Santa Elina where, above the Pleistocene level, traces of an occupation dating to around 6000 B.P. have been unearthed; in Pará, the Gruta do Gavião, where flakes of quartz and amethyst, accompanied by bone remains of small mammals and tortoise, fish bones, and freshwater shellfish, point to a use by humans between about 8000 and 3000 B.P.; but especially the Caverna da Pedra Pintada, occupied, as we have seen, since a little more than 11,000 B.P. (see chapter 3). In fact, only the zones containing rock outcrops are likely to have remains of dwellings in shelters or caves, and such zones are rare. As for open-air camps (which certainly existed for as long as natural shelters were used), apart from the fact that, to discover them, archaeological research in thick forest is not easy—to say the least—it is far more likely that they have been eroded away or been covered by alluvia.

Nevertheless, at the frontier between Brazil and Surinam, work floors made up of concentrations of rhyolite flakes, some of them retouched into crude knives or scrapers, have been found. Attributed to a hypothetical Sipaliwi complex by their discoverer, A. Boomert (1980), they date, in his view, to 8,000 or 7,000 years ago. But this chronological attribution is based only on comparisons with lithic industries that are similar to those found in the north of Venezuela (Las Casitas complex), also as surface finds and likewise undated.

But let us return for a moment to the remains yielded by that astonishing Caverna da Pedra Pintada: the lower occupation levels, dating to about 11,000 to 10,000 years ago, and corresponding to the cultural assemblage baptized "Monte Alegre" by the archaeologists, are followed by an "archaeological silence" of more than two millennia, during which it seems the cave was abandoned. A second occupation then begins, this time of Holocene age (around 7580–6625 B.P.), which corresponds to a new cultural assemblage called "Paituna." Its most striking (and most astonishing) feature is the presence of pottery: a few gray-brown sherds, sometimes soberly decorated with incisions or dots. Yet these are definitely fragments of fired-clay vessels, and they are, at present, the oldest on the American continent (Roosevelt et al. 1996: 380). Certainly, pottery of equivalent age (7080 ± 80 B.P.) had already been reported in 1991 by this same specialist in a shell mound at Taperinha, near Santarém (about 90 kilometers from Pedra Pintada and on the other bank of the Amazon) (Roosevelt et al. 1991). But this discovery had aroused some doubts at that time because of an unconvincing stratigraphic description and a somewhat "forced" use of the C14 dates and their calibration. Must we now accept the evidence and accept that pottery appeared in South America in the eighth millennium? One should recall here the reported presence of a few potsherds unearthed by N. Guidon's team near a hearth dated to 8960 ± 70 B.P. at Sitio do Meio, in Piauí (N. Guidon and A-M. Pessis 1993: 79). However, one needs to remain cautious, because the C14 dates of Pedra Pintada were obtained on bone and shell and not on charcoal; in the same level, Roosevelt herself reports a date, this time obtained by thermoluminescence, of 4710 ± 375 B.P., which would then make the Paituna pottery contemporaneous, but no more than that, with that at Valdivia in Ecuador (see chapter 6).

Away from Amazonia, other biotopes at this time underwent a relatively dense human occupation, the material evidence for which is well preserved and enables one to reconstruct—always approximately, of course—the ways of life, the subsistence, and sometimes even the simple activities of daily life. In the following paragraphs, I shall simply evoke a few examples, taken from highly contrasting environments, of a particularly successful adaptation that nevertheless did not require a farming economy or sedentism, which for the moment remain the monopoly of the Andean area.

The first is that of the groups of coastal fisher-gatherers whose settlements are found along the Atlantic littoral, from Venezuela to Tierra del

Fuego. Their most visible remains are shell mounds of various sizes—the so-called *concheros* of Venezuela, *sambaquis* of Brazil, and *conchales* in Argentina—but the most imposing, both in numbers and volume, are those of Brazil.

PEOPLE OF THE SEA

The People of the Sambaquis

One often still finds the following sentence in books or articles: around 6000 B.P. (or 5000; the date varies according to the authors), settlements of fisher-gatherers "appear" or "spring up" along the coasts. This is quite wrong because, while it is true that the oldest coastal settlements that are visible at present date back to this period, it is highly probable that even older ones preceded them and disappeared because of the postglacial rise in sea level. After a period of particularly pronounced climatic warming between about 8000 and 4000 B.P.—called the "Altithermal" or "Climatic Optimum"—during which the ocean even exceeded its present level by several meters ("Flandrian transgression"), it gradually reached its present level between 6000 and 5000 B.P. But the oldest coastal settlements were then submerged or destroyed. The only ones to survive were those located well back from the shoreline (see chapter 4).

The coast of central and southern Brazil, especially at the back of the great bays, along the low mangrove-bordered shores, or near small brackish lagoons, is peppered with hundreds of *sambaquis*. According to A. Prous (1991), to whom we owe most of the data summarized here, this word is supposedly of tupi origin (from *tamba*, shell, and *ki*, heap). They are indeed accumulations of shells erected by early populations of fisher-gatherers, but their artificial nature was only recognized very late, at the end of the nineteenth century, although several decades earlier the Danish naturalist W. P. Lund had suspected that they were humanly made (see chapter 1). Generally ovoid in plan and dome-shaped, they vary in size, but some of them are enormous: the *sambaqui* of *Garopaba media*, perhaps the biggest shell mound in the world, was destroyed recently, but originally its base measured 400 by 100 meters, with a height of more than 30 meters. On average, the mounds are from 50 to 70 meters long and about 10 meters high. A great thickness, however, is no guarantee of great antiquity or a prolonged occupation: in the *sambaqui* do Macedo, 5 meters of stratified levels accumulated in only two centuries, according to the C14 dates. Most of the *sambaquis* were erected between 5000 and 3000 B.P., although some with a submerged base have yielded dates of 7,000 (Maratúa) and even 8,000 years old (Camboinhas)—dates that are heavily disputed because of the climatic phenomena mentioned earlier.

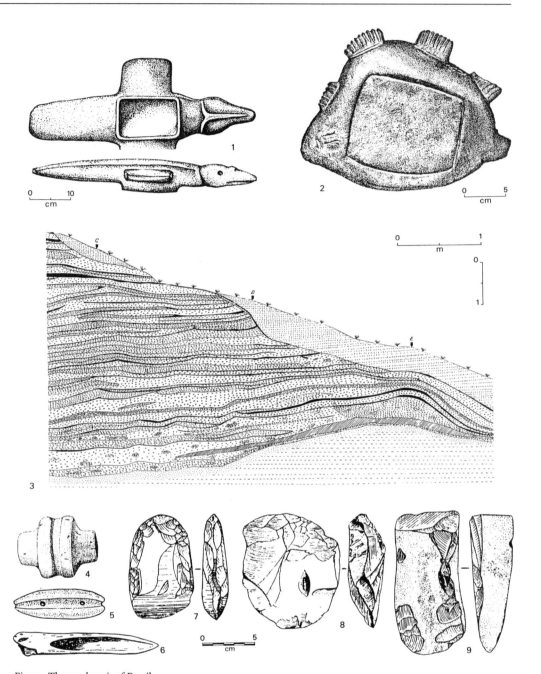

Fig. 22. The *sambaquis* of Brazil.
The *sambaquis* of the Brazilian littoral. 1, 2. Zooliths: saurian, hard rock (*sambaqui do Cubatáhozinho*) and fish, diabase (*Laguna do Imaruí*, Santa Catarina). 3. Partial section of the *sambaqui do Macedo*; the stratigraphy's complexity explains the fact that the excavation of a *sambaqui* and the distinguishing of its occupation levels are particularly difficult. 4–9. Tools recovered in *sambaquis*: geometric polished stone of unknown function (Cabeçuda) (4), net weight of polished stone (5), bone point (6), semipolished ax blade (7), unifacial sidescraper (8), worked ax blade (9) (*sambaqui do Macedo*). This rustic toolkit, in worked or polished stone and in bone, contrasts with the sophistication and aesthetic perfection of the zooliths, objects whose function remains unknown and whose styles are fairly different from one sector of the littoral to another.

Despite their numbers, few of them have yet been the subject of extensive excavations, because their abundance and their composition are also the causes of their rapid destruction: for centuries the *sambaquis* have been exploited as lime quarries, with bulldozers and mechanical shovels doing the work today. Hence Prous (ibid.: 206) remarks that the rarity of scientific work means it is still impossible, for example, to determine whether the *sambaquis* of one region—sometimes grouped in assemblages with a bigger pile in the middle of smaller ones—are contemporaneous. Yet this question is crucial if one wishes to figure out their rhythm of construction, their mode of occupation, and the size of their human populations, because these are indeed dwelling places, and not simply piles of food refuse. Buried between the successively accumulated beds of shells one finds trampled and blackened areas several meters in diameter, probably the remains of hut floors, sometimes postholes arranged in a circle, and often numerous cooking pits and hearths, doubtless with a variety of functions, such as cooking, lighting, or "ritual" (?), when the hearths were close to burials. Some fires (at Forte Marechal Luz) were even lit in whale vertebrae—the upper part of which was hollowed out and still contained charcoal fragments.

What did the builder-occupants of the *sambaquis* live on? I have just mentioned the presence of whale vertebrae, but it is obvious that such prey, made up of individuals who accidentally became beached, must have been exceptional. Other smaller sea mammals, seals and dolphins, were sometimes caught, too. Finally, fishing certainly constituted a preferred source of food, although fish bones are often difficult to see in the midst of the mass of shells. Prous cites the example of one of the rare *sambaquis* to have undergone a detailed study. At Piaçagüera, 120,279 otoliths (a small bone of the inner ear of fishes, which, together with teeth, constitutes one of the main elements for species identification) were recovered, representing a minimum of 20,046 teleosts and a few selachians—rays and even the great white shark (*Carcharodon carcharias*), which suffices to demonstrate the sophistication and the efficacy of the fishing implements and techniques. But obviously it is the volume of shells—of various species but dominated by mangrove oysters, clams, or mussels, depending on their location in relation to the shore—that is the most striking, though this gives an impression that is out of all proportion to their real importance in the diet. In particular, terrestrial hunting was also carried out, and its importance is doubtless undervalued, such is the space occupied by the shells. Moreover, the remains of the terrestrial fauna—bones of large rodents, reptiles, birds, and a few cervids—are relatively rare, as are projectile points. Finally, it is impossible to evaluate the dietary contribution of plant foods, since their remains have generally disappeared, except when carbonized remains have survived, especially those of numerous palm nuts. As for the question of whether the people of the *sambaquis* practiced some kind of agriculture, the answer remains negative for the moment although, according to Prous (ibid.: 256), one cannot rule out the possibility of traces of this being unearthed one day.

With the exception of wood, bark, and plant fibers, all raw materials have survived well in the midst of the shells, so it has been possible to reconstitute the rich and varied panoply of objects and implements (fig. 22). Stone objects dominate, sometimes worked (small raw quartz flakes, ax blades crudely shaped by percussion) but mostly pecked and polished. Among the latter, some are obviously tools, like axes, net weights, and large cobbles with a central cupule, known as *quebracôco* (for opening palm nuts?); but others remain more mysterious, such as the geometrically shaped pieces that are very carefully polished and which often resemble tops or cogwheels, and the famous "zooliths," highly stylized animal sculptures that usually have a central cavity, like a shallow dish, and which differ in type from region to region (fig. 22). These latter objects are so aesthetically successful that, until the 1930s, people refused to believe that their creators were the "primitive" inhabitants of the Brazilian littoral and preferred to see their origin in the Andes. According to Prous, the production of some zooliths doubtless required more than 200 hours, and it is certain that such objects must have played a particular role in the cultural world. However, it has not yet been possible to ascribe any meaning or function to them.

Apart from stone, shell and bone were valued raw materials, easy to work and inexhaustible. Spear points, awls, needles, and hooks made of bones of mammals, birds, or fish; burins and spatulas made of incisors of large rodents; knives, scrapers, and kinds of saws in shells of bivalve mollusks or gastropods; all these types of objects have been found in innumerable quantities in the *sambaquis*. The inhabitants also made vessels or braziers by hollowing out whale vertebrae, small vases out of tympanic bones, and big shovels out of shoulder blades. As for the objects of wood or fiber that have now disappeared, one can sometimes infer their existence: tools of stone or bone that still bear traces of resin imply the existence of handles; similarly, the presence of *sambaquis* on islands that have always been separated from the continent by several kilometers implies the existence of wooden dugouts or bark canoes.

Using and combining all the information provided by the excavations and various analyses that have been carried out, Prous has re-created daily life on the Brazilian coast:

> Hugging the beaches, the dugout boats penetrate the bay bound by rocky elevations and dotted with islets. After reconnoitering the sector and collecting green cobbles on the beach, the arrivals reached the mouth of one of the numerous little rivers flowing down from the mountain. . . . The boats went upstream, struggling against the current, until they reached a place where there was freshwater at low tide. A few people cautiously set foot in the mangrove, seeking an elevated dry spot: an ancient sandy beach or, even better, a rocky outcrop that would constitute solid ground and provide a base in which to polish the axe blades made in the green rocks

from the beach. They found the ideal spot, close to the mangrove that would provide fuel and oysters that were easy to open, near drinkable water, and also close to the free waters of the bay, so full of fish. They all disembarked: small, robust individuals, a few dozen in total, doubtless an exogamous clan, which explains the variety of their physiognomies. The men erected the low, oval huts, measuring up to six meters in diameter, each of them housing a nuclear family. There then began the routine of the new settlement: the children jumped in the mangrove and brought back crustaceans, oysters, curious "fruits" from the red trees; the women did the cooking, filled basketwork vessels with water, or took one of their innumerable baths. "Watch out, children, don't tread on the tail of the little jacarés (caymans)!" While this is going on, the men dive into the bay to collect mollusks on the rocks, and to spear the fish. On returning, they rest for a moment, but continue to take care of their tools: one of them polishes the wood of his bow with a shell, another sharpens the edge of his axe by the water. From time to time, a boat full of adolescents goes upstream to the place where the sea no longer helps them to work the oars. Here they find the mysterious, dense forest where monkeys scream, and where the youngsters hope to kill a wild pig or an enormous tapir. And what if a jaguar were to appear? They don't dwell on this idea. (ibid.: 263–64)

And life goes on in this way, described in a very lively way, from the capture of a school of fish moving upstream in the winter to the butchering of a whale that has been beached (a stroke of luck, because in winter fish become rarer); then the return of summer, the clouds of mosquitoes that plague them, the palm nuts that replace shellfish for meals, after a fashion. Let's hope the cool winter winds return quickly! Finally, as time goes by and oysters become rarer, the people are forced to go farther and farther to seek other species that are harder to collect. So the group splits up, each part settling in a new place, often on a *sambaqui* that has been abandoned by its occupants and which constitutes an ideal spot, nice and dry, elevated and well ventilated, where the mosquitoes will be less virulent.

The *sambaquis* were temporary habitations that were reutilized many times; they were also places of burial. All those that have been studied contained several skeletons buried in pits dug into the mass of shells from the habitation floors. The skeletons are most often in a fetal position, sometimes semiflexed and more rarely completely extended. In the State of Santa Catarina, the pits are sometimes coated with a layer of clay, hardened by fire, and painted red. In other regions, they are delineated by a border of stones, or the body itself is covered with blocks or a slab or protected by whale bones. Grave goods consist of objects linked to diet and the normal equipment of the occupants of the *sambaqui* at this time: food (different shellfish from those in the mass in which the pit was dug, crustacean claws, semicarbonized whale bones); various implements (polished stone axes, tools made of teeth or bone); jewelry made of shells, sharks' teeth, or whale bone; balls of red ocher; and sometimes "zooliths."

In terms of race, the occupants of the *sambaquis* do not constitute a homogeneous group, although some scholars have spoken of a "*sambaqui* race." The only constant features anthropologists have observed on the skeletons (which are usually in a bad state of preservation) are robusticity (greater than that of the people of Lagoa Santa), a relatively small size, a high skull with a receding forehead, and a pronounced sexual dimorphism.

Conchales of the Extreme South and Concheros of the Caribbean Area

Between Winds and Storms in the Magellanic Waters

Unlike the Brazilian *sambaquis,* the hundreds of conchales that are strung out along the coasts of Patagonia—with particular concentrations on both shores of the Magellan Straits and, on the Pacific side, from the island of Chiloe to the Cape Horn archipelago—attracted the attention of archaeologists quite late. Since they are far less spectacular in size and do not constitute an economically exploitable resource (unlike the *sambaquis*), any interest they might have aroused was smothered by the attention being given to the last aboriginal groups that inhabited these regions. Fernández (1982: 107) even observes that it seems to have required the total disappearance of the natives, or their cultural and biological absorption, for this interest finally to be aroused. The first, albeit succinct, observations concerned the Fuegian shell mounds and were made in 1883 by the Italian geologist Domenico Lovisato. They were not to be followed by any truly scientific study until the 1920s, with the research by Lothrop (1928) and Vignati (1926, 1927). But it was Bird's excavations that really began archaeology in Tierra del Fuego. When, in 1932–33, he applied a stratigraphic method that was new and sank his first test pits into the conchales of the island of Navarino, Bird had just completed five years of excavating the camps of fisher-gatherers in northern Chile, which had yielded an incomparable mass of comparative data. Next, from December 1934 until June 1935, accompanied by his wife, Margaret, on the *Hesperus,* a small boat, he carried out research in the Magellan channels, from the island of Chiloe to that of Navarino—which, in view of the region's extreme topographic complexity and the meanders of the route, represents a navigation of almost 2,000 kilometers. As Ortiz Troncoso has stressed, "This exploration was, from every viewpoint, one of the riskiest but also one of the most fruitful in the entire history of South American archaeology" (1985: 21).

At the end of his excavations on Navarino, Bird distinguished two different modes of settlement and of technological culture, which seemed to correspond to two successive cultural facies. During the first, known as the "Shell-knife culture," the human groups along the coast erected oval huts with two

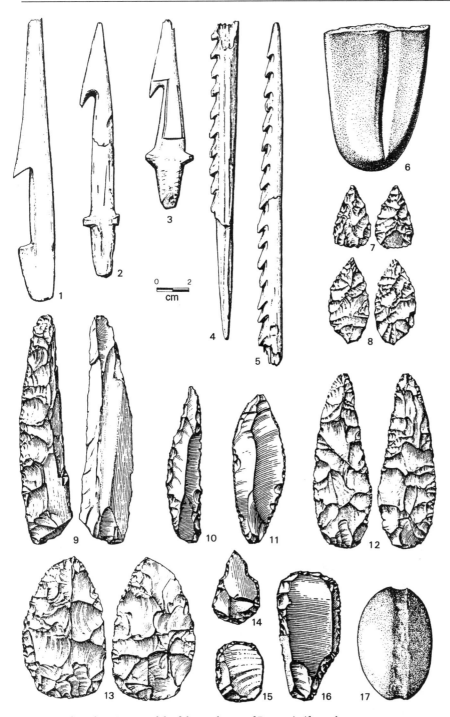

Fig. 23. Technical equipment of the fisher-gatherers of Patagonia (from about 4000 to 2500 B.C.). 1–5. Implements of whale bone: harpoon heads with a single barb and a simple tenon (1), double tenon (2), and sometimes with incised decoration (3), and with multiple barbs (4, proximal fragment , 5, distal fragment). 6. Sharpener-cobble (for sharpening bone points?). 7–17. Obsidian tools: bifacial points (7, 8), knife made on a rod of obsidian (9), unifacial points (10, 11), bifaces (12, 13), scrapers (14–16), grooved sandstone cobble (net-weight?) (17).

entrances. Their technical equipment was extremely simple, consisting of fairly crude stone tools worked by percussion and harpoons with a detachable, single-barbed bone head. But the implement that was apparently the most used, and also the easiest to make, was a knife made from a mussel shell (in these regions, mussels attain or exceed a length of 20 centimeters), from which Bird derived the name he gave to this cultural phase. Their food refuse, mostly made up of shells, was thrown outside through one or other of the openings in the "house." The second cultural facies, called the "Pit-house culture," was characterized by circular dwellings with a single entrance and with a floor that was dug down a few dozen centimeters (Bird thought this was to give the superstructure better support and protection from the wind). The refuse was now tossed out of the single opening. Their technical equipment was more developed, the stone tools (including knives and bifacial projectile points with pressure retouch) were more carefully worked, and the bone harpoon-heads were more elaborate (with multiple barbs). These cultural facies could easily be differentiated by the shape of the shell mounds that gradually accumulated outside, as a double semicircular heap in the first case and a simple mound in the second. However, a short while later, Menghin (1956) undertook some new research in the region of the Beagle Channel and, at this time, cast some doubt on the existence of the "pit-houses"—in his view, the impression of a hollowed-out dwelling was simply due to a raising of the surrounding ground through the peripheral accumulation of refuse.

At the time when he carried out his pioneering research, Bird estimated the age of the oldest archaeological deposits to be a minimum of 1,800 years. No absolute dating method was available in this period, but one should point out that, at the time of his expeditions, interest in "Early Man" had just started to arise in North America, following the discoveries at Folsom (1926) and then Clovis (1935) (see chapter 2). About 15 years later, the invention of the C14 dating method showed that, in reality, his sites were far earlier. Moreover, the prehistoric sites corresponding to the first facies distinguished by Bird, the "Shell-knife culture," continued until the beginning of our own era. The "Pit-house culture" (and Menghin was right, they are not houses) represents only the transitional period between the first culture and that of the historical Yaghans (or Yámanas) (see chapter 7).

The oldest *conchales* have been dated to about 6000 B.P., the explanation for which is more or less the same as that invoked for the Brazilian *sambaquis*: the postglacial rise in sea level. Except that, in these southern regions, which for thousands of years were under the pressure of millions of tons of ice, the slow submersion of the littoral was compensated in part by a rise in the earth's crust (isostasy) following the retreat of the ice and the removal of its weight. This is why sites that were formerly located at the water's edge are today higher up, whereas they should—as in Brazil—now be submerged.

In the labyrinth of Chile's Magellanic archipelagos, pounded by southern storms and drenched with rain, the *conchales* were erected by people who had to move around in boats (hence their name, Canoeros peoples), because the shape and nature of the coast—sheer reliefs plunging perpendicularly into the sea, covered by a hyper-humid and impenetrable southern forest, and numerous glaciers flowing into the ocean—prevent any travel by foot along the shore. Moreover, as Laming-Emperaire remarked (1972), the traces of these settlements are not distributed randomly: they occur either on the continental littoral or on the western edge of the archipelagos, thus leaving a broad median band practically empty (the maritime route that is used by ships today). They are numerous on both banks of the Magellan Straits and those of the Beagle Channel and also occur, albeit increasingly rarely, as far as the southern islands. A thin occupation layer unearthed by D. Legoupil on Herschel Island (close to Hornos Island, the rocky extremity of which constitutes the famous Cape Horn) is the southernmost archaeological site known today on the American continent (Legoupil 1993–94). Although this occupation is very recent (680 ± 60 B.P.), that of the site of Grandi I, discovered on the south coast of Navarino Island, north of the Cape Horn archipelago, dates to 6160 ± 110 B.P. (ibid.). It thus seems clear that the Canoeros occupied all the islands within sight very early—for example, the Isla de los Estados (today on Argentine territory, 31 kilometers off Tierra del Fuego)—but they never reached the Diego Ramirez islands (Chilean territory, 110 kilometers off Cape Horn) (Ortiz-Troncoso 1989: 372). Nevertheless, this demonstrates an astonishing capacity for navigation in these waters that are reputed to be among the most dangerous in the world.

This distribution of the *conchales* and their age have led archaeologists to wonder which peoples (who clearly adapted very quickly—and perfectly—to the maritime environment) had erected them and what was their origin. Several hypotheses have been put forward. According to the first, a territorial expansion by the hunters who then occupied the interior of the lands of Patagonia and Tierra del Fuego gradually pushed back the populations with a lower technological level ("backward" in a sense) until their backs were against the shore. This hypothesis, however, does not tally with the high quality and great specialization of the implements that have been recovered from several sites. According to another hypothesis, there were one or more slow coastal migrations of already well-specialized maritime populations, which had come down from the north (but from where?) along the Pacific coast. Some archaeologists have gone so far as to attribute a North American origin to them, and Menghin, a great supporter of diffusionism, even saw in them the manifestation of a "cultural circle of Eurasian origin." According to a third, more subtle hypothesis, it was simply an adaptation to coastal conditions by populations that had hitherto been exclusively terrestrial (Orquera and Piana 1986–87). For the moment, it is this third hypothesis that seems to have won the support of archaeologists, although a number of points still remain obscure. It is true that almost all the coastal sites discovered so far are located in regions where it was possible at the time to travel between the steppes of the interior and the littoral; hence they are present and even numerous in the south of continental Patagonia, where the barrier of the Andes has almost disappeared. As D. Legoupil has observed, no site earlier than the beginning of our era has yet been discovered in the central zone of the archipelagos (approximately between Wellington Island and the Sea of Skyring), which at the time was still separated from the great continental expanses by the mass of the residual continental glacier of Patagonia (Legoupil and Fontugne 1997: 85). Conversely, it is undeniable that the occupants of the *conchales* used technological equipment that was both sophisticated and original—a highly developed bone industry, implements of pecked and polished stone—having no connection with that of the contemporaneous terrestrial hunters. Finally, as has already been mentioned, they had a mastery of the techniques of navigation that points to long experience. As a matter of fact, the question is not yet settled and research continues.

Let me try to summarize the main stages and principal characteristics of this occupation of the southern coasts from the sixth millennium B.C. onward.

The very first coastal traces detected are in fact older (around 7000 B.P. for the "Componente 1" of the site of Túnel I and layer D of Ponsonby) (Orquera and Piana 1986–87; Legoupil and Fontugne 1997) but doubtless correspond to probably brief incursions by terrestrial hunters who had nothing to do with the maritime adaptations that were to follow. These first occupations have more in common with the earlier ones unearthed in continental Patagonia and in Tierra del Fuego (Marazzi, Tres Arroyos—see chapter 3). Conversely, several slightly more recent sites (6500–5500 B.P.) have yielded very coherent data that, this time, certainly point to an adaptation to littoral life based on an intensive exploitation of maritime resources. Excavated sites are not very numerous (contrary to the Brazilian *sambaquis*), so they can almost all be mentioned here. They can be grouped into two assemblages: on the western side (Chilean archipelagos and western part of the Magellan Straits), Englefield 1 and Bahía Colorada (Emperaire and Laming 1961; Legoupil 1997), and Punta Santa Ana and Bahía Buena (Ortiz-Troncoso 1979) constitute a first assemblage that Legoupil proposes to include within an "Englefield culture" (between c. 6700 and 5100 B.P.) in order to respect the priority of the discoveries and despite the controversies that have legitimately arisen by the first dates obtained for this site.[1] It is characterized by the presence of a superb industry made of obsidian, whose products—bifaces, triangular and lanceolate bifacial points, knives, and scrapers—demonstrate perfect mastery of work involving pressure retouch. It is also distinguished by very elaborate and highly characteristic bone implements (including harpoon heads with a single barb and a cruciform base, barbed points and spatulas, retouchers, and awls), all made with bones of marine mammals (fig. 23). The inhabitants seem to have practiced intensive hunting of small seals or "osos marinos" (*Arctocephalus australis*), since fishing and shellfish collecting are relatively poorly represented. The second assemblage corresponds to

[1]Discovered and excavated by J. Emperaire in 1952, the Englefield shell mound, on the shore of the Otway Sea, had first yielded two C14 dates of surprising antiquity, 9248 ± 1500 and 8456 ± 1500 B.P., which placed it among the oldest sites known in Patagonia, including continental Patagonia. It was therefore considered a reference site, testifying to the antiquity of the maritime peopling of the southern regions, and it is still cited as such in numerous books. However, "we were then [1958] in the infancy of C14 and merely the margin of error of 3,000 years gives one some idea of the reliability of the dates put forward at this time" (Legoupil 1997). In 1986, a sample taken by Legoupil in an unexcavated part of the site yielded the far more plausible date of 6100 ± 110 B.P., which is perfectly consistent with those obtained for the other sites containing similar cultural material.

the sites of Túnel I ("Componente 2") and Lancha Packewaia (Orquera et al. 1977), both located on the south coast of Tierra del Fuego on the edge of the Beagle Channel, far to the east of the preceding sites. Their ages are close to, although slightly younger than, those of the first assemblage (between c. 6200 and 4300 B.P.), and the way of life and technical equipment are by and large comparable. However, fine pieces of obsidian are rare on the Beagle coast and were doubtless obtained through trading.

One still needs to explain why hitherto terrestrial populations (hunters) were led to settle along the coasts. The principal reason was doubtless climatic in nature: between 8500 and 6000 B.P., because of a rise in humidity (leading to a climate that was even more humid than today's—although more than 3 meters of rain still fall every year in these regions!—but no doubt also a bit warmer), the forest invaded the sectors that had hitherto been occupied by a herbaceous steppe that was highly favorable to herds of herbivores (Markgraf in Bird 1988). It is probable that, as the guanaco population became rarer, the importance of terrestrial hunting was reduced, leading to an increasingly specialized exploitation of the littoral.

The Fisher-Gatherers of the Caribbean Littoral

At the other end of South America, the low coasts of the continental Caribbean area that border the Atlantic, often covered with an inextricable jungle of mangroves, are likewise peppered with numerous shell mounds; but these, for the most part, are younger than their southern counterparts. In Colombia, where the oldest examples date to 4500–4300 B.P., their most remarkable characteristic is that none of them reflect a specifically maritime adaptation. On the contrary, they appear to correspond to a uniquely seasonal exploitation of marine resources on the part of populations that were probably based in the interior of the country, although no convincing evidence of them has yet been discovered. Finally, even more astonishing is the fact that, from the start of their accumulation, these Colombian mounds contain pottery, which at this time was still absent from the whole of the continent, except for the Amazonian region of Santarém. This is why I prefer to leave its study until the next chapter. Perhaps older coastal settlements have been submerged, since the evolution of sea level (which, moreover, is still poorly known) differed from region to region.

On the other hand, the northeast coast of Venezuela offers abundant evidence of a littoral occupation by fisher-gatherers, who did not have pottery, contemporaneous with that of the Brazilian, Argentine, and Chilean coasts. The oldest are found on the south coast of the Paria peninsula, where the *concheros* of Ño Carlos and Guayana (c. 6000–5000 B.P.), excavated by M. Sanoja and today located 7 or 8 meters above the present sea level and about 10 kilometers inland—that is, at this period, right on the shore—have yielded a lithic industry of somewhat crude appearance, mostly made up of flakes, clumsily retouched into knives or scrapers, and of worked cobbles (implements used for cutting wood?). It is probable that this equipment was completed with a toolkit of wood, including lances or javelins, indispensable for hunting on sea or land. As in the Brazilian *sambaquis,* the marine fauna, from mangroves or open water—various mollusks and crustaceans, rays, *róbalos* or sea bass, sharks, small cetaceans—dominates, but one also finds (especially in the oldest layers) a few cervid bones, proving that terrestrial hunting was also sometimes practiced. As in Brazil, postholes detected in the fill of the mounds suggest the existence of windbreaks if not of true huts. Conversely, hearths are rare or even, as in the case of Ño Carlos, curiously absent. Finally, as in Brazil, the use of boats seems extremely probable, whether dugouts or rafts (Sanoja 1979).

TERRESTRIAL HUNTERS

Inland, whether on the northern margins of the Andes (highlands of Ecuador and Colombia) or the arid Nordeste and central plateau or Planalto of Brazil, the pampas of Uruguay and Argentina or the steppes of continental Patagonia, no drastic change can be seen between the ways of life described for the preceding period (12,000–8000 B.P.) and those of the period covered in this chapter. The same climatic modifications—a warming and a rise in humidity—certainly affected the environment after 8000 B.P., but where the behavior of the human groups is concerned, the changes do not seem to have had such directly discernible repercussions as in the littoral regions. At most, one can note the growing number of known sites, a probable sign of a population increase.

Interior Plains and Plateaus of Brazil

Several cultural facies or, as one prefers to call them in Brazil, "traditions," coexist here or follow one another at this time. As Prous has stressed (1991: 145), archaeologists distinguish them primarily in terms of their technological equipment—in particular, their panoply of lithic tools—but sometimes also (though more rarely) according to the natural environments they occupied and exploited. This makes their definition all the more precarious and their territorial demarcation often imprecise. Certain traditions coexisted, occupying distinct but neighboring territories; others seem to have followed one another in the same environment. The still excessively common use of "type fossils" (mostly a type of stone tool) does not help to shed light on things insofar as it highlights a single element and thus tends to minimize the importance of the other components of a given cultural assemblage, such as the location and organization of the dwelling, and the means of subsistence.

Some of the sites in caves and shelters that were previously occupied (see chapter 3) continued to be used, although less intensively than in the preceding period, perhaps because of the climatic modifications. Hence, in an increasingly arid Nordeste, the shelters of Toca do Bojo (7180 ± 90 B.P.) and Toca da Boa Vista (7730 ± 140 B.P.), in Piauí, underwent a notable decrease in their frequentation, along with a discernible diminution in the quality of their worked lithic toolkits. The fine, carefully retouched bifacial tools, especially projectile points, became rarer, replaced by cruder (and also more rapidly made) equipment dominated by flakes, with or without retouch. Moreover, open-air settlements multiplied. One finds a similar picture in Goías, where the Itaparica cultural tradition continues, as defined by Schmitz; but its Serranópolis phase (between 9000 and 4000 B.P.) (Schmitz et al. 1981) reflects the same changes in a general way: the fine toolkit on retouched flakes of the preceding Paranaiba phase (11,000–9000 B.P.—see chapter 3) gives way to an industry of irregular flakes with scarcely any retouch. Finally, one finds much the same in Minas Gerais. The sites around Lagoa Santa and in the Serra do Cipo continue to be frequented, but their lithic toolkits likewise undergo a diminution in quality: the bifacial points become rare, the practice of pressure retouch seems to have been abandoned, and most of the "tools" are actually small, raw flakes. Conversely, many implements—kinds of planes and gouges—are henceforth made from the shells of the big terrestrial or aquatic mollusks that also represent a considerable part of the diet. In any case, agriculture does not seem to have been practiced anywhere.

The South of Brazil: Umbú Hunters and Humaitá Fisher-Gatherers

In the same period, on the southern plateaus of Brazil, two "distinct traditions" have been identified: the "Umbú" hunters occupied the open savannas, rich in game, where they set up temporary open-air camps but also used rockshelters like that of Cerrito Dalpiaz (levels I and II: 5950 B.P.) always for short-term but repeated sojourns; the "Humaitá" fisher-gatherers settled on the banks of the tributaries of the Paraná (sites of Porto Gômes, José Vieira, and Alfredo Wagner). The former possessed lithic equipment made of very fine-grained siliceous rocks—flint, chalcedony, agate—which were magnificently suited to working and pressure retouch; the latter used rocks that were less easy to work—basalt, quartzite—but much more resistant. The tools of the former were very finely shaped and in particular comprise beautiful bifacial projectile points, either leaf-shaped or stemmed (the latter perhaps a little later?); big, thin, leaf-shaped knives, so fine that Prous (1986: 259) even compares them to the "laurel leaf" points of the French Solutrean (although obviously there is no cultural correspondence between the two, let alone any chronological link); and various carefully retouched flake tools (scrapers, awls). The tools of the latter group are large and robust but shaped rapidly with little care: choppers, picks with a trihedral section, but above all a characteristic object, a kind of big curved pick with a trihedral or square section, 20 to 40 centimeters long, called a "biface-boomerang" (fig. 24). These very different arrays of tools point to ways of life that

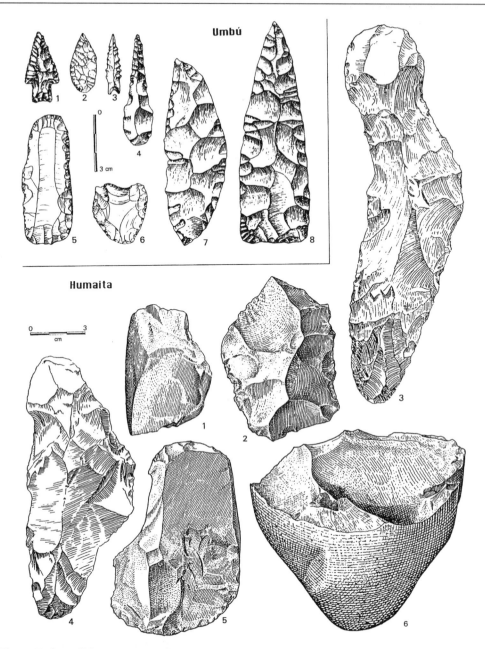

Fig. 24. Umbú tradition. Humaita tradition.
Characteristic tools of the Umbú and Humaita traditions (southern Brazil, Argentina, Uruguay). Umbú tradition: 1–3. Bifacial points of various kinds. 4. Awl. 5, 6. Scrapers. 7. Knife. 8. Big bifacial point. Humaita and Altoparanaense traditions: 1, 2. Flake and bifacial implement (José Vieira, Brazil). 3. Biface-boomerang (Yaguarazapá, Paraguay). 4. Big pick (Eldorado, Argentina). 5, 6. Scraper and chopper. (José Vieira, Brazil)

were likewise very dissimilar. The Umbú groups—which were small, judging by the size of their sites and the density of the remains—practiced terrestrial hunting requiring great mobility (cervids, peccaries, tapirs, armadillos) but also gathered freshwater mollusks, big terrestrial snails (with shells of more than 12 centimeters), and palm nuts. The Humaitá populations fished in the nearby water-courses but especially exploited edible plant species, doubtless digging up roots and tubers with their biface-boomerangs.

Although the excavation of some sites has suggested that the Umbú tradition is earlier than the Humaitá tradition (at the open-air site of Porto Gômes, the two levels were found superimposed in this order), they seem to have coexisted in different environments. Finally, the tradition of the Humaitá fisher-gatherers is directly prolonged and even identified with the culture known as Altoparanaense, which is still called the Itaqui complex or Cuaraimense, defined in Uruguay and in northeast Argentina.[2]

The few sites, "traditions," or cultural facies that have briefly been evoked here do not represent—far from it!—the totality of cultural manifestations of the period that have been identified in Brazil. They merely comprise some examples, but the reader will understand that, within the framework of this book, it is out of the question to describe the innumerable "phases" or "complexes" that have been described (often in a very unequal way) by Brazilian archaeologists, who are extremely active.

Guanaco Hunters of the Southern Steppes

In the immense expanses that had been occupied for almost four millennia by populations of hunters (see chapter 3), life continued without any significant changes—at least in the eyes of the archaeologist, who cannot see, and doubtless never will be able to see, the social and spiritual world—other than those that are discernible in the diversification of technological equipment and the manufacture of toolkits. Moreover, such changes are quite minor, seen against the framework of an immutable subsistence economy based exclusively on hunting: contrary to the other inner regions of South America, whether the highlands on the margins of the Andes or the plateaus of the Brazilian interior, the great prairies of the Uruguayan and Argentine pampa (which are extended southward by the semiarid steppes of Patagonia) offer virtually no plant resources that could constitute a real contribution to the diet.

Consequently, it is hardly surprising that no innovations of any importance, except for those of a technological kind, can be observed during the period 8000–4000 B.P., which corresponds approximately to the Magellan III (c. 8000–6500 B.P.) and Magellan IV (c. 6500–3500 B.P.) phases in Bird's sequence. It is in central Patagonia that this progress was the most remarkable: the so-called Casapedrense tradition (after the eponymous site of Casa de Piedra), which occurs around 7300 B.P. in the province of Santa Cruz, is characterized by intensive and exceptional use of blade debitage, producing

[2]This leads to the following concerns: when will archaeologists ever start to place emphasis on great similarities rather than on small differences? When will they try to develop a unified terminology and systematically carry out comparative observations? This might be the best way to highlight the lines of force, the constants or the true differences, among cultural assemblages, instead of striving to attach their name—or that of the region or site they have just studied—to the slightest manifestation of past human activity.

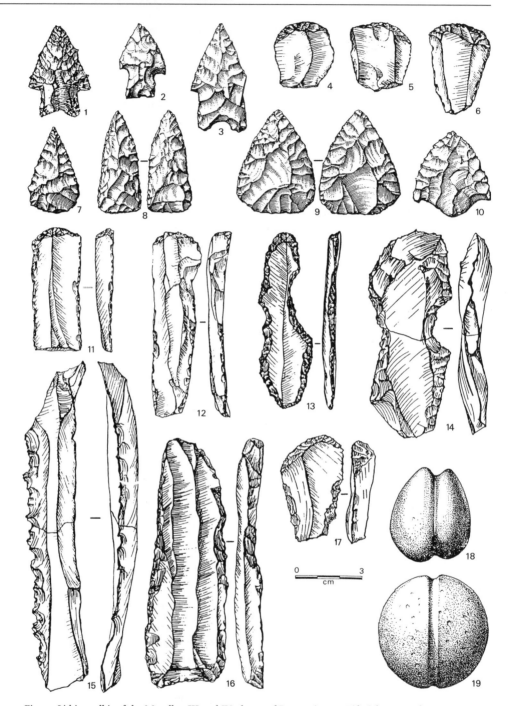

Fig. 25. Lithic toolkit of the Magellan III and IV phases of Patagonia. 1–3. Bifacial stemmed points (Fell's Cave, Magellan IV phase). 4–6. Scrapers (Los Toldos, Patagoniense levels, Magellan IV phase). 7–10. Subtriangular bifacial points (Fell's Cave, Magellan III phase). 11, 12. Scrapers on blades. 13, 14. Strangled blades. 15. Denticulate blade. 16. Blade knife. 17. Scraper (Los Toldos, Casapedrense levels, Magellan III phase). 18, 19. Grooved bolas (Marazzi shelter, middle levels, Magellan IV phase).

very well made elongated tools (particularly blade scrapers and "strangled blades" that recall morphologically comparable pieces in the European Aurignacian) (fig. 25). This is one of the very few blade industries known in South America, and indeed in the entire hemisphere apart from Mexico. The practice of applying marginal and unifacial retouch to flakes and blades, producing quantities of implements suited to cutting or scraping, replaced the bifacial working of the Toldense tradition (see chapter 3), while projectile points, which had been abundant until now, are completely absent. Their disappearance is all the more curious because the faunal remains in the sites are almost entirely guanaco bones, an animal that seems to have been virtually the only one hunted at this time.[3] The only projectile weapons of the Casapedrense tradition are stone bolas, certainly an effective weapon, but the small number of known specimens does not explain the extraordinary quantity of guanacos killed. The Casapedrense tradition, which Orquera (1987) calls enigmatic for this reason and others, is represented in several sites of the province of Santa Cruz: first at Los Toldos, where Menghin identified it for the first time in 1952 and where, after an archaeological silence of one and a half millennia (abandonment of the cave?), it succeeds the Toldense; in the valley of the Río Pinturas—Cueva Grande del Arroyo Feo—where it is partially identified with the regional Río Pinturas II complex;[4] finally, a little farther south, at La Martita, which is its southernmost expression (Aguerre 1981–82, 1987).

In the region of the Magellan Straits, the typical blade industry of the Casapedrense is absent. For example, in Fell's Cave, which had already been occupied for a long time (see chapter 3), the levels dated to between c. 8400 and 6400 B.P. are characterized by the presence of bifacial projectile points which, contrary to earlier types, now possess barbs and a broad bifid stem (fig. 25). Guanaco remains dominate the fauna, but, unlike those in the Casapedrense levels, they are associated with a not inconsiderable quantity of remains of birds (ñandú), fox, and small rodents. Finally, in Tierra del Fuego, the great erratic block of Marazzi, not far from the shore of Bahía Inútil, continues to shelter—very sporadically and for apparently very short-term stops—guanaco hunters who nevertheless did not spurn the resources offered occasionally by the nearby beaches: from time to time a seal, shellfish, or the body of a beached whale (Laming-Emperaire et al. 1972). Sometimes these passing guests even buried one of their dead here: the body of an adult had been laid on the ground, flexed and probably tied up, then burned on the spot. This burial by cremation, dating back to at least 5600 B.P. (it rested on a layer dating to 5570 ± 400 B.P.), recalls those discovered by Bird in the little cave that bears his name, very close to Fell's Cave.

"The Probable Reasons for the Absence of a System"

Most of the cultural facies that I have just briefly described, whether terrestrial or coastal occupations, were to last a long time without undergoing the

[3]With regard to this subject, A. Cardich has put forward a stimulating but as yet unconfirmed hypothesis: following new excavations at Los Toldos, he suggests that the "Casapedrense" may correspond to a period of experimentation with guanaco herding, an experiment that, unlike analogous processes observed in the central Andes of Peru, subsequently came to nothing.

[4]Contrary to the sequence observed in the cave of Los Toldos, where they follow one another, the "Toldense" and "Casapedrense" traditions seem to have coexisted within the regional "Rio Pinturas II" complex: contemporaneous levels unearthed in the famous Cueva de las Manos and in the Cueva Grande del Arroyo Feo have yielded, in the former, a "Toldense"-type industry (with projectile points) and, in the latter, a "Casapedrense"-type industry (blade industry without projectile points). Given our present state of knowledge, as Orquera (1987: 40) has stressed, the idea of a functional complementarity of the sites to explain the disparity in lithic toolkits remains difficult to defend.

radical changes that the central Andean area experienced earlier and would continue to experience (see chapters 6 and 7). Why is there this astonishing timelessness of the hunter-gatherer cultures, sometimes (but not always) also horticulturalist, whereas in many cases nothing in the climatic conditions, the natural environment, and the accessible resources seems to have prevented an evolution taking place that was analogous to and contemporaneous with that of the Andean area?

The title of this section, with its quotation marks, has been purposely borrowed from Alain Testart, author of a brilliant essay on hunter-gatherers. In his view, the evolution of the hunter-gatherer peoples toward sedentism was based above all on their capacity for stockpiling food resources: "What enables the cereal-grower to remain sedentary when he is living on a highly seasonal plant is that, after the harvest, he stockpiles the crop which will allow him to meet his dietary needs for the rest of the year. The gatherer of wild cereals merely has to do the same to remove the need for nomadism . . . nomadism is linked to the absence of storage by a reciprocal causality" (1982: 25). And a bit later he writes, "sedentism is possible when a society, exploiting seasonal food resources that are present in sufficient abundance to constitute the staple food, harvests them en masse and stores them on a large scale" (ibid.: 26). This opinion is immediately qualified by the following observation: "hunter-gatherers can be sedentary when the territory exploited from a site contains a wide variety of exploitable biotic resources according to an annual calendar that includes few gaps" (ibid.: 28). That is, without it being necessary to constitute reserves.

But what have we observed in South America? On the portion of arid or desert coast that borders the Pacific, populations from southern Ecuador to northern Chile either became sedentary very early or the produce from fishing was harvested in massive quantities and stored in one form or another (salted, dried, reduced to flour), or the very abundance of resources taken from nearby terrestrial biotopes, which were not subject to an annual calendar and were complemented by other animal and plant resources, was so great that an already quite large population had no need to move in the course of the annual cycle (see chapter 4). But how can one explain the astonishing stability of the hunting cultures of the tropical eastern South America? Why were settlements ephemeral here, when in the Andes there were permanent and stable villages for centuries? Why were the populations of the tropical lowlands of the east not the first—instead of the Andean populations—to cultivate beans, pimentos, and gourds, when these plants were growing wild before their very eyes, so that domestication and cultivation were thus (theoretically) possible, as was storage, if one remembers what Testart considered to be the determining parameter?

The stability of the material cultures of the extreme south, whether the fisher-gatherers of the Magellanic archipelagos or the terrestrial hunters of continental Patagonia, is perhaps (a little) easier to explain. Where the former are concerned, Legoupil notes: "But it is doubtless permanence—not to say stagnation—that represents the most striking feature of this maritime culture of Patagonia. . . . An excellent balance had already been achieved in the maritime adaptation of the sixth millennium B.P., and environmental pressures were not sufficiently strong to endanger this. It is also obvious that the region's powerful ecological determinism played a decisive role in this process. But beyond this observation, one still needs to determine the real laws that governed this evolution, or rather this nonevolution, while in other parts of the South American continent some highly developed cultures were bursting forth" (1997: 219). One certainly wonders why, despite their own apparently excellent equilibrium, the populations of the Patagonian steppes did not—like their contemporaries in the Cordillera—succeed in domesticating the guanaco, if indeed they even tried (see note 19).

In fact, I can offer no answers to these questions—just two remarks. First, it is always much easier to explain a presence than an absence. Why did something exist? One can always manage to demonstrate this through its antecedents and justify it by what followed. But why did something not exist? The archaeologist may seek the reason in environmental conditions or the level of material culture, but the reason could also—or exclusively—have been social or even religious, domains on which we have little hold. Moreover—and this is a truism—the explanatory hypotheses put forward (or the admissions of ignorance) always depend directly on the state of the known archaeological record and are thus likely to be changed or corrected at any time by new discoveries. Who knows? Perhaps tomorrow we shall discover remains of permanent villages and indisputable evidence for agricultural practices on the banks of the Paraná River dating back to the seventh millennium. The discoveries made in the Caverna da Pedra Pintada, in the heart of Amazonia, show (like those of Monte Verde for an earlier period) the fragility of the "certainties" that have been acquired and how our little scientific world can be shaken from time to time, to its immense benefit. Perhaps we shall discover that some *sambaquis* were occupied throughout the year by a group that also cultivated the lands behind the shore. Nevertheless, it is difficult to imagine that research, which is constantly multiplying, will bring about such a revolution in knowledge that the precocity of Andean development will be called into question as a whole.

6

PEASANTS, ARTISANS, PRIESTS

A FTER THESE FORAYS INTO THE IMMENSE AND DIVERSE TERRITORIES and lifeways in prehistoric South America, we return to the Andean domain. Between about 5000 and 4000 B.P. profound upheavals affected the Andean world once again. Though full of contrasts, this area was culturally coherent. Along the Pacific littoral and in the highlands, varying in time from region to region, there occurred a series of very important economic innovations. This included the start of intensive maize cultivation, the appearance of pottery and weaving, the beginning of hierarchical society and an urban process, and the appearance of the first ceremonial centers. Contrary to deeply held notions, it was not in the central Andes of Peru that this cultural acceleration occurred the earliest and the most splendidly but in the northern area, in the littoral regions of Ecuador and Colombia.

THE MENU GROWS RICHER

Beans, Gourds, and Maize: The American Trilogy

Three plants were crucial to America's economic and cultural development. Later, they were gifts that this continent presented to the Old World, which has since somewhat forgotten the fact. The bean, as we have already seen, was doubtless the first cultivated plant in America. By the seventh millennium (almost 10,000 B.P.), specimens of the earliest domesticated species (*Phaseolus lunatus*) were already present in Guitarrero Cave, followed around 7700 B.P. by specimens of a second species (*Phaseolus vulgaris*). On the coast of Peru, cultivated beans appear later: *P. lunatus* is definitely present at Huaca Prieta around 4500 B.P., *P. vulgaris* would not be cultivated in the littoral regions until the first millennium, during the ceramic period. In Ecuador, a different species, *Canavalia plagiosperma*, was cultivated at Real Alto between 5500 and 5000 B.P., at the start of the site's occupation. The genus *Canavalia*,

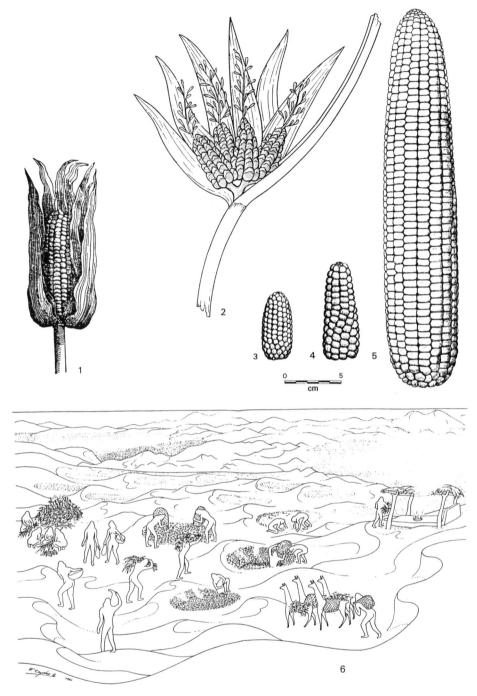

Fig. 26. Maize. 1. The oldest depiction of maize published in Europe (drawing published in F. de Oviedo, *Historia Natural,* Seville, 1535). 2. Idealized depiction ("ideotype") of maize with branching cobs, perhaps, according to Grobman, one of the original forms of wild maize. 3, 4. *Confite Chavinense* and *Proto-Confite Morocho,* first primitive maize cultivated in Peru, present at Guitarrero and Los Gavilanes. 5. Present-day maize cob, according to Beadle, a "biological monstrosity due to a prolonged domestication." 6. Idealized reconstruction of the maize stores at Los Gavilanes (Peru).

doubtless domesticated in Ecuador, was introduced on the coast of Peru between 4500 and 3800 B.P. The cultivation of gourds (*Cucurbita* sp.) and calabashes (*Lagenaria* sp.) is as ancient as that of beans, since evidence of their use dating to around 6000 B.P. has been discovered, once again at Guitarrero but also in the basin of Ayacucho (see chapter 4). As in the case of beans, cultivated cucurbitaceae only appear later on the coast, between 5500 and 4500 B.P. at Ancón, on the central coast of Peru, and a little later still in the north of the country. However, none of these plants would ever play as great a role as maize which, although it was not the first to be cultivated, was very rapidly to acquire particular importance. Its intensive cultivation was to be the foundation for all the "high civilizations," the first of which appeared during the second millennium.

A Complicated Genealogy

The history of *Zea mays* is both highly complex and far from totally clear. Mesoamerica (Mexico) and the Andean area are still arguing over its birth. The debate is made all the more complicated because it can only be resolved by analysis of samples from archaeological sites, and these sites do not always provide the best conditions of preservation nor the best guarantees of antiquity.

According to some specialists such as Paul Mangelsdorf (1974, 1986), the maize that we know is the descendant of a wild ancestral form belonging to the same genus, which remains to be discovered. For others, like George Beadle (1977, 1980) and Walter Galinat (1983, 1985), it derived from a different wild graminea, *teosinte* (*Euchlaena* or *Zea mexicana*), which had no cobs, but prehistoric American populations could have discovered its qualities and selected the rare "mutants" that eventually led them to develop a useful cereal, the primitive maize that was the ancestor of all known maizes. The discussion is far from closed, and it is not my place here to discuss the arguments of the botanists and geneticists. But everyone more or less agrees that this plant, whatever its ancestor, originated in Mesoamerica. However, the trajectory of its diffusion southward and the time this required are not yet known with any certainty.

Domestication raises another problem. For some, the diffusion of an already domesticated maize also occurred out of Mexico and very early.[1] If one accepts that the specimens of primitive maize found in the cave of Tehuacán in Mexico dating to around 7000 B.P. (Coxcatlán phase) are indeed cultivated and not wild, this domestication could have begun in Mexico between 9000 and 8000 B.P. Beadle (1980) estimates that this maize, which has small cobs scarcely 2 centimeters long, nevertheless displays a level of genetic modification that implies a minimum of one or two millennia of previous cultivation. Others believe that the plant found at Tehuacán is still wild. Finally, yet others, such as Alexander Grobman (Grobman and Bonavia

[1] B. D. Smith (1997: 342), using recent AMS radiocarbon dates on early plant remains (maize, bottle gourd, and squash) from Ocampo Caves (Tamaulipas, Mexico), "substantially revises the temporal framework for initial appearance of core domesticates in northeastern Mexico, showing that the transition to food production in Tamaulipas took place more recently than previously thought." No similar work has been conducted in South America.

1978; Grobman 1982) and Duccio Bonavia (Bonavia 1982; Bonavia and Grobman 1989a, b), believe that the diffusion of maize in the Andean area occurred before the appearance of humans in these regions (by means of migratory birds who transported the seeds?) and that it was then a wild maize; there were several independent centers of domestication, one of them in Mesoamerica, another in the central Andean area (and perhaps others in the intermediate areas). The problem of this domestication, like that of the plant's diffusion, from which it must be clearly separated, will really only be resolved when we have abundant reliable archaeological data from the tropical zones between Mesoamerica and the central Andes—data that are still lacking, except for a bit of evidence from Panama (in the Cueva de Los Ladrones) and Colombia (in the Calima valley) where pollen and phytoliths of what seems to be a cultivated maize, recovered from archaeological sediments, are dated to around 7000 B.P. (Piperno 1989; Monsalve 1985).[2] When evidence becomes both more abundant and more conclusive, it will not only shed light on the history of one of the most important plants for prehistoric American people but also will enable one to study the nature of the systems of food production in the tropical region, as well as the nature of human occupations and the processes of diffusion and migration.

For a long time, it was believed that the first cultivated maize in South America appeared in Peru, in parallel with the rise of the Chavín culture (that is, around 3200/3000 B.P.), and that its diffusion in the Andean area was linked to the expansion of this cultural horizon. In fact, as the Peruvian archaeologist Bonavia (1982: 347) reminds us, this plant has even served as a "type fossil" to distinguish the preceramic period (called "premaize") from those that followed. However, various recent discoveries have gradually led to a modification of this hypothesis—except in the eyes of a few stubborn souls who persist in the view that preceramic maize does not exist (McKelvy Bird 1990). Curiously, where this plant is concerned, one encounters points of view that are as distinct and as passionate (and as bereft of impartiality) as on the peopling of America. Be that as it may, archaeological evidence is multiplying, and some of it seems to constitute proof that is difficult to refute: in the highlands of Peru, cultivated maize is present in Guitarrero Cave, in Complex III, for which, unfortunately, we only have a single radiocarbon date of 7730 ± 150 B.P. (Lynch 1980: 306)[3] (see chapter 4). The presence of the two maize cobs, often mentioned, that were discovered in the basin of Ayacucho in a level dating to the Chihua phase (c. 6300–4800 B.P.) has to be treated with caution, because it is not impossible that the stratigraphic context may have been disturbed.

In the Pacific littoral regions, especially Ecuador, maize could also have been cultivated very early: at the site, mentioned above, of Las Vegas, in the southern province of Guayas, phytolith analysis showed that the village's inhabitants were eating maize by the sixth millennium. Elsewhere in the same region, however, the clearest evidence obtained is much later: at Real

[2]However, phytolith analysis is a recent technique, whose results are not accepted by all specialists. Phytoliths are silica particles present in the cells of plants, of which they constitute a kind of "skeleton." Once the plant has died and decomposed, they remain in archaeological soils without being destroyed, and so the analysis of their shape theoretically enables one to identify the family or genus of the original plant.

[3]In 1985, Lynch, after revising the stratigraphy and new radiocarbon dates, proposed making Complex III older by almost two millennia—which would push back the date of maize's appearance at Guitarrero to almost 8600 B.P. (Lynch et al. 1985).

Alto, a large village whose occupation begins around 5500/5400 B.P., maize phytoliths have been identified by 4400 B.P. by D. Pearsall in living floors (Pearsall 1978), and impressions of seeds or maize cobs are observed a little later, around 4300 B.P. (Valdivia 3 phase), in the side of pots (Pearsall and Piperno 1990). According to the analysts, the presence of large-seeded maize at these two sites, but especially at Las Vegas, indicates an already ancient introduction from Mesoamerica, taking into account the time needed for experimentation and the development of its cultivation. However, the particularly ancient evidence yielded by the Las Vegas site remains unique for the moment, and various botanists sometimes express doubts about its reliability. In Peru, cultivated maize appears a little later, on the northern and central coast, at Las Aldas, Culebras, and Los Gavilanes, in contexts that are still indisputably preceramic.

In any case, all the data recovered, both in the Cordillera and on the coast, seem to suggest that maize cultivation began earlier in the valleys or intramontane basins of the Andes than in the coastal regions. This anteriority can be explained if one accepts the model of a first early diffusion from Mesoamerica through Central America to South America, where it followed a terrestrial route, crossing the low-and midaltitude tropical zones of the eastern side of the Andes. Subsequently, it was in these same regions that maize gradually became an important cultivated plant, thanks to the effect of selections that, whether deliberate or not, led to the acquisition of increasingly large cobs and seeds, at the same time that its cultivation gradually spread and the plant slowly adapted to new environments. This process must have occurred in a more or less similar way in various parts of the northern and central Andes. This is how cultivated maize finally appeared on the coast, first in Ecuador and then, a bit later, on the coast of Peru. Elsewhere, particularly in the southern Andes, the proof of a very early presence of cultivated maize remains to be found. Hence, as already mentioned briefly in chapter 4, its presence (with that of beans and pimentos) has been reported in northwest Argentina in a deep level of the cave of Huachichocana dating to around 9000 B.P. (Fernández-Distel 1975, 1985), but this surprising antiquity has not yet convinced everyone—far from it. It is not impossible that the maize remains could be intrusive from more recent upper layers. In northern Chile, a few finds (whose antiquity likewise remains to be proved) have been made in places including Tiliviche (7800–6000 B.P.?) (Nuñez 1986) and Camarones 14 (7400–6600 B.P.?) (Schiappacasse and Niemeyer 1984: 81–83). After about 5000/4500 B.P., on the other hand, one finds cultivated maize in various parts of the Andean area and in well-dated levels.

Between Sea and Desert: Los Gavilanes

But let us return to Peru for a moment. The greatest number of samples of preceramic maize in the entire central Andean area have been found at Los

Gavilanes, a site discovered in 1957 by Lanning, close to the present-day Peruvian township of Huarmey on Peru's north-central coast and excavated by Bonavia (1982) between 1960 and 1979. These include not only quantities of cobs, leaves, and stalks but also abundant pollen and pericarps preserved in human coprolites. After a painstaking study, doubtless the most complete ever devoted to the problem of the ancient cultivation of maize in Peru, it has been possible here to reconstruct the way of life of the first communities of maize cultivators in the most detailed fashion. The site is located at the mouth of the narrow valley of the Río Huarmey, in a sector of the coast with vast beaches separated by sheer promontories. Here and there in the valley itself, the landscape—in which rocky outcrops alternate with sand dunes—is extremely arid. The river is almost dry for much of the year, except from January to May; conversely, the water table is close to the surface of the earth and can easily be reached by means of wells. In this environment, which, according to geological and climatological studies, seems to have varied little during the last four or five millennia, the site of Los Gavilanes extended over almost 2 hectares, not far from the shore, from which it was separated by a range of hills. It is now entirely covered by sand, and nothing—or almost nothing—today enables one to recognize it apart from a series of round, shallow depressions that at first sight suggest a buried assemblage of huts. In fact, these are certainly an ancient settlement, but the depressions mark the locations not of dwellings but of circular pits, with an inverted truncated shape and inner walls lined with stones. The pits contained a variable quantity of maize remains, mostly leaves, stems, and, more rarely, cobs. Forty-seven pits could be counted, and their size varied from 2 to more than 20 meters wide and about 1 to 1.8 meters deep. Between them, and right up to their edges, the ancient floor was scattered with a few lithic objects, some rare flakes and worked-stone discoid tools of an extremely particular kind, as well as abundant dried camelid excrement (Bonavia and Grobman 1979; Bonavia 1982).

Bonavia's analyses have revealed that Los Gavilanes was a place where maize was stored, the first known example of an organized storage system dating back to the preceramic period. The C14 dates have shown that this site underwent three occupation phases spanning the period between 5000 and 3800 B.P. (uncorrected dates), and it was probably during the second period—that is, around 4200/4100 B.P.—that the pit-silos were constructed.

> During the Preceramic V, people who were already familiar with maize settled at Los Gavilones and built stone structures of considerable size. We know nothing of the characteristics and function of these structures. . . . The edifices were subsequently destroyed, for reasons unknown. . . . During the Preceramic VI [4500–3800 B.P.] the site was re-used, and took on another function: it was transformed into a maize store. This is how the pits were made, using the earlier construction materials. The people who did this obviously did not live at the site itself. The stratified refuse [a

small heap unearthed in the southern part of the site] indicates a short occupation, and by few people, and could correspond to the individuals who were in charge of the maintenance of the stores.

Moreover, no trace of dwellings or accumulation of domestic refuse corresponding to this period has been discovered nearby. The habitation areas were doubtless located in the valley itself, close to the cultivated fields, and the maize was brought from the valley to Los Gavilanes. Besides, the presence of a public edifice, probably linked to some form of cult, endows the site with a very specific function. . . .

The maize was brought from the valley to Los Gavilanes, probably intact, with the stems and the rest, carried on men's backs [and llamas' backs, as shown by the presence of abundant excrement close to the pits]. (Bonavia and Grobman 1979: 31–32)

The authors specify that, after the cobs were separated at the site from the stem and leaves (probably used to line the walls and the bottom of the silos), they were then piled up. Sand was mixed in to protect them from insects and diseases and to facilitate their conservation (they note that this is still done today on various parts of the Peruvian coast). This would explain the choice of a desert zone that was protected from winds by the hills that separated it from the ocean. In this way, the maize could be conserved for a year, and Bonavia estimates the total capacity of the 47 pits discovered to be 1,590 meters cubed, that is—taking into account the contribution of sand and assuming that all the silos were full to the brim—between 414 (low estimate) and 460 tons of maize, which could have been enough to maintain a population of 8,760 to 17,500 people, especially since, in addition to the maize, they were cultivating beans, gourds, peanuts, and other plants whose remains are present, although in lesser quantity, in the site.

Los Gavilanes is not the only storage place that existed at this period on the coast. Bonavia has detected several in the same region, including one that contained at least 88 silos, and another with approximately 150. Moreover, it is probable that installations with the same function, if not of the same type, existed at other more or less contemporaneous sites such as Culebras or Aspero, even if, when excavated, they were not detected or interpreted as such (ibid.: 37–39). The existence of such structures obviously implies an already very well organized population of farmers and an already solidly established cultivation of maize. However, this did not prevent the population from also relying heavily on other resources, for example, hunting the cervids that frequented the nearby *lomas* zones and especially gathering marine resources. The discoid stone tools discovered at Los Gavilanes were made unifacially on thin cobbles and characterize the final preceramic of the Peruvian coast. They are called "Culebras discs" because they were first identified at this site. They very probably had a specific function, which Bonavia has tried out with some success: they were used on the rocks that were periodically uncovered by the waves to detach the gastropod mollusks that lived there in colonies (Chitonids or Fissurellids).

The introduction and then intensification of maize cultivation at the end of the preceramic period henceforth gave a decisive impetus to the economic development of the Andean area. Added to the already very extensive assemblage of edible species that had been cultivated earlier, this plant was to make it possible to undertake a considerable qualitative leap by bringing to populations that were steadily growing in numbers this indispensable nutritional complement to beans and gourds.

Elsewhere in South America, the data concerning the first cultivated maize are still rare and poorly founded. In Brazil, in the State of Minas Gerais, an "early" type of maize was discovered in the cave of Varzelândia, associated somewhat doubtfully with a date of 7655 B.P. (Prous 1992: 182). More recently and more credibly, "unexpected" maize seeds were found at Santana do Riacho in domestic hearths earlier than 4000 B.P. (ibid.: 176). However, after 3500 B.P., far more Brazilian sites yield indisputable maize remains.

POTTERS AND WEAVERS

In the first edition of this book, I wrote (in 1995): "two important technological innovations also mark—in the Andean area but also elsewhere in South America—the period stretching from approximately 5000 to 4000 B.P. These were, on the one hand, the cultivation of cotton followed, a bit later, by the 'invention' of weaving and, on the other, the use of vessels of fired clay." I am now forced to note that the panorama has been transformed since then by the apparently well-attested presence, in the Amazonian cave of Pedra Pintada, of ceramic sherds before 6000 B.P., a timely discovery that served to confirm the earlier (1991) but hitherto disputed discovery of pottery in a level that is perhaps even older (see chapter 5).

Hence, whereas the Andean area clearly constituted an early center of "neolithization"—first sedentary settlements, first manipulations of plant and animal species—one of its most important components, pottery, seems to have had a different origin. Although this problem, as far as I am aware, does not arouse such a virulent polemic and such exacerbated positions as that of the first peopling of America, nevertheless it has for a long time kept a lively controversy going—caused as much by the differences in points of view as by the personality of their advocates—and the history of this controversy deserves telling (in the manner of an adventure tale).

Act 1: A Boat from Japan

In 1956, the Ecuadorian archaeologist Emilio Estrada discovered the site of Valdivia on the north coast of the province of Guayas (Estrada 1958). It comprised a group of voluminous mounds located not far from the shore and consisted of the accumulation of refuse of all kinds—shells, remains of fish and crustaceans, plant waste—mingled with numerous fragments of a pottery made with a fairly crude paste but with decoration of surprising variety, involving engraving, champlevé, and pastillage (fig. 27). Excavations were carried out in 1957 with the help of the Americans Betty Meggers and Clifford Evans, and a synthesis was later published by Meggers, Evans, and Estrada (1965). The hypotheses put forward in this work hit the archaeological world like a bombshell. According to Meggers and Evans (Estrada, although a co-author, had died in 1961 and had apparently never pushed his interpretation this far), Valdivia, where the oldest C14 date is around 5150 B.P., was a settlement of fisher-gatherers whose techno-cultural knowledge owed nothing to local adaptations but had been "imported" from Japan. Japanese fishers of the Jomon culture, more specifically from the island of Kyushu—Meggers and Evans went to Japan to confirm their hypothesis—supposedly made an "accidental" maritime crossing (of 8,200 nautical miles), propelled by strong currents, and finally reached the Ecuadorian coast, where they introduced the technique of pottery: "Valdivia pottery is remarkably similar to that of the same age from Kyushu at the opposite edge of the Pacific" (Meggers 1966: 43). Moreover, "pottery from Sobata, Ataka, and Izumi is astonishingly similar to that of early Valdivia. Inside designs on polished or unpolished surfaces present the same combination of concentric rectangles, zones of parallel lines, and incision alternating with punctuation executed with a tool that duplicate the broad, square-ended grooves typical of Valdivia" (ibid.: 44).

The two archaeologists also stress such things as the use, in both traditions, of a shell to make impressions on the malleable clay, the existence of undulating rims made by finger-pressure, and resemblances in shapes. They attribute the differences—on which they place little emphasis—to the inevitable divergences in the style of apprenticeship and the "technical environment" in Japan and America. How did they arrive at a conjecture like this? One has to bear in mind that the discovery of Valdivia occurred in the middle of a period when, in Ecuador (and a number of other countries), diffusionist theories were all the rage. At that time, to "explain" the richness and diversity of early Ecuadorian art, scholars only evoked probable contacts with Mesoamerica, vying with each other to link sites of the Ecuadorian coast, Guatemala, and Mexico. In a context like that, it is hardly surprising that the very first interpretation of the Valdivia culture invoked Mesoamerican influence. As the two archaeologists wrote in one of their first articles about the site, Valdivia constitutes "one more stepping stone to the reconstruction of the early paths of migration and diffusion between Middle and South America" (Evans et al. 1959: 86–87).

However, this first hypothesis of a cultural development linked to Mesoamerica was rapidly abandoned after Estrada discovered that the ceramic material included a very particular kind of sherd with a castellated rim unknown in the Mesoamerican area (fig. 27). Only one contemporaneous cultural complex is known that possesses this kind of rim: the Jomon complex of Japan. In 1961, just before his death, he pointed to the Jomon culture as a possible source of the Valdivia culture. This was when the hypothesis of a transpacific origin for Valdivia pottery was developed, the moment of the transfer occurring during the Middle Jomon phase (c. 5100 B.P.). A little later, Meggers and Evans (1966) also stressed the fact that, quite apart from the pottery, the ways of life of the Jomon and Valdivia populations were astonishingly similar, being based on the exploitation of the maritime environment, complemented by the hunting of small mammals and the gathering of plants. The technical equipment, including lithic material, also appears very similar in its rusticity and simplicity.

There is one difference—albeit a big one: the Jomon pottery in question itself originates from a cultural tradition that was already almost four millennia old, whereas no antecedent is known for the Valdivia culture. Meggers was to emphasize this fact once again in a small work of synthesis published in 1972, which answered all the reservations and criticisms that had been expressed. Whereas the Japanese shell mounds have yielded a long ceramic sequence starting around 9000 B.P., no local antecedent has yet been discovered for the Valdivia pottery (Meggers 1972: 35). More specifically, the hypothesis of an accidental transfer of this technique during the Middle Jomon phase seems to constitute a satisfactory explanation. One has to acknowledge that Meggers and Evans had qualified their demonstration with a series of rigorous conditions: first, that the "cultural traits" in question had to be of similar if not greater age in the "donor" culture; next, that the antecedents of these traits must be present in the donor culture but absent in the "receptor" culture; finally, that their formal aspect must not be linked to any kind of function. They obviously considered all these conditions to have been satisfied.

The idea of transpacific contact between Asia and America was not new. Several spokespersons of the diffusionist school, including major figures such as Gordon Ekholm (1955, 1964) and Robert Heine-Geldern (1959), had already put forward the hypothesis in the 1950s to explain various stylistic similarities detected between the Chinese, Mexican, and Peruvian civilizations. However, this time the case is somewhat more intriguing, insofar as the oldest Valdivia pottery was apparently the work of simple fisherfolk (Meggers et al. 1965: 147–56). Hence this thesis of a contribution from Japan seems to many to be a convenient means of justifying the presence of pottery with already very elaborate decoration in a relatively crude economic context, at the same time as it explains the fact that no evolution in situ has been detected.

The chronological sequence of Valdivia proposed by Meggers and Evans (1965) comprises three phases, A, B, and C, spanning the period between 5150 ± 150 and 3970 ± 65 B.P. (dates obtained at the eponymous site after the excavations of 1957 and 1961). A fourth phase, D, which is not represented at Valdivia itself, is dated to between 3400 and 3000 B.P. (ibid.: 149–50).

Act II: Imported Technique or Local Invention?

As soon as the sensational monograph was published (1965), a number of archaeologists (Donald Collier and several Japanese specialists, among others) were immediately skeptical and severely criticized this diffusionist hypothesis, which undeniably incorporates a certain amount of dogmatism. To many people, the stylistic traits that are singled out for comparison seem so simple that any potter, in any region of the world, could have had the idea. Proof of this can be found in the fact that, if one separated the elements, one would find identical motifs in the Neolithic of numerous parts of the world, including that of Europe. Some, like Lathrap (1967), emphasize that the shapes of the vessels (and not the decorative motifs) that are peculiar to the Middle Jomon phase are curiously absent from the early Valdivian. Or like Bischof (1973) and Lyon (1974), they noted the weakness, or indeed the lack of rigor, of the stratigraphic interpretation of the eponymous site, thus invalidating for the same reason the entire chrono-cultural sequence that had been proposed. Other studies carried out and other criticisms expressed touch on the practical possibility of a maritime voyage of this kind, on the kinds of boats that were probably used at this time, on the direction and force of the marine currents and dominant winds, on the survival of the hypothetical crew of the lost boat, on the possible storms and typhoons, and on the probable duration of such a voyage (estimated at more than 500 days).

In short, the implications of all these criticisms are clear: if the possibility of such an accidental arrival proved to be nil, then the origins of American pottery would have to be sought on the continent itself. It so happens that a site containing pottery that is as old as, or even older than, that of Valdivia has been unearthed in Colombia.

Act III: The Potters of the Caribbean Coast

On the Caribbean coast of Colombia, not far from the present-day city of Cartagena (in other words, away from any possibility of direct maritime contact with the Far East), the site of Puerto Hormiga was discovered and excavated in the 1960s by G. Reichel-Dolmatoff. The report of this investigation was published in 1965, the same year as the Valdivia monograph, but it did not arouse the same immediate interest, for reasons unknown (Reichel-Dolmatoff 1965). The site comprises the remains of a camp of fisherfolk and shellfish-gatherers set up in the low littoral alluvial plain, close to the coastal mangrove from which the occupants apparently derived the bulk of their subsistence. This group of predators—no trace of horticultural practices has been detected at the site—used (and, it seems, manufactured) pottery whose

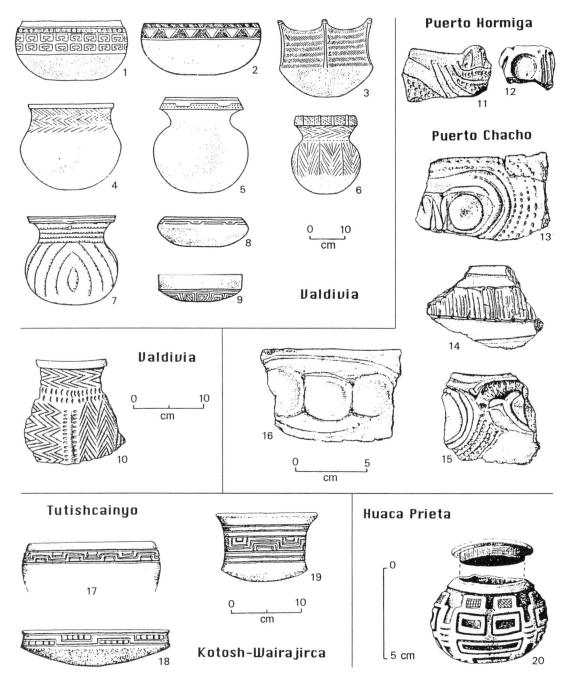

Fig. 27. The first pottery. 1–9. Characteristic forms and decoration of Valdivia ceramics, particularly the castellated rim (3), which suggested to Estrada some relationship with Japan's Jomon pottery. 10. Fragment of Valdivia jar decorated, according to Estrada, with the impression of a maize cob. 11–16. The first Colombian pottery, earlier than that of Valdivia. 17–19. The first Peruvian pottery, this time later than Valdivia. 20. Calabash with pyrograph work, discovered at Huaca Prieta (Peru), with typical Valdivia decoration.

most distinctive feature is that its paste incorporates, in most cases, a temper made up of plant fibers (identifiable from the lightness and porousness of the sherds found, since the firing caused the highly combustible plant particles to disappear). The shapes of the vessels are simple, mostly globular, but the decoration is different from the Valdivian and is already elaborate: incisions, stamped motifs, or ornamentation modeled in relief (fig. 27). The earliest C14 date obtained at Puerto Hormiga was 5040 ± 70 B.P. from shell.

A few years later in the same region, Reichel-Dolmatoff discovered the site of Monsú, made up of several mounds which, this time, contain no shells. It contains a somewhat different pottery. Plant temper is not used here, and the pottery includes two types of vessels (closed globular bowls with no neck and a few dishes or large plates), this time decorated with broad, deep incisions. The discoverer claimed it to be older than that of Puerto Hormiga (5300 ± 80B.P., from shell). In his view, the pottery displayed few resemblances, except that the Monsú pottery used incised-punctuated motifs (an incised line ending in a deeply impressed circular dot), and neither of them can be derived from the Valdivia ceramics. Moreover, the Monsú pottery was the work of a population that, for its subsistence, depended less on the marine environment than at Puerto Hormiga. The excavations of Monsú were published in 1985, and the book was distributed—with a certain sensationalism—at the International Congress of Americanists held in Bogotá. The pottery of Monsú then became "the oldest pottery of the New World," but, in any case, its origins remain unknown.

In 1987, Monsú lost its title. A new site with early pottery was discovered not far from there by the Frenchman Thierry Legros (1990), at Puerto Chacho. As at Puerto Hormiga, it was a shell mound about 100 meters long and 30 meters wide and a little more than 1 meter thick. A painstaking excavation, carefully stripping away the layers, revealed that this mound—which was both a dwelling place and an area for accumulation of food refuse—had four major stratigraphic units. The oldest, dated to a little more than 5300 B.P., contained fragments of an already very elaborate pottery, often with a red slip. The pieces have simple forms and are technically close to those found at Puerto Hormiga, especially through the use of a plant temper and the presence of typical incised-punctuated decoration. However, one finds in them a surprising diversity of decoration: plastic decorations (especially prehensile attachments in the form of animals, mostly of birds) and rectilinear or curvilinear incised motifs in complex combinations (fig. 27). This pottery occurs, without notable modifications, throughout the site's occupation, from about 5300 to 4800 B.P. Puerto Chacho thus becomes, in its turn, the oldest site with pottery on the South American continent. Legros himself observed, however, in a thesis that unfortunately remains unpublished (Legros 1992), that the material denotes "a good mastery of the firing techniques which, together with the decorative imagination and variety which go so far as to define a style one could call 'baroque,' lead one to believe that we are in the presence of an already well established tradition, and that we need to go farther back in the fourth millennium to see the beginnings of this technology" (1992: 62).

However, Puerto Chacho's preeminence was also short-lived, because even older dates were published shortly afterward for the site of San Jacinto I, located in the same region but this time in the hinterland. The pottery, very similar to that of Puerto Hormiga and Puerto Chacho but different from that of Monsú (whose age was apparently greatly overestimated), was dated to 5940 ± 60 B.P. and 5700 ± 430 B.P. (Archila 1993: 34–35; Barnett and Hoopes 1995; Oyuela-Calcedo 1993; Pratt 1999: 71–85; Raymond et al. 1994:33–52). Research is currently continuing in the mountainous hinterland.

Act IV: A Brazil versus Ecuador Match

In the meantime, A. Roosevelt et al. (1991) announced the discovery of an astonishingly ancient pottery in the Santarém region of Brazil. Although the publication in question only deals with the single site of Taperinha, it seems that the site is not unique in the region. Eight other localities have yielded ceramic sherds, with dates spanning the period between 7000 and 5000 B.P. (6980 ± 80 B.P., level 10, uncalibrated date obtained from charcoal; Roosevelt et al. 1991: table 1). Therefore: "Taperinha pottery is at least 1,000 years earlier than northern South American pottery and 3,000 years earlier than Andean and Mesoamerican pottery and could not be derived from them, although the reverse is possible, or independent origins" (ibid.: 1624).

Does the story end there? Of course not, because the "Valdivians" seem to be going all out to regain their ephemeral preeminence. After a painstaking revision of almost a hundred C14 dates obtained over the past 40 years on the principal Valdivian sites, J. Marcos recently modified the chronology of Valdivia and has Phase I starting with a date of 6195 ± 215 obtained at Real Alto (Marcos and Michczynski 1996: 98). The authors place the whole of Phase I between the dates (calibrated this time) of 4460–3755 B.C. (Phase 1a) and 3860–3340 B.P. (Phase 1b) (ibid: 104). So in relation to the very first dates obtained for Valdivia and published in the 1960s, Ecuador has gained a millennium and, without catching up, has moved considerably closer to the age of the Brazilian pottery. In their article, however, Marcos and Michczynski carefully avoid any reference to the problem of origins.

Of course, the conflict between radiocarbon dates that sometimes differ only by several dozen years and whose standard deviations are a frequent occurrence has little significance in itself except when used to raise the ante in the antiquity game, something in which even archaeologists indulge themselves occasionally. In this chapter, I have tried to utilize noncalibrated C14 dates, though this level of precision is not always available. Moreover, it is now known that the dates based on samples of marine shell may be older by several centuries when compared with dates based on charcoal. This renders even more difficult, for instance, efforts to establish a verifiable sequence for the first ceramic complexes for the Caribbean coast or the north-equatorial Pacific littoral. Even so, the dates obtained from Brazilian Amazonia radically modify perspectives on the geographic origin of American ceramics.

Apart from the purely chronological problems posed by the developments of this soap opera, it is equally interesting to look at the way of life of the human groups who manufactured these early ceramics and/or used them. At Taperinha, it was a population settled on the riverbanks, which were liable to flooding. The site itself—a heap of freshwater bivalve shells—yielded not only potsherds but also bone remains of aquatic animals (fish, turtle, mammal). Plant remains are very rare. In Roosevelt's view, "the faunal food remains represent an economy of intensive riverine foraging. . . . Foraging apparently supported relatively permanent settlement, in view of the size of the mound and the pottery, rare among nomads without draft animals" (1991: 1624). So they were predators, but already (partially or totally) sedentary.

The occupants of Puerto Chacho and Puerto Hormiga, at first sight, seem to have been simple fisherfolk. But San Jacinto is located 60 kilometers from the sea, and its occupants, according to Oyuela, were hunter-gatherers and perhaps even horticulturalists, turning to good account all the natural resources peculiar to the humid tropical lowlands. Hence, where the shell mounds by the sea are concerned, Legros does not rule out the possibility that, far from living here permanently, groups of people only came here at a specific time of the year in order to exploit the seasonal resources of the river and the mangrove. It certainly looks as if the important quantities of fish and shellfish taken (the evidence for which is piled up in situ) were not eaten at the site in their totality; one needs to find at these sites possible evidence for conservation and storage (butchering, salting, possibly smoking) and, of course, the traces of the dwelling(s) occupied by the same human groups during the rest of the year located in one or more different ecosystems, and of which San Jacinto doubtless constitutes a promising piece of evidence. Consequently, the final outcome of this hypothesis—the existence of horticulture, practiced by these same groups (who were fisherfolk at certain times of the year) in places located inland—can by no means be ruled out.

The Farmers of Valdivia

A hypothesis of this type—that of an early pottery made not by simple fisher-gatherers but by horticulturalists or farmers—brings us back to Valdivia which, as we have seen, its discoverers had always considered a purely coastal settlement. Certainly, all the Valdivia sites known till then were shell mounds on the ocean shore and indicate an economy based essentially on marine

resources. Yet in the 1960s, at San Pablo, not far from Valdivia, the Ecuadorian archaeologists Carlos Zevallos and Olaf Holm found a carbonized maize
seed encrusted in a sherd of the "Middle Valdivia" (c. 4800 B.P.) (Zevallos
and Holm 1960). This find, and the fact that, according to him, other sherds
of the same period have decoration that strongly resembles plants or stylized maize cobs (fig. 27), led Zevallos—at a time when the Japanese theory
continued to dominate, despite the critics—to propose that the Valdivia
people were perhaps not fisher-gatherers but farmers. However, it was only
in 1971 that another Ecuadorian archaeologist, Presley Norton, revealed what
he had discovered at Loma Alta, still in the same region but this time about
15 kilometers inland, pottery resembling the earliest Valdivian, but even a bit
older than that of the eponymous site, in an ecological and economic context that owes nothing to the maritime environment (Norton 1971). So the
thesis of an accidental and providential arrival of Japanese fishers, already
called into question, is starting to be seriously shaken, insofar as the oldest
known settlements of the region henceforth correspond to groups that settled
well back from the shore, to farmers and not to fisherfolk. Since then, this
picture has been confirmed by several discoveries of Valdivia settlements
located up to 30 kilometers inland but always close to land liable to flooding
and hence easily cultivatable without irrigation.

In 1974, the North American archaeologist Betsy Hill, after completely
reclassifying the ceramic material from different sites and collections, but
especially that of Loma Alta, proposed a new chronology for the Valdivia
culture based on a much more detailed stylistic analysis than that developed
by Estrada, Meggers, and Evans: eight Valdivia phases spanning a period
between 4600 and 3500 B.P., preceded by a pre-Valdivia Loma Alta phase
(5000–4600 B.P.) (Hill 1972–74). If the dates assigned to these different phases
have changed (aged), as we have seen, following their reexamination by
Marcos, the shapes and decoration that are peculiar to each of them, as identified by Hill, remain the same. It would take too long to present this stylistic
chronology here in detail. Instead, I shall simply mention that, in the initial
Loma Alta phase, there exist vessels of various shapes, among which one
finds a predominance of jars with a carefully smoothed surface and sometimes with decoration on the neck of incised or "combed" bands of motifs,
doubtless made with an undulating piece of shell, and deep bowls with a red
slip. Subsequently, the number and importance of the incised decoration
increase, executed on the same shapes after application of the red slip; a
great number of jars also display an undulating rim made by a series of
digital impressions. In the middle period (Valdivia III and IV), the rims often have several vertical extensions; shapes diversify, and many bowls clearly
reproduce halves of calabashes, with a decoration in champlevé that almost
always consists of a stylized representation of a human face. Later (Valdivia
V–VIII), within an even more varied range of shapes and decoration, cari-
nated shapes appear, and at the end of the sequence, trichrome resin-based

decoration (red, yellow, ocher, and white), applied after the pieces were fired. This new technique appears suddenly, with no local known antecedents. In some people's eyes, it reflects an influence from the Amazonian piedmont of Peru, more specifically the valley of Ucayali, where the perhaps slightly older pottery of the Tutishcainyo phase (which was identified by Donald Lathrap but which remains undated—Lathrap considers it similar to another kind of pottery unearthed at Kotosh and attributes the same age to it, approximately 3800 B.P.) comprises the same kind of vessels and decoration (fig. 27) (Lathrap 1970: 84–89; Lathrap et al. 1975: 30). In a general way, the Valdivia pottery seems to have been for primarily domestic use, and all the pieces, except for those of the final period with painted decoration, follow a very uniform technical model. Finally, all of them were manufactured by the coiling method, the only process used in America, where the potter's wheel was to remain unknown until the arrival of the Europeans.

The most important point to note is that the first (for the moment) pottery to appear in the Valdivia region, that of Loma Alta, bears no resemblance to any other, either in South America or elsewhere, including the Jomon pottery of Japan. On the other hand, there seems to be an indisputable filiation between the Loma Alta phase and the Valdivia phases that follow. Moreover, none of the first ceramics discovered in Ecuador or Colombia reflect a sufficiently primitive technology to represent a phase of local invention. What is more, their very diversity suggests independent processes of development, from one or several "centers of invention." In this regard, the discoveries made in Brazil (Taperinha, Pedra Pintada) argue strongly for an origin in the forested zone, probably in many places. These discoveries also spectacularly confirm Lathrap's remarkable intuitions. He quite categorically rejected the "Japanese explanation" very early and postulated in the 1970s that American ceramics had a place of "invention" that was located in the tropical lowlands of the northern subcontinent, somewhere between present-day Venezuela and Ecuador—the same area where, as we saw in chapter 4, the first domestication of the principal South American cultigens was also located. In his view, the diffusion of the two phenomena—horticulture and manufacture of pottery—occurred more or less together from the same region (the tropical forest) toward the coastal regions (the Colombian Caribbean littoral and the south Ecuadorian littoral) after crossing the Andean barrier. In support of this proposition, he enumerated a certain number of resemblances between the Valdivia culture and the cultures of western Amazonia: similarities between Valdivia decorative motifs and Amazonian decoration, the use in both regions of hallucinogenic substances, the use of "little shamans' stools," and the tradition of anthropomorphic figurines, which, as we shall see, is so important in the Valdivia culture (Lathrap 1973a: 176–77). Yet, even if the recent discoveries seem to prove him correct, one cannot help noting that his hypothesis was quite speculative, albeit apparently very stimulating. The same criticisms that he made of the diffusionist theory could also be directed at him, including the use of analogies between plastic techniques that are too general and that of comparisons between cultural and stylistic traits that are widely separated in time.

Once pottery had originated in one or more centers, wherever they might be, ceramic traditions succeeded each other and diversified on the northern littoral at the same time as the use of pottery diffused into the rest of Andean America and toward central and middle America. On the Caribbean coast of Colombia, the earliest Formative, characterized by the material in the lower levels of Puerto Chacho and Puerto Hormiga, is followed by the Canapote and Barlovento phases (between c. 4500/4000 and 3000 B.P.), again defined from the excavation of shell mounds, then by the Malambo (c. 3000–2000 B.P.), during which manioc was apparently cultivated. In Ecuador, the Valdivia tradition, which lasted with a certain homogeneity until about 3500 B.P., was followed in the same region by the Machalilla phase (3500–3100 B.P.), characterized by a far more developed farming economy than before.

On the Atlantic side, the oldest known pottery in Venezuela dates to around 4800 B.P. at Rancho Peludo, but the material—jars of crude paste with thick walls and rarely decorated—bears no resemblance to that of the Colombian or Ecuadorian ceramic complexes, and its dating remains debatable. In Brazil, if one leaves aside the Santarém region, pottery was "introduced" (according to Meggers and Evans) on the Brazilian coast around 5000 B.P.: a shell mound located south of the mouth of the Amazon, in a deep bay close to the coastal mangrove, has yielded crudely made pots with a temper of crushed shell, some of them decorated with incisions while others are coated with red. A (doubtful) date of about 5100 B.P. was obtained for the base of one of the heaps, but other, more reliable dates do not exceed 4500 B.P. (Prous 1992: 471–73).

In the central Andes, no pottery earlier than 3800 B.P. has been discovered. The oldest ceramics in Peru come from the site of Kotosh, near Huánuco in the northern highlands (Waira-Jirca phase, dating to c. 3800 B.P.) and the Amazonian piedmont (Tutishcaynio phase of the valley of Ucayali, undated but comparable, according to Lathrap, to the Kotosh age). This date of 3800 B.P., however, was recently called into question by Henning Bischof, who thinks that pottery did not "arrive" in the Huánuco region before 3500 B.P. (Bischof 1997: 5–6). On the Peruvian coast, the dates accepted hitherto for "initial" ceramics were around 3700 B.P. (3750/3650 B.P. at La Florida), but these, too, have been questioned by Bischof, who sees the appearance of pottery on the nearest coast at 3400/3300 B.P. in the north and 3100 B.P. in the south (ibid.: 7). Perhaps this delay in relation to the northern Andes was caused by the presence of an abundance of calabashes, which made perfect vessels. While pottery was neither manufactured nor used in Peru before 3500 B.P., nevertheless contacts had existed for a long time between the north of the country and Valdivia. At the coastal preceramic site of Huaca Prieta (4500–4000 B.P.), a burial contained two small calabash vessels decorated with a pyrograph depicting a human face; produced in the characteristic Valdivia style, the vessels were very probably imported. Hence either the diffusion of pottery to Peru occurred by following the coast from Valdivia or two independent currents of diffusion existed: one of them originated in the Amazonian forest regions and reached Peru via the eastern piedmont of the Andes; the other followed the littoral. A third hypothesis, recently put forward by Peruvian archaeologists, which proposes the existence of an independent center of invention in Peru, seems very poorly based for the moment.

It was even later, not before 3000 B.P., that pottery at last appeared in the southern Andean regions of northern Chile and northwest Argentina. A number of South American regions were never to use it, at least until the period of European settlement—in the sixteenth century for some, not before the nineteenth for others. Finally, one should not exaggerate the significance of this innovation—certainly it was important from the technological point of view, but its introduction scarcely affected the way of life of the populations who invented or adopted it, except by modifying and facilitating the storage of liquids and the cooking of food, especially plant foods, consumption of which was already preponderant or about to become so.

Cotton and Loom: Two Important Innovations

The first plant fibers to be exploited by the ancient Peruvians came from different species, especially reeds and rushes (*Scirpus* sp. or *Typha angustifolia*) and the agave or cabuya (*Furcraea andina*). As seen in chapter 3, by 8000 B.P. and perhaps even 10,000 B.P., according to Lynch (1980), baskets, cords, or straps of various sizes, and even textiles had been made and used by the occupants of Guitarerro Cave. These are the oldest specimens of textiles known in the Andean area, but it is obvious that, even if material traces of them have not been preserved, all the populations of the period, whether hunters of the highlands or fisherfolk and shellfish-gatherers of the littoral, used various kinds of fibers to make basketry and cords, lines and fishing nets. From 7000 B.P. onward, these objects are encountered in most of the coastal and Andean sites. Moreover, the same is true in other parts of the continent—where the climatic conditions permitted the conservation of such materials—such as on the central Brazilian plateau where, in the shelter of Santana do Riacho, which was used as a cemetery between 10,000 and 6000 B.P., the skeletons of several bodies buried around 7000/6000 B.P. rested in a flexed position, each wrapped in the remains of a netting (a hammock? a shroud?) of small strings of plant fibers (Prous 1986: 263, 1992: 176).

All these first textiles were made by hand using various techniques, such as plaiting, knotting (mostly used for the making of nets), and, a bit later, interlacing and looping, slightly more complex techniques (fig. 28). Around 4500 B.P., when the first pieces made of cotton appeared on the Pacific desert shore of Peru and Chile, they still incorporated the same processes originat-

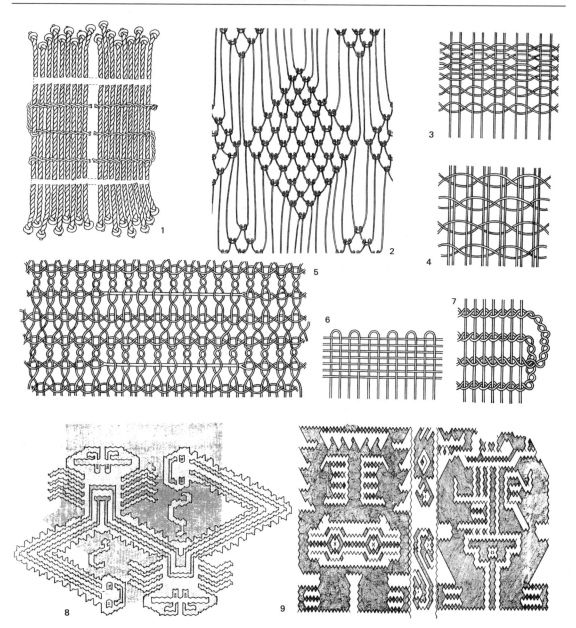

Fig. 28. Peru's textiles. 1. Fragment of a garment or blanket made of twisted cactus fiber, from Paracas. 2. Cotton textile ("knotted looped fabric") from Río Seco. 3–7. Diagrams of the various techniques used at Los Gavilanes for making twined fabrics, nonwoven textiles of cotton or wool. 8, 9. Nonwoven woolen cloths from Huaca Prieta, whose decoration—the combination of a two-headed snake and stylized crabs—was obtained by interlacing the threads and playing on the contrast of the natural tints of the fibers.

ing in basketry, among which interlacing, often considered the ancestor of true weaving, had become predominant. The introduction of cotton henceforth gave the occupants of the preceramic villages of the littoral a very flexible fiber, easy to spin. Cotton therefore originated a more abundant and more diversified textile production, whose creations were sometimes remarkable from an aesthetic point of view, although still made without the help of a loom. Used in its two natural tints, white and brown, and sometimes dyed, cotton made it possible to produce a wide range of decorative effects.

Cultivated cotton appeared relatively late in South America, and we still know nothing of its origins. It is *Gossypium barbadense,* a tetraploid cotton different from the diploid cotton[4] known in the Old World but also different from the cotton that was being cultivated at more or less the same time in Mesoamerica (*G. hirsutum,* tetraploid). Thus there seems to be an independent domestication in each of the two American nuclear areas. In South America, a possible center of domestication could have been extreme northern Peru and southern Ecuador, where a wild form has apparently been detected (Marcos 1988), although Lathrap prefers to suggest—as for the other plant species domesticated on this continent—an origin east of the Andes in the northern Andean piedmont. Be that as it may, without doubt the cultivation and use of cotton gave a decisive impetus to the techniques needed in textile development—an impetus that rapidly led to the appearance of the loom.

The first true "cloths" certainly appeared in Peru and Chile almost at the same time as cotton, in levels that were still preceramic. However, they were exceptional objects, developed with a still rudimentary technique, as shown by the irregularity of the weaving. In particular, it seems that the use of heddles—the pieces that alternately raised part of the warp threads—was still unknown and that this operation was carried out by raising the threads by hand (Doyon-Bernard 1990: 71). In short, this was an intermediate technique between the previously used manual techniques and true weaving on a loom, which has led several specialists to consider the pieces made this way as still "not woven." The most accomplished examples were discovered at Huaca Prieta, on Peru's north coast (Bird 1963, 1985), where anthropomorphic and zoomorphic motifs—birds, two-headed serpents, and a kind of crab—all highly stylized, were created through a delicate and ingenious manipulation of the warp threads (fig. 28). As for the true loom, its place of "invention" could once again be the northern Andean area. Close to the village of Real Alto, Marcos reports that he discovered a ball of fired clay bearing two impressions of textiles. This ball, which came from a concentration of refuse that, in his view, indicates the presence nearby of a potter's workshop (it yielded several shell objects that may have been used to make impressions on clay), is none other than a mass of clay that a potter supposedly transported, while it was still malleable, in a bag made of two different pieces of cloth, which left their imprint on it (Marcos 1988: 303–13). According to this author, these cloths were made of a rather fine cotton, and the technique used to produce them unequivocally demonstrates the use of a loom. They supposedly date to a period before the occupation of the coastal site of Peru, notably Huaca Prieta. The details of this interpretation, with its nested hypotheses, are debatable, as is the sometimes incorrect use of calibration of

[4]Tetraploid: "mutant individuals, mostly from a hybridization, whose set of chromosomes is double that of their parents" (Larousse dictionary); Diploid: "a cell possessing 2 n chromosomes" (ibid.).

absolute dates in which Marcos indulges, depending on whether it suits the theory of a supposed precedence. But it remains true that between 4000 and 3500 B.P., a period that corresponds in Ecuador to the final phases of Valdivia and in Peru to the extreme end of the preceramic and start of the ceramic period, or "Initial period," the production of woven cloths becomes important. Their number and size, like their uniformity, certainly suggest the use of a heddle loom, the efficacy of which definitively superseded that of the other techniques in use until then. These cloths began to be produced en masse for the manufacture of clothing, even if pieces with more elaborate decoration were still obtained by the ancient methods.

Only cotton has been mentioned so far. But it seems that camelid wool, probably used in various forms (unwoven) as soon as the domesticated species appeared (6000–5000 B.P. on the high plateau of central Peru—see chapter 4), and in particular alpaca wool with very long fibers, began to be woven more or less at the same time as cotton. However, the first definite evidence does not come from the highland regions but from the coast, especially that of southern Peru and extreme northern Chile, and date only to the final preceramic (4000/3500 B.P.). In its natural tones, ranging from beige to dark brown, or dyed (red or yellow), and whether mixed with cotton or not, this wool was used to make garments as well as big shrouds.

Woven textiles quickly came to represent the main craft production of the Andean coastal populations. The planting of seeds and the harvesting of cotton, the stockbreeding and shearing of camelids for wool, not to mention the necessary operations of carding and then spinning and then the final weaving—all this production demanded, as Moseley has noted (1975: 68), a great deal of time and energy and a large number of people. He concludes, on the one hand, that the populations (or at least a large part of them) must necessarily have been freed from the worry of securing their daily subsistence, and on the other, that since textile production implies a considerable number of very different and often long operations, it must have been entrusted to specialists. The existence of a food surplus and that of a social division of labor are two features that, in his eyes, characterize the emergence of "civilization" in Peru at the end of the preceramic period but especially from the start of the Initial period.

FIRST TEMPLES, FIRST IMAGES OF THE GODS

Almost a Town: Real Alto

The excavations carried out in the 1970s by Norton at Loma Alta, by various Ecuadorian archaeologists in different parts of the country (from the islands off the south coast to the Amazonian piedmont of the Oriente), and finally by the Ecuadorian Jorge Marcos at the great site of Real Alto, south of the

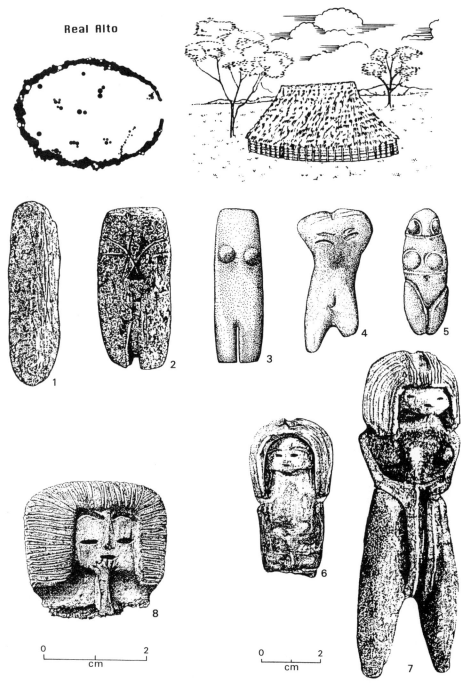

Real Alto

Fig. 29. Valdivia "Venuses." Above: floor-plan and hypothetical reconstruction of a big dwelling whose remains were unearthed at Real Alto. 1–7. "Venuses" of Valdivia, small figurines that were very probably for ritual use; their mode of production and their style evolved through time: first, made of stone and very schematic (1, Valdivia phase 1; 2, Valdivia phase 2); then in clay and increasingly elaborate in form (3–7, Valdivia phase 3) (Museums of the Central Bank of Ecuador, Quito and Guayaquil). 8. A rare variety of bifrons figurine (Museum of the Central Bank of Ecuador, Quito).

Santa Elena peninsula, have culminated in a more complete and also more complex view of the economic and cultural processes of the Ecuadorian Formative (Lathrap and Marcos 1975; Lathrap et al. 1977; Marcos 1986a, 1988).

Real Alto, discovered in 1971 by Marcos, was an area of a dozen hectares in which ceramic sherds abounded on the surface, with several mounds as well as smaller artificial elevations. Founded on a small hill that dominates the alluvial plain of Chanduy and thus protected from floods in the rainy season, the site is about 15 kilometers from the coast. The excavations carried out from 1974 onward by Marcos and a team from the University of Illinois-Urbana affected a large portion of the site, contrary to those carried out until then at Valdivia sites, especially at the eponymous site by its discoverers. The archaeological team believed that big exploratory trenches and the stripping of broad surfaces were the only methods likely to allow a subsequent reconstruction of the modes and stages of construction and use of this vast ensemble.

According to the reconstruction the team produced, the occupation of Real Alto began around 5500/5400 B.P. At first it was just a simple group of elliptical huts, at most 2 to 3 meters in diameter. Each hut had a framework of flexible poles fixed together at the top and leaning on a vertical post that stood slightly off-center toward the entrance. All of this was then covered with an intertwining of stems and bark to produce huts somewhat similar to those built more or less at the same time at Chilca on the Peruvian coast (Donnan 1964) (see chapter 4). No doubt to make the clay floor less slippery during the rainy season, the occupants of the village covered the walkways between the houses with crushed shells of *concha prieta* (*Anadara tuberculosa*), a mollusk that abounds in the coastal mangrove. The village did not contain any construction that differed from the others in size or any kind of artificial mound. At this time, a large part of the occupants' food came from the littoral, where "black shells" that are both tasty and highly nutritious were collected. However, the cultivation of beans (the genera *Phaseolus* and *Canavalia*), achira (*Canna edulis*), and maize (*Zea mays*) was already practiced, and numerous stone metates and manos point to activities of grinding plant products (Marcos 1986a; Pearsall 1988). Finally, the inhabitants made and used pottery, but, according to the archaeologists, it does not belong to the Valdivia tradition.

Around 4500 B.P., "colonizers" of the Valdivia culture arrived, whose pottery corresponds to Meggers's Phase A (or Hill's transition Phase I/II). The agglomeration expanded, still on a more or less circular plan, and the houses were more solidly built. Wooden posts or big reeds, set up vertically, replaced the flexible poles in the framework and were then covered with an interweaving of supple stems that was probably filled in with earth, using the technique of *bahareque* that is still in use today in these regions. These more spacious houses now had a shape that, as Lathrap suggested (Lathrap et al. 1975: 43), recalled that of the malocas built by present-day native groups of

Amazonia intended to house several families who are related through the paternal line. It was at this time that they built a "meeting house," as Marcos calls it (1988: 185), on a small raised artificial platform at the village's southern extremity. At the end of this period there began the construction of a second artificial mound facing the first. It was also at this time that the first storage pits were dug. These were bell-shaped and had walls coated with smoothed clay.

In the Valdivia III phase, the village's structure changed profoundly. It took on a rectangular plan, with more numerous dwellings arranged in concentric rows around a central plaza where the two mounds, built face to face, supported public (ceremonial?) buildings, with a kind of esplanade between them. These dwellings, with a framework of big wooden posts (up to 20 centimeters in diameter) sunk deeply into the ground, became even bigger. Measuring 12 to 13 meters in length and 8 to 9 meters wide, each was able to shelter—according to the archaeologists—about 30 people (fig. 29). Inside, lines of thinner poles point to the existence of dividers, while several hearths, as well as earth ovens, are installed there. In this period, Marcos estimates that the total population could have reached between 1,500 and 3,000 people, which implies a considerable increase in agricultural production in relation to the preceding centuries. During the following phases IV and V, the structure of Real Alto changed little, but the whole village attained its maximal level of development: it comprised about 150 dwellings and now occupied an area of 600 by 400 meters.

An evolution began in Valdivia VI. The residential area was reduced, while the central sector, where the two great mounds stood, assumed more and more importance. The number of inhabitants seems to decrease, while the peasant population dispersed to several satellite villages set up in the surrounding plain, close to the cultivable lands. However, the number of silos increased, a sign that the agricultural surplus continued to be stored at Real Alto, whose role of ceremonial center and in control of production was undeniably reinforced. Again according to Marcos (1986a: 33), although its inhabitants may still have formed a relatively egalitarian society, nevertheless at this moment there appeared a division of labor. The first groups that specialized in supervising production and monitoring its redistribution must have formed at this time. These are the premises of a social stratification that was to become accentuated in the following centuries, gradually expanding throughout the Andean area.

Real Alto was abandoned at the end of the Valdivia VII phase, doubtless between 3900 and 3600 B.P. But there is one feature that has not yet been highlighted—the fact that between the time of their first construction in the Valdivia II phase and the site's abandonment, the two central mounds were reconstructed and enlarged several times, approximately once per century. Excavations have shown that the mound supporting the "meeting house" had been reconstructed five times in 750 years. Each time it was made more imposing and covered with a shiny, yellowish-white coating. As Marcos notes, "it is clear that they considered the maintenance of these ceremonial centers to be very necessary for the well-being of society" (1988: 55).

These successive reorganizations and embellishments increased in scale through time. At periodic intervals, the structures had to be entirely reconstructed, and each construction had to be bigger, finer, and more richly decorated than the preceding ones. But each reconstruction also covered the preceding one without destroying it, thus definitively enclosing and preserving the architectural—and religious—symbols of the previous period. This is a common trait of the ceremonial centers of the Formative period, whether of the Andean area or of Mesoamerica, which all underwent successive phases of reconstruction and enlargement. A little later than at Real Alto, the same process took place in Peru.

As Marcos emphasizes, Real Alto was surely not unique and should not be considered a "center" of development. Its merit lies in its antiquity, its state of preservation, and, I might add, the way in which it was excavated and analyzed, which makes it quite exemplary. At this exceptional site, one can see the beginning of an urban process, the oldest known in the Andean area.

A Thousand Venuses

In the floor of the houses at Real Alto, as at all the Valdivia sites that have been studied since the discovery of the eponymous site, excavation has recovered numerous fragments of very naturalistic anthropomorphic figurines. They accumulated in the habitation floors or in the refuse heaps and are mixed with the thousands of remains of shells, crustaceans, mammals, and various plants, as well as the hundreds of potsherds and remains of stone and shell tools. Most of these figurines measure from 7 to 8 centimeters high, but some are barely 3 centimeters high, and the smallest known is only 2 centimeters high (fig. 29).

In the great majority of cases, they are women represented standing, always naked. Two small clay sausages form the legs, and at their junction is sculpted the upper part of the body, with scarcely a suggestion of hips. The arms are short, only indicated by a relief but not detached from the torso, and are often bent, with hands joined on the stomach; sometimes a bent arm rests on the breasts, which are more or less prominent, while the other supports the chin. A few pieces represent pregnant or obese women or women who are holding a child in their arms, although they remain exceptional. Some rare "abnormal" figurines possess two heads emerging from a single trunk. Finally, one also finds masculine figurines, albeit very few.

However, the dominant characteristic of these statuettes remains the treatment of the head, which was separately modeled, and especially the care devoted to the depiction of the hairstyle, sometimes the subject of a modeled addition. A voluminous hairstyle almost entirely masks the face and falls to the shoulders, whether or not it is separated into two symmetrical masses by a longitudinal line or by a broader band devoid of hair, as if shaved. Sometimes this shaved band is not in the middle but lateral. Finally, even more rarely, some examples have a head with half of its hair shaved, the other half falling amply on the other side, as far as the shoulder. While the face is always expressive, nevertheless its traits are merely indicated by a few horizontal incisions for the eyes and mouth, and the nose is depicted by a thin elongated relief. One notable feature is that, whatever their pose, these figurines all represent, at the front, a woman of voluptuous form and, at the back—because of the peculiar mode of representing the hair (especially those with a median line)—a very explicit depiction of a phallus. Finally, most of them were coated with red or red-brown coloring and then carefully polished.

The stylistic evolution of these "Venuses" has been used a great deal in establishing the Valdivia chronology. The oldest of them are not of clay but of stone: at Valdivia I they are simple little limestone plaquettes on which a few concise incisions are sufficient to indicate the features of the face and sex, and a simple groove or a short notch forms the separation of the legs. No sexual ambiguity is suggested because the other side of the plaquettes is not worked. After Valdivia II, some continued to be made of soft limestone, but most were hand modeled from a mass of clay, using small potters' tools with a blunt end. Their bisexuality is most frequent in this period. Masculine figurines appear in Phase III, while Phase IV sees those (whether feminine or masculine) that are depicted in postures other than upright, especially in a seated position.

It seems that all these statuettes were domestic products. At Real Alto, for example, most have been found in habitation floors associated with hearths and cooking refuse and apparently were "thrown away," even if several have also been unearthed in a "ceremonial" archaeological context (buried close to the mounds or as funerary offerings). Hundreds have been found at the Valdivia sites. If one adds to this the fact that they constitute one of the Pre-Columbian objects most prized by collectors and hence by clandestine excavators, they must doubtless have been made in the thousands through the 1,500 years that the Valdivia culture lasted.

What was the function of these figurines, and what importance did they have in the eyes of these people? There are numerous different opinions, the oldest and still the most widespread being that of a fertility cult in which they played the role of amulets that were relatively devoid of value. Certainly most of them have always been found broken. A leg or the whole lower part of the body is missing. In other cases, headless bodies or just heads have been unearthed. This explains the hypothesis that these statuettes could not have had any real religious importance. But another hypothesis seems more suggestive. According to Marcos, who analyzed the hundreds of specimens recovered at Real Alto, they could be objects associated with shamanic practices during curing treatments. In that case, the breakage would have been intentional, depending on the part of the body that was subject to treatment. He bases his argument on the existence of figurines (masculine or feminine) sitting on small seats, which he compares to the "shamans' stools" still in use in the Amazonian or Caribbean regions (Marcos 1988: 317), an element already used, it will be recalled, by Lathrap to "demonstrate" the Amazonian origin of the Valdivia culture. Moreover, Marcos closely ties the figurines' stylistic evolution to that seen in the economic and social development of Valdivia society: first, this woman-phallus ambiguity embodying the dualist concept of fertility-virility; then more sexually differentiated depictions—mostly feminine—when evidence of task specialization appears in the society; finally, the appearance in the final phases of more elaborate and ornamented figurines—depicting "important personages," priests or shamans?—some of which even seem to be chewing a quid of coca or some other hallucinogenic substance. Marcos states: "We suggest that, if the form corresponds to a specific content, the figurine is the depiction of a superstructural expression, of a substantial necessity, constituted by the need for a greater workforce, on the part of a society which, increasingly every day, exercised its control over the means of production. Consequently it was urgent that this workforce should live and reproduce through ritual forms which assured the curing of its illnesses, the virility of its men, the greater fecundity of its women and of mother earth" (Marcos 1988: 325).

Another hypothesis comes from C. di Capua, who posits that the figurines are connected to a puberty ritual. Thus, "the intense concentration of figurines within habitation areas is overwhelming proof that they functioned in a domestic context. . . . It is difficult to sustain the hypothesis that the Valdivia figurines were used in curing rituals" (di Capua 1994: 231). Furthermore, "The Valdivia figurines that exhibit obvious smoothing on the middle of the head support the hypothesis that in Valdivia society a female puberty ritual was conducted. These figurines represent sexually immature female bodies. . . . Comparisons with ethnographic evidence has reinforced my ideas." He concludes, "In the future it is necessary to test my ideas against more material from good stratigraphic contexts" (ibid.: 245).

Hierarchy and Power

From the fourth millennium onward, the occupation of the desert fringe of the Pacific coast—present-day Peru and northern Chile—became increasingly intensive, as we have seen, because of the rapid development of the farming economy and the social constraints it brought about. Apparently, it was the north and central coasts of Peru that experienced the fastest growth while, in the far south of the country as well as in northern Chile, the adoption of a way of life based on agriculture and the first evidence of social hierarchy are a little later. In Peru, farming took on a predominant role, even

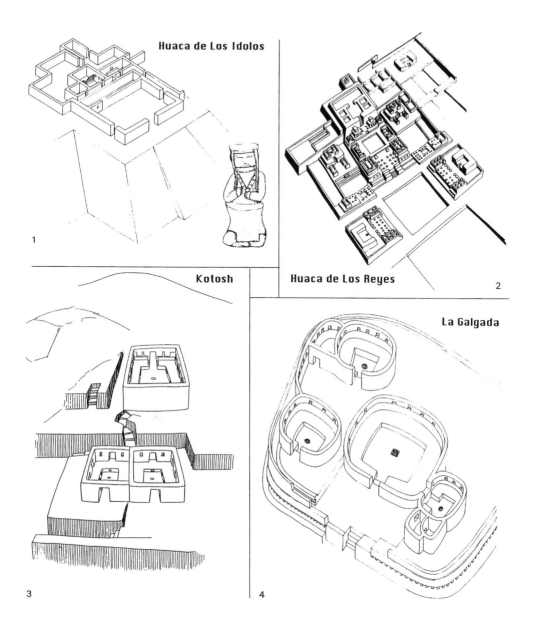

Fig. 30. Peru's first temples. Isometric reconstructions of a few of the most characteristic ceremonial architectural assemblages of the end of the Peruvian preceramic. 1. Huaca de los Idolos at Aspero (one of the oldest examples of monumental architecture in America) and reconstruction of a female statuette in unfired clay, of which a dozen specimens have been found buried in a cache inside one of the buildings. 2. Huaca de los Reyes, the most complex structure in the assemblage at Caballo Muerto, where one can see the U-shaped layout of the structures. 3. Superimposed structures of Kotosh, where the "Temple of Crossed Hands" was erected above the "White Temple" after the latter was filled in. 4. "Temple" of La Galgada, where one can make out, in the center of the constructions that constitute the two last assemblages, the location of a small circular hearth, doubtless for ritual use.

though a large portion of resources continued to be taken from the ocean. Maize cultivation, indubitable evidence for which now appeared, rapidly won a crucial place. Although it could have been practiced without difficulty in the soils of the low coastal valleys that were liable to flooding, without recourse to artificial irrigation its intensification, doubtless caused by increasing demand linked to the demographic growth, soon led (by 4500 B.P.) to the development of complex systems of exploitation and the perfecting of techniques for water collecting and irrigation. The big semipermanent villages that appeared in the preceding period (Paloma by 7500 B.P., Chilca around 5500 B.P.—see chapter 4) were still occupied, but between 5000 and 4500 B.P. the nature of this occupation changed perceptibly. The population grew, fishing was intensified again, and the use of cotton, which had been cultivated from about 4500 B.P. onward, made it possible to manufacture an increasing number of fishing implements (nets and lines) that were also more solid and durable than before. According to Rosa Fung (1988), it was at this time that a complementary economic system began to function between the villages on the shore, mostly occupied by fisherfolk and shellfish-gatherers, and those set up higher in the valleys and occupied by farmers.[5]

However, even more than the setting up of an economy dominated by farming, it was the gradual structuring of complex and hierarchical societies that, in Peru, characterized the final preceramic (5500–3800/3500 B.P.) and then the Initial period (3800/3500–3200/3000 B.P.). Although the latter's beginning is arbitrarily fixed to the appearance of the first pottery on the coast and in the highlands, the social and economic developments that characterize it at first merely continue those of the preceramic period that preceded it. At this time, only the technological and artistic domains took on a new character, because of the introduction of pottery. Social differentiation, which was very pronounced by the final preceramic, is reflected in the construction of big "public" architectural complexes, the first of which appeared after 5000 B.P. Río Seco, Bandurria, Aspero, and Culebras constitute the most representative examples. North of the valley of Chancay, the complex of Río Seco around 4000 B.P. comprises five or six pyramidal mounds of 10 to 15 meters diameter and 3 meters high, each of which supports an edifice with multiple interconnected cells. According to W. Wendt, who excavated the site (1964), the size of these mounds and the quality of their construction, which is different in each case, are clear evidence for a hierarchical distribution of population, the whole site providing shelter for between 2,500 and 3,000 people. At Aspero, built between 4800 and 4600 B.P. at the mouth of the valley of Supe and studied by Feldman (1983, 1985), 17 mounds of varying sizes are distributed over more than 13 hectares. Each supports buildings with stone or adobe (sun-dried earth) walls on a summit platform. Culebras, discovered by Lanning in 1965 at the mouth of the river of the same name, though his excavations have unfortunately never been published despite their importance, was organized on a different plan: no pyramidal mounds but a

[5]There are innumerable publications about this final stage of the preceramic period and the beginning of the ceramic period, known as the "Initial Period" in Peru, and it would be impossible to mention them all here. Most of the data summarized in this chapter have been taken from a few syntheses that have been published in the last decade (Bischof 1998; Bonavia 1991, 1993–95; Fung 1988; Pozorski and Pozorski 1987, 1994).

series of artificial terraces set up on the hillside thanks to massive retaining walls of basalt blocks. Each terrace supported small quadrangular semisubterranean dwellings with adobe walls on a stone foundation and an inner floor covered with carefully smoothed clay (Lanning 1967: 66–69).

El Paraiso (or Chiquitanta), in the low Chillón valley, constitutes one of the biggest preceramic architectural complexes known, not only in Peru but in the whole of Prehispanic America. Occupying almost 60 hectares, it comprises a dozen "units," at least eight of which have been clearly identified: big mounds 3 to 6 meters high, with a summit platform supporting a complex superstructure. Only one, Unit 1, has been excavated and partially (and doubtless excessively) restored by F. Engel (1966). It is a rectangular structure of 60 by 50 meters comprising more than 25 rooms or interior courtyards with stone walls originally coated with smoothed clay, painted with white and red ocher, the whole thing rising more than 6 meters above the ground. This enormous structure merely represents the final stage in a series of successive constructions and fillings, following a procedure that I have already described with regard to Real Alto in Ecuador but which seems, in this case, to have taken place in a relatively short interval of two centuries. The excavations carried out by Engel and then resumed by J. Quilter (1985) demonstrated the structure's multiple function as a dwelling place, a storehouse, and an "administrative-ceremonial center" that could have sheltered about 1,500 people. Quilter's work has also made it possible to take a closer look at an original construction method that is peculiar to the final preceramic at El Paraiso and other contemporaneous sites (for example, Aspero). This consisted of taking stones (rounded cobbles and angular fragments, indiscriminately) and using them to fill big bags of supple basketry with a loose but very solid mesh; these were then piled up to make the artificial platforms that supported the edifices. These bags were very homogeneous in size. The average weight of their contents varied between 23 and 28 kilos, which demonstrates that their manufacture must have been carefully controlled and their size calibrated so as not to exceed the burden that a single man could carry. However, Quilter hesitated to see this clear "organization of work" as proof of a system of labor tax, which Feldman (1983: 212) had already suggested with regard to Aspero (Quilter 1985: 294–96).

On the central coast, by the final preceramic and in a few monumental assemblages (for example, at El Paraiso), there appeared an architectural layout—"U-shaped"—that would become especially predominant a little later during the Initial period and then during the Formative. An imposing principal pyramid, extended by two lateral wings of smaller size, constitutes the bottom of the U. This "central nucleus" was, in turn, flanked by two perpendicular "arms" made up of several truncated pyramids that are joined together (but not always symmetrical), the whole thing encircling one or several central rectangular esplanades, open to the exterior, on the fourth side. As was observed by the Peruvian architect Carlos William (1978–80), who has studied them carefully, these enormous structures must have been very impressive, especially as most of them—as Tom Pozorski and Sheila Pozorski revealed at Pampa de La Llamas-Moxeque, built, in their view, between 4000 and 3500 B.P. in the low Casma valley (Pozorski and Pozorski 1987, 1994), unless it was somewhat later, between 3400 and 3200 B.P., as proposed by Bischof (1998: 62)[6]—were originally decorated with gigantic frescoes painted with vivid colors, contrasting with the green of the surrounding cultivated fields and the grayness of the desert in the background. One of the oldest examples is that of El Olivar, in the same region (start of the Initial period). Of about the same date are the complexes of Las Aldas (Fung 1969; Grieder 1975) and Sechín Alto (Fung and Williams 1977), which are close to those just mentioned and which occupy an impressive surface area. The Sechín Alto complex—the central pyramid, the series of esplanades spread out opposite it, and the constellation of minor edifices that surrounds it—extends over 300 or 400 hectares. According to the Pozorskis, the Sechín Alto complex doubtless served as the capital of a political entity that ruled over the entire valley (Pozorski and Pozorski 1994: 51). Other more or less imposing complexes were built on the north and central coasts: in the north, Caballo Muerto, in the Moche valley, between 3500 and 3100 B.P. (Pozorski 1983); in the center, La Florida, in the Rimac valley, around 3750–3600 B.P. according to the Pozorskis (1990: 488–89) but about three centuries later in Bischof's view (1997: 10–11); and Garagay, in the Chillón valley (Ravines and Isbell 1975). Each displays specific architectonic characteristics.

In the highlands of Peru, the process was analogous, although a bit later. It was around 4500 B.P. that the first preceramic "temples" were built, on a far more modest scale than the enormous coastal complexes that characterize what is called the "Mito" tradition. In reality, these temples are merely simple monocellular constructions; most are rectangular, but some, like La Galgada (c. 3800 B.P.) in the high Santa valley (or Callejon de Huaylas) (Grieder and Mendoza 1985) and Piruru in the high Marañon valley (Bonnier 1987, 1997), have walls with rounded corners (fig. 30). Each of these little constructions has a single entrance and functions apparently quite independently, which differentiates them from the big coastal complexes with their multiple and interconnected "cells" reached only by a communal entrance. The earliest discovery of these "ceremonial" (?) structures in the northern Cordillera is that of Kotosh, in the high Huallaga valley, excavated in the 1960s by a team from the University of Tokyo led by Seiichi Izumi (Izumi and Sono 1963). Three edifices that are considered preceramic were unearthed: the Templo Blanco, the Templo de las Manos Cruzadas, and the Templo de los Nichitos. All three were built one above the other after the preceding one had been abandoned and filled in, following the process we have already seen applied at Real Alto in Ecuador and which the Japanese archaeologists called "temple entombment" (fig. 30). The three buildings are of modest size and rectangular in shape, with the interior surface of the

[6]H. Bischof questions the dates published by different specialists for the sites mentioned here. In general, Bischof's criticism is that they "disregarded material evidence as a chronological criterion," and systematically gave preference to the results from C14 analyses. He then carries out a relatively severe revision of the chronology that has hitherto been proposed for this crucial period to the preceramic-Initial period transition, and in several cases makes it markedly younger (Bischof 1998).

walls coated with smoothed clay and containing a series of trapezoidal niches. In the Temple of Crossed Hands, under two of these niches was a bas-relief of molded clay depicting two crossed human forearms, which gave the edifice its name. Finally, all of them along the interior walls have a kind of bench surrounding a depressed area, the center of which is occupied by a circular hearth, which was itself hollowed out (and whose precise function remains unknown). Other comparable architectural complexes, whose successive phases of building and filling-in stretch from the final preceramic to the Initial period, have been discovered at Shillacoto (Izumi et al. 1972), not far from Kotosh, and at Huaricoto (Burger and Salazar-Burger 1985) in the high Santa valley.

The function of all these buildings, whether on the coast or in the mountains, still remains a matter of conjecture, despite the abundant literature they have inspired. Perhaps they were indeed ceremonial centers—this certainly seems more plausible in the case of the vast coastal complexes than in that of the more modest mountain complexes—but no indisputable archaeological evidence has as yet provided definitive proof of this. Perhaps it is slightly hasty to call a building a "sanctuary," a carefully prepared and cleaned surface a "sacrosanct surface," and an interior floor with a central hearth an "altar" without having any absolute proof. So all this is probable but not certain. Moreover, examples of a similar "power" of vocabulary could easily be found in the archaeological literature concerning the prehistory and protohistory of the Old World. Hence in my opinion it is preferable to speak of buildings "for public use," because everyone agrees that these structures were not used as dwellings. With regard to the U-shaped coastal complexes, Williams (1978–80) has put forward an original interpretation: rather than places intended to cater to large assemblies of people, these were "agro-religious complexes" where the plants that were of major economic importance at this time were cultivated "ritually." He observed that they were all located in the middle of cultivable soils that were easy to irrigate, that their U shape is always parallel to the river courses and open to the east or northeast (the source of the water), and finally that, in an angle of this U, there is always a passage left open (which he believed were intended for facilitating its drainage). Here again, we have an interesting and original interpretation but one that remains difficult to prove.

The nature of the power that controlled their construction of these buildings is equally difficult to define. At most, one can imagine that, within the framework of an already very evolved social organization, this power was held by a theocratic (or warrior?) elite in charge of controlling the exploitation of the land—since the construction, the maintenance, and use of an irrigation network is inconceivable (in the case of the coastal complexes) without a centralized control—and the distribution of resources on a scale that was no longer local but largely regional. As Fung concluded at the end of a masterly synthesis of the data concerning this period: "In the name of the gods which its own members created and qualified as part of a powerful repressive apparatus, the minority gained control of the labor force, thereby disposing of sufficient manpower to achieve increasingly grandiose public buildings" (1988: 94).

The Sacred Shell

Everything that has been evoked so far—the existence of a controlling elite and centralized power on the scale of several valleys, the mastery of a sophisticated hydraulic technology, the multiplication of public buildings— clearly implies not only a strict control of the means of production but also the ability to organize this production and the distribution of produce. In the case of an agriculture (mostly of maize) that had become intensive and closely dependent on irrigation, this entailed deciding the times for sowing and harvesting, as well as a judicious distribution of water. In other words, this involved knowing, as it were, how to predict time. This is where an element appears that might seem incongruous and yet whose importance has never ceased to intrigue specialists in Andean archaeology—the *mullu,* the Quechua name for *Spondylus princeps,* a big bivalve mollusk with an intensely red and white shell covered with long spines, which abounds in the warm tropical waters that bathe the southern littoral of Ecuador where the Gulf of Guayaquil marks the southern limit of its habitat.

Why should we be concerned here with this warm-water shellfish, when the littoral waters of Peru and Chile are generally cold, very cold even, because of the action of the Humboldt Current, and when the very presence of this current gives this Pacific littoral fringe its extreme aridity and its wealth of marine fauna? The fact is that torrential rains do sometimes hit this coast, when the equatorial current of El Niño (to which the Ecuadorian coast owes the warmth of its waters) descends southward, bringing warm waters along the coast of Peru and thus provoking major formations of clouds and diluvial precipitation, which cause a veritable disaster. We now know (in fact, it is quite a recent discovery) that this is a phenomenon called ENSO (El Niño Southern Oscillation), which is infinitely more complex, with effects that are felt on a planetary scale (but its explanation does not fall within the scope of this book). Whether it be El Niño in popular parlance or ENSO in scientific terms, the effects are the same: rivers burst their banks; entire villages, roads, aqueducts, and canals are destroyed; species of fish that are commonly fished by the local populations desert the area; and marine animals die by the thousand. Peru has suffered this phenomenon on various occasions in the past—a particularly violent Niño doubtless occurred shortly after 3200 B.P., which caused among other things the destruction of the temple of Cerro Sechín (Bischof 1997: 4) (see chapter 7)—and recently in 1982–83 and especially 1997–98. The arrival of El Niño, and especially its strength, remain unpredictable, while all agricultural production, indeed all of coastal life, depends, today as in the past, on the alternation of dry years, during which the rivers only bring a feeble trickle of water to the desert, with humid or excessively humid years, when their floods devastate everything in their path. One can therefore appreciate the serious extent of the consequences that the sudden arrival of a Niño could have had in the period that concerns us here, in an economy that was henceforth dominated by agriculture, and also the interest that people would have taken in trying to predict these catastrophic effects, since they could not stop them. But if our current technical knowledge does not enable us to predict Niño years, how could they have managed this 3,000 years ago? It does seem that they at least tried, if one believes the judicious and brilliant hypothesis put forward by Marcos following his research on the Valdivia culture.

Several archaeologists—Holm in the 1950s, then Allison Paulsen (1974) and John Murra (1975)—who were intrigued by the quantities of spondylus shells unearthed in the dwellings, temples, and tombs; by their astonishing geographical distribution from Ecuador to Chile; and by the long duration of their usage from the Valdivia period to the Spanish Conquest, had already wondered about the role of this shellfish in the Prehispanic Andean world. However, Marcos was the first to put forward an explanation for this amazing and very ancient distribution. In his view, the spondylus shells were not sought for their beauty or their rarity but because of the mollusk's behavior, which the Valdivia people would have had occasion to observe very early, being skilful fisherfolk as well as farmers. This mollusk, which is found exclusively in the equatorial waters that are warmed by the Niño current where it lives at a depth of between 10 and 25 meters, is extremely sensitive to temperature and can move rapidly. If the waters grow cold and the current slows or moves away from the coast, the populations of spondylus also move and are no longer accessible except at a great depth. If the current's effect increases and warms the coastal waters to a latitude farther south than usual, this indicates an impending season of heavy rain, and the spondylus shellfish will be found at a lesser depth and also move southward. This is the source of the hypothesis: "In accordance with the existing evidence, we suggest that the ritual use of Spondylus princeps in the Andes was based on its usefulness through time on the Ecuadorian coasts to specialists in climatic prediction, in order to determine the cycles of rain and drought, and events as important as the phenomenon of El Niño, which could affect food production in Andean America so dramatically" (Marcos, cited by Lumbreras 1988: 357–58).

But Marcos went even further. He noticed that in the Valdivia occupation levels of Real Alto (around 4500 B.P.) there were numerous fragments, carefully cut out, of the white part of the spondylus shell, its red edge being systematically absent; however, at Cerro Narrio, in the highlands of the interior, the more or less contemporaneous levels contain either intact spondylus valves or pieces of jewelry—beads, pendants, or rings—made out of the red part of the shell, as well as little anthropomorphic figurines, likewise sculpted out of the colored portion. Almost in the same period, red fragments of spondylus are also present on the Peruvian coast, especially at the big "public" site of Aspero. Marcos therefore supposes that although the Valdivia people may have perceived very early that it was important to monitor carefully the spondylus populations close to their coast and the numbers and the depth where they were found, nevertheless they attached no value to the shells themselves. However, the news of spondylus's astonishing predictive power rapidly reached the interior of the country, where agriculture is always at the mercy of an episode of drought. Since spondylus could help protect against this, whole shells or, failing that, their red part—the most characteristic part—were needed. Spondylus progressed from being a simple bio-indicator on the coast to acquiring a ritual value and, especially, becoming the object of a very active "commerce," whose network extended farther and farther. In the Valdivia region during this time, spondylus shells were collected in increasing quantities to satisfy this growing demand. Many shells were cut up on the spot, and the white part, which was of no interest, was discarded, while the precious red part or whole shells were transported to the Cordillera and exchanged for various products from the highlands or the raw materials that were lacking on the coast (copper, obsidian, camelid wool, salt).

As one moves forward in time, spondylus shells are found farther and farther south, until they reach Chile and even northwest Argentina. In all cases, they were either offerings linked to domestic rituals, part of funerary assemblages, or simple items of jewelry, sometimes of very small size (which proves the price that was attached to them). At the end of the second millennium, depictions of spondylus were integrated into religious iconography on the monumental sculptures and the bas-reliefs that decorated the temples—for example, at Chavín de Huantar (fig. 32)—as well as on innumerable ceramic vases associated with other, generally frightening supernatural figures, such as entities with a cayman's body and a feline mouth or birds of prey with enormous talons, all of them mythical creatures that were more or less linked to the cult of water and fertility (see chapter 7).

The *mullu* was to remain closely related to fertility rituals until the Spanish Conquest, and several chroniclers of the sixteenth and seventeenth centuries (Bernabé Cobo, Francisco de Avila) mention its importance and its use in ceremonies where, in the form of whole or crushed shells, it constituted the offering that was supposedly the most prized—the "food" of the gods, indispensable to make it rain. In the state hierarchy of the Inca empire, a special official, the *mullu-chaski-camayoq* ("he who is in charge of transporting the mullu") supervised its distribution in the sanctuaries. At this time, it still constituted one of the most important products of trade between the Andean peoples, the subject of an intensive traffic by land and sea. The famous Relación by Sámano-Xérez relates the meeting, in 1525 off the

Ecuadorian coast, and the capture by the Spanish pilot Bartolomé Ruiz, of a raft that had left the coast of Manabí and was heading north, loaded with a great quantity of varied merchandise, as well as spondylus shells: "They were carrying all that to exchange it for marine shells from which they made beads of the color of coral, and the vessel was loaded with these" (quoted in Rostworowski 1970: 151).

7

EPILOGUE: CIVILIZATION

A ROUND 3,500 YEARS AGO IN THE ANDEAN AREA TIME SPEEDED UP ONCE more. Within two or three centuries, the region saw the birth of the "high civilizations," by which I mean societies that were completely sedentary and numerically important with an economy based almost exclusively on agriculture and which display a highly evolved social and political organization. Since, strictly speaking, this period lies outside the field of prehistory, I shall merely point out things it owed to the preceding period.

A transformation of this kind only really took place in the Andean area, in the broadest sense,[1] both along the Pacific littoral and in the highlands, although it is not yet possible to determine with any certainty where the process of "becoming civilized" began. For some, the impulse that changed "maritime realms" into "agricultural states" (to use Feldman's expression) came from the coast of Peru. For others, the first impetus came from the Amazonian forest which, moreover, is where they locate the origins of agricultural practices (see chapters 4 and 6). In fact, neither of these two positions has proved totally convincing, because a number of the hypotheses involved are more like speculations rather than veritable demonstrations. However, each of them uses some attractive arguments.

CHAVÍN

In 1919, on the eastern side of Peru's White Cordillera, Peruvian archaeologist J. Tello "discovered" the imposing ruins of Chavín de Huantar. In fact, they had obviously been known to the local populations for a long time and had attracted the attention of the Spanish chroniclers in the sixteenth century. The cleric Vasquez de Espinosa visited them around 1616, describing them in detail. During the nineteenth century, numerous naturalists or travelers rediscovered them or paid them some attention—Raimondi in 1837 and Wiener in 1880, and in 1874 the "Raimondi stela"[2] (fig. 31), one of the

[1]A hypothesis expressed in a somewhat polemical tone by the North American archaeologist A. C. Roosevelt claims that an urban civilization also developed in Amazonia, where the Marajó culture, from about 3,500 years ago until the fourteenth or fifteenth centuries A.D., in her view constituted one of the most important complex societies of prehistoric America and even one of the great tropical realms of the world, equivalent to the most evolved Andean and Mesoamerican civilizations (Roosevelt 1991). However, a number of specialists still find this interpretation highly exaggerated.

[2]These paragraphs devoted to Chavín owe a great deal to L. G. Lumbreras, *Chavín de Huantar en el Nacimiento de la Civilización andina* (1989), which is the source of most of the data concerning the history of the study of Chavín, as well as the genesis and significance of the different theories put forward about it.

site's most famous sculptures, was taken to Lima. Around 1893, Middendorf was apparently the first European to have the intuition that this was a very important and extremely ancient monument, dating to long before the Incas, to whom the majority of Peru's Prehispanic monuments were then attributed in a great jumble: "In a very remote period, long before the Incas extended their domination to this region, between both Cordilleras and the upper course of the Marañon, in the valleys that join to form the Conchucos, and probably much farther north, there lived a civilized people which was probably in close relations with the tribes of the coastal valleys, even though this has not yet been proved. . . . Chavín was one of the centers of this realm, but not its capital, because in this spot the valley is very narrow and does not provide enough space to establish a city" (Middendorf [1895] 1970: 129).

However, the site's importance would not really be recognized until Tello's explorations and, especially, until he put forward his interpretation, which was to be the origin of a long controversy that has not yet been closed. In his view, this place was the "cradle" of an ancestral culture that gave rise to all the later cultures of Prehispanic Peru. This filiation is supposedly reflected in the diffusion throughout the whole country and even beyond, and during the entire time span of the Prehispanic period, of the cult of a feline god. The grimacing stone heads fixed in a long frieze in the wall of the main temple of Chavín de Huantar; the labyrinth of dark, narrow galleries that runs through the edifice, at the heart of which stands the great idol of the Lanzón; and that impressive image, endlessly repeated, of a divinity with snakes for hair and long, curved fangs—all of these things certainly evoke a complicated cult devoted to frightening supernatural beings and the deification of a fauna that was as foreign to the coastal plain as to the highlands of the Cordillera. Tello recognized this principal figure as that of a jaguar, a forest animal, and therefore declared it to have originated in the forest. But in the 1920s and 1930s when he published his first interpretations—including the famous *Wirakocha,* in which he undertook a long analysis of the Andean mythical bestiary that he believed was completely dominated by the image of a big primordial feline—Uhle's theories still held sway. According to Uhle, the great cultures of ancient Peru were of Mesoamerican origin (none of the ceremonial centers of the end of the preceramic period, which were mentioned in the previous chapter, had been discovered). For the supporters of this diffusionist way of thinking, the "Chavín culture" must have the same origin and, more specifically, arose out of the culture of the Olmecs of Mexico. Others went even farther, like R. Heine-Geldern, who thought he could see the trace of Chinese art in the depiction of an "Asiatic tiger." However, as one might imagine, this theory was rapidly abandoned.

Sierra or Coastal Desert?

Whereas several major North American archaeologists—W. C. Bennett, A. L. Kroeber, G. R. Willey, J. M. Corbett—henceforth quite logically set about

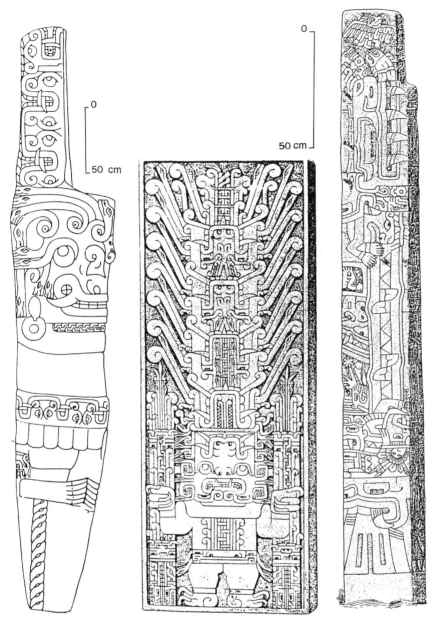

Fig. 31. The gods of Chavín. 1. The *Lanzón,* doubtless the oldest idol of Chavín de Huantar, located at the heart of the Old Temple and which Rowe called the "smiling God" because of its mouth with turned-up corners. 2. The Raimondi stela, a later work, engraved with a depiction of the "Staff God," a creature with a feline face and with a high headdress made up of monstrous heads decorated with a profusion of scrolls and serpents; this figure displays the peculiarity that one can look at it from both directions (Lima, National Museum of Anthropology and Archaeology). 3. The Tello obelisk, decorated with an engraved figure that several specialists interpret as that of a big cayman, which would confirm if not its origin then at least the strong influence of Amazonian origin that affected the Chavín culture in its late phase (Lima, National Museum of Anthropology and Archaeology).

seeking proof of the validity of Tello's proposals through fieldwork and through the objects unearthed on the coast or in the highlands, around 1940 the Peruvian R. Larco Hoyle, owner of a big hacienda in the Chicama valley on the north coast and an amateur archaeologist (but with great knowledge of his region), discovered a style of pottery that he called "Cupisnique," which he considered to be the prototype of the pottery discovered at Chavín itself. As he wrote in 1945: "The presence of the feline in decorative art originates in Nepeña, a place which we consider to be the main religious center from which the feline cult spread throughout all of ancient Peru. Consequently, Chavín is not the work of a mountain culture, but the main exponent of the architecture of the men of Nepeña" (Larco Hoyle 1945: 2).

Casma and Nepeña were two northern coastal valleys that he thus thought to be the cradle of the culture that had been wrongly called "Chavín," but where he would be very hard pressed to justify the past or present existence of any feline dangerous enough to have inspired such mystic terror! However, during the 1950s and 1960s, while a few researchers like M. Coe or F. Kauffmann Doig continued to cling to the "Olmec hypothesis," the theory of a coastal origin gained strength through research by R. Fung, E. Lanning, and then T. C. Patterson and M. Moseley, into the establishments and ceremonial centers of the preceramic period or the very beginning of the ceramic period, known as the Initial period, or Early Formative (see chapter 6).

THE TEETH OF THE GREAT CAYMAN

Between 1970 and 1980, in several publications, D. Lathrap in his turn developed and presented a revolutionary new theory, one that was quite close to some aspects of Tello's ideas but even more audacious: Amazonia was indeed the cradle of Andean culture; cultural development had occurred early here, and cultural influences had moved up the great rivers from the central Amazon and thus reached the regions of the Cordillera and then the coast, first affecting Ecuador and then more distant regions, as far as Mexico. I have already evoked this theory with regard to the appearance of Andean agriculture (chapter 4) and the origins of the Valdivia culture (chapter 6). Moreover, in Lathrap's view, the Chavín "beast" is not a feline but a cayman, an equally dangerous animal, and more specifically the black cayman *Melanosuchus niger*, a species peculiar to the Amazon River and the lower course of its principal tributaries—an animal that supposedly embodied the cosmos everywhere. Taking the hypothesis to extremes, he maintained that all the cosmological models developed in nuclear America—including, therefore, Central America and Mexico—had this black cayman as a prototype, although when this species did not exist in the surrounding environment it was sometimes replaced by a local species with an equivalent power to ter-

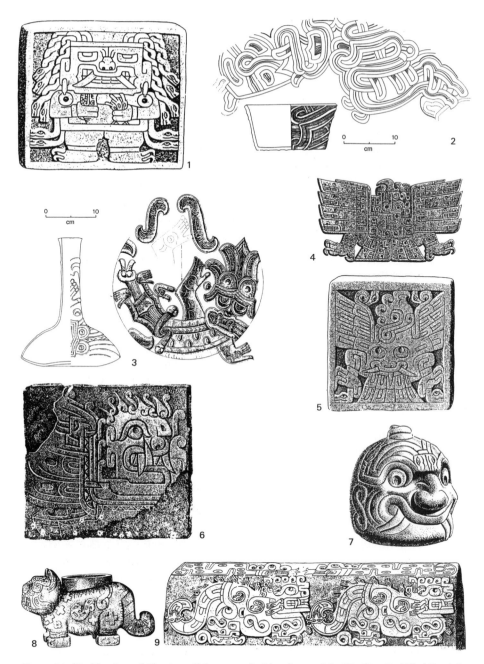

Fig. 32. Mythical bestiary of Chavín. 1. Slab engraved with a figure of the "Smiling God," holding in his hands a strombus and a spondylus, both shells that symbolize, according to Lathrap and Burger, the balance of the universe between the male (strombus) and female (spondylus) principles (Chavín de Huantar, patio of the New Temple). 2, 3. Pottery decoration that is characteristic of Chavín imagery: a combination of feline elements (mouth and fangs) and the figure of a monstrous saurian. 4–6. Slabs engraved with the "felinized bird of prey" motif. 7. Monstrous head with feline fangs decorating the exterior wall of the temple. 8, 9. The jaguar motif, sculpted in the round (ceremonial mortar in black stone, University Museum, Philadelphia) and engraved on the "Cornice of the felines" of the Ancient Temple.

rify. In his view, it was not so much in the whole animal as in its fangs, even exclusively in its fangs, that the universe's force and regulatory power are embodied. This hypothesis was presented again in an article that was enthusiastic in tone and deliberately provocative, although often confused, and which was called "Jaws" after the successful movie of the time. It was based on a painstaking revision of Chavín religious iconography, as expressed in a few of the main engraved or sculpted works. In all of them he recognized the figure of the cayman, whose teeth had allegedly become "the most important icon ordering the organization of Nuclear American ceremonial architecture" (Lathrap 1985: 245).

In other words, the diffusionist explanation had reappeared but in a different direction from that proposed by Uhle, Coe, or Kauffman Doig, because Lathrap found the Amazonian cayman in all religious imagery, from Mexico (Olmecs) to Panama (Coclé) and even Chile, from the mouth of the Amazon (Santarem) to Colombia and Peru. In his view, too, the most complete and detailed depiction of the Great Cayman, symbol of the cosmos, is found in the "Tello Obelisk." In 1919, Tello found the big monolith lying on the ground at some distance from the edifice of which it must originally have constituted one of the main idols, if not *the* main idol. Accompanied by the harpy eagle, it is the Sky, flanked by the two sacred shells Spondylus and Strombus, and rules over the Water and the Underworld, while cultivated plants of tropical origin (manioc, gourds, pimento), symbols of fertility, escape from its nose and mouth (fig. 31).

Naturally, other readings are possible, because Chavín's art on stone is extremely difficult to decipher. As was well demonstrated by J. Rowe (1967), this art is based on the systematic utilization of a particular mode of representation, in which each of the parts of the mythical figure depicted—the Tello Obelisk is his example here, and the principal figure is thus interpreted as that of a cayman—comprises a perfectly identifiable animal form, with only a graphic relationship between this form and the anatomical section it embodies. According to this "code," the cayman's belly is represented by an immense mouth with crossed fangs; its genitalia by a monstrous feline head from which there emerges a "tongue" in the form of arborescence and with eyes; its tail by another head with feline fangs, and so forth. Rowe showed that this labyrinthine complexity probably resulted from the use of visual metaphors. In reference to those used long ago in the poetry of the court of medieval Norway, he called these *kennings,* which can be translated (albeit imperfectly) as "keys" or "signifiers." The graphic depictions of Chavín were thus governed by a system of conventions in which each element of a complex motif was always represented by the same figure or part of a figure, the latter mostly zoomorphic: hair and cephalic appendages by serpents, tongues by tails or legs, mouths by feline jaws (fig. 32). Hence behind an apparent abundance there lies hidden a codified execution, governed by very strict norms and using only a small number of graphic units with a perfectly well defined symbolism. This is what produced these extraordinary puzzles in which, in order to be intelligible, the work had to be capable of being "read" and clearly could only be read by "initiates"—which we are not and shall never be.

CHAVÍN, MELTING POT OR CROSSROADS?

At present, the question of the origins of the Chavín phenomenon remains unsolved. A theory similar to Tello's has been defended with talent by G. Lumbreras who in the late 1960s carried out an important program of excavations at the site itself, whereas the "coastal hypothesis" is defended with equal brilliance by R. Burger and H. Bischof, the former having worked at Chavín after Lumbreras and the latter at the coastal sites.

As seen in the preceding chapter, the desert littoral of Peru is dotted with great centers that were both residential and ceremonial—including Caballo Muerto, Las Aldas, Pampa de las Llamas-Moxeque, Garagay—and their architecture, their decoration, and the cultural material that has been recovered from them (mostly pottery) often display astonishing similarities to those of Chavín. Before they were well studied and dated, it was thought, as Burger (1992) recalls, that these ensembles were contemporary, or slightly more recent than Chavín—"provincial manifestations," so to speak, that were subject to the direct influence of the more complex and older Andean center. Recent radiocarbon dates have demonstrated that the construction of several of these coastal architectural complexes had begun around 3500 B.P. and even, like those of the valley of Casma, at the beginning of the fourth millennium B.P., that is, before the start of construction of the Chavín de Huantar ensemble, which (according to the supporters of this theory) began shortly after 3000 B.P. Other monuments of the littoral region, which are a little later, seem to be contemporaneous with the first building phase of the Chavín temple, as shown by stylistic comparison of the sculpted or modeled works that adorn them. Another clue to the earlier date of several coastal complexes is the adoption at Chavín de Huantar of the characteristic U-shape of those coastal sites that are unquestionably older (see chapter 6). Hence, according to Burger and Bischof (1994, 1998), the first phase of development only affected the north coast of Peru, and the site of Chavín de Huantar attained its architectural and artistic zenith somewhat later. It was only then that depictions of animals and plants peculiar to the low tropical regions appeared in religious imagery, pointing to influences that did indeed come from Amazonia at that time.

Naturally, it is not up to me to choose between the two hypotheses and decide which is true and which false. I shall confine myself to the observation that, for the most part, the contradictory propositions are based on the importance and reliability attributed to the radiocarbon dates. Lumbreras is a defender of the earlier date of Chavín in relation to the coastal centers; although he has recently qualified his position, he believes that Chavín de Huantar's first ceremonial buildings were constructed in 3300 B.P. In Burger's view, this was not before 2900 B.P. The site's zenith and the phase of its greatest influence supposedly began around 2800 B.P. in Lumbreras's view, but 2500 B.P. in Burger's view. It is now known that the production of C14 dates rarely leads to coherent and universal results and, especially, that these dates only have meaning when they are closely integrated with their archaeological context. It is also known that a number of archaeologists sometimes have a tendency to retain the dates that suit them and to discard as "invalid" or "aberrant" those that do not "fit" what they want to prove. But here the gap between the dates retained by either side takes on a remarkable importance. According to the "long" chronology, that of Lumbreras, Chavín is certainly the origin of the civilization of the same name and the precursor of all the Andean "high civilizations" that followed. The ceremonial sites on the coast (including Caballo Muerto, Las Aldas, Moxeque, and Garagay) or in the Andes (Pacopampa and Kuntur Wasi), even those that already existed, merely adopted its ideology. According to the "short" chronology—supported by Burger and Bischof—it was the other way round, with the big centers mentioned earlier reaching their zenith between 3200 and 2900 B.P. and being the origin of the "Chavín phenomenon." Today, the most "fashionable" theory is the one maintained by Burger, which has met with support from other specialists such as Feldman, Kano, and Pozorski. Hence, as Burger writes: "The Old Temple seems a combination of elements drawn mainly from coastal antecedents. The U-shaped monumental platform, for example, is apparently based on the architectural patterns of the central coast, while the small, semisubterranean Circular Plaza fronting the central complex appears to be modeled on the layout of the north-central coast centers. The concept of decorating the exteriors of ceremonial buildings with bas-relief and modeled public art also has antecedents in the clay friezes of the central and north coast" (1992: 156).

Moreover, no matter which region developed earlier than the other, it is undeniable in any case that, during the first millennium B.C. and at the latest around 2400 B.P., Chavín de Huantar became a major cultural center whose influence henceforth superseded that of the littoral. It was now a religious center of the first magnitude. By means of interregional exchanges, it imposed the cult of its gods from the extreme north of Peru to the valleys of the south, both inter-Andean (Ayacucho) and coastal (Ica). In the same period, the great coastal centers entered a decadent phase, as shown by the partial destruction and the abandonment of several temples.

Hence Chavín represents the point where cultural currents from both coast and forest converged and were integrated. It was not a beginning but the culmination of a long process, which corresponds to the transition from a way of life that had remained relatively rural and village-based to another that was infinitely more complex. It certainly implied the appearance of a state and other sociopolitical institutions that characterize "civilization." While the other centers in the Andes or on the coast were clearly in decline, Chavín also became the center of an extremely active network of contacts and trade that linked regions as remote as the coastal and mountainous south of Ecuador, where another flourishing "formative" culture developed, that of Chorrera, and extreme northern Chile. There is evidence for this in the presence in the engraved imagery of Chavín of two shells originating in the warm tropical waters, the Spondylus and the Strombus, cult objects (as fertility symbols) that were the basis of a vast inter-Andean traffic that had been active since the preceramic period (see chapter 6). As Lathrap wrote fifteen years later: "It was in 1967, I believe, when I first noticed that the Smiling God in the often-illustrated panel from Chavín de Huantar was not simply standing there grinning, but was doing something important. In fact, he was balancing the male principle of order and culture, represented by the conch, held in his right hand, against the female principle of chaos and regeneration, represented by the spondylus, held in his left hand. He was maintaining the balance of the cosmos with precisely the same ritual that was performed by modern Kogi [a tribe occupying the Sierra Nevada de Santa Marta in northern Colombia] priests at burials" (Lathrap 1985: 241). (I shall refrain from commenting on the assimilation of femininity with chaos.)

Also in Lathrap's view, and he was followed by Burger on this point, Chavín functioned as an axis mundi, a "cosmological center" that played the role of mediator between natural and cultural forces. It must be acknowledged that Lathrap's prose is not always free of pomposity and even confusion. Lumbreras proposes a simpler reading of the role of the Spondylus in Chavín culture and imagery. According to Lumbreras, it was used as a bio-indicator to foresee meteorological events or variations in marine currents. Thanks to this, it was capable of anticipating climatic alterations, linked to the El Niño phenomenon, which were catastrophic for agriculture; it seems that the Andean populations had ascribed this role to it since the Valdivia period in Ecuador (see chapter 6).

In conclusion, although Lathrap's provocative and attractive hypotheses (on which I spent a great deal of time in the preceding chapters) apparently remain valid where the undeniably tropical origin of numerous American cultigens is concerned (as has been confirmed by botanists and geneticists) and probable where the likely location of the place(s) where pottery was invented is/are concerned (somewhere in the low tropical lands of northern Amazonia), it seems that one cannot agree with him completely when he proclaims that a "tropical forest culture" was timeless and preeminent over any other form of cultural development. The Great Forest as a devouring womb is a fantasy as old as the forest itself.

DISMEMBERED BODIES AND SEVERED HEADS:
CERRO SECHÍN

If we return to the relative chronological position of the ceremonial ensembles and to the origin of Chavín ideology and imagery, doubtless one of the most impressive sites—the subject of a long debate as to whether it was earlier than Chavín de Huantar (now apparently confirmed)—is the monumental ensemble of Cerro Sechín, located on the north coast of Peru in the low valley of the Río Casma. The site was recognized and described for the first time by Tello in 1937, then studied by specialists as eminent as W. C. Bennett, J. Bird, G. R. Willey, and A. H. Sawyer—who all considered it earlier than, or at best contemporaneous with, Chavín de Huantar. It was again excavated in the 1970s by a German-Peruvian team (Samaniego et al. 1985: 165–90). Nevertheless, the predominant view continued to be that, as Tello had first thought, this was a later work than Chavín. Now, however, it appears to have been demonstrated that its construction preceded that of the Chavín temple by several centuries.

Today, as described by H. Bischof after some major work of clearance and restoration (Bischof 1984, 1995), the ensemble takes the form of a building 52 meters square, with rounded corners—a solid structure constituting a massive platform about 4 meters high which in turn supported a smaller construction. The main access, on the north side, was by a staircase. Excavation has also made it possible to discover that the fill making up this big platform contained some older constructions, and four successive building phases have been identified. Rebuilding by covering over is an Andean custom that seems to have appeared for the first time in Ecuador, at the site of Real Alto (see chapter 6).

But the most spectacular aspect of Cerro Sechín is its mural art. The oldest works are two felines—pumas according to Bischof—and a man depicted head downward, eyes closed (a corpse?), all painted on the oldest building, built of sun-dried bricks (adobe), which belongs to phase I (that begins perhaps c. 3800 B.P.). Later (phase III), two big bas-relief fish in polychrome clay flanked the entrance staircase on the north facade. Finally, the great stone platform, which was more recent (phase IV, c. 3300 B.P.?), was entirely surrounded by a frieze of granite slabs decorated with almost 400 engraved works. Warriors wearing plumed helmets and armed with clubs or arrows, and sometimes carrying a severed human head as a trophy, are depicted in two rows that meet on both sides of the main entrance. These standing figures, which look like victors, alternate with depictions of dislocated, mutilated, dismembered, or disemboweled bodies, severed human heads from which spurted a stream of blood, or heads piled up like Mexican *tzompantli*, or torn-out eyes and viscera, or defleshed vertebral columns (fig. 33). This parade of horror, as Bischof writes, "forms an eternal procession, full of pride and power, that circulates around the building and enables one to identify it

Fig. 33. Cerro Sechín. This ceremonial complex, built in the low valley of the Río Casma, comprises an exterior wall—corresponding to the last building phase, around 3300–3200 B.P.—which is fitted with engraved slabs depicting an alternation of armed and plumed warriors in a hieratic pose (1), naked corpses cut in two (2, 3), torn-out viscera (4), severed heads or limbs (5, 6), fleshless vertebral columns (7), or piles of heads (8). The excavations by Samaniego and Bischof revealed that these works were earlier than the construction of the first temples of Chavín de Huantar.

as a place reserved for rituals or ceremonial gatherings restricted to a particular group, for example victorious warriors" (1984: 367).

In any case, the ensemble bears witness to the degree of violence that had been attained and the role that it played in ideology, if not in daily life. As Bischof has also remarked, the power reflected in this frieze is ambivalent: it is both a magical power, obtained through the capture and sacrifice of victims, and a political power that affirmed the preeminence of one group over its neighbors. Finally, in this wall impregnated with ferocity, one observes the absence of any animal elements, whereas fish and felines were depicted on the older buildings swallowed up by the final edifice. Depictions of various zoomorphic beings most often adorned the coastal or Andean "temples," which are considered to be more or less contemporaneous with Cerro Sechín: a monstrous "felinized" crustacean at Garagay (central coast), enormous modeled feline silhouettes at Huaca de los Reyes, Pampa de Las Llamas, and Punkuri (north coast)—a little later, Chavín was to produce an amalgamation and synthesis of all these depictions.

THE TWILIGHT OF CHAVÍN

Around 2400 B.P. (according to Lumbreras) or 2200 B.P. (according to Burger), the temple of Chavín de Huantar seems to have been abandoned and partly destroyed, for reasons that still remain a mystery. Throughout the territory that had hitherto been under its influence, cultural ties slackened, which probably reflects a gradual disintegration of the religious influence it had exerted till then. Over almost all of Peru, ceremonial buildings were abandoned or reoccupied by new populations, while new edifices were constructed on these same sites and often with their own materials. Little by little, the great habitation centers, both coastal and Andean, were freed from Chavín's aesthetic and ideological canons, while a process of stylistic decomposition began in art, probably reflecting this disintegration.

In the whole of the Andean world, from Ecuador to Chile, local particularisms were now gradually to express themselves. Each natural unit—a valley or intramontane basin—became the center of a "culture" whose separate identity was expressed above all in ceramic art. A similar process can be observed in Colombia and northwest Argentina, regions that were not included, at least directly, in the Chavín sphere of influence. In all these regions, the mastery of agricultural and craft techniques reached a level that was never again to be surpassed. This is particularly notable in the case of weaving and metallurgy, the progress and diffusion of which had been stimulated by the religious expansion of Chavín and the increasing production of luxury goods that was linked to it. But it was now, in what for a while became a strictly regional framework, that the so-called classic Andean civilizations developed, some of which were to see their power grow until they formed veritable little states. "Prehistoric" times were now left far behind.

ELSEWHERE, A VERY LONG "PREHISTORY"

However, South America is not limited to the Andean area, and, outside this privileged region, a large part of South American territory continued to be occupied by populations that remained at an "archaic" stage. Hence the Venezuelan *concheros* continued, until the early centuries A.D., to be occupied by fisher-hunter-gatherers who had no pottery and, apparently, no agriculture. New shell mounds—El Bajo, Las Varas—were formed between 5000 and 4000 B.P. in the Paria peninsula and were still (at this time) on the edge of the mangrove, the source of the bulk of their subsistence. Their technological equipment was as rustic as ever, although next to the worked cobbles and the big flakes a few objects of polished stone appeared—ax blades, pestles, and small vessels—as did bone points (for hunting and fishing?) and a kind of gouge made of big shells, whose function remains uncertain. No plant remains have yet been found in these mounds, but, according to Sanoja (1959), the traces of use-wear on the ax blades "could correspond" to the felling of trees as well as clearing undergrowth or digging, "perhaps associated" with primitive horticultural practices. These hypotheses are linked, and they are expressed in the conditional here because they need better support, since the first convincing evidence of horticulture in Venezuela does not date back farther than about 2500 B.P. The coastal settlements belonging to the "Manicuaroid series" defined by Cruxent and Rouse (1961) seem even more "conservative" and are represented by the camps of Cubagua, Manicuare, and Punta Gorda (4000–2000 B.P.), where subsistence was still based largely on fishing and collecting mollusks, with little or no contribution from terrestrial hunting. This way of life, exclusively turned toward the sea, was even to last beyond the arrival in the early centuries of groups with farming and pottery who came from the lower and middle Orinoco.

On the Brazilian littoral, it has not been possible to determine the age of the last *sambaquis* any more exactly than that of the first. Around 3000 B.P., most of them seem to cease to be occupied (though some would still be occupied until the early centuries A.D.). From that time onward, the littoral settlements assumed a different character: what Prous (1992) calls "littoral camps" (*acampamentos litorâneos*) still corresponds to a way of life based on the exploitation of the marine environment, but fishing became more important than mollusk collecting, and shells henceforth formed only isolated pockets in the occupation layers established on dunes or at the top of ancient *sambaquis*. The study of the skeletons found in the burials of the period seems to indicate that this was a new population that probably came from the plateaus of the interior. When the Portuguese conquest took place in the sixteenth century A.D., all the settlements of *sambaqui* type or the littoral camps were uninhabited, and the tales of the first travelers do not mention the Indians eating shellfish.

Farther south, at the frontier between Brazil and Uruguay, the late coastal occupations, in the early centuries A.D., but especially from the tenth century onward, were to take on a different form. In this region, which is liable to flooding and sprinkled with numerous lagoons whose waters are very rich in plankton, people built earthen mounds called *cerritos*. They occupied these on a regular basis in order to take advantage of the seasonal abundance of the migratory fish. So these are relatively recent sites, and all (or nearly all) contain pottery. Prous even cites the case of a Uruguayan *cerrito* where cow bones were found at a depth of 50 centimeters, evidence for an occupation later than the arrival of the Europeans (1992: 299).

If we now turn to the interior, a similar situation can be observed. In the Nordeste and on the central plateau of Brazil, the first evidence for cultivated food plants (bean and calabash in Piauí) does not date back farther than the final centuries B.C., although Prous, as we have seen, has proposed a slightly earlier date (4500–3000 B.P.) on the basis of plant remains unearthed at Santana do Riacho. The lithic technology remains highly conservative until the beginning of the third millennium B.P. In the south, the "archaic" traditions of hunting, fishing, and gathering likewise remained very active after 3000 B.P. The "Humaitá" fisher-gatherers continued to set up open-air camps on the riverbanks. Although temporary, these camps sometimes include a highly developed layout. At Alfredo Wagner, the most recent occupation layer, dating to about 3000 B.P., contained the remains—exceptionally well preserved by the marsh that covered them—of a hut with a floor paved with cobbles and a roofing of pine branches and bark (Rohr 1967). However, according to Prous, the presence of polished axes in these camps, or that of a polished edge on the large bifacial picks, could be evidence (as in the case of the Venezuelan shell mounds) of "agricultural experiments requiring the felling of trees for slash-and-burn cultivation" (1986: 259), thereby suggesting a relatively sedentary way of life. But this (indirect) evidence remains extremely meager.

At the southern extremity of the continent, whether on the continental plain of Patagonia or the coastal fringes of the Magellan Straits, a more or less comparable continuity can be observed. The Casapedrense was to be followed, in central Patagonia, by the Patagonian (Rio Pinturas III tradition in the valley of the Rio Pinturas roughly from the first to the seventh century A.D.) and, in the region of the Magellan Straits, by the largely historical Magellan V phase. Guanaco hunting continued to constitute the basis of economic life, and the toolkits scarcely changed. The whole gives the impression of great cultural stability due, it seems, to the absence of all demographic or climatic pressure (the environment and climate were more or less the same as today). The final traces of these occupations come from the Aonik'enk group or its immediate ancestors. It was the Aonik'enk hunters whom the Europeans encountered when they arrived in these lands. Still nomadic, the Aonik'enk remained in place until their final extermination at the start of the twentieth century. There is an analogous situation in the interior of Tierra del Fuego where the last "prehistoric" occupations detected in the archaeological sites were followed by those of the Selk'nam (or Onas) groups of the historical period. In the region of the Magellan Straits, the fisher-gatherer way of life was also to last without discontinuity, and the accumulation of shell mounds was to continue until the beginning of the twentieth century, the work of the Yámanas (or Yaghans) and Alakaluf ethnic groups.

Hence the European conquest in the sixteenth century took place in a varied context where, side by side, one found hierarchical, sedentary societies of food producers and hunting groups that had remained seminomadic and where pottery, already present for more than 4,000 years in one place, only appeared 1,000 or even 2,000 years later elsewhere and sometimes had not even been adopted at all. Everywhere the arrival of Europeans caused an abrupt drop in indigenous population numbers if not their disappearance, pure and simple, through the spread of infectious diseases or deliberate extermination—and this until the dawn of the twentieth century.

This book opened with a controversy—that of the first peopling of South America—and it closes with another: that of the origins of "civilization" in this same continent. Both of these questions are fundamental, and both remain unsolved despite the proliferation of research and of the sites or objects unearthed and despite the constant progress in techniques of the excavation, recovery, dating, and analysis of remains which, through the ceaselessly increasing contribution of disciplines such as physics, chemistry, the life sciences, and earth sciences, make it possible to scrutinize the very heart of the slightest fragment of material left by people in any place whatsoever. Certainly, the gaps in the puzzle are being filled in little by little, while an increasingly dense and coherent picture of prehistoric occupation is being produced. But there are still some major "blanks." And somewhat paradoxically, that enables me to end this book on an optimistic note: the prehistorians of America still have some prime times ahead of them.

Bibliography

GENERAL WORKS

BONAVIA D., 1991. *Peru. Hombre e Historia. De los origenes al siglo XV,* Edubanco, Lima.

BONNICHSEN R. and TURNMIRE K. L., eds., 1991. *Clovis: Origins and Adaptations,* Center for the Study of Early Man, Oregon State University, Corvallis.

BROWMAN D., ed., 1978. *Advances in Andean Archaeology,* Mouton, La Haye.

BRUHNS K. O., 1994. *Ancient South America,* Cambridge University Press, Cambridge.

BRYAN A. L., 1965. *Paleo-american Prehistory,* Pocatello ("Occasional Papers of the Idaho State University Museum," 16).

BRYAN A. L., 1983. "South America." In Shutler R., ed., *Early Man,* pp. 137–46.

BRYAN A. L., 1986. *New Evidence for the Pleistocene Peopling of the Americas,* Center for the Study of Early Man, University of Maine, Orono.

BRYAN A. L., ed., 1978. *Early Man in America from a Circum-Pacific Perspective,* University of Alberta, Edmonton ("Occasional Papers of the Department of Anthropology," 1).

CRUXENT J. and ROUSE I., 1961. *Arqueología Cronológica de Venezuela,* Pan American Union, Washington, D.C. ("Estudios monográficos," 6).

DONNAN C. B., ed., 1985. *Early Ceremonial Architecture in the Andes,* Dumbarton Oaks Research Library and Collection, Washington, D.C.

FERNÁNDEZ J., 1982. *Historia de la Arqueología argentina,* Asociación cuyana de Antropología, Mendoza.

GUILAINE J., ed., 1986. *La Préhistoire. D'un continent à l'autre,* Larousse, Paris.

HIDALGO J., SCHIAPACASSE V., NIEMEYER H., ALDUNATE C. and SOLIMANO I., 1989. *Culturas de Chile. Prehistoria, desde sus origenes hasta los albores de la Conquista,* Ed. Andrés Bello, Santiago.

HUMPHREY R. L. and STANFORD D., eds., 1979. *Pre-Llano Culture in the Americas: Paradoxes and Possibilities,* Anthropological Society of Washington, Washington, D.C.

JENNINGS J. D., ed., 1978. *Ancient Native Americans,* W. H. Freeman, San Francisco.

JENNINGS J. D., ed., 1983. *Ancient South Americans,* W. H. Freeman, San Francisco.

JENNINGS J. D. and NORBECK E., eds., 1964. *Prehistoric Man in the New World,* University of Chicago Press, Chicago.

KAULICKE P., 1993. *Los origenes de la civilización andina,* Ed. Brasa S. A., Lima.

KEATINGE R. W., ed., 1988. *Peruvian Prehistory,* Cambridge University Press, Cambridge.

LANNING E. P., 1967. *Peru before the Incas,* Prentice Hall, Englewood Cliffs.

LAVALLÉE D., 1985. "L'occupation préhistorique des hautes terres andines," *L'Anthropologie,* 89 (3), Paris, pp. 409–30.

LAVALLÉE D., 1986. "Cultures préhistoriques de Mésoamérique et d'Amérique du Sud." In Guilaine J., ed., *La Préhistoire*, pp. 123–37.

LAVALLÉE D., 1990. "L'Amérique du Sud précéramique," *Encyclopaedia Universalis*, 2, Paris, pp. 161–69.

LAVALLÉE D., 1992. "L'Amérique: Le milieu naturel. Les gisements pléistocènes— Amérique moyenne, centrale et méridionale." In Garanger J., ed., *La Préhistoire dans le monde*, PUF, Paris, pp. 699–716 (avec P. Plumet) et 766–801 (Coll. "Nouvelle Clio").

LAVALLÉE D., 1994. "Le peuplement préhistorique de la Cordillère des Andes," *Bulletin de la Société Préhistorique Française*, 91 (4–5), Paris, pp. 264–74.

LAVALLÉE D., 1995. *Promesse d'Amériqu: La Préhistoire de l'Amérique du Sud*, Hachette, Paris (Coll. "La Mémoire du temps").

LEROI-GOURHAN A., ed., 1993. *Dictionnaire de la Préhistoire*, Presses universitaires de France, Paris (2nd ed.).

LYNCH T. F., 1978. "The South American Paleo-Indians." In Jennings J. D., ed., *Prehistoric Man*, pp. 455–89.

LYNCH T. F., 1983. "The Paleo-Indians." In Jennings J. D., ed., *Prehistoric Man*, pp. 87–137.

MACNEISH R. S. et al., 1980–83. *Prehistory of the Ayacucho Basin, Peru* (3 vols.). R. S. Peabody Foundation for Archaeology, University of Michigan Press, Ann Arbor.

MARCOS J., ed., 1986. *Arqueología de la costa ecuatoriana. Nuevos enfoques*, Espol, Guayaquil ("Biblioteca Ecuatoriana de Arqueología").

MARTIN P. S. and WRIGHT H. E., eds., 1967. *Pleistocene Extinctions: The Search for a Cause*, Yale University Press, New Haven.

MEGGERS B., ed., 1992. *Prehistoria Sudamericana. Nuevas perspectivas*, Taraxacum, Washington, D.C.

MOSELEY M., 1993. *The Incas and Their Ancestors*, Thames and Hudson, London.

ORQUERA L. A., 1987. "Advances in the Archaeology of the Pampas and Patagonia," *Journal of World Archaeology*, 1 (4), pp. 333–413.

PROUS A., 1986. "L'archéologie au Brésil. 300 siècles d'occupation humaine," *L'Anthropologie*, 90 (2), pp. 257–306.

PROUS A., 1992. *Arqueologia Brasileira*, Ed. Universidade de Brasilia, Brasilia.

ROUSE I. and CRUXENT J. M., 1963. *Venezuelan Archaeology*, Yale University Press, New Haven ("University Caribbean Series," 6).

SCHMITZ P. I., 1987. "Prehistoric Hunters and Gatherers of Brazil," *Journal of World Prehistory*, 1 (1), pp. 53–126.

SCHOBINGER J., 1988. *Prehistoria de Sudamérica. Culturas precerámicas*, Alianza Editorial, Barcelona.

SHUTLER R., ed., 1983. *Early Man in the New World*, Sage, Beverly Hills.

VAN DER HAMMEN T., 1986. *The Palaeoecology of Tropical South America*, Netherlands Foundation for the Advancement of Tropical Research (Wotro), La Haye, pp. 35–91.

VAN DER HAMMEN T., 1992. *Historia, Ecología y Vegetación*, Corporación Araracuara, Bogotá.

WENDORF F. and CLOSE A. E., eds., 1983. *Advances in World Archaeology*, Academic Press, New York.

WILLEY G. R., 1966 and 1971. *An Introduction to American Archaeology*, vol.1, *North and Middle America*; vol. 2, *South America*, Prentice Hall, Englewood Cliffs.

WILSON D., 1999. *Indigenous South Americans of the Past and Present: An Ecological Perspective*. Westview Press, Boulder.

CHAPTER 1. THE DISCOVERY OF A WORLD

ACOSTA J. de [1590], 1962. *Historia natural y moral de las Indias*, Fondo de Cultura Economica, Mexico (Biblioteca americana 38).

ADAM J. P., 1975. *L'archéologie devant l'imposture,* Robert Laffont, Paris.

ALCINA FRANCH J., 1985. *Los Origenes de América,* Ed. Alhambra, Madrid.

AMEGHINO F., 1880–81. *La Antigüedad del Hombre en La Plata,* Masson, Paris and Buenos Aires.

AMEGHINO F., 1909. "Las formaciones sedimentarias de la región litoral de Mar del Plata y Chapadmalan," *Anales del Museo Nacional de Buenos Aires,* 17, pp. 343–428.

BAULNY O., 1968. "Une gloire française oubliée: Alcide d'Orbigny, père de l'américanisme moderne," *Americana,* 1, Paris.

BENNASSAR B. and BENNASSAR L., 1991. *1492. Un monde nouveau?* Perrin, Paris.

BEUCHAT H., 1912. *Manuel d'archéologie américaine,* A. Picard, Paris.

BOMAN E., 1908. *Antiquités de la région andine de la République argentine et du désert d'Atacama,* Mission scientifique G. de Créqui-Montfort and E. Sénéchal de la Grange, Imprimerie nationale, Paris (2 vols.).

BOMAN E., 1919. "Encore l'homme tertiaire dans l'Amérique du Sud," *Journal de la Société des Américanistes,* 11, Paris, pp. 657–64.

CABRERA J., 1976. *El mensaje de las piedras grabadas de Ica,* Inti-Sol Ed., Lima.

CASTELLANOS A., 1923. "La limite plio-pléistocène et le problème de l'homme tertiaire dans la République argentine," *Revista de la Universidad Nacional de Córdoba,* 1–2–3, Córdoba.

CASTELLANOS A., 1927. "Apuntes sobre el Homo Chapadmaensis n. sp.," *Trabalhos da Sociedade Portuguesa de Antropologia e Etnologia,* 3/3, Pôrto.

CASTELLANOS A., 1929. "Nuevos restos del hombre fósil (nota informatica)," *Physis,* Sociadad Argentina de Ciencias Naturales, Buenos Aires, pp. 175–81.

CASTELLANOS A., 1934. "Conexiones sudamericanas en relación con las migraciones humanas," *Quid Novi?* 6, Buenos Aires, pp. 1–11.

CHARROUX R., 1974. *L'énigme des Andes,* Robert Laffont, Paris.

CHAUNU P., 1976. *Les Amériques. 16e 17e 18e siècles,* Armand Colin, Paris.

DARWIN C., 1839. *Narrative of the Surveying Voyages of HMS "Adventure" and "Beagle" between 1826 and 1836, III,* London.

FERNÁNDEZ J., 1982. *Historia de la arqueología argentina,* Asociación cuyana de antropología, Mendoza.

GARCILASO de la VEGA Inca [1609], 1982. *Commentaires royaux sur le Pérou des Incas,* translated by R. L. F. Durand, Maspero, Paris.

HOCH E. and PROUS A., 1985. "A contribucão de P. W. Lund à arqueologia européia e brasileira," *Arquivos,* 10, Belo Horizonte, pp. 170–76.

HRDLIČKA A., 1913. "Early Man in South America," *Proceedings of the International Congress of Americanists* (Buenos Aires 1910), 18, London, pp. 10–21.

HUMBOLDT A. von and BONPLAND A., 1961. *Voyage aux régions équinoxiales du Nouveau Continent,* Club des Libraires de France, Paris (1st ed., Paris 1814).

LAMING-EMPERAIRE A., 1979. "Mission archéologiques franco-brésiliennes à Lagoa Santa, Minas Gerais, Brésil—Le Grand Abri de Lapa Vermelha," *Revista de Pré-Historia,* 1/1, Instituto de Pré-Historia, Universidade de São Paulo, São Paulo, pp. 53–89.

LAMING-EMPERAIRE A., 1980. *Le problème des origines américaines,* Maison des Sciences de l'Homme et Presses Universitaires de Lille, Paris.

LEHMANN-NITSCHE R., 1907. "Nouvelles recherches sur la formation pampéenne et l'homme fossile de la République argentine (recueil de contributions scientifiques)," *Revista del Museo de La Plata,* 14, pp. 143–479.

LHOTE H., 1972. "L'Amérique et l'Atlantide," *Bulletin de la Société des Explorateurs et Voyageurs Français,* 22, Paris.

LUND P. W., 1950. *Memórias sobre a Paleontologia brasileira,* revised and with a commentary by Carlos de Paula Couto, Instituto Nacional do Livro, Rio de Janeiro.

MAHN-LOT M., 1970. *La découverte de l'Amérique,* Flammarion, Paris ("Questions d'Histoire," 18).

ORBIGNY A. d', 1835–45. *Voyage dans l'Amérique méridionale*, Bertrand, Paris-Strasbourg (9 vols.).

ORBIGNY A. d', 1839. *L'homme américain de l'Amérique méridionale, considéré sous ses aspects physiologiques et moraux*, Pitois-Levrault, Paris (2 vols.).

OSTOYA P., 1962. "Le succès d'un mauvais livre : le Matin des Magiciens," *La Nature*, June, Paris, pp. 263–64.

OUTES F. and BRUCH C., 1951. *Los Aborigenes de la República argentina*, Ed. Estrada, Buenos Aires (10th ed.).

PAUWELS L. and BERGIER J., 1960. *Le Matin des Magiciens. Introduction au réalisme fantastique*, Gallimard, Paris.

RIVET P., 1943. *Les origines de l'homme américain*, L'Arbre, Montréal.

RIVIALE P., 1996. *Un siècle d'archéologie française au Pérou (1821–1914)*, L'Harmattan, Paris.

RONSIN A., 1979. *Découverte et baptême de l'Amérique*, Ed. Georges Le Pape, Montréal.

TODOROV T., 1982. *La Conquête de l'Amérique*, Le Seuil, Paris.

UHLE M., 1903. *Pachacámac. Report of the William Pepper Peruvian Expedition of 1896*, Department of Anthropology, University of Pennsylvania, Philadelphia.

UHLE M., 1910. "Uber die Frühkulturen in der Umgebung von Lima," *Proceedings of the 16th International Congress of Americanists*, A. Hartleben's Verlag, Wien and Leipzig, pp. 347–70.

UHLE M., 1913. "Die Müschelhügel von Ancón," *Proceedings of the 18th International Congress of Americanists*, London, pp. 22–49.

UHLE M., 1919. "La Arqueología de Tacna y Arica," *Boletin de la Sociedad ecuatoriana de estudios históricos americanos*, Quito.

ULLOA A. de, 1772. *Noticias americanas. Entretenimiento historico-físico sobre la América meridional y la septentrional oriental*, Madrid.

ULLOA A. de and JUAN J., 1826. *Noticias secretas de América*, London.

VIGNAUD H., 1917. *Améric Vespuce. 1451–1512*, E. Leroux, Paris.

CHAPTER 2. THE FIRST OCCUPANTS

ADOVASIO J. M., 1993. "The Ones that Will Not Go Away." In Soffer O. and Praslov N. D., eds., *From Kostenki to Clovis. Upper Palaeolithic-Paleo-Indian Adapatations*, Interdisciplinary Contributions to Archaeology, Plenum Press, New York, pp. 199–218.

ADOVASIO J. M., BOLDURIAN A. T., and CARLISLE R. C., 1988. "Who Are Those Guys? Some Biased Thoughts on the Initial Peopling of the New World." In Carlisle R. C., ed., *Americans before Columbus: Ice-Age Origins*, Department of Anthropology, University of Pittsburgh, Pittsburgh, pp. 45–61.

ADOVASIO J. M., DONAHUE J., CUSHMAN K., CARLISLE R. C., STUCKENRATH R., GUNN J. D., and JOHNSON W. C., 1983. "Evidence from Meadowcroft Rockshelter." In Shutler R., ed., *Early Man*, pp. 163–89.

ADOVASIO J. M., DONAHUE J., and STUCKENRATH R., 1990. "The Meadowcroft Rockshelter Radiocarbon Chronology 1975–1990," *American Antiquity*, 55, pp. 348–54.

ARDILA G. and POLITIS G., 1989. "Nuevos datos para un viejo problema," *Boletin del Museo de Oro*, 23, Bogotá, pp. 3–45.

BELTRÃO M. C., 1974. "Datacões arqueologicas mais antigas do Brasil," *Anais da Academia Brasileira de Ciências*, 46, pp. 211–51.

BELTRÃO M. C. and DANON J., 1987. "Evidence of Human Occupations during the Middle Pleistocene at the Toca da Esperança in the Central Archaeological Region, State of Bahia, Brazil," *Sessão regular da Academia Brasileira de Ciencias* (23.06.87).

BELTRÃO M. C. et al., 1982. "Sur l'arrivée de l'homme en Amérique: datations par thermoluminescence des silex brûlés du site archéologique de Alice Boër (Brésil)," *Comptes-rendus de l'Académie des Sciences,* série 2, 95, Paris, pp. 629–32.

BERNARD J., 1983. *Le Sang et l'Histoire,* Buchet/Chastel, Paris.

BIRD J., 1951. "South American Radiocarbon Dates," *American Antiquity,* 17, pp. 37–49.

BONNICHSEN R., 1978. "Critical Arguments for Pleistocene Artifacts from the Old Crow Basin, Yukon: A Preliminary Statement." In Bryan A. L., ed., *Early Man,* pp. 102–18.

BONNICHSEN R., 1979. *Pleistocene Bone Technology in the Beringian Refugium,* Musée national de l'Homme, Ottawa (Coll. Mercure).

BRAY W., 1986. "Finding the Earliest Americans," *Nature,* 321, p. 726.

BRAY W., 1988. "The Paleoindian Debate," *Nature,* 332, p. 107.

BRYAN A. L., 1979. "The Stratigraphy of Taima-Taima." In Ochsenius C. and Gruhn R., eds., *Taima-Taima : A Late Pleistocene Paleo-indian Kill in Northernmost South America—Final Reports of 1976 Excavations,* pp. 41–52.

BRYAN A. L., 1986. *New Evidence for the Pleistocene Peopling of the Americas,* Center for the Study of Early Man, University of Maine, Orono.

BRYAN A. L. and BELTRÃO M. C., 1978. "An Early Stratified Sequence near Rio Claro, East Central São Paulo State, Brazil." In Bryan A., ed., *Early Man,* pp. 137–46.

BRYAN A. L. and GRUHN R., 1989. "The Evolutionary Significance of the American Lower Paleolithic." In Mirambell L., ed., *Homenaje a J. L. Lorenzo,* INAH, Mexico, pp. 81–102 (Serie Prehistoria).

BRYAN A. L. et al. , 1978. "An El Jobo Mastodon Kill at Taima-Taima, Venezuela," *Science,* 200, pp. 1275–77.

CARDICH A., 1978. "Recent Excavations at Lauricocha and Los Toldos." In Bryan A. L., ed., *Early Man,* pp. 296–302.

CARDICH A., 1980. "Origen del hombre y de la cultura andina," *Historia del Peru,* 1, Mejia Baca, Lima, pp. 31–156.

CARDICH A. et al., 1973. "Secuencia arqueológica y cronología radiocarbónica de la cueva 3 de Los Toldos (Santa Cruz, Argentina)," *Relaciones,* 7, Buenos Aires, pp. 85–123.

CARDICH A. et al., 1981–82. "Arqueología de las cuevas de El Ceibo, provincia de Santa Cruz, Argentina," *Relaciones,* 14, Buenos Aires, pp. 173–209.

CAVALLI-SFORZA L. L., 1991. "Genes, Peoples, and Languages," *Scientific American.*

CHAUCHAT C. and DRICOT J., 1979. "Un nouveau type humain fossile en Amérique du Sud : l'Homme de Paiján (Pérou)," *Comptes-rendus de l'Académie des Sciences,* t. 289, Paris, pp. 387–89.

CINQ-MARS J., 1990. *Investigaciones arqueológicas en los abrigos rocosos del Tequendama : 11,000 años de prehistoria en la planicie de Bogotá,* Bogotá, Banco Popular.

CORREAL G., 1981. *Evidencias culturales y megafauna pleistocénica en Colombia,* Bogotá, Finarco.

CRAWFORD M. H., 1998. *The Origins of Native Americans: Evidence from Anthropological Genetics,* Cambridge University Press, Cambridge.

CRUXENT J. M., 1970. "Projectile Points with Pleistocene Mammals in Venezuela," *Antiquity,* 44, pp. 223–25.

DELIBRIAS G. and GUIDON N., 1986. "L'abri Toca do Boqueirão da Pedra Furada," *L'Anthropologie,* 90 (2), pp. 307–16.

DELIBRIAS G., GUIDON N., and PARENTI F., 1988. "The Toca do Boqueirão do Sitio da Pedra Furada : Stratigraphy and Chronology." In Prescott J. R., ed., *Early Man in the Southern Hemisphere,* Suppl. to *Archeaometry: Australasian Studies,* University of Adelaide (Australia), pp. 3–11.

DILLEHAY T., 1984. "A Late Ice-Age Settlement in Southern Chile," *Scientific American,* 251, pp. 106–17.

DILLEHAY T., 1997. "¿Donde estan los restos óseos humanos del periodo pleistoceno tardío?," *Boletin de Arqueología* PUCP, 1, Pontificia Universidad Católica del Perú, Lima, pp. 55–63.

DILLEHAY T. et al., 1986. "Monte Verde : adaptación humana en el centro-sur de Chile durante el Pleistoceno Tardio," *Journal de la Société des Américanistes,* 72, pp. 87–106.

DILLEHAY T., ed., 1989. *Monte Verde: A Late Pleistocene Settlement in Chile,* vol.1, Smithsonian Institution, Washington, D.C.

DILLEHAY T., ed., 1997. *Monte Verde: A Late Pleistocene Settlement in Chile,* vol. 2, Smithsonian Institution, Washington, D.C.

DILLEHAY T. and MELTZER D., eds., 1991. *The First Americans: Search and Research,* CRC Press, Boca Raton.

DINCAUZE D., 1984. "An Archaeological Evaluation of the Case for Pre-Clovis Occupations." In Wendorf F. and Close A., eds.,. *Advances in World Archaeology,* pp. 275–323.

ELIAS S. A., SHORT S. K., PHILLIPS R. L., 1992. "Paleoecology of Late-Glacial Peats from the Bering Land Bridge, Chukchi Sea Shelf Region, Northwestern Alaska," *Quaternary Research,* 38 (3), pp. 371–78.

ERLANDSON, J. M. et al., 1996a. "An Archaeological and Paleontological Chronology for Daisy Cave (CA-SMI-261), San Miguel Island, California," *Radiocarbon,* 38 (2), pp. 355–73.

ERLANDSON, J. M. et al., 1996b. "Further Evidence for a Terminal Pleistocene Occupation of Daisy Cave, San Miguel Island, California," *Current Research in the Pleistocene,* 13, Center for the Study of the First Americans, Oregon State University, Corvallis, pp. 13–15.

FAGAN B., 1990. "Tracking the First Americans," *Archaeology,* November/December, pp. 14–20.

FLADMARK K. R., 1979. "Routes: Alternative Migration Corridors for Early Man in North America," *American Antiquity,* 44, pp. 55–69.

FLADMARK K. R., 1982. "Le peuplement de l'Amérique," *La Recherche,* 137, Paris, pp. 1110–18.

FLADMARK K. R., 1983. "Times and Places: Environmental Correlates of Mid-to Late Wisconsinan Human Population Expansion in North America." In Shutler R., ed., *Early Man,* pp.13–42.

FRISON G. C. and WALKER D. N., 1990. "New World Palaeoecology at the Last Glacial Maximum and the Implications for New World Prehistory." In Soffer O. and Gamble C., eds., *The World at 18000 BP,* London, Unwin Hyman, pp. 312–30.

GIBBONS A., 1993. "Geneticists Trace the DNA Trail of the First Americans," *Science,* 259, pp. 312–13.

GIBBONS A., 1998. "Mother Tongues Trace Steps of Earliest Americans," *Science,* 279, pp. 1306–7.

GOWLETT J. A. J., 1986. "Problems in Dating the Early Human Settlement of the Americas." In Gowlett J. A. J. and Hedges R. E. M., eds., *Archaeological Results from Accelerator Dating,* Oxford University Committee for Archaeology, Oxford, pp. 51–59.

GREENBERG J. H., 1987. *Language in the Americas,* Stanford University Press, Stanford.

GREENBERG J. H. and RUHLEN M., 1992. "Linguistic Origins of Native Americans," *Scientific American,* 267, pp. 94–99.

GREENBERG J. H., TURNER II C. G., and ZEGURA S. L., 1986. "The Settlement of the Americas : A Comparison of the Linguistic, Dental, and Genetic Evidence," *Current Anthropology,* 27, pp. 477–97.

GREEMAN E. F., 1963. "The Upper Palaeolithic and the New World," *Current Anthropology,* 4 (1), pp. 41–66.

GRUHN R., 1978. "A Note on Excavations at El Bosque, Nicaragua, in 1975." In Bryan A. L., ed., *Early Man,* pp. 261–62.

GUERIN C., 1991. "La faune de vertébrés du Pléistocène supérieur de l'aire archéologique de São Raimundo Nonato (Piaui, Brésil)," *Comptes-Rendus de l'Académie des Sciences,* 312, Paris, pp. 567–72.

GUIDON N., 1984. "Les premières occupations humaines de l'aire archéologique de São Raimundo Nonato, Piaui, Brésil," *L'Anthropologie*, 88 (2), pp. 263–71.

GUIDON N., 1986. "Las unidades culturales de São Raimundo Nonato, Sudeste del Estado de Piaui." In Bryan A. L., ed., *Early Man*, p. 171.

GUIDON N., 1989. "On Stratigraphy and Chronology at Pedra Furada," *Current Anthropology*, 30 (5), pp. 641–42.

GUIDON N. and ARNAUD B., 1991. "The Chronology of the New World: Two Faces of One Reality," *World Archaeology*, 23 (2), pp. 167–78.

GUIDON N. and DELIBRIAS G., 1986. "Carbon-14 Dates Point to Man in the Americas 32,000 Years Ago," *Nature*, 321, pp. 769–71.

GUIDON N. and PESSIS A.M., 1996. "Falsehood or Untruth?" *Antiquity*, 70, pp. 408–15.

HAYNES C. V., 1969. "The Earliest Americans," *Science*, 166, pp. 709–15.

HAYNES C. V., 1980. "When and from Where Did Man Arrive in Northeastern North America : A Discussion." In Newman W. S. and Salwen B., eds., *Amerinds and Their Paleoenvironments in Northeastern North America*, New York Acadamy of Sciences, 228, pp. 165–66.

HAYNES C. V., 1988. "Geofacts and Fancy," *Natural History*, 97 (2), pp. 4–11.

HOPKINS D. M., MATTHEWS J. V., and SCHWEGER C. E., eds., 1982. *Palaeoecology of Beringia*, Academic Press, New York.

HRDLIČKA. A., 1912. *Early Man in South America*, Bulletin 52, Bureau of American Ethnology, Smithsonian Institution, Washington, D.C..

IRVING W. N., 1987. "The First Americans. New Dates from Old Bones," *Natural History*, 96 (2), pp. 8–13.

KIDDER A. V., 1927. "Early Man in America," *Masterkey*, 1 (5), pp. 5–13.

KIRK R. and SZATHMARY E., 1985. "Out of Asia : Peopling the Americas and the Pacific," *Journal of Pacific History*, Canberra.

KRIEGER A., 1964. "Early Man in the New World." In Jennings J. and Norbeck E., eds., *Prehistoric Man*, pp. 23–81.

KUZMIN, Y. V., 1996. "The Colonization of Eastern Siberia: An Evaluation of the Paleolithic Age Radiocarbon Dates," *Journal of Archaeological Science*, 23, pp. 577–85.

KUZMIN, Y .V. and ORLOVA L. A., 1998. "Radiocarbon Chronology of the Siberian Paleolithic," *Journal of World Prehistory*, 12 (1), pp. 1–53.

LACOMBE J. P. and CHAUCHAT C., 1986. "Il y a 10 000 ans, l'Homme de Paijan," *Archéologia*, 209, pp. 44–47.

LAMING-EMPERAIRE A., 1979. "Missions archéologiques franco-brésiliennes de Lagoa Santa, MG., Brésil. Le Grand Abri de Lapa Vermelha," *Revista de Pre-historia*, 1, São Paulo, pp. 53–90.

LAMING-EMPERAIRE A., 1980. *Le problème des origines américaines*, Ed. de la Maison des Sciences de l'Homme, Presses universitaires de Lille (Cahiers d'Archéologie et d'Ethonologie d'Amérique du Sud).

LAMING-EMPERAIRE A. et al., 1975. *Grottes et abris de la région de Lagoa Santa, Minas Gerais, Brésil*, E.P.H.E., Paris (Cahiers d'Archéologie d'Amérique du Sud, 1).

LANNING E. P., 1973. "Burin Industries in the Pleistocene of the Andes," *Estudios Atacameños*, 1, Univ. del Norte, San Pedro de Atacama, pp. 25–30.

LAUGHLIN W. S. and HARPER A. B., eds., 1979. *The First Americans: Origins, Affinities and Adaptations*, Gustav Fisher, New York-Stuttgart.

LAVALLÉE D., 1985. "L'occupation préhistorique des hautes terres andines," *L'Anthropologie*, 89 (3), pp. 409–30.

LAVALLÉE D., 1986. "Cultures préhistoriques de Mésoamérique et d'Amérique du Sud." In Guilaine J., ed., *La Préhistoire, d'un continent à l'autre*, Larousse, Paris, pp. 123–37.

LAVALLÉE D., 1989. "Un homme en Amérique il y a 300 000 ans?" *Les Nouvelles de l'archéologie*, 36, pp. 14–16.

LAVALLÉE D., 1990. "Le peuplement de l'Amérique," *Encyclopaedia Universalis*, 2, pp. 84–86.

LAVALLÉE D., 1991. "Les gisements pléistocènes (Amérique moyenne et centrale, Amérique du Sud." In Garanger J., ed., *La Préhistoire dans le Monde*, P.U.F., Paris, 1991, pp. 706–16 (Coll. Nouvelle Clio).

LEROI-GOURHAN A., 1991. "La préhistoire du Japon dans ses phases climatiques," *L'Anthropologie*, 29 (1–2), pp. 115–22.

LORENZO J. L and MIRAMBELL L., 1986. "Preliminary Report on Archaeological and Paleoenvironmental Studies in the Area of El Cedral, San Luis Potosi, Mexico." In Bryan A. L., ed., *Early Man*, pp. 107–13.

LORENZO J. L., MIRAMBELL L., et al., 1986. "The Antiquity of Man in South America," *Quaternary Research*, 4, pp. 356–77.

LYNCH T. F., 1978. "The South American Paleo-Indians." In Jennings J. D., ed., *Ancient Native Americans*, pp. 455–89.

LUMLEY H., DE MORAES M. A., COUTINHO BELTRÃO M. C., YOKOYAMA Y., LABEYRIE J., DANON J., DELIBRIAS G., FALGUÈRES C., and BISCHOFF J. L., 1987. "Présence d'outils taillés associés à une faune quaternaire datée du Pléistocène moyen dans la Toca da Esperança, Région de Central, Etat de Bahía, Brésil," *L'Anthropologie*, 91 (4), Paris, pp. 917–42.

LUMLEY H. et al., 1988. "Découverte d'outils taillés associés à des faunes du Pléistocène moyen dans la Toca da Esperança, Etat de Bahía, Brésil," *Comptes-Rendus de l'Académie des Sciences*, t.306, Paris, s.II, pp. 241–47.

LYNCH T. F., 1983. "The Paleo-Indians." In Jennings J. D., ed., *Ancient South Americans*, pp. 87–137.

LYNCH T. F., 1990a. "Glacial-Age Man in South America? A Critical Review," *American Antiquity*, 55, pp. 12–36.

LYNCH T. F., 1990b. "El Hombre de la Edad Glacial en Sudamerica: une Perspectiva Europea," *Revista de Arqueologia Americana*, 1, pp. 141–85.

LYNCH T. F., 1991. "Lack of Evidence for Glacial-Age Settlement of South America: Reply to Dillehay and Collins and to Gruhn and Bryan," *American Antiquity*, 56, pp. 348–55.

MACNEISH R. S., 1976. "Early Man in the New World," *American Scientist*, 63 (3), pp. 316–27.

MACNEISH R. S., 1996. "Pendejo Pre-Clovis Proofs and Their Implications," *Fumdhamentos*, Revista da Fundação do Homen Americano, 1 (1), São Raimundo Nonato, pp. 171–200 (Proceedings of the International Meeting on the Peopling of the Americas, 1993).

MACNEISH R. S. et al., 1981. *Prehistory of the Ayacucho Basin, Peru*. Vol. 2: *Excavations and Chronology*. R. S. Peabody Foundation for Archaeology, University of Michigan Press, Ann Arbor.

MACNEISH R. S. et al., 1983. *Prehistory of the Ayacucho Basin, Peru*. Vol. 4: *The Preceramic Way of Life*. R. S. Peabody Foundation for Archaeology, University of Michigan Press, Ann Arbor.

MANSUR-FRANCHOMME E., 1986. *Microscopie du matériel lithique : traces d'utilisation, altérations naturelles, accidentelles et technologiques. Exemples de Patagonie*, CNRS, Bordeaux ("Cahiers du Quaternaire").

MELTZER D., 1989. "Why Don't We Know When the First People Came to America?" *American Antiquity*, 54, pp. 471–90.

MELTZER D., 1993. "Pleistocene Peopling of the Americas," *Evolutionary Anthropology*, 1 (5), pp. 157–69.

MELTZER D., ADOVASIO J., and DILLEHAY T., 1994. "On a Pleistocene Human Occupation at Pedra Furada, Brazil," *Antiquity*, 68, pp. 695–714.

MENDES CORREA A. A., 1925. "O significado genealogico do *Australopithecus* e do crânio de Tabgha e o arco antropofilético indico," *Trabalhos da Sociedade Portuguesa de Antropologia e Etnologia*, 2 (3), Pôrto.

MENGHIN O., 1957. "Vorgeschichte Amerikas." In Oldenburg R., ed., *Abriss der Vorgeschichte*, Munich, pp. 162–218.

MERRIWETHER D. A. et al., 1996. "MtDNA Variation Indicates Mongolia May Have Been the Source for the Founding Population of the New World," *American Journal of Human Genetics*, 59, pp. 204–12.

MIRAMBELL L., 1994. "Recherches récentes sur le stade lithique au Mexique," *Bulletin de la Société Préhistorique Française*, 91 (4–5), pp. 240–45.

MORLAN R. E., 1979. "A Stratigraphic Framework for Pleistocene Artifacts from Old Crow River, Northern Yukon Territory." In Humphrey R. L. and Stanford D., eds., *Pre-Llano Culture*, pp. 125–45.

MORLAN R. E., 1983. "Pre-Clovis Occupations North of the Ice-Sheets." In Shutler R., ed., *Early Man*, pp. 47–63.

MORLAN R. E., 1988. "Pre-Clovis People: Early Discoveries of America?" In Carlisle R. C., ed., *Americans before Columbus: Ice-Age Origins*, Department of Anthropology, University of Pittsburgh, Pittsburgh, pp. 31–43.

MORLAN R. E., and CINQ-MARS J., 1989. "The Peopling of the Americas as Seen from Northern Yukon Territory." In Tomenchuk J. and Bonnichsen R., eds., *The First World Summit Conference on the Peopling of the Americas (Abstracts)*, University of Maine at Orono, pp. 11–12.

NELSON D. E. et al., 1986. "New Dates on Northern Yukon Artifacts: Holocene Not Upper Pleistocene," *Science*, 232 (4551), pp. 749–51.

NICHOLS J., 1990. "Linguistic Diversity and First Settlement of the New World," *Language*, 66, pp. 475–521.

PARENTI F., 1993. "Le gisement quaternaire de la Toca do Boqueirão da Pedra Furada (Piaui, Brésil) dans le contexte de la préhistoire américaine. Fouilles, stratigraphie, chronologie, évolution culturelle." Thèse de Doctorat, Paris, EHESS.

PARENTI F., FONTUGNE M., and GUERIN C., 1996. "Pedra Furada in Brazil, and Its 'Presumed' Evidence: Limitations and Potential of the Available Data," *Antiquity*, 70, pp. 416–21.

PARENTI F., MERCIER N., and VALLADAS H., 1990. "The Old Hearths of Pedra Furada, Brazil: Thermoluminescence Analysis of Heated Stones," *Current Research in the Pleistocene*, 7, pp. 36–38.

PARENTI F. and TORRONI A., 1994. "Archeologia preistorica e analisi del DNA mitocondriale nella questione del popolamento delle Americhe," *Rivista di Antropologia*, 72, Roma, pp. 1–14.

PEYRE E., 1993. "Nouvelle découverte d'un homme préhistorique américain : une femme de 9700 ans au Brésil," *Comptes-Rendus de l'Académie des Sciences*, 316, pp. 839–42.

PLUMET P., 1991. "Les gisements pléistocènes (Amérique du Nord)—Le Nord et le premier peuplement de l'Amérique." In Garanger J., ed., *La Préhistoire dans le Monde*, P.U.F., Paris, pp. 705–06 et 716–65 (coll. Nouvelle Clio).

PLUMET P., 1994. "Le premier peuplement de l'Amérique et de l'Arctique? Etat des problèmes," *Bulletin de la Société Préhistorique Française*, 91 (4–5), pp. 228–39.

POWERS, W. R., 1996. "Siberia in the Late Glacial and Early Postglacial." In Straus, L. G., Eriksen B. V., Erlandson J. M., and Yesner D. R., eds., *Humans at the End of the Ice Age: The Archaeology of the Pleistocene-Holocene Transition*, Plenum Press, New York, pp. 229–42.

POWLEDGE T. M. and ROSE M., 1996. "Colonizing the Americas: The Great DNA Hunt, Part II," *Archaeology*, November-December, pp. 58–66.

PROUS A., 1986. "Os mais antiguos vestigios arqueológicos no Brasil central." In Bryan A. L., *New Evidence*, pp. 173–82.

PROUS A., 1991 and 1992–93. "Santana do Riacho," *Arquivos do Museu de Historia Natural* (12, 13/14), Universidade Federal de Minas Gerais, Belo Horizonte.

PROUS A., 1995. "Archaeological Analysis of the Oldest Settlements in the Americas," *Brazilian Journal of Genetics*, 18 (4), pp. 689–99.

REYNOLDS T. E. G., 1986. "Toward Peopling the New World : A Possible Early Palaeolithic in Tohoku District, Japan," *American Antiquity*, 51, pp. 330–32.

RIVET P., 1943. *Les origines de l'homme américain,* Ed. de l'Arbre, Montreal.

ROUSE I. and CRUXENT J. M., 1963. *Venezuelan Archaeology,* Yale University Press, New Haven ("University Caribbean Series," 6).

SCHOBINGER J., 1988. "200.000 años del hombre en América : que pensar?" *Espacio, Tiempo y Forma,* Revista de la Facultad de Geografía e Historia, Univ. Nac. de Educación a distancia, Madrid, pp. 375–95 (Serie 1, Prehistoria, 1).

SIMPSON R. D., PATTERSON L., and SINGER C., 1986. "Lithic Technology of the Calico Mountains Site, Southern California." In Bryan A. L., *New Evidence,* pp. 89–105.

SOFFER O. and PRASLOV N. D., eds., 1993. *From Kostenki to Clovis: Upper Palaeolithic Paleo-Indian Adaptations,* Plenum Press, New York.

SORG M., 1985. "New Date for Old Crow Caribou Flesher," *Mammoth Trumpet,* 2, (2), Orono, p. 1.

TANKERSLEY K. and MUNSON C., 1992. "Comments on the Meadowcroft Rockshelter Radiocarbon Chronology and the Recognition of Coal Contamination," *American Antiquity,* 57, pp. 321–26.

TAYLOR R. E. et al., 1985. "Major Revisions in the Pleistocene Age Assignments for North American Human Skeletons by C-14 Accelerator Mass Spectrometry: None Older than 11,000 C-14 years BP," *American Antiquity,* 50, pp. 136–40.

TORRONI A. et al., 1993. "MtDNA Variation of Aboriginal Siberians Reveals Distinct Genetic Affinities with Native Americans," *American Journal of Human Genetics,* 53, pp. 591–608.

TORRONI A. et al., 1994. "Mitochondrial DNA 'Clock' for the Amerinds and Its Implications for Timing Their Entry into North America," *Proccedings of the National Academy of Science, USA,* 91, pp. 1158–62.

TURNER II C. G., 1988. "Ancient Peoples of the North Pacific Rim." In Fitzhugh W. and Crowell A., eds., *Crossroads of Continents. Cultures of Siberia and Alaska,* Smithsonian Institution Press, Washington, D.C., pp. 111–16.

VAN DER HAMMEN T., 1978. "Stratigraphy and Environments of the Upper Quaternary of the El Abra Corridor and Rockshelter (Colombia)," *The Quaternary of Colombia,* 6, Elsevier, Amsterdam, pp. 111–62.

VAN DER HAMMEN T., 1992. *Historia, ecologia y vegetación.* COA-FEN, Bogotá.

WALLACE D. C. and TORRONI A., 1992. "American Indian Prehistory as Written in the Mitochondrial DNA: A Review," *Human Biology,* 64 (3), pp. 403–16.

WATERS M. R., 1985. "Early Man in the New World : An Evaluation of the Radiocarbon Dated Pre-Clovis Sites in the Americas." In Mead J. I. and Meltzer D. J., eds., *Environments and Extinctions: Man in Late Glacial North America,* Center for the Study of Early Man, Orono.

WEST F. H., 1996. *American Beginnings. The Prehistory and Palaeoecology of Beringia,* University of Chicago Press, Chicago.

WILLEY G. R., 1966 and 1971. *An Introduction to American Archaeology,* vol.1, *North and Middle America*; vol. 2, *South America,* Prentice Hall, Englewood Cliffs.

WORMINGTON M., 1957. *Ancient Man in North America,* Denver Museum of Natural History, Denver (Popular Series 4).

CHAPTER 3. THE TIME OF THE HUNTERS

AB'SABER A., 1977, "Espaços ocupados pela expansão do climas secos na America do Sul por ocasão dos periodos glaciais quarternários," *Paleoclimas,* 3, Universidade de São Paulo, São Paulo.

ALDENDERFER M., 1989. "Archaic Period Settlement Patterns in the Sierra of the Osmore Basin." In Rice D., Stanish C., and Scarr P., eds., *Ecology.*

ALDENDERFER M., 1990. "Cronología y definición de fases arcaicas en Asana, sur del Perú," *Chungará*, 24–25 (1990), Universidad de Tarapacá, pp. 13–35.

ALDENDERFER M., 1998. *Montane Foragers: Asana and the South-Central Andean Archaic*, University of Iowa Press, Iowa City.

ARDILA G., 1991. "The Peopling of Northern South America." In Bonnichsen R. and Turnmire K. L., eds., *Clovis*, pp. 261–82.

ASCHERO C., 1979. "Un asentamiento acerámico en la quebrada Inca-Cueva. Informe preliminar sobre el sitio Inca-cueva 4," *Actas de las Jornadas de Arqueología del Noroeste Argentino*, Buenos Aires, pp. 159–63.

BARBOSA A. S., SCHMITZ P. I., and MIRANDA A. F. de, 1976. "Um sitio paleo-indio de Goías. Novas contribuções ao estudo do paleo-indio de Goías, *Anúario de Divulgação Cientifica*, 3–4, UCG, Goiâna, pp. 21–29.

BATE L. F., 1982. *Origenes de la comunidad primitiva en Patagonia*, Escuela Nacional de Antropología e Historia, Mexico.

BELL R. E., 1965. *Investigaciones arqueológicas en el sitio de El Inga, Ecuador*, Casa de la Cultura Ecuatoriana, Quito.

BIRD J. B., 1946. "The Archaeology of Patagonia." In Steward J. H., ed., *Handbook of South American Indians*, 1, Bureau of American Ethnology, Smithsonian Institution, Washington, D.C., pp. 587–94.

BITTMAN B. and MUNIZAGA J. R., 1979. "El arco en América: Evidencia temprana y directa de la cultura Chinchorro (Norte de Chile), *Indiana*, 5, Berlin, pp. 229–51.

BONAVIA D. and CHAUCHAT C., 1990. "Presencia del Paijanense en el desierto de Ica," *Bulletin de l'Institut Français d'Etudes Andines*, 19 (2), pp. 399–412.

BORRERO L .A., 1986. "Cazadores de Mylodon en la Patagonia Austral." In Bryan A. L., ed., *Early Man*, pp. 281–94.

BORRERO L. A., LANATA J. L., and BORELLA F., 1988. "Reestudiando huesos : nuevas consideraciones sobre sitios de Ultima Esperanza," *Anales del Instituto de Patagonia*, 18, Punta Arenas, pp. 133–56.

BRYAN A. L., 1991. "The Fluted-Point Tradition in the Americas: One of Several Adaptations to Late Pleistocene American Environments." In Bonnichsen R. and Turnmire K. L., eds., *Clovis*, pp.15–34.

BRYAN A. L. and GRUHN R., eds., 1993. "Archaeological Investigations at Six Caves or Rockshelter in Interior Bahía, Brasil," *Brazilian Studies*, Univ. of Oregon.

CARDICH A.,1964. "Lauricocha. Fundamentos para una prehistoria de los Andes centrales," *Studia Praehistorica*, 3, Centro Argentino de Estudios Prehistóricos, Buenos Aires.

CARDICH A., 1977. *Las culturas pleistocénicas y postpleistocénicas de Los Toldos y un bosquejo de la prehistoria de Sudamérica*, Obras del Centenario del Museo de La Plata, 2, La Plata.

CARDICH. A, 1984. "Paleoambientes y la más antigua presencia del hombre," *Las Culturas de América en la época del descubrimiento. Culturas indígenas de la Patagonia*, Ed. Cultura Hispánica, Madrid, pp. 13–36.

CARDICH A., CARDICH L., and HAJDUK A., 1973. "Secuencia arqueológica y cronología radiocarbónica de la cueva 3 de Los Toldos (Santa Cruz, Argentina)," *Relaciones*, 7, Buenos Aires, pp. 85–123.

CARLISLE R. C., ed., 1988. *Americans before Columbus: Ice-Age Origins*, Department of Anthropology, University of Pittsburgh, Pittsburgh).

CAVELIER I. and MORA S., eds., 1995. *Ambito y ocupaciones tempranas de la América tropical*, Fundación Erigaie, ICAN, Bogotá.

CAVIGLIA S. E., YACOBACCIO H. D., and BORRERO L. A., 1986. "Las Buîtreras : Convivencia del Hombre con la Fauna Extinta en Patagonia Meridional." In Bryan A. L., ed., *Early Man*, pp. 295–318.

CHAUCHAT C., 1992. *Préhistoire de la côte nord du Pérou: le Paijanien de Cupisnique*, CNRS Editions, Bordeaux ("Cahiers du Quaternaire," 18).

CHAUCHAT C., ed., 1998. *Sitios arqueológicos de la zona de Cupisnique y margen derecha del valle de Chicama*. Instituto Nacional de Cultura de la Libertad, Trujillo et Institut Français d'Etudes Andines, Lima.

COLINVAUX P. A., 1989a. "Ice-Age Amazon Revisited," *Nature*, 340 (6230), pp. 188–89.

COLINVAUX P. A., 1989b. "Le passé et l'avenir de la forêt amazonienne," *Pour la Science*, juillet, Paris, pp. 86–92.

COLTRINARI, L., 1992, "Paleoambientes Quarternários na América do Sul: Primeira Aproximaçã," *Anais* 3 Congreso de ABEQUA, Belo Horizonte, pp. 13–42.

CORREAL G., 1979. *Investigaciones arqueológicas en abrigos rocosos de Nemocón y Sueva*, Finarco, Banco de la República, Bogotá.

CORREAL G., 1981. *Evidencias culturales y megafauna pleistocénica en Colombia*, Finarco, Banco de la República, Bogotá.

CORREAL G., 1990. "Evidencias culturales durante el Pleistoceno y Holoceno de Colombia," *Revista de Arqueologia Americana*, 1, pp. 69–90.

CORREAL G. and VAN DER HAMMEN T., 1977. *Investigaciones arqueológicas en los abrigos rocosos del Tequendama*, Banco Popular, Bogotá.

CUNHA L., 1994, "Le site d'Alice Boër (Brésil)," *L'Anthropologie*, 98 (1), Paris, pp. 110–27.

D'ANS A.-M., 1982. *L'Amazonie péruvienne indigène*, Paris, Payot.

DELIBRIAS G. and FONTUGNE M., 1992. "L'apport des datations carbone 14," *Les Dossiers d'Archéologie—Brésil*, 169, Dijon, pp. 6–7.

DILLEHAY T. et al., 1992. "Earliest Hunters and Gatherers of South America," *Journal of World Prehistory*, 6 (2), pp. 145–204.

DILLEHAY T., ed., 1997. *Monte Verde. A Late Pleistocene Settlement in Chile*, vol. 2, Smithsonian Institution, Washington, D.C.

DOLLFUS O. and LAVALLÉE D., 1973. "Ecología y ocupación del espacio en los Andes tropicales durante los últimos veinte milenios," *Bulletin de l'Institut Français d'Etudes Andines*, 2 (3), Lima, pp. 75–92.

DUPLESSY J. C. and RUDDIMAN W. F., 1984. "La fonte des calottes glaciaires," *La Recherche*, 156, Paris, pp. 806–18.

EMPERAIRE J., LAMING-EMPERAIRE A., and REICHLEN H., 1963. "La grotte Fell et autres sites de la région volcanique de la Patagonie chilienne," *Journal de la Société des Américanistes*, 52, Paris, pp. 167–254.

FALGUERES C., FONTUGNE M., CHAUCHAT C., and GUADELLI J.-C., 1994. "Datations radiométriques de l'extinction des grandes faunes pléistocènes du Pérou," *C. R. Acad. Sci.* Paris, t. 319, série 2, pp. 261–66.

FERNANDEZ-DISTEL A., 1986. "Las cuevas de Huachichocana. Su posición dentro del *und Vergleichenden Archäologie*, 8, Bonn, pp. 353–430.

FLEGENHEIMER N., 1987. "Recent Research at Localities Cerro la China et Cerro El Sombrero, Argentina," *Current Research in the Pleistocene*, 4, Center for the Study of Early Man, Orono, pp. 148–49.

FUNG R., CENZANO C., and ZAVALETA A., 1972. "El taller lítico de Chivateros, valle del Chillón," *Revista del Museo Nacional*, 38, Lima, pp. 61–72.

GRADIN C. J., ASCHERO C., and AGUERRE A. M., 1976. "Investigaciones arqueológicas en la Cueva de las Manos, Estancia Alto Río Pinturas (Provincia de Santa Cruz), *Relaciones de la Sociedad Argentina de Antropología*, X, Buenos Aires, pp. 183–227.

GRADIN C. J., ASCHERO C., and AGUERRE A. M., 1979. "Arqueología del área Río Pinturas (Provincia de Santa Cruz)," *Relaciones de la Sociedad Argentina de Antropología*, 13, Buenos Aires, pp. 183–227.

GRAHAM A., ed., 1973. *Vegetation and Vegetational History of Northern Latin America*, Elsevier, Amsterdam.

GROOT A.M., 1995. "Checua: un aporte para el conocimiento del precerámico de la sábana de Bogotá." In Cavelier I. and Mora S., eds., *Ambito y ocupanciones tempranas*, pp. 45–58.

GUERIN C., 1991. "La faune de vertébrés du Pléistocène supérieur de l'aire archéologique de São Raimundo Nonato (Piaui, Brésil)," *Comptes-Rendus de l'Académie des Sciences*, 312 (2), Paris, pp. 567–72.

HURT W. and BLASI O., 1969. "O Projeto arqueológico Lagoa Santa, Minas Gerais, Brasil," *Arquivos Museu Paranaense*, 4, Curitiba.

KAPLAN L., 1980. "Variation in the Cultivated Beans." In Lynch, T. F., *Guitarrero Cave*, pp. 145–49.

KAULICKE P., 1981. "Des Abri Uchkumachay und seine zeitliche Stellung innerhalb der lithischen Perioden Perus" *Allgemeine und Vergleichende Archäologie-Beitrage*, 2, Deutsches Archäologisches Institut, Bonn.

KEEFER D. et al., 1998. "Early Maritime Economy and El Niño Events at Quebrada Tacahuay, Peru," *Science*, 281, pp. 1833–35.

LABEYRIE J., ed., 1974. *Les méthodes quantitatives d'étude des variations du climat au cours du Pléistcène*, Colloque international du CNRS (Gif, June 1973), CNRS, Paris.

LAMING-EMPERAIRE A., LAVALLÉE D., and HUMBERT R., 1972. "Le site de Marazzi en Terre de Feu," *Objets et Mondes*, 12 (2), Paris, pp. 225–44.

LAMING-EMPERAIRE A., PROUS A., VILHENA DE MORAES A., and BELTRÃO M., 1975. *Grottes et abris de la région de Lagoa Santa, Minas Gerais, Brésil*, E.P.H.E, Paris ("Cahiers d'Archéologie d'Amérique du Sud," 1).

LANNING E. P., 1965. "Early Man in Peru," *Scientific American*, 4, pp. 68–76.

LANNING E. P., 1967. *Peru before the Incas*, Prentice Hall, Englewood Cliffs.

LANNING E. P., 1973. "Burin Industries in the Pleistocene of the Andes," *Estudios Atacameños*, 1, Univ. del Norte, San Pedro de Atacama, pp. 25–30.

LAVALLÉE D., 1985. "L'occupation préhistorique des hautes terres andines," *L'Anthropologie*, 89/3, Paris, pp. 409–30.

LAVALLÉE D., 1994. "Le peuplement préhistorique de la Cordillère des Andes," *Bulletin de la Société Préhistorique Française*, 91 (4–5), Paris, pp. 264–74.

LAVALLÉE D., 1997. "Territorio, recursos líticos y estrategias de aprovisionamiento en la cuenca del alto Shaka (Junín, Perú)." In Varon R., ed., *Arqueología, Antropologia e Historia en los Andes, Homenaje a Maria Rostworowski*, Lima, IEP, pp. 353–78.

LAVALLÉE D. et al., 1985. *Telarmachay. Chasseurs et pasteurs préhistoriques des Andes*, Editions ADPF-ERC, Paris.

LAVALLÉE D., et al., 1999. "Pescadores-recolectores arcaicos del extremo sur peruano," *Bull. Inst. fr. etudes andines*, 28 (1), Lima, pp. 13–52.

LLAGOSTERA A., 1979. "9,700 Years of Maritime Subsistence on the Pacific: An Analysis by Means of Bioindicators in the North of Chile," *American Antiquity*, 44, pp. 309–24.

LLAGOSTERA A., 1992. "Early Occupations and the Emergence of Fishermen on the Pacific." In Sandweiss D. H. et al., eds., *Andean Past*, 3, Latin American Studies Program, Cornell University, Ithaca, pp. 87–109.

LÓPEZ CASTAÑO C. E., 1995. "Dispersión de puntas de proyectil bifaciales en la cuenca media del río Magdalena." In Cavelier I. and Mora S., eds., *Ambito y ocupanciones tempranas*, pp. 73–82.

LYNCH T. F., 1971. "Preceramic Transhumance in the Callejon de Huaylas, Peru," *American Antiquity*, 36, pp. 139–48.

LYNCH T. F., 1978. "The South American Paleo-Indians." In Jennings J. D., ed., *Prehistoric Man*, pp. 455–89.

LYNCH T. F., 1980. *Guitarrero Cave*, Academic Press, New York.

LYNCH T. F., 1983. "The Paleo-Indians." In Jennings J. D., ed., *Ancient South Americans*, pp. 87–137.

LYNCH T. F., 1989. "Chobshi Cave in Retrospect." In Sandweiss D. H., ed., *Andean Past*, 2, Latin American Studies Program, Cornell University, Ithaca, pp. 1–32.

LYNCH T. F., 1990a. "Glacial-Age Man in South America? A Critical Review," *American Antiquity*, 55, pp. 12–36.

LYNCH T. F., 1990b. "El Hombre de la Edad Glacial en Sudamerica: une Perspectiva Europea," *Revista de Arqueologia Americana*, 1, pp. 141–85.

LYNCH T. F., 1991. "Paleoindians in South America: A Discrete and Identifiable Cultural Stage?" In Bonnichsen R. and Turnmire K. L., eds., *Clovis*, pp. 255–60.

LYNCH T. F. and POLLOCK S., 1981. "La arqueología de la Cueva Negra de Chobshi," *Miscelánea Antropológica Ecuatoriana,* 1, Guayaquil and Quito, pp. 92–119.

LYNCH T. F. et al., 1985. "Chronology of Guitarrero Cave, Peru." *Science,* 229, pp. 864–67.

MACNEISH. R. S. et al., 1980–83. *Prehistory of the Ayacucho Basin,* Peru, R. S. Peabody Foundation for Archaeology, University of Michigan Press, Ann Arbor (3 vols.).

MARKGRAF V., 1989. "Palaeoclimates in Central and South America since 18,000 B.P. Based on Pollen and Lake-Level Records," *Quaternary Science Reviews,* 8, pp. 1–24.

MARTIN P .S., 1967. "Pleistocene Overkill." In Martin P. and Wright H. E., eds., *Pleistocene Extinctions,* pp. 75–120.

MARTIN P. S., 1973. "The Discovery of America," *Science,* 179, pp. 969–74.

MARTIN P. S. and KLEIN R., 1984. *Quaternary Extinctions : A Prehistoric Revolution,* University of Arizona Press, Tucson.

MASSONE M., 1987. "Los cazadores paleoindios de Tres Arroyos (Tierra del Fuego)," *Anales del Instituto de Patagonia,* 17, Punta Arenas, pp. 47–60.

MASSONE M., 1991. "El estudio de las cenizas volcánicas y su implicancia en la interpretación de algunos registros arqueológicos de Chile austral," *Anales del Instituto de Patagonia,* 20, Punta Arenas, pp. 111–15.

MAYER-OAKES W. J., 1986a. "Early Man Projectile and Lithic Technology in the Ecuadorian Sierra." In Bryan A. L., ed., *Early Man,* pp. 133–56.

MAYER-OAKES W. J., 1986b. "El Inga: A Paleoindian Site in the Sierra of Northern Ecuador," *Transactions of the American Philosophical Society,* Philadelphia, 76.

MENGONI GOÑALONS G. L., 1986. "Patagonian Prehistory: Early Exploitation of Faunal Resources (13,500–8500 B.P.)." In Bryan A. L., ed., *Early Man,* pp. 271–80.

MILLER E. T., 1987. "Pesquisas arqueológicas paleoindígenas no Brasil ocidental," *Estudios Atacameños,* 8, San Pedro de Atacama, pp. 37–61.

MONTANE J., 1968. "Paleo-Indian Remains from Laguna Tagua-Tagua, Central Chile," *Science,* 161, pp. 1347–48.

MOSIMANN J. E. and MARTIN P. S., 1975. "Simulation Overkill by Paleoindians," *American Scientist,* 63, pp. 304–13.

NAMI H., 1987a. "Cueva del Medio: A Significative Paleoindian Site in Southern South America," *Current Research in the Pleistocene,* 4, Center for the Study of Early Man, Orono, pp. 157–59.

NAMI H., 1987b. "Cueva del Medio: perspectivas arqueológicas para la Patagonia austral," *Anales del Instituto de Patagonia,* 17, Punta Arenas, pp. 73–106.

NAMI H. and MENEGAZ A., 1991. "Cueva del Medio: aportes para el conocimiento de la diversidad faunística hacia el Pleistoceno-Holoceno en la Patagonia austral," *Anales del Instituto de Patagonia,* 20, Punta Arenas, pp. 117–32.

NUÑEZ L., 1983. "Paleoindian and Archaic Cultural Periods in the Arid and Semi-arid Regions of Northern Chile." In Wendorf F. and Close A. E., eds., *Advances in World Archaeology,* pp. 161–203.

NUÑEZ L., 1989. "Hacia la producción de alimentos y la vida sedentaria." In Hidalgo J. et al., eds., *Culturas de Chile,* pp. 81–105.

NUÑEZ L. and SANTORO C., 1988. "Cazadores de la puna seca y salada," *Estudios Atacameños,* 9, Universidad del Norte, Antofagasta, pp. 11–60.

NUÑEZ L. and SANTORO C., 1990. "Primeros poblamientos en el Cono sur de América (XII-IX Milenio a.P.)," *Revista de Arqueología Americana,* 1, pp. 90–140.

NUÑEZ L. and ZLATAR V., 1978. "Tiliviche-1b y Aragón-1 (estrato V): Dos comunidades precerámicas coexistentes en Pampa del Tamarugal, Norte de Chile," *3 Congreso peruano del Hombre y la Cultura andina,* 2, Lima, pp. 734–56.

NUÑEZ L. et al., 1983. *Ocupación paleoindia en Quereo, reconstrucción pluridisciplinar en territorio semi-arido de Chile,* Universidad del Norte, Antofagasta.

OSSA P., 1973. "A Survey of the Lithic Ceramic Occupation of the Moche Valley, North Coastal Peru: With an Overview of Some Problems in the Study of the Early Human Occupation of West Andean South America." Ph. D. diss., Harvard University.

OSSA P., 1978. "Paiján in Early Andean Prehistory: The Moche Valley Evidence." In Bryan A. L., ed., *Early Man,* pp. 290–95.

PEYRE E., 1993. "Nouvelle découverte d'un Homme préhistorique américain: une femme de 9 700 ans au Brésil," *Comptes-Rendus de l'Académie des Sciences,* 316, série 2, Paris, pp. 839–42.

POLITIS G., 1984. "Investigaciones arqueológicas en el Area interserrana Bonaerense," *Etnia,* 32, pp. 7–52.

POLITIS G., 1991. "Fishtail Projectile Points in the Southern Cone of South America." In Bonnichsen R. and Turnmire K. L., eds., *Clovis,* pp. 287–302.

POLITIS G., and GUTIÉREZ M.A., 1998. "Gliptodontes y cazadores-recolectores de la region pampanea (Argentina)," *Latin American Antiquity,* 9 (2), pp. 111–34.

PRIETO A., 1991. "Cazadores tempranos y tardios en la cueva 1 del Lago Sofía," *Anales del Instituto de Patagonia,* 20, Punta Arenas, pp. 75–99.

PROUS A., 1980–81. "Fouilles du grand Abri de Santana do Riacho (Minas Gerais) Brésil," *Journal de la Société des Américanistes,* 67, Paris, pp. 163–83.

PROUS A., 1991. "Les fouilles de la Lapa do Boquete," *Journal de la Société des Américanistes,* 77, Paris, pp. 77–109.

PROUS A., 1992. *Arqueologia Brasileira,* Ed. Universidade de Brasilia, Brasilia.

PROUS A., JUNQUEIRA P. A., and MALTA I. M., 1984. "Arqueología do Alto Médio São Francisco. Região de Janúaria e Montalvânia," *Revista de Arquelogia,* Museu Paraense E. Goeldi, 2 (1), pp. 59–72.

PROUS A. and MALTA I. M., eds., 1991. "Santana do Riacho-I," *Arquivos do Museu de Historia Natural,* 12, Belo Horizonte.

RASMUSSEN K.A., 1998. "Exploring the Origin of Coastal Sedentism in the South-Central Andes." Ph.D. diss., University of California (UMI Dissertation Services).

RICE D., STANISH C., and SCARR P., eds., 1989. *Ecology, Settlement and History in the Osmore Basin,* BAR Intern. Series 545, Oxford.

RICHARDSON III J., 1978. "Early Man on the Peruvian Coast: Early Maritime Exploitation and the Pleistocene and Holocene Environment." In Bryan A. L., ed., *Early Man,* pp. 274–89.

RICK J., 1980. *Prehistoric Hunters of the High Andes,* Academic Press, New York.

ROOSEVELT A., 1991. *Moundbuilders of the Amazon,* Academic Press, San Diego.

ROOSEVELT A. et al., 1996. "Paleoindian Cave Dwellers in the Amazon: The Peopling of the Americas," *Science,* 272, pp. 373–84.

SANDWEISS D. H. et al., 1989. "Early Maritime Adaptations in the Andes: Preliminary Studies at the Ring Site, Peru." In Rice D., Stanish C,. and Scarr P., eds., *Ecology,* pp. 35–84.

SANDWEISS D. H. et al., 1998. "Quebrada Jaguay: Early South American Maritime Adaptations," *Science,* 281, pp. 1830–32.

SCHMITZ P. I., 1987. "Prehistoric Hunters and Gatherers of Brazil," *Journal of World Prehistory,* 1 (1), pp. 53–126.

SCHMITZ P. I., 1990. "O povoamento pleistocénico do Brasil," *Revista de Arqueología Americana,* 1, pp. 33–68.

SCHMITZ P. I., BARBOSA A. S., and RIBEIRO M. B., eds., 1981. *Temas de Arqueologia brasileira,* Anuário de Divulgacão Cientifica, Instituto Goiano de Pré-historia e Antropologia, Universidade Católica de Goiás, Goiania.

SCHNELL R., 1987. *La flore et la végétation de l'Amérique tropicale,* Masson, Paris (2 vols.).

SCHOBINGER J., 1988. *Prehistoria de Sudamérica. Culturas precerámicas,* Alianza Editorial, Barcelone.

SMITH T. E., 1980. "Plant Remains from Guitarrero Cave." In Lynch T. F., ed., *Guitarrero Cave,* pp. 87–118.

STOTHERT K. E., 1988. *La Prehistoria temprana de la Peninsula de Santa Elena, Ecuador. Cultura Las Vegas,* Museo del Banco Central del Ecuador, Guayaquil et Quito ("Miscelánea Antropológica Ecuatoriana," 10, monografía).

TEMME M., 1982. "Excavaciones en el sitio précérámico de Cubilán (Ecuador)," *Miscelánea Antropológica Ecuatoriana,* Museo del Banco Central, Guayaquil ct Quito, pp. 135–64.

USSELMANN P., 1989. "Evolución del clima y sus consecuencias a lo largo del litoral pacífico de los Andes centrales desde el fin de la última glaciación." In Bouchard J. F. and Guinea M., eds., *Relaciones interculturales en el área ecuatorial del Pacífico durante la Epoca precolombina,* BAR Intern. Series 503, Oxford, pp. 237–46.

VACHER S., JEREMIE S., and BRIAND J., eds., 1998. *Amérindiens du Sinnamary (Guyane): archéologie en forêt équatoriale,* MSH, Paris (Coll. "Documents d'Archéologie Française").

VAN BUREN G. E., 1974. *Arrowheads and Projectile Points.* Arrowheads Publishing, Garden Grove.

VAN DER HAMMEN T., 1978. "Stratigraphy and Environments of the Upper Quaternary of el Abra Corridor and Rockshelters (Colombia)," *Palaeostratigraphy, Palaeoclimatology Palaeoecology,* 25, pp. 179–90.

VAN DER HAMMEN T., 1981. "Environmental Changes in the Northern Andes and the Extinction of Mastodon," *Geologie en Minjbouw,* 60, pp. 369–72.

VAN DER HAMMEN T., 1992. *Historia, Ecología y Vegetación,* Corporación Araracuara, Bogotá.

VAN DER HAMMEN T. and CORREAL G., 1978. "Prehistoric Man on the Sábana de Bogotá: Data for One Ecological Prehistory." In Van der Hammen T., ed., *The Quaternary of Colombia,* 6, Elsevier, Amsterdam, pp. 179–90.

VILHENA VIALOU A. et al., 1995. "Découverte de Mylodontinae dans un habitat préhistorique daté du Mato Grosso (Brésil): l'abri rupestre de Santa Elina," *Comptes-rendus de l'Académie des Sciences de Paris,* 320, series UUa, pp. 655–61.

CHAPTER 4. THE ANDEAN BOOM

ALLISON M. J., 1985. "Chile's Ancient Mummies," *Natural History,* 94, pp. 74–81.

ARRIAZA B. T., 1995. *Beyond Death: The Chinchorro Mummies of Ancient Chile,* Smithsonian Institution Press, Washington, D.C.

BENFER R. A., 1984. "The Challenges and Reward of Sedentism: The Preceramic Village of Paloma, Peru." In Cohen M. N. and Armelagos G., eds., *Paleopathology at the Origin of Agriculture,* Academic Press, New York, pp. 531–58.

BENFER R. A., 1986. "Holocene Coastal Adaptations: Changing Demography and Health at the Fog Oasis of Paloma, Peru, 7,800–5,000 B.P." In Matos R. et al., eds., *Andean Archaeology,* pp. 45–64.

BENFER R. A., 1990. "The Preceramic Period Site of Paloma, Peru: Bioindications of Improving Adaptation to Sedentism," *Latin American Antiquity,* 1, pp. 284–318.

BIRD J. B., 1943. "Excavations in Northern Chile," *Anthropological Papers of the American Museum of Natural History,* 38 (4), New York.

BIRD J. B., 1946. "The Cultural Sequence of the North Chilean Coast." In Steward J., ed., *Handbook of the South American Indians,* 2, Bureau of American Ethnology, Bulletin 143, Smithsonian Institution, Washington, D.C., pp. 587–94.

BONAVIA D., 1982. *Los Gavilanes. Mar, desierto y oasis en la historia del hombre,* Cofide and Deutsche Archäologisches Institut (Bonn), Lima.

BONAVIA D., 1993. "La papa: apuntes sobre sus origenes y su domesticación," *Journal de la Société des Américanistes,* 79, Paris, pp. 173–87.

BONAVIA D., 1993–95. "La domesticación de las plantas y los origenes de la agricultura en los Andes centrales," *Revista Historica,* 38, Academia Nacional de la Historia, Lima, pp. 77–107.

BONAVIA D. and GROBMAN A., 1978. "El origen del maïs andino." In Hartman R. and Oberem U., eds., *Estudios Americanistas* 1, St. Augustin, pp. 82–91.

CAUVIN J., 1992. "Problèmes et méthodes pour les débuts de l'agriculture: le point de vue de l'archéologue." In Anderson P., ed., *Préhistoire de l'agriculture. Nouvelles approches expérimentales et ethnographiques*, Editions du CNRS, Paris, pp. 265–68.

COHEN M. N., 1978. "Population Pressure and the Origins of Agriculture: An Archaeological Example from the Coast of Peru." In Browman D., ed., *Advances in Andean Archaeolgoy*, pp. 91–132.

DONNAN C. B., 1964. "An Early House from Chilca, Perú," *American Antiquity*, 30, pp. 137–44.

ENGEL F., 1966. *Geografía humana prehistórica y agricultura precolombina de la Quebrada de Chilca*, Universidad agraria La Molina, Lima.

ENGEL F., 1980. *Prehistoric Andean Ecology: Man, Settlement and Environment in the Andes—Paloma*, Department of Anthropology, Hunter College, City University of New York, New York.

FELDMAN R. A., 1992. "Preceramic Architectural and Subsistence Traditions." In Sandweiss D. H. et al., eds., *Andean Past*, 3, pp. 67–86.

FLANNERY K. V., ed., 1986. *Guilá Naquitz. Archaic Foraging and Early Agriculture in Oaxaca, Mexico*, Academic Press, New York.

FUNG R., 1982. "El temprano surgimiento el el Perú de los sistemas socio-políticos complejos: planteamiento de una hipotesis de desarrollo original," *Primer Simposio de correlaciones antropológicas andino-mesoamericano* (25–31 July 1971, Salinas), ESPOL, Guayaquil, pp. 457–93.

FUNG R., 1988. "The Late Preceramic and Initial Period." In Keatinge R. W., ed., *Peruvian Prehistory*, pp. 67–96.

GUILAINE J., 1992. "Nous, les enfants du Néolithique," *Sciences et Vie*, 178, Paris, pp. 163–64 (Special issue, "Néolithique, la première révolution sociale").

GUILLEN S. E., 1992. "The Chinchorro Culture: Mummies and Crania in the Reconstruction of Preceramic Coastal Adaptation in the South Central Andes," Ph.D. diss., University of Michigan.

IJZEREEF G. F., 1978. "Faunal Remains from the El Abra Rockshelters (Colombia)." In Van der Hammen T., ed., *The Quaternary of Colombia*, 6, Elsevier, Amsterdam, pp. 163–77.

LANNING E. P., 1963. "A Preagricultural Occupation on the Central Coast of Peru," *American Antiquity*, 28, pp. 360–71.

LANNING E. P., 1965. "Early Man in Peru," *Scientific American*, 213 (4), pp. 68–76.

LANNING E. P., 1967. *Peru before the Incas*, Prentice Hall, Englewood Cliffs.

LATHRAP D. W., 1970. *The Upper Amazon*, Thames and Hudson, London.

LATHRAP D. W., 1971. "The Tropical Forest and the Cultural Context of Chavín." In Benson E. P., ed., *Dumbarton Oaks Conference on Chavín*, Dumbarton Oaks Library and Collection, Washington, D.C., pp. 73–100.

LAVALLÉE D., 1989. "Quelques aspects de la néolithisation andine." In Aurenche O. et Cauvin J., eds., *Néolithisations*, BAR Intern. Series 516, Oxford, pp. 319–32.

LAVALLÉE D., 1990. "La domestication animale en Amérique du Sud. Le point des connaissances," *Bulletin de l'Institut Français d'Etudes Andines*, 19 (1), Lima, pp. 25–44.

LAVALLÉE D., JULIEN M., WHEELER J. C., and KARLIN C., 1985. *Telarmachay. Chasseurs et Pasteurs préhistoriques des Andes*, 1, Ed. ADPF-ERC, Paris.

LLAGOSTERA A., 1979. "9,700 Years of Maritime Subsistence on the Pacific: An Analysis by Means of Bioindicators in the North of Chile," *American Antiquity*, 44, pp. 309–24.

LLAGOSTERA A., 1989. "Caza y Pesca marítima (9.000 a 1.000 a.c.)." In Hidalgo J. et al., eds., *Culturas de Chile*, pp. 57–79.

LLAGOSTERA A., 1992. "Early Occupations and the Emergence of Fishermen on the Pacific Coast of South America." In Sandweiss D .H. et al., eds., *Andean Past*, 3, pp. 87–110.

LYNCH T. F., 1973. "Harvest Timing, Transhumance, and the Process of Domestication," *American Anthropologist*, 75, pp. 1254–59.

LYNCH T. F., 1980. *Guitarrero Cave: Early Man in the Andes,* Academic Press, New York.

MACNEISH R. S. et al., 1980–83. *Prehistory of the Ayacucho Basin, Peru* (3 vols.). R. S. Peabody Foundation for Archaeology, University of Michigan Press, Ann Arbor.

MANZANILLA L., ed., 1988. *Coloquio V.Gordon Childe. Estudios sobre las revoluciones neolítica y urbana,* Instituto de Investigaciones Antropológicas, UNAM, Mexico.

MATOS R., TURPIN S. A., and ELING H. H., eds., 1986. *Andean Archaeology,* Papers in Memory of Clifford Evans, Institute of Archaeology, UCLA (Monograph 27).

MOSELEY M., 1975. *The Maritime Foundations of Andean Civilization,* Cummings, Menlo Park.

MOSELEY M., 1992a. *The Incas and Their Ancestors: The Archaeology of Peru,* Thames and Hudson, London.

MOSELEY M., 1992b. "Maritime Foundations and Multilinear Evolution: Retrospect and Prospect." In Sandweiss D. H. et al., eds., *Andean Past,* 3, pp. 5–42.

MOSELEY M. and FELDMAN R., 1988. "Fishing, Farming and the Foundations of Andean Civilisation." In Bailey G. and Parkington J., eds., *The Archaeology of Prehistoric Coastlines,* Cambridge University Press, pp. 125–47.

NUÑEZ L., 1983. *Paleoindio y Arcaico en Chile. Diversidad, secuencia y procesos,* I.N.A.H., Mexico ("Serie Monografías" 3).

OSBORN A., 1977. "Strandloopers, Mermaids and Other Fairy Tales: Ecological Determinants of Marine Resources Utilization—The Peruvian Case." In Binford L., ed., *For Theory Building in Archaeology,* Academic Press, New York, pp. 157–205.

PICKERSGILL B., 1972. "Cultivated Plants as Evidence for Cultural Contacts," *American Antiquity,* 37, pp. 97–104.

PICKERSGILL B. and HEISER JR. C., 1978. "Plants Domesticated in the New World Tropics." In Browman D., ed., *Advances in Andean Archaeology,* pp. 133–65.

QUILTER J., 1989. *Life and Death at Paloma: Society and Mortuary Practices in a Preceramic Peruvian Village,* University of Iowa Press, Iowa City.

QUILTER J., 1992. "To Fish in the Afternoon: Beyond Subsistence Economies in the Study of Early Andean Civilization." In Sandweiss D. H. et al., eds., *Andean Past,* 3, pp. 111–25.

RAYMOND J. S., 1981. "The Maritime Foundations of Andean Civilization: A Reconsideration of the Evidence," *American Antiquity,* 46, pp. 806–21.

REITZ E. J., 1988. "Faunal Remains from Paloma, an Archaic Site in Peru," *American Anthropologist,* 90, pp. 310–22.

RICK J. W., 1980. *Prehistoric Hunters of the High Andes,* Academic Press, New York.

SANDWEISS D. H., RICHARDSON III J. B., REITZ E. J., HSU J. T., and FELDMAN R. A., 1989. "Early Maritime Adaptations in the Andes: Preliminary Studies at the Ring Site, Peru." In Rice D. et al., eds., *Ecology, Settlement and History in the Osmore Basin,* BAR Intern. Series 545, Oxford.

SANDWEISS D. H. et al., eds., 1992. *Andean Past,* 3, Latin American Studies Program, Cornell University, Ithaca.

SAUER C. O., 1952. *Agricultural Origins and Dispersals,* MIT Press, Cambridge.

SCHIAPPACASSE V. and NIEMEYER H., 1984. *Descripción y análisis interpretativo de un sitio arcaico temprano en la Quebrada de Camarones,* Museo Nacional de Historia Natural, Universidad de Tarapacá (Publicación ocasional 41).

SMITH JR. C. E., 1988. "Evidencia arqueológica actual sobre los inicios de la agricultura en América" In Manzanilla L. ed., *Coloquio Gordon Childe,* Instituto de investigaciones antropológicas, UNAM, Mexico, pp. 91–112.

STOTHERT K. E., 1988. *La Prehistoria Temprana de la Peninsula de Santa Elena, Ecuador: Cultura Las Vegas,* Museos del Banco Central del Ecuador, Guayaquil et Quito ("Miscelánea Antropológica Ecuatoriana," 10, Monografía).

STOTHERT K. E., 1992. "Early Economies of Coastal Ecuador and the Foundations of Andean Civilization," In Sandweiss D. H. et al., eds., *Andean Past,* 3, pp. 43–54.

TRIGGER B. G., 1989. *A History of Archaeological Thought,* Cambridge University Press, Cambridge.

UHLE M., 1917. "Los aborigenes de Arica," *Publicaciones del Museo de Etnología y Antropología de Chile,* 1 (4–5), pp. 151–76.

UHLE M., 1922. *Fundamentos etnicos y arqueológicos de Arica y Tacna,* Sociedad Ecuatoriana de Estudios Históricos, Universidad Central, Quito.

WEIR G. and DERING P., 1986. "The Lomas of Paloma: Human-Environment Relations in a Central Peruvian Fog Oasis: Archaeobotany and Palynology." In Matos R. et al., eds., *Andean Archaeology,* pp. 18–44.

WHEELER J. C., 1984. "On the Origin and Early Development of Camelid Pastoralism in the Andes." In Clutton-Brook J. and Grigson G., eds., *Animals and Archaeology 3: Early Herders and Their Flocks,* BAR Intern. Series 202, Oxford, pp. 395–410.

WILSON D. J., 1981. "Of Maize and Men: A Critique of the Maritime Hypothesis of State Origins on the Coast of Peru," *American Anthropologist,* 83, pp. 93–120.

WING E. S., 1977. "Animal Domestication in the Andes." In Reed C., ed., *Origins of Agriculture,* Mouton, The Hague, pp. 837–59.

WING E. S., 1978. "Animal Domestication in the Andes." In Browman D., ed., *Advances in Andean Archaeology,* pp. 167–88.

CHAPTER 5. THE OTHER SIDE OF THE CORDILLERA

AGUERRE A. M., 1981–82. "Los niveles inferiores de la Cueva Grande (Arroyo Feo), Area Rio Pinturas, Pcia. de Santa Cruz," *Relaciones,* 14, Buenos Aires, pp. 211–39.

AGUERRE A. M., 1987. "Investigaciones arqueológicas en el Area de La Martita," Dpto Magallanes, Pcia. de Santa Cruz, *Primeras Jornadas de Arqueología de la Patagonia,* Gobierno de la Pcia. de Santa Cruz, Serie Humanidades 2, Rawson, pp. 11–16.

BATE L. F., 1982. *Origenes de la comunidad primitiva en Patagonia,* Escuela Nacional de Antropologia e Historia, Mexico.

BIRD J. B., 1938. "Antiquity and Migrations of the Early Inhabitants of Patagonia," *Geographical Review,* 28 (2), pp. 250–75.

BIRD J. B., 1943. "Excavations in Northern Chile," *Anthropological Papers of the American Museum of Natural History,* 38 (4), pp. 173–318.

BIRD J. B., 1948. "The Archaeology of Patagonia." In Steward J., ed., *Handbook of South American Indians,* 1, Bureau of American Ethnology, Bulletin 143, Smithsonian Institution, Washington, D.C., pp. 17–24.

BIRD J. B., 1988. *Travels and Archaeology in South Chile,* ed. J. Hyslop, University of Iowa Press, Iowa City.

BOOMERT A., 1980. "The Sipaliwi Archaeological Complex of Surinam: A Summary," *Nieuwe West-Indischgids,* Utrecht, pp. 94–107.

CARDICH A. et al., 1973. "Secuencia arqueológica y cronología radiocarbónica de la cueva 3 de Los Toldos (Santa Cruz, Argentina)," *Relaciones,* 7, Buenos Aires, pp. 85–123.

DARWIN C. [1875] 1979. *Voyage d'un naturaliste. De la Terre de Feu aux Galapagos,* Maspero, Paris ("La Découverte").

EMPERAIRE J. and LAMING A., 1961. "Les gisements des îles Englefield et Vivian dans la mer d'Otway (Patagonie australe)," *Journal de la Société des Américanistes,* 50, Paris, pp. 7–77.

EMPERAIRE J., LAMING A., and REICHLEN H., 1963. "La grotte Fell et autres sites de la région volcanique de la Patagonie chilienne," *Journal de la Société des Américanistes,* 52, Paris, pp. 167–254.

FERNÁNDEZ J., 1982. *Historia de la Arqueología argentina,* Asociación cuyana de Antropología, Mendoza.

GRADIN C., 1985. "Arqueología y Arte rupestre de los cazadores de la Patagonia," *Culturas Indígenas de la Patagonia,* ed. Cultura Hispánica, Madrid, pp.37–58 ("Las Culturas de América en la Epoca del Descubrimiento").

GRADIN C., ASCHERO C., and AGUERRE A. M., 1979. "Arqueología del área Rio Pinturas," *Relaciones,* 13, pp. 183–228.

GUIDON N. and PESSIS A. M., 1993. "Recent Discoveries on the Holocenic Levels of Sitio do Meio Rock-shelter, Piauí, Brasil," *Clio,* 1 (9), pp. 77–80.

LAMING-EMPERAIRE A., 1972. "Sites préhistoriques de Patagonie chilienne," Objets et Mondes, 12 (2), Paris, pp. 201–24.

LAMING-EMPERAIRE A., LAVALLÉE D., and HUMBERT R., 1972. "Le site de Marazzi en Terre de Feu," *Objets et Mondes,* 12 (2), Paris, pp. 225–44.

LEGOUPIL D., 1993–94. "El archipielago del Cabo de Hornos y la costa sur de la isla Navarino: poblamiento y modelos económicos," *Anales del Instituto de Patagonia,* 22, Punta Arenas, pp. 101–21.

LEGOUPIL D. (dir.), 1997. *Bahia Colorada. Les premiers chasseurs de mammifères marins de Patagonie australe,* ed. ADPF-ERC, Paris.

LEGOUPIL D. and FONTUGNE M., 1997. "El poblamiento marítimo en los archipielagos de Patagonia : núcleos antiguos y dispersión reciente," *Anales del Instituto de Patagonia,* 25, Punta Arenas, pp. 75–87.

LOTHROP S. K., 1928. *The Indians of Tierra del Fuego,* Museum of the American Indian, Heye Fund, New York ("Contributions," 10).

LOVISATO D., 1883. "Di alcune armi e ustensili dei Fueghini e degli antichi Patagoni," *Atti della Reale Academia dei Lincei,* 11, Rome, pp. 194–202.

LUBBOCK J., 1865. *Prehistoric Times, as Illustrated by Ancient Remains, and the Manners and Customs of Modern Savages,* William and Norgate, Londres.

MASSONE M., 1985. "El poblamiento humano aborigen de Tierra del Fuego," *Culturas Indígenas de la Patagonia,* ed. Cultura Hispánica, Madrid, pp. 131–44 ("La Culturas de América en la Epoca del Descubrimiento").

MENGHIN O., 1952. "Fundamentos cronológicos de la Prehistoria de Patagonia," *Runa,* 5, Buenos Aires, pp. 23–43.

MENGHIN O., 1956. "Existe en Tierra del Fuego la auténtica casa-pozo?" *Runa,* 7 (1), Buenos Aires, pp. 107–12.

ORQUERA L. A., 1987. "Advances in the Archaeology of the Pampa and Patagonia," *Journal of World Prehistory,* 1, pp. 313–413.

ORQUERA L. A. and PIANA E. L., 1983. "Adaptaciones maritimas prehistóricas en el litoral magallanico-fueguino," *Relaciones,* 15, Buenos Aires, pp. 225–35.

ORQUERA L. A. and PIANA E. L., 1986/87. "Composición tipológica y datos tecnomorfológicos y tecnofuncionales de los distintos conjuntos arqueológicos del sitio Túnel I (Tierra del Fuego, República argentina)," *Relaciones,* 17, Buenos Aires, pp. 201–39.

ORQUERA L. A., SALA A. E., PIANA E. L., and TAPIA A. H., 1977. *Lancha Packewaia. Arqueología de los canales fueguinos,* Ed. Huemul, Buenos Aires.

ORTIZ-TRONCOSO O., 1979. "Punta Santa Ana et Bahía Colorada: deux gisements sur une ancienne ligne de rivage dans le détroit de Magellan," *Journal de la Société des Américanistes,* 66, Paris, pp. 133–204.

ORTIZ-TRONCOSO O., 1985. "Arqueología del estrecho de Magallanes y canales del sur de Chile," *Culturas Indigenas de la Patagonia,* ed. Cultura Hispánica, Madrid, pp. 113–29 ("Las Culturas de América en la época del descubrimiento").

ORTIZ-TRONCOSO O., 1989. "Ancestros de los pescadores australes." In Hidalgo J. et al., eds., *Culturas de Chile,* pp. 367–79.

ORTIZ-TRONCOSO O., 1991. "Desarrollo histórico de las investigaciones arqueológicas en Patagonia y Tierra del Fuego," *Anales del Instituto de la Patagonia,* 20, Punta Arenas, pp. 29–44.

PROUS A., 1986. "L'archéologie au Brésil. 300 siècles d'occupation humaine," *L'Anthropologie*, 90 (2), pp. 257–306.

ROOSEVELT A. C. et al., 1991. "Eighth Millennium Pottery from a Prehistoric Shell Midden in the Brazilian Amazon," *Science*, 254, pp. 1621–24.

ROOSEVELT A. C. et al., 1996. "Paleoindian Cave Dwellers in the Amazon: The Peopling of the Americas," *Science*, 272, pp. 373–84.

SANOJA M., 1979. "Los recolectores tempranos del Golfo de Paria, Edo Sucre, Venezuela," *Economia y Ciencias Sociales*, 4, pp. 98–111.

SCHMITZ P. I., BARBOSA A. S., and RIBEIRO M. B., eds., 1981. Temas de Arqueologia brasileira. In *Simposio Goiano de Arqueologia*, 3, Instituto Goianio de Pré-Historia e Antropologia, Goiânia.

TESTART A., 1982. *Les chasseurs-cueilleurs ou l'origine des inégalités*, Société d'Ethnographie, Paris.

VIGNATI M., 1926. "Consideraciones generales relativas al instrumental humano hallado en conchales fueguinos," *Physis*, 8 (30), Sociedad Argentina de Ciencias Naturales, Buenos Aires, pp. 396–401.

VIGNATI M., 1927. "Arqueología y Antropología de los 'conchales' fueguinos," *Revista del Museo de La Plata*, 30, Buenos Aires, pp. 79–143.

CHAPTER 6. PEASANTS, ARTISANS, AND PRIESTS

ANGULO VALDES C., 1992. "Modos de vida en la prehistoria de la llanura atlántica de Colombie." In Meggers B., ed., *Prehistoria Sudamericana*, pp. 253–70.

ARCHILA S., 1993. "Medio ambiente y arqueología de las tierras bajas del Caribe colombiano," *Boletin del Museo de Oro*, 34–35, Bogotá, pp. 111–64.

BARNETT W. K. and HOOPES J. W., 1995. *The Emergence of Pottery: Technology and Innovation in Ancient Societies*, Smithsonian Institution Press, Washington, D.C.

BEADLE G. W., 1977. "The Origin of *Zea Mays*." In Reed C. E., ed., *Origins of Agriculture*, Mouton, The Hague, pp. 615–55.

BEADLE G. W., 1980. "The Ancestry of Corn," *Scientific American*, 242, pp. 112–19.

BIRD J. B., 1963. "Preceramic Art from Huaca Prieta, Chicama Valley," *Ñawpa Pacha*, 1, Berkeley, pp. 29–34.

BIRD J. B., 1985. *The Preceramic Excavations at the Huaca Prieta, Chicama Valley, Perú*, New York, ed. J. Hyslop, Anthropological Papers of the American Museum of Natural History, 62 (1).

BISCHOF H., 1973. "The Origin of Pottery in America. Recent Radiocarbon Notes from Southwestern Ecuador," *Actes du XLᵉ Congrès International des Américanistes* (1972), Rome, pp.268–81.

BISCHOF H., 1979. "San Pedro und Valdivia—Frühe Keramikkomplexe an der Küste Südwest-Ekuadors," *Beiträge zur Allgemeinen und Vergleichenden Archäologie*, 1, Deutsche Archäologisches Institut, Verlag C. H. Beck, Munich, pp. 335–89.

BISCHOF H., 1997. "Cronología y Cultura en el Formativo Centroandina." Communication au 49e Congreso Internacional de Americanistas (Quito, 7–10 juillet 1997).

BISCHOF H., 1998. "El Periodo Inicial, el Horizonte Temprano, el Estilo Chavín y la realidad del proceso formativo en los Andes Centrales." In *Encuentro Internacional de Peruanistas* (3–6 September 1996), Universidad de Lima ed., Lima, pp. 57–76.

BONAVIA D., 1993–95. "La domesticación de las plantas y los rigenes de la agricultura en los Andes centrales," *Revista Historica*, 38, Academia Nacional de Historia, Lima, pp. 77–107.

BONAVIA D. and GROBMAN A., 1979. "Sistema de depósitos y almacenamiento durante el periodo precerámico en la costa del Perú," *Journal de la Société des Américanistes*, 46, Paris, pp. 21–42.

BONAVIA D. and GROBMAN A., 1989a. "Andean Maize: Its Origins and Domestication." In Harris D. R. and Hillman G. C., eds., *Foraging and Farming*, pp. 456–70.

BONAVIA D. and GROBMAN A., 1989b. "Preceramic Maize in the Central Andes: A Necessary Clarification," *American Antiquity*, 54, pp. 836–40.

BONAVIA D., ed., 1982. *Los Gavilanes. Mar, oasis y desierto en la historia del hombre.* Cofide et Institut archéologique allemand, Lima.

BONNIER E., 1987. "Les architectures précéramiques dans la Cordillère des Andes. Piruru face à la diversité des données," *L'Anthropologie*, 91 (4), Paris, pp. 889–903.

BONNIER E., 1997 . "Preceramic Architecture in the Andes: The Mito Tradition," In Bonnier E. and Bischof H., eds., *Arquitectura y Civilización*, pp. 121–43.

BONNIER E. and BISCHOF H., eds., 1997. Arquitectura y Civilización en los Andes Prehispánicos, *Archaeologica Peruana* 2, Sociedad Arqueológica Peruano-Alemana, Reiss-Museum Mannheim.

BRAY W., HERRERA L., and CARDALE SCHRIMPF M., 1985. "Report on the 1982 Field Season in Calima," *Pro Calima*, 4, Bogotá, pp. 2–26.

BURGER R. L., 1992. *Chavín and the Origins of Andean Civilization*, Thames and Hudson, London.

BURGER R. L. and SALAZAR-BURGER L., 1985. "The Early Ceremonial Center of Huaricoto." In Donnan C. B., ed., *Early Ceremonial Architecture*, pp. 111–38.

DI CAPUA C., 1994. "Valdivia Figurines and Puberty Rituals: An Hypothesis," *Andean Past* 4, pp. 229–79.

DONNAN C. B., 1964. "An Early House from Chilca, Perú," *American Antiquity*, 30, pp. 137–44.

DONNAN C. B., ed., 1985. *Early Ceremonial Architecture in the Andes*, Dumbarton Oaks Research Library and Collection, Washington, D.C.

DOYON-BERNARD S. J., 1990. "From Twining to Triple Cloth: Experimentation and Innovation in Ancient Peruvian Weaving," *American Antiquity*, 55, pp. 68–87.

ECKHOLM G. E., 1964. "Transpacific Contacts." In Jennings J. and Norbeck E., eds.. *Prehistoric Man*, pp. 485–510.

ECKHOLM G. E., 1995. "The New Orientation toward Problems of Asiatic-American Relationships," *New Interpretations of Aboriginal American Culture History*, Anthropological Society, Washington, D.C., pp. 55–109.

ENGEL F., 1966. "Le complexe précéramique d'El Paraiso, Pérou," *Journal de la Société des Américanistes*, 46, Paris, pp. 67–155.

ESTRADA E., 1958. *Las Culturas Pré-Clásicas, Formativas o Arcaicas del Ecuador*, Public. du Museo V. E. Estrada, 5, Guayaquil.

EVANS C., MEGGERS B., and ESTRADA E., 1959. *Cultura Valdivia*, Public. du Museo V.E.Estrada, 6, Guayaquil.

FELDMAN R. A., 1983. "From Maritime Chiefdom to Agricultural State in Formative Coastal Peru." In Leventhal R. M. and Kolata A. L., eds., *Civilization in the Ancient Americas*, University of New Mexico Press, Albuquerque, and Peabody Museum of Archaeology and Ethnology, Harvard University, Cambridge, pp. 289–310.

FELDMAN R. A., 1985. "Preceramic Corporate Architecture: Evidence for the Development of Non-Egalitarian Social Systems in Peru." In Donnan C. B., ed., *Early Ceremonial Architecture*, pp. 71–92.

FERNÁNDEZ-DISTEL A., 1975. "Restos vegetales de etapas arcaicas en yacimientos del N.O. de la República Argentina (Pcia. de Jujuy)," *Etnía*, 22, pp. 11–24.

FERNÁNDEZ-DISTEL A., 1985. "Huachichocana: informes específicos. Ficha técnica de la cueva CH III," *Paleoetnológica*, 1, Buenos Aires, pp. 9–11.

FUNG R., 1969. "Las Aldas, su ubicación dentro del proceso histórico del Perú antiguo," *Dédalo*, 5 (9–10), Museu de arte e arqueología, Universidade de São Paulo, São Paulo.

FUNG R., 1988. "The Late Preceramic and Initial Period." In Keatinge R. W., ed., *Peruvian Prehistory*, pp. 67–96.

FUNG R. and WILLIAMS LEON C., 1977. "Exploraciones y excavaciones en el valle de Sechin, Casma," *Revista del Museo Nacional*, 43, Lima, pp. 111–55.

GALINAT W. C., 1983. "The Origin of Maize as Shown by Key Morphological Traits of Its Ancestor, Teosinte," *Maydica*, 28, pp. 121–38.

GALINAT W. C., 1985. "Domestication and Diffusion of Maize." In Ford R. I., ed., *Prehistoric Food Production in North America*, Anthropology Papers 75, Museum of Anthropology, University of Michigan, Ann Arbor, pp. 245–82.

GARTELMANN K. D., 1985. *La Huellas del Jaguar. La arqueología en el Ecuador*, Quito.

GRIEDER T., 1975. "A Dated Sequence of Building and Pottery at Las Haldas," *Nawpa Paccha*, 13, Institute of Andean Studies, Berkeley, pp. 99–112.

GRIEDER T. and BUENO MENDOZA A., 1985. "Ceremonial Architecture at La Galgada." In Donnan C. B., ed., *Early Ceremonial Architecture*, pp. 93–110.

GROBMAN A., 1982. "Maíz (*Zea mays*)." In Bonavia D., *Los Gavilanes*, pp. 157–79.

GROBMAN A. and BONAVIA D., 1978. "Preceramic Maize on the North-central Coast of Peru," *Nature*, 276, pp. 386–87.

HAAS J., POZORSKI S., and POZORSKI T., eds., 1987. *The Origins and Development of the Andean State*, Conference at Dumbarton Oaks (8–10/10/1982), Dumbarton Oaks Research Library and Collection, Washington, D.C.

HARRIS D. R. and HILLMAN G. C., eds., 1989. *Foraging and Farming: The Evolution of Plant Exploitation*, Unwin Hyman, London ("One World Archaeology," 13).

HEINE-GELDERN R., 1959. "Representation of the Asiatic Tiger in the Art of the Chavin Culture: A Proof of Early Contacts between China and Peru," *Actas del 33o Congreso Internacional de Americanistas (1958)*, San José de Costa Rica, pp. 321–26.

HILL B., 1972–74. "A New Chronology of the Valdivia Ceramics Complex From the Coastal Zone of Guayas Province, Ecuador," *Ñawpa Paccha*, 10–12, Berkeley, pp. 1–32.

IZUMI S., CUCULIZA P. J., and KANO C., 1972. *Excavations at Shillacoto, Huánuco, Perú*, University Bulletin Museum 3, University of Tokyo, Tokyo.

IZUMI S. and SONO T., 1963. *Excavations at Kotosh, Peru*, University of Tokyo Expedition 1960. Andes 2, Kadokawa, Tokyo.

IZUMI S. and TERADA K., 1972. *Excavations at Kotosh, 1963 and 1966. Andes 4*, University of Tokyo Press, Tokyo.

LANNING E. P., 1967. *Peru before the Incas*, Prentice Hall, Englewood Cliffs.

LATHRAP D. W., 1967. "Review of Early Formative Period of Coastal Ecuador: The Valdivia and Machalilla Phases," *American Anthropologist*, 69, pp. 96–98.

LATHRAP D. W., 1970. *The Upper Amazon*. Thames and Hudson, London.

LATHRAP D. W., 1973. "The Antiquity and Importance of Long Distance Trade Relationships in the Moist Tropics of Pre-Columbian South America," *World Archaeology*, 5 (2), pp. 170–86.

LATHRAP D. W., COLLIER D., and CHANDRA H., 1975. *Ancient Ecuador: Culture, Clay and Creativity, 3000–300 BC*, Field Museum of Natural History, Chicago.

LATHRAP D. W. and MARCOS J., 1975. "Informe preliminar sobre las excavaciones del sitio Real Alto por la misión antropológica de la Universidad de Illinois," *Revista de la Universidad Católica*, 3(10), Quito, pp. 41–46.

LATHRAP D. W., MARCOS J., and ZEIDLER J., 1977. "Real Alto: An Ancient Ceremonial Center," *Archaeology*, 30 (1), New York, pp. 2–13.

LAVALLÉE D., 1989. "Quelques aspects de la néolithisation andine." In Aurenche O. et Cauvin J. eds., *Néolithisations*, BAR Intern. Series, 516, Oxford, pp. 319–32.

LEGROS T., 1990. "Les premières céramiques américaines," *Dossiers de l'Archéologie—Les Amériques. De la Préhistoire aux Incas*, 145, Dijon, pp. 60–63.

LEGROS T., 1992. "Puerto Chacho et les premiers céramistes américains." Thèse de Doctorat, Université Paris I-Panthéon-Sorbonne, Paris.

LEVENTHAL R. M. and KOLATA A. L., 1983. *Civilization in the Ancient Americas: Essays in Honor of Gordon R. Willey*, University of New Mexico Press, Albuquerque.

LUMBRERAS L. G., 1988. "Childe y la tesis de la revolución urbana : la experiencia central andina." In Manzanilla L., ed., *Coloquio V. Gordon Childe. Estudios sobre las revoluciones neolítica y urbana,* Instituto de Investigaciones Antropológicas, UNAM, Mexico, pp. 349–66.

LYNCH T. F., 1980. *Guitarrero Cave: Early Man in the Andes,* Academic Press, New York.

LYNCH T. F., GILLESPIE R., GOWLETT J., and HEDGES R., 1985. "Chronology of Guitarrero Cave, Peru," *Science,* 229, pp. 864–67.

LYON P., 1974. "Early Formative Period of Coastal Ecuador: Where Is the Evidence?" *Ñawpa Paccha,* 10–12, Berkeley, pp. 33–48.

MANGELSDORF P. C., 1974. *Corn: Its Origins and Improvement,* Belknap Press, Harvard University, Cambridge.

MANGELSDORF P. C., 1986. "The Origin of Corn," *Scientific American,* 255 (2), pp. 80–86.

MARCOS J., 1986a. "De ida y vuelta a Acapulco con mercaderes de Mullu." In Marcos J., ed., *Arqueologia de la costa ecuatoriana,* pp. 163–96.

MARCOS J., 1986b. "Intercambios a larga distancia en América: el caso del Spondylus." In Marcos J., ed., *Arqueologia de la costa ecuatoriana,* pp.197–206.

MARCOS J., 1988. *Real Alto. La historia de un centro ceremonial Valdivia,* 2 vols., ESPOL, Guayaquil ("Biblioteca Ecuatoriana de Arqueología," 4 et 5).

MARCOS J. and MICHCZYNSKI A., 1996. "Good Dates and Bad Dates in Ecuador," *Andes,* 1, Boletin de la Misión Arqueológica Andina, Universidad de Varsovia, pp. 93–114.

MARCOS J., ed., 1986. *Arqueologia de la costa ecuatoriana. Nuevos enfoques,* ESPOL, Guayaquil ("Biblioteca ecuatoriana de arqueología," 1).

MCKELVY BIRD R., 1990. "What Are the Chances of Finding Maize in Peru Dating before 1000 B.C.? Reply to Bonavia and Grobman," *American Antiquity,* 55, pp. 828–40.

MEGGERS B., 1966. *Ecuador,* Praeger, New York.

MEGGERS B., 1972. *Prehistoric America,* Aldine, Chicago.

MEGGERS B. and EVANS C., 1966. "A Transpacific Contact in 3000 BC," *Scientific American,* 214 (1), pp. 28–35.

MEGGERS B., EVANS C., and ESTRADA E., 1965. *Early Formative Period of Coastal Ecuador: The Valdivia and Machalilla Phases.* Smithsonian Institution, Washington, D.C. ("Smithsonian Contributions to Anthropology," 1).

MONSALVE J. G., 1985. "A Pollen Core from the Hacienda Lusitania," *Pro Calima,* 4, Bogotá, pp. 40–44.

MOSELEY M. E., 1975. *The Maritime Foundation of Andean Civilization,* Cummings, Menlo Park.

MURRA J. V., 1975. *Formaciones económicas y políticas del mundo andino,* Instituto de Estudios Peruanos, Lima, pp. 255–67.

NORTON P., 1971. "Preliminary Observations on Loma Alta, an Early Valdivia midden in Guayas Province, Ecuador." In Marcos J. and Norton P., eds., *Primer simposio de correlaciones antropologicas andina-mesoamericano,* ESPOL, Guayaquil, pp. 101–19.

NORTON P., 1982. "Preliminary Observations on Loma Alta, an Early Valdivia Midden in Guayas Province, Ecuador," *Primer Simposio de Correlaciones Antropológicas Andino-Mesoamericano (Salinas, 1971),* ESPOL, Guayaquil, pp. 101–19.

NORTON P., 1977. "The Loma Alta Connection," Communication présentée au 42e Annual Meeting of the Society for American Archaeology, New Orleans (multigraphiée).

NORTON P. and GARCIA M. V., 1992. *5000 años de ocupación. Parque nacional,* Centro Cultural Artes and Ed. Abya-Yala, Quito.

NUÑEZ L., 1986. "Evidencias arcaicas de maíces y cuyes en Tiliviche : hacia el semisedentarismo en el litoral fértil y quebradas del norte de Chile," *Chungará,* 16–17, Universidad de Tarapacá, pp. 25–47.

OYUELA-CALCEDO A., 1993. "Sedentism, Food Production, and Pottery Origins in the Tropics: The Case of San Jacinto I," Ph.D. diss., University of Pittsburgh.

PATTERSON T. C., 1985. "The Huaca La Florida, Rimac Valley, Peru." In Donnan C. B., ed., *Early Ceremonial Architecture*, pp. 59–70.

PAULSEN A., 1974. "The Thorny Oyster and Voice of God: Spondylus and Strombus in Andean Prehistory," *American Antiquity*, 39, pp. 597–607.

PEARSALL D. M., 1978. "Phytolith Analysis of Archaeological Soils: Evidence for Maize Cultivation in Formative Ecuador," *Science*, 199, pp. 177–78.

PEARSALL D. M., 1986. "La circulación primitiva del maíz entre Mesoamérica y Sudamérica." In Marcos J., ed., *Arqueologia de la costa ecuatoriana*, pp. 231–58.

PEARSALL D. M., 1988. *La producción de alimentos en Real Alto*, ESPOL, Guayaquil ("Biblioteca Ecuatoriana de Arqueología," 2).

PEARSALL D. M. and PIPERNO D. R., 1990. "Antiquity of Maize Cultivation in Ecuador : Summary and Reevaluation of the Evidence," *American Antiquity*, 55, pp. 324–37.

PIPERNO D. R., 1989. "Nonaffluent Foragers: Resource Availability, Seasonal Shortages, and the Emergence of Agriculture in Panamanian Tropical Forests." In Harris D. R. and Hillman G. C., eds., *Foraging and Farming*, pp. 538–54.

PIPERNO D. R. et al., 1985. "Preceramic Maize in Central Panama: Phytolith and Pollen Evidence," *American Anthropologist*, 87, pp. 871–78.

POZORSKI S. and POZORSKI T., 1987. *Early Settlement and Subsistence in the Casma Valley*, University of Iowa Press, Iowa City.

POZORSKI S. and POZORSKI T., 1990. "Reexamining the Critical Preceramic/Ceramic Period Transition: New Data from Coastal Peru," *American Anthropologist*, 93, pp. 481–91.

POZORSKI S. and POZORSKI T., 1994. "Early Andean Cities," *Scientific American*, 270 (6), pp. 46–51.

POZORSKI T., 1983. "The Caballo Muerto Complex and its Place in the Andean Chronological Period Sites of Peru," *Annals of the Carnegie Museum*, 52 (1), Pittsburgh, pp. 1–40.

PRATT A. F., 1999. "Determining the Function of One of the New World's Earliest Pottery Assemblages: The Case of San Jacinto, Colombia," *Latin American Antiquity*, 10 (1), pp. 71–85.

PROUS A., 1986. "L'archéologie au Brésil. 300 siècles d'occupation humaine," *L'Anthropologie*, 90 (2), pp. 257–306.

PROUS A., 1992. *Arqueologia brasileira*, Ed. Universidade de Brasilia, Brasilia.

QUILTER J., 1985. "Architecture and Chronology at El Paraiso, Peru," *Journal of Field Archaeology*, 12, pp. 279–97.

QUILTER J., 1991. "Problems with the Late Preceramic of Peru," *American Anthropologist*, 93, pp. 450–54.

RAVINES R. and ISBELL W., 1975. "Garagay: sitio ceremonial temprano en el valle de Lima," *Revista del Museo Nacional*, 41, Lima, pp. 253–72.

RAYMOND J. S., 1994. "La vida ceremonial en el Formativo temprano de Ecuador." In Millones L. and Onuki Y., eds., *El mundo ceremonial andino*, Ed. Horizonte, Lima, pp. 27–46.

RAYMOND J. S., et al., 1994. "Una comparación de las tecnologías de la cerámica temprana de Ecuador y Colombia." In Shimada I., ed., *Tecnología y organización de la producción cerámica prehispánica en los Andes*, Pontificia Universidad Católica de Perú, pp. 33–52.

REICHEL-DOLMATOFF G., 1965. "Excavaciones arqueológicas en Puerto Hormiga, départamento de Bolivar," *Antropología*, 2, Universidad de los Andes, Bogotá.

REICHEL-DOLMATOFF G., 1985. *Monsú. Un sitio arqueológico*, Banco Popular, Bogotá.

ROOSEVELT A. C., 1996. "Paleoindian Cave Dwellers in the Amazon: The Peopling of America," *Science*, 272, pp. 373–84.

ROOSEVELT A. C., HOUSLEY R. A., IMAZIO DA SILVEIRA M., MARANCA S., and JOHNSON R., 1991. "Eighth Millennium Pottery from a Prehistoric Shell Midden in the Brazilian Amazon," *Science*, 254, pp. 1621–24.

ROSTWOROWSKI DE DIEZ CANSECO M., 1970. "Mercaderos del valle de Chincha en la época prehispánica: un documento y unos comentarios," *Revista Española de Antropología Americana,* 5, Madrid, pp. 135–77.

SCHIPPACASSE V. F. and NIEMEYER H. F., 1984. *Descripción y análisis interpretativo de un sitio arcaico temprano en la quebrada de Camarones,* Publicación ocasional 41, Museo Nacional de Historia Natural, Universidad de Tarapacá.

SMITH B. D., 1997. "Reconsidering the Ocampo Caves and the Era of Incipient Cultivation in Mesoamerica," *Latin American Antiquity,* 8 (4), pp. 342–83.

STOTHERT K. E., 1985. "The Preceramic Las Vegas Culture in Coastal Ecuador," *American Antiquity,* 50, pp. 613–37.

WENDT W. E., 1964. "Die Praekeramische Seidlung am Rio Seco," *Baessler Archiv,* 11 (2), pp. 225–75.

WILLIAMS LEON C., 1978–80. "Complejos de pirámides con planta en U, patrón arquitectónico de la costa central," *Revista del Museo Nacional,* 44, Lima, pp. 95–110.

ZEVALLOS MENENDEZ C., 1966–71. *La agricultura en el Formativo temprano del Ecuador (cultura Valdivia),* Ed. Ecuador S. A., Guayaquil.

ZEVALLOS MENENDEZ C. and HOLM O., 1960. *Excavaciones arqueológicas en San Pablo: Informe preliminar,* Casa de la Cultura Ecuatoriana, Guayaquil.

CHAPTER 7. EPILOGUE

BENSON E. P., ed., 1971. *Dumbarton Oaks Conference on Chavín,* Dumbarton Oaks Library and Collection, Washington, D.C.

BISCHOF H., 1984. "Zur Entstehung des Chavín-Stils in Alt-Peru" *Beiträge zur Allgemeinen und Vergleichenden Archäologie,* 6, Bonn, pp. 355–452.

BISCHOF H., 1994. "Toward the Definition of Pre-and Early Chavin Art Styles in Peru," In Sandweiss D., ed., *Andean Past,* 4, Latin American Studies Program, Cornell University, Ithaca, pp. 169–228.

BISCHOF H., 1995. "Cerro Sechin y el arte temprano centro-andino," *Arqueología de Cerro Sechin,* t. 2, Pontificia Universidad Católica del Perú, Lima.

BISCHOF H., 1996. "Analisis iconográfico y del estilo en la elaboración de cronologías: El caso del Formativo Centroandino, *Andes,* 1, Varsovia, pp. 61–91.

BISCHOF H., 1998. "El Periodo Inicial, el Horizonte Temprano, el Estilo Chavín y la realidad del proceso formativo en los Andes Centrales." In *Encuentro Internacional de Peruanistas* (3–6 September 1996), Universidad de Lima ed., Lima, pp. 57–76.

BURGER R. L., 1981. "The Radiocarbon Evidence for the Temporal Priority of Chavín de Huantar," *American Antiquity,* 46, pp. 592–602.

BURGER R. L., 1988. "Unity and Heterogeneity within the Chavín Horizon." In Keatinge R. W., ed., *Peruvian Prehistory,* pp. 99–144.

BURGER R. L., 1992. *Chavín and the Origins of Andean Civilization,* Thames and Hudson, London.

BURGER R. L. and SALAZAR-BURGER L., 1993. "The Place of Dual Organization in Early Andean Ceremonialism: A Comparative Review." In Millones L. and Onuki Y., eds., *El mundo ceremonial andino,* Ed. Horizonte, Lima, pp. 97–116.

COE M., 1962. "An Olmec Design on an Early Peruvian Vessel," *American Antiquity,* 27, pp. 579–80.

CRUXENT J. and ROUSE I., 1961. *Arqueología Cronológica de Venezuela,* Pan American Union, Washington, D.C. ("Estudios monográficos," 6).

FELDMAN R.A., 1983. "From Maritime Chiefdom to Agricultural State in Formative Coastal Perú." In Leventhal R. M. and Kolata A. L., eds., *Civilization in the Ancient Americas,* University of New Mexico Press, Albuquerque, and Peabody Museum of Archaeology and Ethnology, Harvard University, Cambridge, pp. 289–310.

FUNG R., 1981. "Sobre el origen selvático de la civilización Chavín," *Amazonia Peruana*, 4 (8), Lima, pp. 77–92.

FUNG R., 1982. "El temprano surgimiento en el Perú de los sistemas socio-políticos complejos: planteamiento de una hipótesis de desarrollo original," *Primer Simposio de Correlaciones Antropológicas Andino-Mesoamericano* (25–31 juillet 1971, Salinas), ESPOL, Guayaquil, pp. 457–93.

FUNG R., 1988. "The Late Preceramic and Initial Period." In Keatinge R. W., ed., *Peruvian Prehistory*, pp. 67–96.

KANO C., 1979. "The Origins of the Chavín Culture," *Studies in Pre-columbian Art and Archaeology*, 22, Dumbarton Oaks, Washington, D.C.

KAUFFMANN DOIG F., 1963. "Origen mesoamericano de Chavín," *Nueva Corónica*, 1, Universidad San Marcos, Lima, pp. 148–59.

LANNING E. P., 1967. *Peru before the Incas*, Prentice Hall, Englewood Cliffs.

LARCO HOYLE R., 1945. *Los Cupisniques*, Sociedad Geográfica Americana, Buenos Aires.

LATHRAP D. W., 1970. *The Upper Amazon*, Thames and Hudson, London.

LATHRAP D. W., 1971. "The Tropical Forest and the Cultural Context of Chavín." In Benson E. P., ed., *Dumbarton Oaks Conference on Chavín*, pp. 73–100.

LATHRAP D. W., 1982. "Complex Iconographic Features Shared by Olmec and Chavín and Some Speculations on Their Possible Significance," *Primer Simposio de Correlaciones Antropológicas Andino-Mesoamericano* (25–31 July 1971, Salinas), ESPOL, Guayaquil, pp. 301–27.

LATHRAP D. W., 1985. "Jaws: The Control of Power in the Early Nuclear American Ceremonial Center." In Donnan C. D., ed., *Early Ceremonial Architecture*, pp. 241–68.

LAVALLÉE D., 1985. "Origine et expansion de la culture Chavín," *Grand Atlas de l'Archéologie*, Ed. Encyclopaedia Universalis, Paris, pp. 364–65.

LAVALLÉE D. and LUMBRERAS L. G., 1985. *Les Andes. De la Préhistoire aux Incas*, Gallimard, Paris ("L'Univers des Formes").

LUMBRERAS L. G., 1989. *Chavín de Huantar en el nacimiento de la Civilización andina*, INDEA, Lima.

LUMBRERAS L. G., 1993. *Chavín de Huantar: excavaciones en la Galeria de las Ofrendas*, KAVA, von Zabern, Mainz ("Materialen für Allgemeinen und Vergleichenden Archäologie," 51).

MIDDENDORF E. [1895] 1970. "Las ruinas de Chavín." In Bonavia D. and Ravines R., eds., *Arqueología peruana: precursores*, Casa de la Cultura del Perú, , pp. 119–32.

RAVINES R., 1984. "Sobre la formación de Chavín : Imágenes y Símbolos," *Boletin de Lima*, Lima, pp. 27–45.

ROHR J. A., 1967. "O Sitio arqueologico de Alfredo Wagner S.C. VI 13," *Pesquisas*, 17, São Leopoldo, pp 1–23.

ROOSEVELT A. C., 1991. *Moundbuilders of the Amazon: Geophysical Archaeology on Marajó Island, Brazil*, Academic Press, San Diego.

ROWE J. H., 1967. "Form and Meaning in Chavín Art." In Rowe J. H. and Menzel D., eds., *Peruvian Archaeology: Selected Readings*, Peek Publications, Palo Alto.

SAMANIEGO L., VERGARA E., and BISCHOF H., 1985. "New Evidence on Cerro Sechin, Casma Valley, Peru." In Donnan C. B., ed., *Early Ceremonial Architecture*, pp. 165–90.

SANOJA M., 1959. "Origines of the Cultivation around the Gulf of Paria, Northern Venezuela," *National Geographic Research*, (4), pp. 446–58.

TELLO J. C., 1923. *Wirakocha*, Univ. Nac. Mayor de San Marcos, Lima.

TELLO J. C., 1929. *Antiguo Perú*, Primera Epoca, Edit. Excelsior, Lima.

TELLO J. C., 1942. "Origen y Desarrollo de las Civilizaciones Prehistóricas Andinas," *Actas y Trabajos del 37 Congreso Internacional de Americanistas* (1939), 1, Lima, pp. 589–720.

TELLO J. C., 1960. *Chavín, cultura matriz de la civilización andina*, Univ. Nac. Mayor de San Marcos, Lima.

Acknowledgments

There remains one final, pleasant task to carry out, that of thanking all the people without whom this book would have been impossible. The individuals to whom I am indebted are so numerous that a full list would be endless. They include all those whose names appear in the bibliography and who permitted me (albeit usually without knowing it) to quote and comment on their works.

For the illustrations, I have been fortunate enough to beneWt from the skilled talents of Francine Chassagnac, George Clément, Jean-Pierre Magnier, and Danièle Molez, whose maps or original drawings brought a positive gloss to an iconography of sometimes uneven quality.

Several colleagues and friends—in fact the two go together—gave me even more direct help by accepting the task of reading and criticizing the manuscript's successive drafts. For this I oVer my warmest thanks to Claude Baudez, Claude Chauchat, Marie-France Fauvet-Berthelot, Michèle Julien, Claudine Karlin, Suzana Monzón, Fabio Parenti, Jacques Pelegrin, and Denis Vialou. However, I hope they will forgive me if I have not always completely followed their advice.

Finally, I would like to give particular thanks to my friend Paul Bahn who undertook the translation of this book into English. *Traduttore, traditore* (translator, traitor) goes the Italian expression, but it is quite wrong here. Paul pointed out several errors to me, suggested rectiWcations, and opened up new leads. I would also like to thank him for sending me several sources that were not available in France. This joint work was not only a pleasure but also an enriching experience.

Index

Acosta, José de, 10, 14

Adovasio, J., 39–40

agriculture: earliest evidence for in Peru, 92, 134–39; economic and cultural development in 5000–4000 B.P. period, 169–76; and establishment of permanent villages in Near East, 126n1; and origins of pottery, 183–87; and social organization of Pacific coast cultures, 196–202, 204; and Valdivia tradition, 192. *See also* beans; irrigation; maize; plant resources

Aguerre, A., 111

Alakaluf ethnic group, 221

Aldenderfer, M., 94

Alice Boër (Brazil), 46, 53

Allison, M., 133

Almagro, Diego de, 5

alpaca, 141, 143, 145. *See also* camelids

Altoparanaense culture, 163

Amazonia: and cultures of post-Pleistocene period, 103–105; and influences on Chavín culture, 210–13, 215; and Marajó culture, 207n1. *See also* Brazil

Ameghino, C., 28

Ameghino, F., 25–28, 32

Amerindians. *See* Indians

"Amotape" complex, 97

Andes: and Chavín culture, 207–19; and geography of South America, x; and glaciation at end of Pleistocene, 72; and origins of pottery, 176–87; post-Pleistocene cultures of Central, 90–93; post-Pleistocene cultures of dry and salt punas, 93–96. *See also* Cordillera

Angrand, Léonce, 19

animals, domestication of in Andes, 139–45. *See also* camelids; hunting and hunters

Aonik'enk group, 221

Aragón (Chile), 101, 130–31

archaeology: development of scientific, 29–30; early recordings of sites and monuments, 19, 20; establishment of in Argentina, 25; similarities and differences in comparative observations, 163n2

Ardila, G., 47

Argentina: beginnings of archaeology in, 25; and earliest evidence for agriculture, 173; high plateaus and post-Pleistocene cultures, 94; hunting and pampas in post-Pleistocene period, 108–10; and sites prior to 10,000 B.P., 51; and spondylus shells, 204. *See also* Patagonia; Tierra del Fuego

Argentine Scientific Society, 25

Arroyo Seco (Argentina), 110

art. *See* ceremonial centers; rock art; Venus figurines; zooliths

arthritis, 116

Asana (Peru), 94

Aschero, C., 94

Asia: and European "discovery" of New World, 2; prehistory of eastern, 61–62; transpacific contact between Americas and, 178–79. *See also* Japan

Aspero (Peru), *197*, 198, 199, 204

Atahualpa (Inca), 5

Atlantic coast: and cultural innovation in "Neolithic" period, 149–60; and cultures of plateaus in post-Pleistocene period, 105–108. *See also* Brazil

Atlantis, and European theories on origins of Amerindians, 11–12

atlatl, 87

Australia, and theories on origins of Amerindians, 63

Ayacucho (Peru), 90

Bahamas, and Atlantis controversy, 12

Bahía Colorada (Chile), 158

Baixão do Perna (Brazil), 44, 106

Balboa, Francisco Nuñez de, 4

Bandelier, A., 21

Bandurría (Peru), 198

Barbosa, A., 106

Barlovento phase, 186

Barra do Antonião (Brazil), 69, 106

baskets and basketry, 187, 188

Baulny, O., 16

Beadle, G., 171

beans: and earliest evidence for agriculture in Peru, 92, 135–36, 169; and Valdivia culture, 192. *See also* agriculture; plant resources

Bell, R., 89

Beltrão, M., 46, 56

Benalcázar, Sebastián de, 5

Benassar, Bartolomé, 8

Benfer, R., 129,130

Bennett, W. C., 208, 210, 216

Bergier, J., 13

Bering Straits and Beringia, 57–58, 60

Bernard, J., 65

Bible, and European images of Amerindians, 9–10

Bird, J., 50, 68, 111, 133, 154, 156, 216

Bischof, H., 179, 186, 200, 213, 214, 216, 218, *217*